The Poems of Anne, Countess of Winchilsea

THE DECENNIAL PUBLICATIONS OF
THE UNIVERSITY OF CHICAGO

THE DECENNIAL PUBLICATIONS

ISSUED IN COMMEMORATION OF THE COMPLETION OF THE FIRST TEN
YEARS OF THE UNIVERSITY'S EXISTENCE

AUTHORIZED BY THE BOARD OF TRUSTEES ON THE RECOMMENDATION
OF THE PRESIDENT AND SENATE

THESE VOLUMES ARE DEDICATED

TO THE MEN AND WOMEN
OF OUR TIME AND COUNTRY WHO BY WISE AND GENEROUS GIVING
HAVE ENCOURAGED THE SEARCH AFTER TRUTH
IN ALL DEPARTMENTS OF KNOWLEDGE

THE POEMS OF ANNE COUNTESS OF WINCHILSEA

THE POEMS OF ANNE COUNTESS
OF WINCHILSEA

.

FROM THE ORIGINAL EDITION OF 1713 AND FROM UNPUBLISHED MANUSCRIPTS
EDITED WITH AN INTRODUCTION AND NOTES

BY

MYRA REYNOLDS
OF THE DEPARTMENT OF ENGLISH

THE DECENNIAL PUBLICATIONS
SECOND SERIES   VOLUME V

.

CHICAGO
THE UNIVERSITY OF CHICAGO PRESS
1903

PREFACE

THIS edition of the Poems of Anne, Countess of Winchilsea, is based on a small volume of verse published by her in 1713, on two unpublished manuscripts, and on poems scattered through various *Miscellanies*. These sources are more fully described in the *Introduction*, and the *Table of Contents* indicates in which of them each poem is found. In preparing the present text for publication the volume of 1713 has been considered authoritative for the poems it includes, but there has been incorporated into the text the list of *Errata* published in that volume. For poems occurring in both manuscripts the folio has been accepted as the best authority, inasmuch as it is later than the octavo and was apparently revised by the author or under her supervision.

There has been no modernization of the text, except that in some instances titles are not given with the original amplitude and variety of capitalization, and brackets are not used to mark triplets. Beyond these slight changes the various accepted texts are exactly followed. Some of the poems could doubtless have been made more pleasing to the eye and more easily intelligible by a series of editorial changes. It must be admitted that as the poems stand they show an orthography which, though often quaint and a valuable indication of contemporary pronunciation, is also often inconsistent and the outcome of carelessness or possibly of ignorance. The punctuation is sometimes so scanty, sometimes so elaborate, as to obscure the text. And there is an irritating excess of capitals and italics. But in spite of these facts, more seemed to be lost than gained by any attempt to make the poems conform to exact canons or to

modern taste. Since so many of them are now published
for the first time, it seemed best on the whole to follow the
original sources exactly. In order to avoid encumbering
the poems with references, the *Notes* are printed in a
separate section at the end of the volume.

I cannot bring forward this edition of Lady Winchilsea's
poems without an expression of my sense of indebtedness to
Mr. Frederic Ives Carpenter, of the Department of English
in the University of Chicago, through whose mediation the
manuscripts were given to me to edit, and whose aid has
been constant throughout the perplexities incident to the
production of this volume; to the Earl of Winchilsea, not
only for the use of the octavo manuscript in his possession, but for access to other manuscript material valuable in
connection with Lady Winchilsea's life, and for introductions
whereby it became possible to visit the places most closely
associated with her poems; and to Mr. Edmund Gosse for
the use of his most important folio manuscript volume of
Lady Winchilsea's work, and for many valuable suggestions
in connection with the *Introduction* and the *Notes*.

TABLE OF CONTENTS

[In the following table are marks showing in which of the original sources each poem is found. The volume of 1713 is indicated by *; the folio MS. by †; the octavo MS. by ‡; Birch's *General Dictionary* by ‖].

INTRODUCTION

LADY WINCHILSEA was born in 1661 and died in 1720. Her poems were written after 1685. During the period from 1685 to 1720 she takes rank as a minor writer in all the popular literary forms except comedy. Love songs, sacred songs, pindarics, satires, epistles, fables, translations, tragedies, verse criticism, and one prose critical essay, come within the compass of her works. Her poems are frequently commonplace in substance and even more frequently crude in form. Only now and then does she reach an excellence that would make them of importance apart from their place in literary history. Yet, taken as a whole, her work proves to be of unusual interest. This is due, in part, to the social environment and the literary associations of which the poems give so detailed and clever a picture, and in part to Lady Winchilsea's own personality, as revealed in her work. But the chief elements of interest arise from the fact that she was a heretic in her own day, a protestant, both consciously and unconsciously, against the religious, social, and literary canons then in vogue; and from the further fact that some of her heresies became the orthodox faith of later generations. Her education and her literary activities fall entirely within the compass of the classical period, but her poems show romantic tastes unparalleled in her own day, and not afterward so highly developed before Cowper. She was hardly strong enough to be counted one of the influences in bringing about changes in taste, but she distinctly foreshadows such changes, and it is on her delicate originality and independence of judgment that her claim to literary recognition must rest.

I

SKETCH OF LADY WINCHILSEA'S LIFE

Anne Kingsmill was descended from a very ancient Hampshire family. This family, whose original name was Castelayne, resided at Basingstoke from the twelfth to the sixteenth century. One of its members, for a personal service done to King John, had the grant of the Royal Mill at Basingstoke, and he took thereafter the name of Kingsmuln. Early in the reign of Edward I. the mill was alienated by Hugh de Kingsmuln, but the name was retained. During succeeding generations the family held a position of importance in Hants. It was at the house of Richard Kyngesmylle, bailiff of Basingstoke, that Catherine of Aragon and her suite were entertained for a night on her way to be married to Prince Arthur. Richard's son, Sir John Kingsmill, was judge of the common pleas, and one of the feoffees in the will of Henry VII. His son, Sir John Kingsmill, was high sheriff of Hants and purchased from the crown various manors, among them that of Sydmonton, with which this branch of the family is afterward associated. Of the seventeen children of this Sir John several were of high distinction. Thomas was professor of Hebrew at Oxford; Richard was attorney at the court of wards under Elizabeth; Sir George, judge of the common pleas, married a direct descendant of Edward I. by Eleanor his wife. One daughter married Sir James Pilkington, Bishop of Durham, and another married Richard Cooper, ancestor to the first Earl of Shaftesbury. The Constance Kingsmill who married the son of Sir Thomas Lucy, the supposed original of Shakespeare's "Justice Shallow," was probably a niece of this Sir John. A cousin, William Kingsmill, was the last prior of St. Swithun's Priory, Win-

Ancestry

chester, and the first dean of Winchester Cathedral. His initials, "W. K.," and the Kingsmill arms, are carved on the oak stalls of the choir. Anne's great grandfather, who was high sheriff under James I. and Elizabeth, was esteemed "the wisest gentleman of his country." Her father, Sir William Kingsmill, married Anne Haselwood, one of the nine children of Sir Anthony Haselwood and Elizabeth Wilmer, of Maidwell, Northamptonshire. Anne Haselwood's brother, Sir William Haselwood, succeeded his father in 1660. His estate that year was rated at £3,000 *per annum*. His daughter Elizabeth, "whose excellent character would fill a volume," became in 1685 the third wife of Viscount Hatton of Kirby. Another daughter, Penelope, was the first wife of Sir Henry Seymour, *alias* Portman, of Orchard-Portman, in Somersetshire. Anne Haselwood's sisters, Catherine and Elizabeth, married, respectively, Sir Thomas Cave and Sir William Langham. It will thus be seen that through both father and mother Anne Kingsmill was related to families of high repute.

Sir William Kingsmill and his wife Anne had three children, William, Bridget, and Anne. Sir William died when Anne, who was born in April, 1661, was **The Family** but five months old. In his will, after solemnly "bequeathing his soul to his Saviour Jesus Christ through whose merits he hopes to join the Saints and Angels, and his body to the dust whence it came," he shows his confidence in his "Ladie and loving wife" by making her his sole executrix during the minority of his son, William, then a child of two or three years, to whom the estates were bequeathed. Provision was likewise made for his daughters, a sum of £2000 being set aside to be invested for Bridget and paid to her with all the interest accruing therefrom on her twenty-first birthday or on her marriage. A sum of £1500 was similarly set apart as Anne's portion. The authority vested in the wife was to remain in force during her widowhood or her after-marriage " to any man whatsoever if so it should come to pass according to her good will and pleasure." That it did so come to pass, and that with almost indecorous promptitude, is shown by the marriage license issued in October, 1662, to "Sir Thomas Ogle, Kt., of Wickin, in Barewell, Co. Suffolk, Bach^r, 24, and Dame Anne Kingsmill of Sydmonton, Co. South^{ton}, widow, above 80." The only child of this second marriage was Dorothy Ogle, born in 1663. In 1664 the mother died, leaving four children under seven years of age. In her will she says: "Out of the assurance I have of the prudent love and care of my dear husband, Sir Thomas Ogle, I doe wholly give and bequeath to him all my possessions, and I doe hereby wholly give, assign, remit and bequeath the education and government of all my children unto the said Sir Thomas Ogle, to be brought up in the fear of God and good nurture according to their quality, as he in his discretion shall think fit." In what way the young widower fulfilled this momentous trust must, unfortunately, be left largely to the imagination. Beyond the fact that he became Major of H. M. Holland Regiment in 1665, we have no record of him except that he died in 1671. His daughter Dorothy was left as the ward of Sir Richard Campion (or Champion), but there is no statement as to the disposition made of the other children. It would perhaps be most natural to suppose that they would go to Sir William Haselwood, their mother's brother, and their intimacy with his daughter Elizabeth would lend color to that supposition. But wherever they were, Anne and Bridget, if we may judge by a few letters preserved among the Hatton MSS. in the British Museum, received a more thorough education than Dorothy. Bridget's letters are smooth, formal, highbred and tolerably correct, while Dorothy's orthography and sentence structure follow no law more imperative than her immediate whim. But whether the sisters were educated together or not, there was always a close bond between Anne and Dorothy. In a poem written to Dorothy from Kirby in 1688 Anne dwells with eager affection on the "lost pleasures" of their former companionship, and demands that time shall pay back the days and hours of their separation. Their "soft endearing life" together makes her think of Heaven as the place when they shall learn new mysteries of love. "Teresa," as Dorothy is poetically called, also appears in the *Dialogue between Teresa and Ardelia*, as the wisest and most loving counsellor of the unhappy Ardelia. Dorothy was maid of honor to the Princess of Denmark, and died unmarried at the age of twenty-nine. The original draft of her will is among the Hatton manuscripts and is worth quoting in full:

In the name of God Amen I Dorothy Ogle of Maidwell in ye County of Northton, spinster for the settling of my temporall estate Doe make this my last will & testament in manner following first I give & bequeathe to ye Right Honble the Lord Viscount Hatton his Ladyes picture then I give unto ye Lady Hatton my bible and common prayer booke then I give to my cozen Mrs Elizabeth Hatton my tea table dishes and gilt spoones then I give to my sister Bridget Kingsmill my bed then I give to my sister ffinch my cabinet and 5 yards of new-point. then I give unto my serv^t Mary Rice all the residue ·of my books, my watch & all my wairing Apparell [three words undecipherable] dresing glasse & Boxes and all the rest & residue of my Goods, Chattells & personall estate what soever I give and bequeath to the aforesaid Lady Viscountess Hatton who I doe hereby ordaine & make the sole executrix of this my last will and testament In witness whereof I have hereunto set my hand & seale this eight day of Augt 1692.

Sealed and published by ye above named

Dorothy Ogle to be her last will and testament in ye presence of us; and by us subscribed in ye presence of ye testator.

Jere Bellyrout
John Hatton
  his mark
Will ∧ Dawson

my mind and desire
is that my cozen M^{rs}
Portman have my Shag-
green tooth-pick case
in remembrance of me.

Of "sister bidy," as Dorothy called her, we know practically nothing except that she died unmarried in 1719–20. William was knighted and married as soon as he attained his majority. His relation to his sisters does not seem to have been close. In a codicil to his will he left Anne and Bridget £100 each, but his great ambition was to bequeath his estates so that they would remain under the Kingsmill name. He died in 1698 leaving a son of four who lived to the age of eighty-one unmarried. The estate, which was a large one, was apparently managed by Anne's husband, in whose note-book are many records of accounts paid for " my nephew Kingsmill," even the house servants receiving their wages through Mr. Finch. At the death of this nephew, the last male heir, the estates devolved upon a granddaughter whose husband took the name of Kingsmill. His nephew, the distinguished Admiral Sir Robert Kingsmill, a friend of Nelson, succeeded to the estates in 1805.

In 1683 we find Anne Kingsmill as one of the six maids of honor of Mary of Modena. Gregario Leti, historio-

As Maid of Honor grapher to Charles II., gives the list of the ladies who made up the household of the duchess in that year. First, there was Penelope O'Brien, Countess of Peterborough, who spoke French well, drew a salary of 1600 crowns, and had been with the duchess since her marriage. A more exciting personality was Susanna Armine, the famous Lady Belasyse, who, coming to court as a very young widow in 1670, had so attracted James by her

wit, gayety, and remarkable powers of mind that he had
"honorably wooed her for his wife." Of Lady Belasyse
Mary of Modena never felt the slightest jealousy. It
was Catharine Sedley, the maid of honor drawing the
highest salary, intrepid, brilliant, conscious of her power
over James, and unscrupulous in her use of it, who roused
all the fierce antagonism in the nature of the Italian wife,
and brought discord into the court circle. Of the other
maids of honor Anne Killigrew was the most famous. She
died of smallpox in her twenty-fifth year. But she had
already shown superior ability in both poetry and painting.
She was a pupil of Lely and her royal master and mistress
sat to her for their portraits. If we may trust Dryden's *Ode
to Mistress Anne Killigrew*, her pencil was also skilled
in the representation of landscapes. Dryden was her
master in poetry, and she was not a pupil of whom he
needed to be ashamed. The thin volume of her published verse shows a vigor and a bitterness not to be
looked for in a maid of honor. There is no hint of
interest in nature, no tenderness, no lightness, almost no
beauty or grace. The poems are marked instead by a crude
virility. They are apparently genuine in their Carlylean
scorn of fools, and of men who will expose themselves to
hostile arms, or give themselves to "toylsome study" "all
for the praise of Fools." "O famisht soul," she exclaims,
"which such thin food can feed." She hates war, but she
shows admiration for strength and daring, and she scorns
weakness. There is in her poems no contemplative religious
spirit, but there is a stern morality, and an emphatic recognition of reason as man's supreme guide. There would seem
to be valid reasons in the law of affinities for a warm friendship between the two Annes. They were both, Miss Strickland says, "much beloved by her [Mary of Modena], were
ladies of irreproachable virtue, members of the Church of

England, and alike distinguished for moral worth and
literary attainments." But if such a friendship did exist
there is no hint of it in the poetry of either. Their minds
were stretched to a contemplation of the progress of man
through the "Inextricable Mazes of Life to his probable
final Ruine," and they could not turn the uncertain and difficult stream of their verse into merely domestic or friendly
channels. Both were, however, ardently devoted to Mary
Beatrice, and it is not strange that the young, unhappy
duchess, "so innocently bred," so religiously inclined, found
in them most congenial companionship. The two Annes
vied with each other in their scorn of vice and frivolity, and
their association with their blameless mistress creates at
once in the midst of the stifling court life of Charles II.'s
day a little oasis of moral purity, and of spiritual and intellectual aspiration. To the court in general, Miss Strickland
adds, Anne Kingsmill was well-known as the beautiful and
witty maid of honor.

In her youthful days Anne had looked forward to life
and recognition at court as "an earthly paradise," but her
Marriage to disappointment there had been intense. Almost
Mr. Finch her only unquestioned source of happiness,
aside from her love for her royal mistress, was her acquaintance with Mr. Heneage Finch. Ardelia had early declared
hostility to love, "however painted o'er and seeming soft"
his addresses might be, but she was at last forced to admit
that Mr. Finch's constant passion had found the way "to
win a stubborn and ungrateful heart." Mr. Finch was at
that time a commoner with but a remote chance of an earldom, but as the oldest living son of Lord Winchilsea, and
the uncle of Charles, the heir to the title, he was treated
with consideration in court circles. He had been bred
to arms, and was at this time captain of the halbardiers
of the Duke of York, and likewise gentleman of the

bedchamber. But though brought up to arms and forced
by circumstances into public life, not Anne Kingsmill herself had a more genuine love for studious retirement than
possessed the mind of this captain and courtier. Doubtless
no dignity of these days was more prized by him than the
D. C. L. bestowed upon him by Oxford when he went thither
with James, May 22, 1683.

How long Anne's stubborn heart resisted Mr. Finch's
constancy cannot be definitely told, but the marriage license
reads as follows :

14 May, 1684. Appeared personally Collonell Heneage Finch
of Eastwell in ye County of Kent, Batchelor, aged ab. 27 years,
and alleadged that he intends to marry with Madam Anne Kingsmill of ye Parish of St. Martins in ye fields in ye county of Midd'l
a spinster aged ab. 18 years at her own disposal he not knowing
any lawful let or impediment to hinder ye said intended marriage
of ye truth of which he made oath and prayed a Lycence for them
to be married in the Chapple of St. James in ye parish of St. Martin
in ye ffields after.

The "spinster ab. 18 years" is a delicious bit of
coquetry, a charming subjugation of the independent maid
of honor to the prejudices of her day. She was certainly twenty-two. A relentless cordon of dates makes
escape impossible. But who can censure the smooth little
"about" which let Anne into the paradise of eighteen,
if he but recalls the fact that in her day and circle, from
fourteen to eighteen were the marriageable ages, that to be
twenty-one was to rank as "ancient," while to be twenty-
three was to be off the stage? Anne's mother had indulged
in a like evasive phrase, when, in her second wedding license,
she put herself on record as "above thirty." The marriage
probably took place on the following day, a day commemorated thirty-nine years later in Lord Winchilsea's private
journal by the simple entry, "May 15, 1684. Most blessed
day." And though succeeding years held much in the way

of deprivation and anxiety and grief, this marriage was the beginning of Anne Finch's real and permanent happiness.

Miss Strickland speaks of Mrs. Finch as "a favorite Maid of Honour of the Queen." This is, however, a mistake. On **Domestic** the occasion of Anne's marriage she left the **Happiness** service of Mary of Modena. But Mr. Finch was still in the retinue of the Duke of York, and Mr. and Mrs. Finch therefore lived in Westminster. It was the preference of both that they should order their lives in as simple and retired a fashion as court demands would permit. Ardelia's poetic aspirations had been no secret to Mr. Finch in her maid of honor days, and now in the independency and privacy of their own home he not only indulged her verse, but even now and then "requir'd her rhymes." When he went away for the day he liked to have a poem waiting for him at night, and he enjoyed versified letters. Ardelia had come into a new freedom. She and her husband were most unfashionably happy together. She was not ashamed to declare that all her hopes and joys were bound in him. Occasional brief separations caused genuine grief to both of them. When Mrs. Finch was at Tunbridge Wells for the waters in the summer of 1685, her husband's loneliness made him urge her to shorten her stay. Only the first stanza of her answer is decipherable in the manuscript, but that in its simplicity and directness of statement shows something of the feeling between them:

> Daphnis your wish no more repeat
> For my return nor mourn my stay,
> Lest my wise purpose you defeat,
> And urged by love I come away.
> My own desires I can resist
> But blindly yield if you persist.

Ardelia gaily describes the consternation of the Muses when they were called upon for aid in praising her husband.

> A *Husband!* echo'd all around:
> And to *Parnassus* sure that sound
> Had never yet been sent.

At least no such compromising request had been received at the sacred Mount "since Grizzel's Days," and it would have gone hard with Ardelia's poem had she not luckily found in her own breast so many tender memories that the aid of the Nine was superfluous. Domestic felicity of this idyllic sort was certainly not in harmony with the prevailing court standards. This age had defined courtship as a "witty prologue to a dull play;" marriage was but "an ecclesiastical mouse-trap," and all marriage was said "to end in repentance;" while the accepted similes for a wife were "a clog," "a tether-stake," "a yoke," "a galling load." In such a state of public opinion a home-life so unaffectedly good, so frankly happy, as that of this court-bred lady and gentleman was of itself a mark of distinction.

With the accession to the throne of James in February, 1685, Mr. Finch became more than ever occupied with public affairs. He was colonel in the army; he was groom of the bedchamber to the king; he was three years deputy lieutenant for the county of Kent; and he sat one year as member of parliament for Hythe. During this period Mr. and Mrs. Finch lived in London with but occasional short visits in other parts of England. A brief stay in Somersetshire in 1688 (probably in the summer) had, as its outcome, the following statement made by Lord Winchilsea August 12, 1722:

I do affirm that in the year 1688, Mrs. Mompesson (wife to Thomas Mompesson, esq. of Bruham, in Somersetshire, a worthy and a very good woman) told me and my wife, that Archbishop Juxon assured her, that to his certain knowledge the ΕΙΚΩΝ ΒΑΣΙΛΙΚΗ was all composed and written by King Charles the First.—Although in the following book the King's book is thoroughly vindicated, and proved to be of his Majesty's composing, I am willing to add this circumstance from Mrs. Mompesson with whom and her husband my wife and I at this time sojourned.   WINCHILSEA.

This "statement" shows the eagerness with which Mr. and Mrs. Finch followed up whatever pertained to the fame or fortunes of the Stuarts. The revolution was therefore to them a momentous and lamentable event as a result of which the course of their lives was suddenly and violently changed. So closely, indeed had they identified themselves with the Stuart interests that Mr. Finch found it impossible to take the vows of allegiance to the new monarch.

The first two or three years after the revolution, accordingly, were trying ones. During these years we find Anne in various places of temporary refuge, but with no fixed home. In December, 1688, immediately after the flight of James, she went to Kirby and spent some time with her cousin Elizabeth, the Viscountess Hatton. In July, 1689, she was at Eastwell on a visit. At some date near this she was at Godmersham, where she wrote *Aristomenes*. Her retirement to Wye college belongs somewhere in this period. The succor offered by Lady Thanet to Ardelia in her hour of sorest need may indicate that for a time Hothfield was her refuge. At any rate there was quite a prolonged period during which Mr. and Mrs. Finch felt great anxiety concerning their "much-diminished bread" and their possible future place of abode. Just when they were finally domiciled at Eastwell is a little uncertain. Ardelia says in her *Preface* that their removal into the solitude and security of the country was due to the "generous kindness of one who possessed the most delightful seat in it," but she does not say whether this was her husband's father or nephew. Heneage, the second earl, died in September, 1689, so the invitation may have come from him, and the poem of July, 1689, may mark the beginning of the permanent Eastwell sojourn. But this is unlikely.

All the further references to the earl in this preface seem consistent with her later very warm friendship for the young earl, Charles, and inconsistent with other references to her husband's father. Moreover, a poem to Lady Worsley, written after 1690, speaks as if Anne were still in some place of retirement with the future not yet determined upon. It was almost certainly Charles, the third earl, who invited them to make their home at Eastwell.

For Anne and her husband the change was complete. There were practically no ties that bound the family to the new court, for although the second earl, in spite of the long and devoted services of his house to the Stuart cause, had at last declared in favor of William and Mary, and at the revolution had been counted of so much importance that his public offices had been renewed, his early death had broken the only possible link between his family and the reigning powers. Charles was too young for statecraft, while Heneage Finch, Anne's husband, as a non-juror, could have no part in public affairs. This entire severance from court activities could not, however, have been a matter of unmixed grief to Ardelia and her husband. To be together on this beautiful estate would, on the contrary, have been cause for unmixed joy had it not been for the fate of their royal master and mistress. Their loyalty to the Stuarts was no ephemeral passion, and nearly all the poems of this period are dominated by a melancholy born of the disasters of that unhappy house. Ardelia writes concerning the composition of *Aristomenes*:

I must acknowledge, yt the giving some interruptions to those melancholy thoughts, which possesst me, not only for my own, but much more for the misfortunes of those to whom I owe all imaginable duty, and gratitude, was so great a benefit, that I have reason to be satisfied with the undertaking, be the performance never so inconsiderable. And, indeed, an absolute solitude (which often was my lott) under such dejection of mind, could not have been

supported, had I indulged myself (as was too natural to me) only
in the contemplation of present and real afflictions, which I hope
will plead my excuse, for turning them for relief, upon such as
were imaginary, and relating to persons no more in being.

These words fairly describe the state of mind in which
many of the early poems were composed. *The Petition for
an Absolute Retreat*, *A Fragment*, and *Lines to Lady
Worsley* recount Ardelia's own unhappiness. *The Change*,
which for its gentleness and dignity, for its pathetic sweetness, is one of her most charming poems, is a little allegory
of the selfishness and insincerity of courtiers. The obscured
sun no longer followed by the flowers it had brought into
being, the dried-up river deserted by the fish it had nourished, the ruined mansion forsaken by the guests it had
cherished, are evidently but successive pictures of the dis-
crowned king. *The Losse* commemorates the breaking of
some close personal tie. Could the Urania of the poem be
possibly Mary of Modena herself ?

> Urania is no more, to me she is no more,
> All these combined can ne'er that loss deplore.

But whoever the heroine, the genuineness of the grief
cannot be questioned, a genuineness not lessened by the
Shelley-like lament that grief itself is mortal. The verses
On the Death of King James bring to an end the series of
poems especially marked by the bitterness of the revolution.
It is a long, heavy poem, in parts incomplete and crude, but
it is of distinct value as showing James II. and Mary of
Modena from the point of view of one of their own household.

This last poem was not written till 1701, and in spite of
the indignant sorrow and rebuke, the passionate loyalty, that
flamed up anew in its many stanzas, the twelve years had
already brought their gift of healing, and Ardelia had found
at beautiful Eastwell a more serene and deeply satisfying

life than could have opened before her had the highest court
honors been hers.

It is difficult to think of the present splendid mansion at
Eastwell Park as connected in any intimate way with Arde-
Eastwell   lia.   The eighteenth century house was built by
The Mansion   the Italian architect, Bonomi, under the direction of George Finch Hatton, the eighth Earl of Winchilsea.
And that house has been remodeled and enlarged on so
magnificent a scale by the present owner, Lord Gerard, as
hardly to suggest the house of a century ago.   Yet the house
to which Mr. and Mrs. Finch went was nevertheless of excep-
tional interest.   It dated, in its seventeenth century form,
from 1589, in which year Sir Moyle Finch obtained permission from Queen Elizabeth to inclose one thousand acres
and to embattle his house.   The original building was of the
sixteenth century, having been built by Sir Thomas Moyle
in about 1544, and having come into the Finch family
through the marriage of Thomas Finch, Esq., and Catherine
Moyle.   The wife of Sir Moyle Finch, their son, was the rich
heiress of Sir Thomas Heneage.   She was a woman, glad, it
is true, to be assured of an appropriate local habitation, but
more ambitious of a name.   Nine years after the death of
her husband her energetic use of the resources at her command was crowned by the title of Viscountess Maidstone,
and, five years later, in 1628, by that of Countess of Winchilsea, both titles with reversion to heirs male.   So that
the house to which Anne came in 1690 was of interest to her
not only as a fine English mansion a century old, with portions of it boasting an additional half century as well, but it
must have had a stronger personal attraction as the home of
her husband's family since the days of Catherine Moyle and
Elizabeth Heneage, the heiresses to whom they owed rank
and fortune.

Of Ardelia's associations with the estate itself we may

speak more confidently. Yet even here reservations must
be made. We must free ourselves, for instance, from the
glamor of certain historical associations that date back only
to the days when H. R. H. the Duke of Edinburgh, made
Eastwell his home, when members of the royal family
planted trees that still bear their names, when Edward VII.,
then Prince of Wales, drank tea on the balcony of the beautiful winter-garden. We must banish, too, from our mental
picture of Ardelia's home most of the luxuries, perhaps most
of the conveniences of the modern estate. The electric light
plant and the gas plant must give way to candles. For the
present elaborate system of water-works we must substitute
Mr. Finch's "darling spring" whence water was brought to
the house in a cart "driven by one of the underkeepers in a
green coat with a hazelbough for a whip." For the modern
splendor of equipment and service we must figure to ourselves very simple domestic arrangements. The completion
of the house, the building in of wide glass windows, the
plotting of gardens, the fair ordering of the trees, terraces,
and lawns adjacent to the house were all improvements not
accomplished till ten or twelve years after Ardelia's arrival
at Eastwell.

But in spite of all the enlargements and modifications
and improvements made from 1700 to 1900, there are yet
large portions of the estate that must be today
as they were when Ardelia first went to Eastwell. The following notes, taken, in substance, from the
Eastwell Blue Book of the present day, give the very details
urged in enthusiastic praise by earlier topographical writers:

The Park

Near the church of Boughton Aluph is the Pilgrim's Road,
marked by yew trees supposed: to have been planted by pilgrims
on their way to Canterbury to show other pilgrims the way. Near
Timber Gate Lodge is a grand avenue of beeches with large
stretches of fern. In one place are twelve yew trees near together
— wierd in shape, colossal in proportion, hoary in antiquity. If

they could speak they would probably tell us of forest chases in the
time of Alfred the Great, if not of Egbert, the first king of England, who ascended the throne in 827. . . . . We pass through
hills, slopes, undulations, and levels, which, with their ancient
timber and high fern, form the very ideal of an ancestral park of
the ancient noblesse. Here and there through the Park are stumps
of trees that were flourishing before Duke William of Normandy
became William I. of England. . . . . The ride through the woods
on a sultry day is most delightful; the complete shelter and
obscured sky, the brown carpet of dried beech-leaves and
beech-husks, the startling of the deer, the voices of nature, the
absence of any sight or sound to indicate that one is in a country of
human beings combining to add a charm of repose and of poetic
seclusion. The church of St. Cosmos and the embattled tower and
beacon turret of the church are very ancient. In this churchyard
is a yew, old in the time of William the Conqueror. This church
stands in a lovely spot surrounded by greenery where no sound
reaches it but the voices of birds and occasional animals. . . . . At
Challocks Church bottom formerly stood the straight oak which,
because of its shape and colossal proportions, was worth more than
£100 for the timber there was in it. A former Lord Winchilsea
refused that sum for it. . . . . The Star Walk is still traceable but
much overgrown. . . . . Mt. Pleasant is a circular eminence surrounded by ancient yew trees standing at intervals as solitary sen-
tinels. From this point the view is remarkable. At our back is the
wooded park with its undulations, its mansion, gardens and lake,
with the tower of Eastwell church peeping up through the trees.
On our left the horizon line is formed by Wye church and Wye
Downs. Spread out before us are villages, parks, county seats, hop
gardens, fruit gardens, orchards, cornfields, woods, plantations and
meadows. In the distance we descry the coast town of Hythe, and
on a clear day we may see the English channel with its passing
shipping.

The majesty and dream-like loveliness of this park could
not have been less in the seventeenth century. Lady Winchilsea says of it:

And now whenever I contemplate the several beautys of this
Park, allow'd to be (if not of the Universal yett) of our British
World infinitely the finest,

A pleasing wonder through my fancy roves,
Smooth as her lawns, and lofty as her Groves.
Boundless my Genius seems, when my free sight,
Finds only distant skys to stop her flight.
Like mighty Denhams, then, methinks my hand,
Might bid the Landskip, in strong numbers stand,
Fix all its charms, with a Poetick skill,
And raise its Fame above his Cooper's Hill.

This, I confess, is what in itts self itt deserves, but the unhappy difference is, that he by being a real Poet, cou'd make that place (as he sais) a Parnassus to him; whilst I that behold a real Parnassus here, in that lovely Hill, which in this Park bears that name, find in myself so little of the Poet, that I am still restrained from attempting a description of itt in verse, tho' the agreeableness of the subject has often prompted me most strongly to itt.

The central figure in the family circle when Mr. and Mrs. Finch went to Eastwell was, of course, Charles, the young earl, then eighteen or nineteen years of age. His sister Mariamne was three years older, while his mother, Elizabeth Wyndham, a widow from his birth, was still a young woman. Charles was the grandson of the second earl by his second wife, Mary Seymour, of whose eleven children five, at least, were still living. Of these, Frances was the wife of Viscount Thynne of Longleat. Leopold was warden of All-Soul's College, Oxford. The sons possibly still at Eastwell were Lashley and Henry, young men between twenty-two and eighteen years of age. Two daughters, Catherine and Elizabeth, between ten and fifteen, were children of the third wife. Elizabeth Ayres, the fourth wife, was still living, and though technically the grandmother of the earl, was a young woman of twenty-eight, with a son John, of seven, who became the fifth earl, and a little daughter, Anne, of two. It is possible that not all these persons lived at Eastwell. But it was at any rate a large, a young, and a curiously complex family circle into

which Heneage and Anne Finch came after the wreck of
their fortunes in 1688.

That Anne was speedily at home with her husband's kin
is apparent from various bits of playful verse commemorating
domestic happenings, the best of these being the charmingly
light and deft *Lines on a Punch Bowl*, addressed to her
brother Lashley. But her meed of serious verse was naturally reserved for Charles. He was the earl; he was her
generous and hospitable host; he was young, gay, handsome; she approved of his management of Eastwell; he
approved of her poetry. The ties were certainly strong.
Fortunately Charles was not only knowing in all the rules of
poetry, and at his pleasure capable of putting them in practice, but he was also indulgent to the gentle craft of poesy
when practiced by others. It was, indeed, his lordship's
commendation of some lines of hers that led Ardelia to her
final joyous renunciation of the vows so often and so
straitly made to forego the unfeminine seductions of the
pen. In the *Prologue to Aristomenes* we have a very
pleasant picture of the shy Ardelia and the poetically
inclined young earl by the good winter's fire in the drawing-
room at Eastwell, while she, with outward dash and fun, but
with hardly concealed inward trepidation, presents to this
much-dreaded critic who had the rules of Horace at his
tongue's end her "wholly tragicall" play.

The social joys of Eastwell were not, however, limited to
the family. Ardelia, who says of herself,

Lady   I who to my heart just bounds had sett,
Winchilsea's And in my friendship scorn'd to be coquette
Friendships   Or seem indulgent to each new Adresse,

really did, in spite of this reserve, walk in the footsteps of
the Matchless Orinda in her capacity for devoted attach-
ments, and were it not for the disguise of fanciful names,
we should be introduced through her poems to a wide circle.

But though certain Oranias and Uranias remain unidentified, in many cases the disguise is penetrable, and sometimes the real names are used.

One group of poems shows the close relationship always maintained between Ardelia and the family of Lord Thanet, of Hothfield. Catherine Cavendish was four years younger than herself, but she was married to Lord Thanet in 1684, only a few months after the marriage of Anne Kingsmill and Mr. Finch. Inasmuch as all the poems addressed to Arminda refer to her as "my Lady Thanet," they must all date after 1684. *The Inquiry After Peace*, a poem inserted in a letter to Lady Thanet, and the *Petition for an Absolute Retreat* show that in hours of foreboding or of actual disaster, Ardelia's instinctive refuge was "the great Arminda."

> What Nature, or refining Art,
> All that Fortune cou'd impart,
> Heaven did to *Arminda* send ;
> Then gave her for *Ardelia's* Friend.

The good Lord Thanet evidently agreed with Ardelia's estimate of his young wife. He outlived her for many years, but had carved on his tombstone as the most notable fact in his career that he had been married to Catherine Cavendish, and that he "believed no woman on earth would have made him so happy as she did;" so Mr. and Mrs. Finch were not alone in their unfashionable domestic felicity. The daughter, Catherine Tufton, chose Ardelia as the recipient of "the first letter that ever she writt," and she is thereupon celebrated as the high-born Serena, fair and young. Of more interest is the probable relation between Ardelia and the second daughter, Anne Tufton, who was married in 1708-9, when she was but fifteen or sixteen, to the Earl of Salisbury. Is she then the "Salisbury" praised in the *Nocturnal Reverie?* Leigh Hunt, in *Men, Women, and Books*, says positively, but without giving his authority, that the "Salisbury"

of the poem is Frances Bennett, the wife of the fourth Earl
of Salisbury; while Jane Williams in *Literary Women of
England*, says, with equal positiveness and equal absence
of a citation of authority, that this "Salisbury" is the Lady
Anne Tufton. Wordsworth suggested that the lines in question marred the poem and should be omitted. Such a
course would certainly save controversy. With no actual
proof at hand, only the probabilities of the case can be
stated, and these are all in favor of Anne Tufton. The comparatively late date of the poem is indicated by the fact that
it appears in neither manuscript. The latest possible date
for it would be 1713, the date of its publication, and the
earliest possible date, if Anne Tufton is the "Salisbury,"
would be 1709. In these years the young countess would
be between sixteen and twenty, with Lady Winchilsea twenty-
two years older, a disparity of age that might tell against a
close friendship between the two countesses, but would certainly be no bar to an adroit compliment from the older lady
to the daughter of her dearest friend. And there is no
record of any friendship with Frances Bennett.

Another family closely connected with the Finches was
that of the Thynnes of Longleat. Ardelia visited often at
The Thynnes   this noble estate, and the mansion, and espe-
of Longleat   cially the gardens, the most splendid and costly
example of the formal garden at that time in England, never
failed to arouse her enthusiasm. The Thynne family, also,
both collectively and individually, received their meed of
eulogistic verse. The poems run along from 1690 to 1714,
and show a steadfast and intimate friendship. The death of
young James Thynne is made the occasion for an enumeration
of the renowned ancestors of the family. Of these distinguished persons none attracted Ardelia more than "that
matchless Female," the Lady Packington, who was supposed
by many to be the author of *The Whole Duty of Man*, and who

> of each Sex the two best Gifts enjoy'd,
> The Skill to write, the Modesty to hide.

Grace Stroud, the wife of Henry Thynne, is the Cleone of the poems. Her husband is Theanor, and is always spoken of with a certain awe because of his knowledge of the fine arts. As a judge of tapestry, painting, and poetry his opinions seemed beyond contradiction. Ardelia must have had more than one thrill of gratified pride as she found her own poems praised from time to time by so competent a critic. When, seven years after his death, she sent her volume of poems to his daughter, the young Countess of Hertford, she rests her modest plea on the father's favor rather than on her own merits. It is interesting to see Lady Hertford, the friend in later years of Thomson, Savage, and Shenstone, begin thus early her role as patroness of letters.

Frances, the daughter of Viscount Weymouth, married Sir Robert Worsley in 1690. Lady Worsley is the "Utresia" who had "so obligingly desired Ardelia to correspond with her by Letter." Ardelia's response to the request of this petted child of fortune, beautiful in her fresh and smiling bloom, universally beloved, encompassed with present joys and rich in hope, is couched in complimentary terms that would certainly stimulate Lady Worsley's side of the correspondence. But though extravagant, the praise Ardelia gives is evidently from her heart. She speaks only what she feels. A little hint of the permanence of this friendship is found in a letter from Lady Marrow to Lady Kay, quoted on page xliv. In Ardelia's *Answer to Ephelia* the reference to "your large Pallace" as their "place of meeting, love and liberty," would seem definitely to affix the "Ephelia" to some one of the Longleat ladies. The date of the poem, which is about 1690–1, would still further confine the allusion to the Viscountess Weymouth or to the Lady Worsley, and Anne's intimacy with the latter would make her the more probable one.

In that case the "Ephelia" of the little poem on *Friendship* is doubtless also Lady Worsley. That she should be "Utresia," in one poem and "Ephelia" in another is no more surprising than that Mr. Finch should figure as both "Daphnis" and "Flavio." Lady Worsley's daughter is celebrated in some gay little verses in honor of the marriage of Edward and Elizabeth Herbert, which must have taken place about 1709, when the bride and groom were respectively fourteen and seventeen. Cupid, having lost Elizabeth Herbert, is comforted by the thought that he may still find a suitable mate in the young Worsley, who was then fifteen, and who was married the next year to Lord Cartaret.

One of the prominent figures at Longleat at this time was Elizabeth Singer, afterward Mrs. Rowe, whose pen-name was Philomela. In 1694, when a young lady of twenty, she was on intimate terms with the family, and Mr. Henry Thynne taught her Latin and Italian. A collection of her poems was published in 1696 and was much admired. The friendship between Elizabeth Singer and Lady Hertford was warm and was life-long. One would expect from the circumstances that Ardelia and Philomela would have found much in common, but their extant letters and poems do not reveal any especial friendship. Ardelia refers once in *The Miser and the Poet* to the poems of Philomela, and a letter from Mrs. Rowe to Lady Hertford, in 1720, the year of Lady Winchilsea's death, written to condole with Lady Hertford for the death of "My Lady ——," may refer to Lady Winchilsea. The letter closes: "'Tis impertinent to reason, and against the dictates of nature, or else you might satisfy yourself with the extraordinary character she left behind her and her rest from the misfortunes of life." But this letter is indecisive, and there are no further indications of any acquaintance between the two poetesses.

There was also resident at Longleat the saintly Bishop

Ken, the author of several widely-known hymns, as "Awake My Soul" and "Glory to Thee, My God, This Night." He was one of the nonjuring bishops, and at this time living in retirement under the protection of Viscount Thynne. Ardelia was much impressed by the beauty and consistency of Bishop Ken's life. She even goes so far as to say, in her poem on the hurricane of 1703, that the bishop's mansion at Wells would never have been so scourged by the wild winds had Bishop Ken not been supplanted by Bishop Kidder. On the whole, we may safely say that Longleat was the source to Ardelia of much personal happiness, and of much in the way of poetical guidance and inspiration.

Ardelia's long, dignified, and rather heavy poem on the death of Sir William Twysden, shows how intimately she knew him and how genuinely she admired him. The Twysdens were also her husband's relatives, for Sir William was the great-grandson of the famous Elizabeth Heneage, the first Countess of Winchilsea. When Anne visited at the Twysden estate it must have been with an envious pleasure that she gazed upon certain heirlooms there. Sir William owned the picture of the first Lady Winchilsea and "the blew case of gold in which it is," and also a dozen of silver plates that had been given by the said Lady Winchilsea as a legacy to Sir William's grandmother, "having the said Ladies armes on the one side and coronet of an Earle over them, and on the backside a Coronet and over against it A. T.," the initials of the grandmother, Anne Twysden. There was also "a gold booke" and "a gold bole and cover to it belonging," which had apparently come from the same source. Sir William was learned in history, genealogies and heraldry. He was, according to Ardelia, a clear-sighted and moderate patriot; an author himself of no mean rank; and a gentleman of fine taste, high breeding, and affable manners.

Ardelia's personal poems do not bear the stamp of conventional eulogy. In an interchange of formal literary
compliments she could be as verbose and vapid as the law
governing such effusions seemed to demand. But poems
written to people for whom she had a personal friendship
are quite different in tone. They strike a modern reader
as having a good deal of what Dr. Johnson would call
"encomiastic fervor," but they likewise have the stamp of
genuineness. These eulogies are Ardelia's deliberate esti-
mates of the friends she praises. The total effect of her
rather prolific and almost wearisomely minute personal poems
is to introduce us to a company of sweet-spirited, quick-
witted, beautiful, and virtuous women; to a company of men
patriotic, well educated, of high breeding, refined manners,
and cultivated tastes. It is worth a moment's pause to note
the marked contrast between the social life thus indicated
and that presented by contemporary writers, such as Pope,
Swift, or Prior. Certainly no Jeremy Collier would have
been needed had all the aristocracy been such as Ardelia
portrays. Either she had a gift for eliciting and seeing
only the best in her friends, or she decisively rejected all
who were not of the best; or, the more probable hypothesis,
her pictures of Lord Thanet and Viscount Thynne and Sir
William Twysden, of Arminda and Cleone, and Serena, and
Ephelia, and Utresia, and the rest of the goodly squires
and dames, as truthfully represent the times as Pope's
Chloes and Atossas and Sapphos, his Bufos and Bubos
and Lord Fannys. Ardelia merely brings into the light a
typical group of the best portion of the English aristocracy
of her day.

Life at Eastwell was further varied by visits to different
watering-places, and by winters in London. Ardelia's town-
house was in Cleveland Row, a short street adjacent to St.
James's palace. Charles Jervas, the artist who painted a

portrait of Pope, and whose house was often Pope's head-
quarters in London, lived but a short distance away, in
Cleveland Court. Lady Winchilsea knew Jervas, and admired
his work, especially the portrait of her friend, the lovely
Mrs. Chetwynd. It was at the house of Jervas that Pope
was staying when Lady Winchilsea invited him to the famous
dinner which was followed by the dramatic recital destined
to play so interesting a part in the relations between Pope
and Ardelia.

Visits to the more noted watering-places were not infrequent. We have seen the depression of spirit engendered by
the public and private disasters incident on the revolution.
But Ardelia's peace of mind was assailed by another and
even more insidious foe. That "anxious Rebell," her heart,
was reinforced by another enemy within the gates. She was,
in fact, an unfortunate victim of the Spleen, a fashionable
eighteenth century distemper, the protean woes of which
had early cradled her into song. Many were her ineffectual
attempts to find relief through visits to various health resorts.
Of these Tunbridge Wells with its "quick spring of spirit-
eous water" was the most fashionable, and its fame as a cure
for the Spleen was long-lived. We find Lady Winchilsea
here once in 1685 and again in 1706.

A less noted resort, but one much frequented by the
gentry and lauded by medical men was, at Astrop, a small vil-
lage near London. A "Learned Physician" in 1668 gave
four pages to an encomium of the well dedicated to St. Rum-
bald, a child which spake as soon as he was born. This
well, says the Learned Physician, "openeth, astringeth, and
consolidateth egregiously." It takes away "ecrementitious
Humidities of the Brain . . . . opens the obstructions of the
Liver and Spleen, cures the Flatus Hypochondriacus, and the
Palpitation and Trembling of the Heart proceeding from
thence. . . . . It fastens the Teeth though ready to drop

out. . . . . It comforts the Nerves, helps the Gout. . . . .
strengthens broken Bones. . . . . takes away the swelling
and pains of the Spleen . . . . and cures Aches and Cramps
in any part of the body whatsoever." But even this concen-
trated apothecary's shop proved unavailing in Lady Winchilsea's case. Neither Tunbridge nor Astrop gave her the
branch of healing spleenwort with which Pope's Umbriel
safely penetrated to the cave of the gloomy goddess. Her
poem on *The Spleen* is of the first-hand, naturalistic order.
It has none of the glittering generalities born of vague knowledge. So full and accurate is its account of symptoms that
it achieved prompt professional recognition. Dr. Stukeley
published it in his treatise on the spleen, for the purpose, as
he said, of helping out his own description. Lady Winchilsea admits that the spleen is often counterfeited, but
maintains that the real disease is of the gravest sort. The
sufferer is afflicted by insomnia or by boding dreams and
terrifying visions. There are successive moods of stupid
discontent, wild anger, panic fear. Spleen blights the ablest
minds with self-doubt. It enters the realm of religion and
perplexes men with endless, foolish scruples. It fills the
heart with fancied griefs. It creates an abnormal love of
solitude. Various early poems, as *On Grief, To Sleep, To
Melancholy*, express in other terms the extreme depression
of spirits against which the sufferer from the spleen had to
contend. Ardelia addresses Melancholy as her "old invet'-
rate foe," who in spite of mirth, music, poetry and friendship,
in spite even of " the *Indian* leaf and parch'd *eastern* Berry"
still holds his throne in her darkened heart. In despairing
surrender she exclaims:

> To thee, great Monarch, I submitt,
> Thy Sables and thy Cypress bring,
> I own thy Pow'r, I own thee King,
> Thy title in my heart is writt,
> And till that breaks I ne'er shall freedom gett.

It is probable, however, that as the years went by her health improved. Her spirits certainly did. When she was at Tunbridge in 1706 she was sufficiently at leisure from herself to examine into the love-making then so popular a pastime at the Wells and to write it up with fine scorn. And she threw a playful jibe at the doctors who thought to cure the spleen with a formula. Further proof of this increased gayety of spirit is in a letter, written August 1708, from Lady Morrow to her daughter, Lady Kay:

Friday last I went to town. . . . .From the Vice Chamberlain I went to see Mrs. Finch, she ill of the spleen. Lady Worsley has painted a pretty fire-screen and presented her with; and notwithstanding her ill-natured distemper, she was very diverting—Mrs. Finch I mean.

It is not certain that Ardelia ever discovered Green's famous remedy for the spleen,

Throw but a stone, the Giant dies,

but it is more than probable that the simple life at Eastwell, the long, entrancing walks in the park, and the peace growing out of congenial companionships and congenial occupations were better cures than Tunbridge or Astrop.

No record of Ardelia's life at Eastwell would be satisfactory without as full an account as possible of the "one from whom she was inseparable." In her description of her ideal retreat from the world the one person needed to make its charms complete was

A *Partner*, suited to my Mind,
Solitary, pleas'd and kind ;
Who, partially, may something see
Preferred to all the World, in me ;
Slighting, by my humble Side,
Fame and Splendour, Wealth and Pride.

Inasmuch as this was a description after the event, the lines may be counted a fairly accurate, though they are not

an adequate, picture of Heneage Finch in this Eastwell life.
In a poetical appeal to Dafnis written about 1700, in which
Ardelia urges him to leave his usual occupations for a walk
in the fields, we have incidentally a summary of the interests
of this retired courtier and soldier. He follows with steady
attention all the details of the campaigns in behalf of his
old Master James, and the work of Vauban, Lewis's chief
engineer, is minutely studied. But there are other and more
peaceful interests. Mr. Finch is attracted by geographical research and is absorbed in the work of Nicolas and Guillaume
Sanson, the French geographers. He busies himself with
mathematical drawing. He particularly enjoys doing illu-
minations on vellum. Against the tyranny of these pursuits
Ardelia makes playful protest. The partner entirely suited
to her mind should discover that reading even the softest
poetry about nature could not vie with seeing nature itself,
that the best "carmine and imported blew" cannot compete
with the bright colors of the corn-flower and the poppy, that
faery circles on the green are of more worth than the truest
line compasses can draw, and that all Sanson's facts about
the universe are as naught before the joy of one perfect
English day spent among the fields and groves. So eager a
delight in outdoor life must have been infectious, and we can
hardly imagine Dafnis insensible to Ardelia's pleadings.
His interest in Eastwell, however, took another and more
learned direction, that of antiquarian research. He was an
enthusiastic believer, for instance, in the legend that Richard
Plantagenet had served as a brick-layer at Eastwell when
the house of Sir Moyle Finch was built; that Sir Moyle, on
discovering the royal workman, had granted him his wish
for a palace of one room built in a field; and that an ancient
unmarked tomb in Eastwell Church covered the remains of
the hapless Richard. It was through Mr. Finch that the
legend first saw light. Dr. Brett related the story in a let-

ter published in Peck's *Desiderata Curiosa* (1732), saying
that he had his information from Heneage, Earl of Winchilsea, whom he visited at Eastwell Park in 1720. An anonymous tract, entitled *The Parallel*, and published in London,
1744, tells the story of Richard, and closes with these words:

> This house of Eastwell Place came afterwards into possession
> of the eldest Branch of the noble Family of Finch, and it is to the
> laudable curiosity of the late Heneage, Earl of Winchilsea, a Noble-
> man whose virtues threw a Shade on the age in which he lived,
> that we owe the several particulars I have given the Reader. They
> were frequently the topic of that good man's Conversation, who
> would sometimes show that Spot in his Park, upon which the
> House of old Richard stood, and which had been pulled down by
> the Earl's Father. "But I," said the most worthy Lord, "had it
> reached my Time, would sooner have pulled down that," pointing
> to his own House. As a testimony to the Truth of this remarkable
> History he was wont to produce the following Entry in the Register
> of the Parish Church at Eastwell: "Anno Domini 1555 Richard
> Plantagenet was buried the 22nd December, Anno ut supra."

Mr. Finch's antiquarian tastes and learning received
early and frequent recognition. Harris, in his *History of
Kent*, records the accidental discovery, in 1703, of a small
urn of reddish earth and of the skeleton of a child, in a
cutting along the wagon-way near Wye. In 1713 he
writes of it :

> The Report of this Discovery brought the Right Honourable
> Colonel Heneage Finch (now Earl of Winchilsea) whose inquisitive
> genius inclines him to a curious search after Antiquities, and of
> which he hath a nice Relish and is an excellent Judge, to come out
> and examine this place more narrowly which was done the same
> year.

The results of this investigation were all left in the hands
of Lord Winchilsea. Dr. Stukeley says that during the nine
years he lived in London (1717-1726) he had "the greatest
intimacy with Thomas, Ld Pembroke, Heneage Earl of
Winchelsea, Sir Isaac Newton — in short with the whole sett

of learned men and Vertuoso's w^h at that time abounded," and his *memoirs* contain numerous references to Lord Winchilsea's antiquarian zeal and learning.

Lord Winchilsea's closest associates, besides his chaplain, Mr. Creyk, were Lord Hertford and Dr. Stukeley. They styled themselves Druids and had fanciful names, Dr. Stukeley being Chyndonax; Lord Hertford, Segonax; and Lord Winchilsea, Cyngetorix. Their special search was for *Durolenum*, and Lord Winchilsea enthusiastically declared that if he should be so happy as to succeed in the search he would have "O brave Cyngetorix" engraved on his tombstone.

Another form of antiquarian research carried on in the main by Charles, and one perhaps more in accord with Ardelia's taste, was the hunt for old books and manuscripts. In an account of Thomas Britton, the famous musical smallcoal man, we have a very pleasant picture in which the Earl of Winchilsea is one of the figures:

About the beginning of this century, a passion for collecting old books and manuscripts reigned among the nobility. The chief of those who sought after them were the Duke of Devonshire, Edward, Earl of Oxford, and the Earls of Pembroke, Sunderland and Winchilsea. These persons in the winter season, on Saturdays, the Parliament not sitting on that day, were used to resort to the city, and, dividing themselves, took several routes, some to Little Britain, some to Moorfields, and others to different parts of the town, inhabited by book-sellers; there they would enquire into the several shops as they passed along for old books and manuscripts; and sometime before noon would assemble at the shop of Christopher Bateman, a book-seller, at the corner of Ave-Maria-lane in Paternoster-row; and here they were frequently met by Bagford, and other persons engaged in the same pursuits, and a conversation always commenced on the subject of their inquiries.

And presently along would come Thomas Britton in his blue linen frock and with his sack of small coal on his back, and join them.

Most of the antiquarian research of which we find definite record occurred in the years 1720–1726, or after Lady Winchilsea's death, but inasmuch as Lord Winchilsea was elected president of the Society of Antiquaries as early as 1717, and was recognized as early as 1703 as the natural judge and custodian of antiquarian treasures found in that region, we cannot escape the conclusion that Roman roads, Roman ruins, mortuary urns, ancient brasses and coins, and worm-eaten manuscripts loomed large among the interests of this Eastwell life.

From Lord Winchilsea's antiquarian labors and letters we get more than a hint of his character. He shows himself capable of strong enthusiasms, and he is prompt, energetic, and optimistic in carrying them out. He is, withal, gay in spirit, and with a sense of humor that turns even his failures into fun. He lives an easy, genial, unambitious life. His interests are varied and dilletante. If *Durolenum* remains elusive, why there are still manuscripts to be illuminated. If the "blew and carmine" fail, the rabbit burrows still hold out possibilities in the way of urns and rings and bones. He has no occupation so strenuous or important as to interrupt the peaceful tenor of his days.

But antiquarian research was far from being his only interest. From a leather-bound, silver-clasped duodecimo copy of *Rider's Almanac*, on the blank pages of which Lord Winchilsea recorded important domestic incidents, we gain many suggestive hints concerning life at Eastwell. The *Almanac* is for 1723, but the events recorded are not merely of that year. He apparently made the little book a repository for any family dates or happenings that seemed interesting to him. The dates from 1713 to 1719 have chiefly to do with "my several Tryalls in Chancery," and there are dates of important deeds of sale, showing that after the death of Charles there were many imperative demands on the time and thought of the new earl in the way of business management. The dates of births, marriages, and deaths in the families of various friends are also carefully noted. He sets down the day he was weighed and the "16 stone and 12 lbs." registered by the scales. We find that a "horse-hair peruque" costs £2, 10s. Among scattered financial transactions is a list of fees headed, "Given away at Marlborough House, Aug. 18, 1723." These fees range from a guinea each to seven of the more important servants down to 2s 6d for the "Kitchin-Boy;" and aggregate £14 6s. 6d. An interesting list of "Books which I have Subscribed for" certainly shows, in spite of the incorrect citation of titles, some learning and a catholic taste, for it includes such volumes as "*Carmina Quadragesimila;*" "*Recuille des Piers antique graves;*" "*Monfaucons Supplim, 5 vol.;*" "*King of Sweden's Travels;*" "*Cardinal Wolsey's Life;*" "*Querels Testament;*" "*Sr. Ra. Winnwood's Letters;*" "*Rev. Lewis' Isle of Thanet;*" "*Mr. Breval's Book;*" and "*Dr. Barwick's Life.*" If any room in the present house can be definitely associated with Ardelia it must be the stately library, where are doubtless still many of the books selected by Anne Finch and her husband, and perhaps also some of those illuminated by him.

Along with notes on books are jottings of another sort, as a record of the "large ripe scarlet strawberrys from Brook Garden," presented to Mr. Finch, October 8; or the account of "a Buck which, having been almost killed by another Buck in the Park, had been gott by the Keeper into the Green Garden" where "from being a very lean Buck—after his recovery he grew so fatt that he cutt as deep as the length of this mark on the Haunches, viz. two inches and a half."

Through the pleasant intimacy of this little book we gain confirmations of the attractive impression already made by Mr. Finch through his wife's poems and his own letters, an

impression further confirmed by G. Vertue's print of his
lordship, which shows a portly man with straight nose, dark
eyes, a white, curled wig, and a very kindly expression.

Lord Winchilsea died in 1726. A Latin eulogy of him
is quoted in *The Gentleman's Magazine* for October, 1783.
It is entitled "*In Obitum Prænobilis Viri*, HENEAGII FINCH,
*Comitis de Winchilsea, Epicedium et Apotheosi, Prid. Cal.
Oct. 1726.*" But this tribute is less satisfying than the fol-
lowing brief note from Lord Hertford to Dr. Stukeley:

> The concern you express for the loss of Lord Winchilsea can-
> not but be pleasing to me; for I should be very sorry that you, for
> whom he had a just value, should not have grieved with the rest of
> his friends; and I think I may call the whole world so, for sure he
> had no enemy nor was he one to anybody.

The final impression made by these scattered facts concerning Lord Winchilsea is that he was as well fitted by
temperament and tastes to find permanent joy in the retirement at Eastwell as was Ardelia herself. If she loved nature
and poetry with emphasis on the nature, and he loved nature
and antiquities with emphasis on the antiquities, that was
only enough of a difference to give needed variety. They
were both simple and unambitious in their desires. They
were loyal to their friends. Their minds were alert and
their interests always along scholarly or poetical lines. They
very nearly made real Wordsworth's maxim of plain living
and high thinking.

**Lady Win-
chilsea's
Death** Lady Winchilsea died six years before her
husband. Her death is thus recorded in
"*Mawson's Obits.*"

On Friday, 5th of August, 1720, dyed at her own house in
Cleveland Row the Right Honble Anne Countess of Winchilsea, and
was on Tuesday following privately Interred according to her desire
at Eastwell in Kent, the ancient seat of that noble family. She
was Dau'r of Sr Wm Kingsmill of Sidmonton, a very ancient family
in Hantshire.

The facts in this notice and in parts its phraseology
are identical with a brief statement in Lord Winchilsea's
journal, from which I have already freely quoted. The
authorship of the little sketch is left doubtful, but the fact
that Lord Winchilsea preserved it shows that it was satisfactory to him. There is, perhaps, no more fitting way to
close this outline of Ardelia's life than by quoting the exact
words recorded in her husband's private journal:

My Dear Wife's just character finely drawn by —— and published in the publick prints after her Decease.

On Friday the fifth instant died at her own house in Cleaveland
Row the R^t Honourable Anne Countess of Winchilsea and was on
Tuesday following (privately according to her own desire) carried
down to Eastwell in Kent, the ancient seat of that noble Family,
and Interred there. She was a Daughter of Sr Wm Kingsmill of
Sidmonton, a very ancient Family in Hampshire, and had been Maid
of Honour to her late Majesty Queen Mary when Dutchess of York,
till married to the Honble Coll. Heneage Finch who on the death of
his Nephew the late Earl of Winchelsea succeeded to that Honour: To draw her Ldysp's just character requires a masterly pen
like her own. We shall only presume to say she was the most
faithfull servant to her Royall Mistresse, the best wife to her noble
Lord, and in every other relation public and private so illustrious
an example of all moral and divine virtues: in one word a Person of
such extraordinary endowments both of Body and Mind that the
Court of England never bred a more accomplished Lady nor the
Church of England a better Christian.

II

THE PROGRESS OF LADY WINCHILSEA'S FAME

The relation between Ardelia and contemporary poets is
a matter of considerable interest. She early received an
enthusiastic welcome into the guild from sub-
Early Tributes ordinate craftsmen. In a package of manuscript poems in the possession of the Duke of Marlborough

at Blenheim is *An Ode on Love, inscribed to the Honourable Mrs. Finch.* It is four and one-half pages long, and is
apparently one of the earliest tributes to her work. Another
example of "private homage from an unknown muse" is
from the very modest pen of honest Will Shippen, a par-
liamentary Jacobite and a poet on his own account. He
bases his admiration of her "wondrous sweetness" and "manly
strength" on the poems that appeared in Gildon's *Miscellany*
in 1701, and on *All is Vanity*, which, though not published
till 1713, was written before the death of Dryden in 1700.
Shippen may have known all these poems in manuscript, but
it seems probable that his eulogy was called forth by Mrs.
Finch's first appearance in print in 1701.

A congratulatory poem from Mrs. Randolph and an even
more congratulatory response from Mrs. Finch would, if
interpreted as seriously as they were written, enthrone both
ladies high in poetic realms. The description of Mrs. Finch
as the Elisha on whom fell the mantle of Cowley, the recognition of her as the rightful heir of Orinda's fame, carried
praise to dizzy heights. But the conventional extravagance
of eulogy is so vague that we cannot determine just which
poem Mrs. Finch had sent for Mrs. Randolph's inspection.
The only one referred to is *The Pastoral* published by Gildon. Of Mrs. Randolph's other work I find no trace except
a commonplace poem, *On the much lamented death of the
Incomparable Lady, the Honorable Lady Oxenden. A
Pindarique Ode.* This *Ode* is preserved in a curious old scrap-
book in the British Museum, a volume made up of clippings
of verse by women, from newspapers, annuals, books, and
with a few manuscript items. None of these early poems
calls Mrs. Finch "Ardelia." This pen-name was not made
public, it seems, till her fame was somewhat established.

In Prior's *Miscellaneous Works* published in 1740, is a
little poem called *Lines to Prior by a Lady Unknown.*

This poem, no trace of which is to be found elsewhere, is ascribed by Mr. Adrian Drift, Prior's executor, to Anne, Countess of Winchilsea. There is no evidence that **Matthew Prior** Lady Winchilsea knew Prior, nor can the slight personal allusions in this poem be taken as indicating any first-hand knowledge of the poet. Such knowledge might easily have come, however, with sufficient minuteness and directness from Longleat through Elizabeth Singer, to whom Prior, in the intervals of his attendance on the king as gentleman of thé bed-chamber, was paying vain addresses. The poem must be an early one, its spirit and phraseology having little likeness to any of Lady Winchilsea's work except her first drama. Certainly the hysterical emotion with which the lady speaks of herself as "A Virgin-heart fraught with secret wishes," "a love-sick maid whose passion is raised to excess by the swelling numbers of the poet," is quite out of keeping with the usual dignified and delicate reticence of Lady Winchilsea's personal allusions. The lines are an acknowledgment of poetical indebtedness to Prior, a point to be more fully discussed in connection with Ardelia's songs.

Nicholas Rowe's estimate of Lady Winchilsea's poems is recorded in *An Epistle to Flavia. On the sight of two* **Nicholas Rowe** *Pindaric Odes on the Spleen and Vanity. Written by a Lady, her Friend.* This dates before any published work of hers, for it is evident that the poems had been transmitted to Rowe through some trusted intermediary with many cautions as to secrecy. Rowe's praise is unqualified. Ardelia is a "divine nymph" whose inspiration comes from heaven. She alone has not bowed the knee to false gods of wit, she is the only rival of Pindar short of the celestial choirs. Rowe approved of Ardelia's caution in keeping her poems from the public eye, but lines such as his would not have made her averse to the

proposals of Gildon in 1701. Later Rowe sent down to
Eastwell copies of his *Imitations* of Horace's *Odes*. In
1713 Ardelia wrote a prologue to be spoken by Mrs. Oldfield,
at the presentation of Rowe's tragedy, *Jane Shore*. These
facts would seem to indicate a literary friendship of considerable strength. A personal acquaintance is highly probable,
but of that I find no direct proof.

Swift's *Letters* and *Journal to Stella* show that by 1710
he was on familiar terms with Charles, the third Earl of

Jonathan Swift
Winchilsea, who, in spite of his Jacobite ancestors, had so far submitted to the revolution
government as to deserve and receive valuable public appoint-
ments from William, and later from Anne. Swift says of
him, "Being very poor he complied too much with the government he hated;" but that the two men were on especially
good terms is apparent from the words in which Swift
informs Stella of the death of the handsome young earl:
"Poor Lord Winchilsea is dead, to my great grief. He was
an worthy, honest gentleman, and particular friend of mine;
and what is yet worse, my old acquaintance, Mrs. Finch, is
now Countess of Winchilsea, the title being fallen to her
husband but without much estate." Swift's intimacy with
Lord Winchilsea and also with Lady Worsley, one of Anne
Finch's closest friends, would certainly imply that Swift had
frequent opportunities of meeting the lady of whom he
speaks thus cavalierly. To offset this note to Stella we may
turn to Swift's poem, *Apollo Outwitted, to Mrs. Finch under
the name of Ardelia*. This was published in *Miscellanies
in Prose and Verse* in 1711, but would seem to have been
written some years earlier. It very possibly belongs to the
September-October, 1708, spent by Swift in Kent. Ardelia
is represented as having adroitly won from Apollo the gift of
song but without having granted his suit. In revenge the
god exclaims that, though he cannot revoke his gift, he will

afflict the prudish lady with pride and modesty so stubborn
that her verse shall remain unknown:

> And last my vengeance to complete,
> Mayst thou descend to take renown,
> Prevailed on by the thing you hate,
> A Whig! and one that wears a gown!

The verses are, on the whole, playful and gallant and would
indicate nothing but friendly relations. But the last lines
show that, whatever concessions her nephew Charles felt to
be the logical outcome of his necessities, Ardelia's allegiance
to the old order was unfaltering and outspoken. It would
not, indeed, be difficult to imagine after-dinner conversations
in which the statements of that very positive defender of the
Whigs, Dr. Swift, might have elicited not only those
"flashes of Ardelia's eyes" before which Apollo was
abashed, but even more emphatic retorts not contributory to
final amity. The evidence is too scanty for an exact statement of the attitude of Swift toward Mrs. Finch, but it
would seem to be more friendly than that of Pope.

The actual relationship between Lady Winchilsea and
two others of her fellow poets, Pope and Gay, is not easily
Alexander Pope determined. In years she was much their
and John Gay senior. When she first braved the publicity of
Gildon's *Miscellany* in 1701 Pope was but a lad of thirteen,
studying versification under his father's strict tutelage in
Binfield, and Gay, a youth of sixteen, in the free grammar
school of Barnstaple, was devoting himself to dramatic per-
formances under his "rhyming pedagogue," R. Luck, A. M.
But the next decade brought great changes. The young
men had come to London and were on friendly terms in the
same literary coterie. Gay was not yet widely known, but
Pope's *Pastorals*, his *Essay on Criticism*, and his *Rape of
the Lock*, had made him the most talked-of poet in England.
Lady Winchilsea had also advanced. Not only had her

work been accepted by Gildon, and received flattering
tributes from Rowe and Swift, not to mention minor bards,
but her *Spleen* had attained to the dignity of a second
edition, and she had the inner, supporting consciousness of a
stately volume of verse practically ready for publication.
Yet in comparison with Pope Ardelia was hardly even the
"minor excelsitude" Mr. Gosse has so aptly called her.
When her volume of verse appeared in 1713 it was Pope's
criticism that she coveted and which she proceeded in a
feminine fashion to obtain.   Perhaps her husband's recent
accession to the title gave her courage.   At any rate she
issued a bold invitation, which Pope accepted but which he
commemorated in the following words in a letter to Caryll,
dated December 15, 1713 :

> The fact is, I was invited to dinner to my Lady Winchilsea, and
> after dinner to hear a play read, at both which I sat in great dis-
> order with sickness at my head and stomach.

The situation has picturesque possibilities.   Did Ardelia do
the reading ?   Did Pope adopt the suffering posture of the
portrait by Kneller ?   Evidently the trials inseparable from
literary dictatorship began early with Pope, and Lady
Winchilsea's dinner was one of the experiences that later
occasioned the humorous complaints to Dr. Arbuthnot :

> A dire dilemma! either way I'm sped,
> If foes they write, if friends they read me dead.
>   Siezed and tied down to judge, how wretched I!
>   Who can't be silent, and who will not lie ;
>
> .   .   .   .
>
> I sit with sad civility, I read
> With honest anguish and an aching head.

Courthope conjectures that the play read to Pope was
Aristomenes.   But this play was already in print and Pope
could have read it at his leisure.   It is more probable that
it was *Love and Innocence,* the play still in manuscript.   In

either case the strain on Pope's stock of "sad civility" must have been considerable, and it may be set down to his credit that author and critic parted on good terms. They were certainly friends in 1714 when the first separate edition of the *Rape of the Lock* came out. To Ardelia's playful protest against the satiric lines on women, Pope responded in a highly eulogistic *Impromptu* in which, even if perchance the "sickness at his head and stomach" had proved too much for his gallantry at the memorable dinner, he made amends by acknowledging Ardelia the bright particular star among female wits. Her gay answer is written in an intimate, friendly, bantering tone such as she could not assume. It marks the moments when she was least self-conscious and restrained, when she was most at ease, most certain of pleasing. Another evidence of literary amity is that when the quarto edition of Pope's *Works* came out in 1717, one of the seven commendatory poems he saw fit to print was by Lady Winchilsea. This poem, doubtless with Pope's consent, appeared also in the publications of 1727 and 1732. Either Pope liked the lady, or he liked the lady's verses, or he liked to have a countess speak well of him, even if her admiration found but bald and prosaic expression.

There is, however, another side to the picture. There are certain serious lapses from this attitude of friendship. In the second *Epistle*, written about twelve years after Lady Winchilsea's death, the lines,

> Arcadia's Countess here in ermined pride,
> Is there, Pastora by a fountain side,

are said by Croker to refer to Lady Winchilsea. "She is," he adds, "here and elsewhere sneered at." The "elsewhere" in Croker's note, if it is not a mere guess, probably refers to the farce *Three Hours after Marriage* which is commented on in the next section. In this farce the satiric flings at Lady Winchilsea doubtless express more exactly the attitude of Pope and Gay toward her as a female wit, and toward female wits in general, than does the gallant eulogy of Pope's *Impromptu*. And that their attitude is but the attitude of their age, may be indicated by a brief statement of the position accorded the learned lady by contemporary comedy.

Mrs. Behn's *Sir Patient Fancy* (1678) gives us in Lady Knowell one of the earliest examples in the restoration **The Learned** period of the English female pedant. Lady **Lady in Comedy** Knowell is especially distinguished by her use of big words in the style of Mrs. Malaprop. "I have consented to marry him" she says, "in spite of your Exprobations;" "I saw your reclinations from my Addresses;" "There is much Volubility and Vicissitude in Mundane Affairs." Her devotion to the classics is of the most effusive sort. To Leander she exclaims,

Oh the delight of Books! When I was their age I always employed my looser hours in reading—if serious, 'twas *Tacitus*, *Seneca*, *Plutarch's Morals*, or some such useful Author; if in an Humour gay, I was for Poetry, *Virgil*, *Homer*, or *Tasso*.

Yet this classical lady is represented as rivaling her frivolous daughter in the pursuit of amorous adventure. Mrs. Behn doubtless took the suggestion for this character from Moliére's *Femmes Savantes* (1672), the acknowledged source of Wright's *Female Virtuosos* (1693). Wright's Lady Meanwell, Mrs. Lovewit, and Catchat, were meant to be English versions of the Philaminte, Armande and Bélise of the French comedy. But though Moliére's general plot structure is followed and the characters certainly find their originals in his play, yet the kind of learning the ladies have is based on Shadwell's *Virtuoso* (1676), rather than on the *Femmes Savantes*. They are scientific in their tastes. Lady Meanwell is also public-spirited, and she invents a "Mathematical Engin" to keep the streets of London dry and clean.

"'Tis but setting up Timber Posts round about the City, and then fixing a pair of Bellows on every one of 'em to blow the clouds away." Mrs. Lovewit has made an exact collection of all the plays that ever came out, and she has devised a limbeck where all the quintessence of wit that is in them is to be extracted and sold by drops to the poets of this age. Catchat is teaching a flea to sing by note and expects soon to have the little creature ready for the opera. Sir Maurice Meanwell embodies the protest against these learned ladies.

Lady M. How now, Sir Maurice, is the merry God Dancing a Jigg within the inclosure of your Brains? You forget yourself strangely, methinks.

Sir Maur. 'Tis to you, Sister, I speak, what a Devil have you to do with Jingling and Poetry. (*To Catchat.*)

Catch. Lord, Sister, what a strange compound your Husband is of Vulgar and clownish atoms?

Sir Maur. A pretty thing indeed, to see those long spectacles of yours, set on the top of my house, for you to peep, and tell how many Hackney Coaches are going in the Moon.

Lovew. Oh the illiterate Brute! thus to affront a telescope. [*Aside.*]

Sir Maur. I am no Scholar, not I, and I thank my Stars for it, but with your leave, so much common sense has taught me, that all the Study and Philosophy of a wife, should be to please her Husband, instruct her Children, have a Vigilant Eye over Domestick Affairs, keep a good order in her Family, and stand as a Living Pattern of Virtue, and Discretion to all about her.

Lady M. Sir Maurice like another Solon, is now setting up for a lawgiver, Poor Soul!

Sir Maur. The Women of Old did not read so much, but lived better; Housewifery was all the Knowledge they aspired to; now-adays Wives must Write forsooth, and pretend to Wit, with a Pox.

Catch. 'Tis the partial, and foolish Opinion of Men, Brother, and not our Fault has made it ridiculous nowadays; for a Woman to pretend to Wit, she was born to it, and can shew it well enough, when occasion serves.

Vanbrugh's *Æsop* (1697) gives us Hortentia, " the wise

lady, the great scholar that nobody can understand." Her
lover tells her Æsop's fable of the nightingale that tried to
imitate a linnet, and adds :

> From that day forth she chang'd her note,
> She spoil'd her voice, she strain'd her throat ;
> She did as learned women do,
> Till everything
> That heard her sing
> Would run away from her — as I from you.

Wright's play was revived at Lincoln's Inn Fields in
January, 1721, in order to anticipate Cibber's *Refusal*, likewise an adaptation of the *Femmes Savantes*, which appeared
at Drury Lane the next month. In the twenty-eight years
between Wright's first production of *The Female Virtuosos*
and Cibber's *The Refusal*, the learned woman is a not infrequent comic character, and she is often given pungency by
traits drawn from some well-known original. Mrs. Manley in
The Lost Lover (1696) even ventured to name her "affected
poetess," Orinda, the pseudonym under which Mrs. Catherine
Phillips had subdued the world. *Female Wits: or the
Triumvirate of Poets at Rehearsal*, by W. M. (1697) made
prompt use of three ladies who had recently made their literary debut. Calista was Catherine Trotter, then but eighteen
years of age, and the author of but a single poor tragedy,
Agnes de Castro. She was treated more lightly than the
others, and was merely " bantered for pretending to understand Greek and to set herself up for a critic." The heroine, Marsilia, was Mrs. Manley, whose tragedy, *The Royal
Mischief*, had appeared in 1696 and is the drama supposed to be in rehearsal by the players. Mrs. Pix, whose
portly figure, good nature, and love for wine were well
known, appeared as Mrs. Wellfed, "a fat female author, a
good, sociable, well-natured companion that will not suffer
martyrdom rather than take off three bumpers in a hand."

The *Comparison between the Two Stages* (1702), attributed to Gildon, is also severe on the female wits of his day, with especial reference to Mrs. Manley. A dialogue between Rambler, Sullen, and the Critick illustrates the attitude toward women playwrights. Rambler brings forward Mrs. Manley's *The Lost Lover* for comment, but the Critick is roused to fury by the mere mention of a play by a lady and exclaims:

I hate these Petticoat-Authors; 'tis false Grammar, there's no Feminine for the Latin word, 'tis entirely of the Masculine Gender, and the language won't bear such a thing as a she-author.

Sullen insists that " 'twas a Lady carry'd the Prize of Poetry in France t'other day," and that "there have been some of that sex in England who have done admirably," and Rambler proposes a toast to "the Fair Author of the Fatal Friendship," but the Critick is not so easily to be appeased.

Mrs. Centlivre's *Basset-Table* (1705) gives disagreeable prominence to a learned young lady, but Mrs. Centlivre, herself a writer of plays, adroitly places her heroine in the scientific rather than the literary realm. Her Valeria is a younger sister of Wright's Lady Meanwell in that she professes to find a microscope more interesting than a man. The physical peculiarities of flesh-flies and tapeworms rouse her to an ecstacy of admiration. In her search for knowledge she calmly dissects her pretty dove, and is with difficulty restrained from dissecting her lover's Italian greyhound. She prefers the "immense pleasures of dear, dear Philosophy" to converse with beings so unenlightened and irrational as would-be suitors, and it is not strange that they declare her "fitter for Moorfields than Matrimony." The lady who represents "common sense" in the play urges that "Philosophy suits the Female Sex as Jack-boots would do," but Valeria defends even the Jack-boots. The character of Valeria doubtless gained in raciness from the various references to the famous Mary Astell, whose *Serious Proposal to the*

Ladies appeared in two parts in 1694 and 1697. In 1705 the third edition of her *Reflections on Marriage* was accompanied by a new *Preface*, a plea for women not equaled before Mary Wolstoncraft. Mary Astell's proposed "college for the education and improvement of the female sex" was for years a theme provocative of coarse raillery, and Mrs. Centlivre was not above throwing a stone or two at so well marked a target. Her Common Sense Lady says sarcastically to Valeria:

> Well, Cousin, might I advise, you should bestow your fortune on founding a College for the study of Philosophy where none but women should be admitted; and to immortalize your name they should be called Valerians, ha, ha, ha!

Charles Johnson's "female philosopher," Florida (*Generous Husband*, 1711), Cibber's "female philosophic saint," Sophronia, and her young step-mother, the learned "translator of the passion of Byblis" (*The Refusal*, 1721), have less direct personal reference; though the education of Cibber's ladies, who ostentatiously read Latin and quote Latin and who can talk Latin by the hour with Lady Wrangle's uncle, the bishop, their instructor, doubtless refers to Mary Astell, who, as was well known, had been early inducted into the classics by her uncle, a clergyman.

In this comic procession of the seventeenth and eighteenth century Minervas Lady Winchilsea was given a bitter pre-eminence by satirists so clever and unscrupulous as Pope and Gay. On January 16, 1717, there appeared on the stage of Drury Lane a farce entitled *Three Hours after Marriage*. It ran feebly seven nights and was then hissed off the stage. It was published under Gay's name, but was known to be the joint work of Pope, Arbuthnot, and Gay. The character of Phœbe Clinket is attributed to Gay by Mr. Austin Dobson in his article on Gay in the *Dictionary of National Biography*, and is there

said to be a satire on Lady Winchilsea. Evidently the
authority for these statements is Baker's *Biographica Dra-
matica.* In Baker's analysis of the farce occurs this passage:

Phœbe Clinket was said to be intended for the Countess of
Winchilsea, who was so much affected with the itch of versifying
that she had implements of writing in every room in the house that
she frequented. She was also reported to have given offence to one
of the triumvirate by saying that Gay's Trivia showed that he was
more proper to walk before a chair than to ride in one.

Baker's account did not appear till 1764, forty-seven
years after the play, and was based on rather vague rumor.
More exact information as to the apportionment of work
among the triumvirate is to be found in a farce called *The
Confederates*, in which the trio were savagely attacked by
John Durant Breval under the pseudonym of "Joseph Gay."
The Confederates appeared almost immediately after the
Three Hours after Marriage and doubtless embodies the
general opinion at that time as to the authorship of different
parts of the play. The first scene of *The Confederates* is in
a room in the Rose-Tavern near the Play-House. Arbuthnot listens at the door while Pope soliloquizes as follows:

> *Thus* in the Zenith of my Vogue I Reign
> And bless th' Abundance of my fertile Vein;
> My pointed Satire aim alike at All,
> (Foe to Mankind) and scatter round my Gall:
> With poyson'd Quill, I keep the world in Awe.
> And from My Self my own THERSITES draw.
> This very Night, with Modern Strokes of Wit,
> I charm the *Boxes*, and divert the Pit ;
> Safe from the Cudgel, stand secure of Praise ;
> Mine is the Credit, be the Danger Gay's.
> *Arb.* (*coming forward*).
> Hold, Brother! thou forget'st the Scenes I made ;
> This Boast of thine, is but a Gasconade.

> . . . .

> *P.* Know, Caledonian, Thine's a simple Part,
> Scarce anything but some Quack-Terms of Art,

Hard Words, and Quibbles; but 'tis I that sting,
And on the Stage th' *Egyptian Lovers* bring ;
Miss Phœbe, Plotwell, Townley, all are Mine,
And Sir *Tremendous*—Fossile's only Thine.

The character of Fossile in the play was meant as a satire
on Dr. Woodward, a well-known geologist, and it may easily be
that Arbuthnot was the only one of the triumvirate sufficiently versed in scientific terms to reel off the jargon put
into the mouth of this virtuoso. Sir Tremendous, a satirical
portrait of John Dennis, must almost certainly be the work
of Pope, who could hardly be expected to keep his hands off
if his arch-enemy were thus to be exposed to a drubbing.
Many strokes in the character of Plotwell are said to be
levelled at Cibber, hence this character, too, may naturally
be ascribed to Pope. Gay may have had some private grudge
against Lady Winchilsea, as Baker says, and may have had
a hand in the portrayal of Phœbe Clinket, but that this
character was virtually Pope's is explicitly stated, not only
by *The Confederates*, but also by the *Complete Key* by "E.
Parker, Philomath," published a few months after the play.
It is in this *Key*, too, that we find Lady Winchilsea given
as the original of Phœbe. The *Key* reads as follows:

Phœbe Clinket. This character is a very silly Imitation of the
Bays in the Rehearsal, but is design'd to Redicule the Countess of
W—n—ea, who, *Pope* says, is so much given to writing of Verses
that she keeps a Standish in every Room of the House, that she
may immediately clap down her Thoughts, whether upon *Pindaric,
Heroic, Pastoral* or *Dramatical Subjects.* This punning Character was drawn by Pope.

So far as the plot is concerned Phœbe Clinket is an
unimportant character in the farce. After the first act she
comes in but twice, once to claim as her own the much-
maligned invention whereby the two lovers, disguised as a
mummy and a crocodile, gain access to their mistress; and
again when a letter, which announces that her play, the off-

spring of her brain, has been refused by the theater, is by
a vulgar series of double meanings interpreted into an
acknowledgment by her of a crime that should be laid at the
door of Mrs. Townley, the immoral heroine of the farce.
The character of Phœbe Clinket is drawn merely for the
purpose of caricaturing a learned lady. A brief analysis of
the first act will serve to show the points of general satire as
well as the points to be interpreted as especially applying to
Lady Winchilsea.

When Mrs. Clinket appears on the stage she has on an
ink-stained dress, and pens are stuck in her hair. She is
accompanied by her maid carrying strapped to her back a
desk on which her mistress may write. The following conversation shows the authoress in the throes of creation:

Maid. I had as good carry a raree-show about the street. Oh!
how my back aches!

Clink. What are the labours of the back to those of the brain?
Thou scandal to the muses, I have now lost a thought worth a
folio, by thy impertinence.

Maid. Have I not got a crick in my back already, that will
make me good for nothing, with lifting your great books?

Clink. Folio's call them and not great books, thou monster of
impropriety. But have patience, and I will remember the three
gallery-tickets I promised thee at my new Tragedy.

Maid. I shall never get my head-cloaths clear-starch'd at this
rate.

Clink. Thou destroyer of learning, thou worse than a bookworm! Thou hast put me beyond all patience. Remember thou
my lyric ode bound about a tallow-candle; thy wrapping up snuff
in an epigram; nay, the unworthy usage of my Hymn to *Apollo*,
filthy creature! read me the last lines I wrote upon the *Deluge*, and
take care to pronounce them as I taught you.

Maid. *Swell'd with a dropsy, sickly Nature lies,*
   And melting in a diabetes, dies.

         [*Reads with an affected Tone.*]

Clink. Still without cadence!

Maid. *Swell'd with a dropsy—*

Clink. Hold! I conceive——
>*The roaring seas o'er the tall woods have broke*
>*And Whales now perch upon the sturdy Oak.*

Roaring? Stay. Rumbling, roaring, rustling.
No; raging seas. (*Writing.*)
>*The raging seas o'er the tall woods have broke*
>*Now, perch, thou whale, upon the sturdy oak.*

Sturdy oak? No; steady, strong, strapping, stiff—stiff. No, stiff is too short.

>(*Fossile and Townley come forward.*)
>*What feast for fish! Oh too luxurious treat!*
>*When hungry dolphins feed on butcher's meat.*

Foss. Neice, why neice, neice! Oh, *Melpomene,* thou goddess of tragedy, suspend thy influence for a moment, and suffer my niece to give a rational answer. This lady is a friend of mine.

Clink. Madam, excuse this absence of mind; my animal spirits had deserted the avenues of my senses, and retired to the recesses of the brain, to contemplate a beautiful idea. I could not force the vagrant creatures back again into their posts, to move those parts of the body that express civility.

Mistress Clinket's eagerness to get her play, the theme of which is *The Universal Deluge; or The Story of Deucalion and Pyrrha,* on the stage, leads her to invite Sir Tremendous and some of the players to a private reading of the tragedy in her own parlor. But in order to escape the prejudices sure to bias their judgments if the play is known to be by a woman, she introduces young Mr. Plotwell as the author, while she poses as a lady patroness of letters willing to encourage obscure merit by this preliminary reading at her tea-table. The indifference with which Mr. Plotwell submits his supposed play to the critics, allowing them to blot or insert at their pleasure; Phœbe's frantic defense of every mooted point; her unconcealed agony as the players and Sir Tremendous confide to her that the young gentleman knows nothing of poetry, that his play neither can take nor ought to take, make a very clever situation. The stage directions in the tragedy give rise to a violent discussion. Clinket reads aloud:

The scene opens, and discovers the heavens cloudy. A prodigious shower of rain, at a distance appears the top of the mountain, Parnassus, all the fields beneath are overflowed, there are seen cattle and men swimming. The tops of the steeples rise above the flood, with men and women perching on their weathercocks.

The bone of contention here is whether the use of weathercocks must not be regarded as an anachronism; and whether, indeed, according to the latest theories concerning the flood, the stones were not all dissolved, in which case the steeples themselves, being without foundations, could not support men and women. Plotwell carelessly abandons stones, steeples, weather-cocks, and all to the learning of the critics; but Phœbe declares that this cavil is leveled at the whole drama, for the theory of dissolved stones would make the reparation of the human race by Deucalion and Pyrrha an impossibility. Portions of the opening passage of the tragedy are defended with spirit by Clinket as having the fire of Lee and the tenderness of Otway. But as the criticism grows in severity, she exclaims in angry protest: "Were the play mine, you should gash my flesh, mangle my face, anything, sooner than scratch my play." And when finally the diction, the metaphors, whole speeches, the fable, the characters are declared "monstrous," "abominable," "execrable," her agony overcomes her prudence, and crying out, "I'm butcher'd! I'm massacred!" she falls in a faint. But the crisis of her misery does not come until her uncle flings her papers into the fire, declaring that thus only can she be cured of the poetical itch.

Clink. Ah! I am an undone woman.

Plotw. Has he burned any bank-bills, or a new *Mechlin* head-dress?

Clink. My works! My works!

1st Play. Has he destroyed the writings of an estate, or your billet-doux?

Clink. A pindaric ode! five similes! and half an epilogue!

2nd Player. Has he thrown a new fan, or your pearl neck-lace into the flames?

Clink. Worse, worse! The tags of the acts of a new Comedy! a Prologue sent by a person of quality! three copies of recommendatory verses! and two Greek mottos!

When the play is finally refused, Phœbe is unhappy but philosophical. She reflects on the egregious stuff that passes current on the stage, and comforts herself with the thought that she is but one of the famous daughters of Apollo to suffer because of the "wrong *gout* of the rabblement." And she felicitates herself that whatever may be said of her judgment and correctness, no one excels her in readiness and fertility.

Mrs. Clinket is a prude as well as a pedant. She calls herself a "platonic lady" in matters of love, and boasts that in her plays she does not allow "the libertinism of lip-embraces," for, though Aristotle never actually prohibited kissing on the stage, she is "unwilling to stand even on the brink of an indecorum." Phœbe is very religious and very severe on the corrupt plays so popular in London. She chooses the Deucalion and Pyrrha version of the "Universal Deluge" for her tragedy because she counts neither the stage nor the actors of her day "hallowed enough for sacred story." In her attitude toward her own plays Phœbe is a combination of pompous self-conceit and of extreme sensitiveness to criticism. Her ruling passion is her desire to get her plays before the public. For that she scorns delight and lives laborious days.

We learn from the *Complete Key* that some touches in this satiric portrait refer to Margaret, Duchess of Newcastle, but that in general the Countess of Winchilsea is the one ridiculed. Yet the authors of the farce were careful not to make the application too minutely exact. In two important respects Phœbe Clinket does not even remotely suggest Lady Winchilsea. The supposed tragedy is, in its theme and in the substance and style of the quoted passages, entirely unlike any work of hers. It would better serve as a travesty of some passages in Dryden's heroic tragedies. And then, again, Ardelia was as averse to any public presentation of her plays as Phœbe Clinket was eager for it. The impassioned "Advertisement" to *Love and Innocence*, written years before the appearance of Pope's farce, is as genuine a personal appeal as was ever buried away in a manuscript. Even after the lapse of years, even if her plays had admirable dramatic qualities, one would hardly feel at liberty to put them on the stage in the face of such a protest. And every other indication in Ardelia's poems or prose writings emphasizes her spirit of self-depreciation, her morbid shrinking from any but the most intimate and friendly audience. Hence the satire is in this, its chief point, wide of the mark. Many minor points, however, could easily be made to apply. Lady Winchilsea's learning, her devotion to literary pursuits, her fecundity in verse, her irritable shrinking from adverse criticism, her determined opposition to amatory themes, her preference for divine and moral songs, her detestation of the modern stage, are traits that tally with the burlesque portrait. The story of the "standish in every room," if not a malicious invention of Pope's, would of course be most wittily burlesqued by the desk strapped to the maid's back, and would be sufficient to locate the character, but the story itself rests only on the doubtful authority of Pope.

But in so far as the character did suggest Lady Winchilsea to hearers or readers, it was an intolerable affront. She was made not merely ridiculous, butodious. Swift's treatment of Mary Astell as Madonella in the *Tatler* papers, and his vulgar account of the supposed foundation and disruption of her college, were no more unjust and libelous than was Pope's treatment of Lady Winchilsea in this play. Lady Mary Wortley Montagu as Sappho in Pope's *Epistle II.* had really less right to complain.

There is probably a reference to this play in Gay's *Welcome from Greece.* Among the illustrious ladies who crowd the quay to welcome Pope are "Winchilsea, still meditating song," while "afar off is frolic Bicknell," the actress who played Phœbe Clinket. The conjunction of names may be fortuitous, but it probably has covert reference to the play.

This play was, unhappily, one of the last important notices of Lady Winchilsea's work during her lifetime. But there **Recognition After 1725** were some minor indications of favorable recognition. Steele and Fenton published some of her poems in their *Miscellanies* of 1714 and 1717; Harris in his *History of Kent* (1719) included her *Fanscomb Barn,* with a laudatory account of her writings; and immediately after her death Dr. Stukeley republished her *Spleen.* Twenty-two years later, however, Pope, in the final edition of his works, omitted her previously published commendatory verses, because, says Mr. Elwin, they were "intrinsically worthless and the author's name no longer carried weight." This note probably represents the state of the case, and the revival of interest in Lady Winchilsea soon after Pope's death must be due to Birch's *General Dictionary* (1734–1741), which pub- **Birch's General Dictionary** lished six of her poems, five of them being from the manuscript in the possession of the Countess of Hertford, and added a brief life, giving the facts repeated in later biographical notices. During the next thirty years Lady Winchilsea's name appears with some frequency.

The purpose of John Duncomb's *Feminead* (1751) was to reveal to "lordly man" the glories of a sister-choir. In

this chivalrous enterprise he counts himself but as the coadju-
tor of his friend Richardson, whose "Pamela" and "Clarissa"
John Duncomb's had proved him "the sex's champion and
Feminead constant patron." Duncomb heads the list of
"lettered nymphs" with the chaste Orinda, but Ardelia, who
is commended in a foot-note as a "lady of great wit and
genius," makes a close second. It is her *Spleen* that rouses
Mr. Duncomb's admiration.

> Who can unmoved hear Winchilsea reveal
> Thy horrors, Spleen! which all, who paint, must feel.
> My praises would but wrong her sterling wit,
> Since Pope himself applauds what she has writ.

In 1752 George Ballard in his *Memoirs of several Ladies
who have been celebrated for their writings or skill in the*
Ballard's *learned languages, arts, and sciences*, referred
Memoirs to Lady Winchilsea as "a lady of excellent
genius especially in poetry," and quoted her answer to
Pope's *Impromptu.*

Cibber in the *Lives of the Poets* (1753) quotes Pope's
Impromptu with the comment: "The answer which the
Cibber's Lives countess makes to the above is rather more
of the Poets exquisite than the lines of Mr. Pope; he is
foiled at his own weapons, and outdone in the elegance
of compliment." Referring to the poems in Birch's *Dictionary* he says:

> If all her poetical compositions are executed with as much
> spirit and elegance as these, the lovers of poetry have some reason
> to be sorry that her station was such as to exempt her from the
> necessity of more frequently exercising a genius so furnished by
> nature to have made a great figure in that divine art.

Of the "excellent picturesqueness" of her *Spleen* he
speaks in the warmest terms, and affirms that this poem
alone would give her a "very high station among the inspired
tribe."

In 1755 there appeared a compilation entitled *Poems by Eminent Ladies*. It was designed, the preface tells us, as **Eminent Ladies** "a solid compliment to the sex," and was put forward as a convincing proof that "great abilities are not confined to men, and that genius often glows with equal warmth and perhaps with more delicacy in the breast of a female." Twelve poems by Lady Winchilsea are quoted in this volume. and for the first time the selections are made, not from Birch's *Dictionary* but from the *Miscellany Poems* of 1713, nine of the twelve being fables. Wordsworth commented most unfavorably on the literary insight that could choose to represent Lady Winchilsea by these selections.

In Walpole's *Royal and Noble Authors* (1758) is the note which Wordsworth found so scanty and unsatisfactory when he was in search of information concerning Ardelia.

The *Biographia Brittanica* (1763), Gough's *Anecdotes of British Topography* (1768), Granger's *Biographical Dictionary* (1769), echo in brief and perfunctory fashion the critical dicta of their predecessors.

There is, then, through the century an unemphatic, uncritical, but persistent literary tradition that Lady Winchilsea's claim to a niche in the Temple of Fame could not be entirely ignored. She was a countess, she wrote *The Spleen*, and Pope had praised her. These are the chief points on which eulogy was based. But we have also indications of a recognition much more spontaneous and pleasing. In 1763 Anna Seward, a mature little lady of fifteen, was **Anna Seward** engaged in a serious literary correspondence well calculated to awaken parental fears lest she should become "that dreaded phenomenon, a learned lady." In the midst of counsel to a friend "the morning sun of whose youth is with difficulty escaping from the unwholesome mists of a foolish love affair," we come upon the following bit of criticism:

The last words of that sentence bring to my recollection a pleasing little poem, to which, in infancy, I have often listened with delight from the lips of my mother, who used frequently to repeat it as she sat at work. She had learnt it from a lady who was the friend of her youth.

Wholly without literary curiosity, as she never saw it printed, so she never asked after the author; consequently could give me no information on that subject. She had never taken the trouble of copying it; therefore was it mine as it was hers, by oral tradition, before I attained my tenth year. Its easy and tuneful numbers charmed; and, with a great deal of giddy vivacity on a thousand occasions, I had yet an inherent fondness for seeing the perspectives of opening life through the clare-oscure of a meditative fancy, particularly where the sombre tints were ultimately prevalent.

Behold this little orphan ode which I have searched for in vain through the pages of our poets.

Lady Winchilsea's *Progress of Life* is then quoted entire with many slight inaccuracies such as would result from oral transmission, but substantially identical with the form given in the volume of 1713. The "friend of Mrs. Seward's youth" must have been alive in Lady Winchilsea's day. It would be interesting to know who started the little poem on its oral way. It is at any rate a charming picture that we get of the gentlewoman at her needlework, perhaps—like the lady of the ballad,—letting "her silken seam fall till her tae" as she yields her spirit to the musical flow and pensive moralizing of Ardelia's verse; and of the child lured from her play by the charm of the words as they fall from her mother's lips. Another manuscript copy of this poem is to be found in a volume in the possession of Mr. George Finch-Hatton. If we may judge by verbal inaccuracies, this poem, too, had been orally transmitted to the writer. Such facts are evidences of an undercurrent of popularity, and popularity of the sort that would have been most pleasing to Ardelia.

Miss Seward's letter continues in a strain of elegant criticism. She endeavors to date the poem by internal evidence. She feels a lack of "polished accuracy;" she discovers one "inadmissible inversion;" she is conscious of some failures in the matter of "verbal perspicuity." But she rejoices in the truth and pathetic sweetness of the poem, and she considers the stanzas after the fourth as "poetically faultless." Miss Seward's letter is the first instance of detailed criticism applied to Lady Winchilsea's verse.

This letter was published without comment in Walter Scott's edition of Miss Seward's *Poetical Works.* Scott's failure to find parentage for the orphan ode is noted by "J. H. R." in *The Gentleman's Magazine* (1812), and he felicitates himself on having found the author. In looking over a volume of old poems he chanced upon this one ascribed to "Anne, Countess of Winchilsea, who lived in the reign of Queen Anne." He then points out the most interesting of the variations resulting from oral transmission:

The second stanza is thus printed in Miss Seward's Works:

How pleasing the world's prospect lies;
  How tempting to look through!
Parnassus to the Poet's eyes,
Nor Beauty, with her sweet surprise,
  Can more inviting shew.

But in the volume I have mentioned, it is inserted in the following manner:

How pleasing the world's prospect lies;
  How tempting to look through!
Not Canaan to the Prophet's eyes,
Nor Pisgah, with her sweet surprise,
  Can more inviting shew.

Miss Seward's version certainly preserves more poetical beauty, though perhaps the latter one is most correct. The Ode in general is very excellent, and is written in that style of chaste simplicity which was so peculiar to the Poets in the reign of Anne.

Was it the lady with the needlework, or the friend of her youth, or perhaps the swan of Lichfield herself, that thus substituted a bit of poetical paganism for Ardelia's honest Hebraisms? Scott, it seems, did not know Lady

Southey's Specimens   Winchilsea. Southey knew her but slightly. He includes her in his *Specimens* (1807) with the laconic comment: "Her poems were praised by Rowe and by Pope; and they deserved praise." He publishes nothing of hers except portions of her *Petition for an Absolute Retreat.* Much more space is devoted to Anne Killigrew, to Mary Barber, to Constantia Grierson, to Elizabeth Rowe. But Wordsworth made amends for all omissions.

The modern interest in Lady Winchilsea's work and the transfer of emphasis from her poems on man to her hitherto

William Wordsworth   unnoticed poems on nature date from the publication of Wordsworth's *Essay, Supplementary to the Preface* (1815), in which occurred the well-known passage:

Now it is remarkable that, excepting the Nocturnal Reverie of Lady Winchilsea, and a passage or two in the Windsor Forest of Pope, the poetry intervening between the publication of the Paradise Lost and the Seasons does not contain a single new image of external nature, and scarcely presents a familiar one from which it can be inferred that the eye of the Poet had been steadily fixed upon his object, much less that his feelings had urged him to work upon it in the spirit of genuine imagination.

In 1820 Wordsworth sent Lady Mary Lowther a unique present. It was a manuscript volume of extracts from the poems of Lady Winchilsea and kindred writers. Wordsworth had made the selections and a "female friend" had transcribed them for him. In the accompanying *Sonnet to Lady Mary Lowther* he explained that he had "culled this store of lucid crystals from a Parnassian Cave seldom trod." This volume is probably the one referred to by Christopher North when he says, " We never had in our hands the poems of Anne, Countess of Winchilsea, printed in 1713; but we well remember reading some of them in beautiful manu-

script years ago at Rydal Mount." This book is probably
still in existence somewhere, and the publication of it would
be a most interesting addition to our stock of Words-
worthiana.

That Wordsworth's interest in Lady Winchilsea's poems
was genuine and permanent is evinced in his correspondence
with the Rev. Alexander Dyce, whose *Specimens of British
Poetesses* appeared in 1825. The volume made its way
slowly and in time attracted the favorable attention of
Wordsworth. He wrote from Rydal Mount, October 16,
1829, to Mr. Dyce as follows:

By accident, I learned lately that you had made a Book of
Extracts, which I had long wished for opportunity and industry
to execute myself. I am happy it has fallen into so much better
hands. I allude to your *Selections from the Poetry of English
Ladies*. I had only a glance at your work; but I will take this
opportunity of saying, that should a second edition be called for,
I should be pleased with the honor of being consulted by you
about it. There is one poetess to whose writings I am especially
partial, the Countess of Winchelsea. I have perused her poems
frequently, and should be happy to name such passages as I think
most characteristic of her genius, and most fit to be selected.

Wordsworth's glance at the book must have been of the
most casual sort, for he not only misquoted the title, but he
is ignorant of the fact that Mr. Dyce's *Selections* included
The Spleen, Life's Progress, The Atheist and the Acorn,
and *A Nocturnal Reverie* by Lady Winchilsea, and that he
quoted in her praise Wordsworth's own words in the *Essay*
of 1815. But the next letter to Mr. Dyce shows that a copy
of the *Specimens* had been sent Wordsworth, and that he
had given it diligent attention. The letter is undated but
bears the postmark 1830. After some preliminary discussion he writes:

I now come to Lady Winchelsea. First, however, let me say a
few words on one or two other authoresses of your "Specimens."
British poetesses make but a poor figure in the "Poems by Emi-

nent Ladies." But observing how injudicious that selection is in
the case of Lady Winchelsea, and of Mrs. Aphra Behn (from whose
attempts they are miserably copious) I have thought something
better might have been chosen by more competent persons who had
access to the volumes of the several writers. . . . .

Could you tell me anything of Lady Mary Wortley Montagu
more than is to be learned from Pope's letters and her own? She
seems to have been destined for something much higher and better
than she became. A parallel between her character and genius
and that of Lady Winchelsea, her contemporary (though somewhat
prior to her) would be well worth drawing.

And now at last for the poems of Lady Winchelsea. I will
transcribe a note from the blank leaf of my own edition written
by me before I saw the scanty notice of her by Walpole. (By the
by, that book has always disappointed me when I have consulted
it on any particular occasion.) The note runs thus: 'The "Fragment," p. 18, seems to prove that she was attached to James II.,
as does p. 74, and that she suffered by the Revolution. The most
celebrated of these poems, but far from the best is "The Spleen."
"The Petition for an Absolute Retreat," and the "Nocturnal Reverie,"
are of much superior merit. See also for favorable specimens, p. 56;
"On the Death of Mr. Thynne," p. 134 [*Moral Song*]; and p. 13,
"Fragment." The Fable of 'Love, Death, and Reputation,' p. 160,
is ingeniously told.' Thus far my own note. I will now be more
particular. P. 4, 'Our Vanity,' etc., and p. 153 are noticeable as
giving some account from herself of her authorship. See also p.
193, where she alludes to 'The Spleen.' She was unlucky in her
models, Pindaric Odes, and French Fables. But see p. 49, 'The
Blindness of Elymas,' for proof that she could write with powers of
high order when her own individual character and personal feelings were not concerned. For less striking proofs of this power see
p. 238, 'All is Vanity;' omitting verses 5 and 6, and reading "clouds
that are lost and gone," &c. There is merit in the two next stanzas; and the last stanza toward the close contains a fine reproof for
the ostentation of Louis XIV., and one magnificent verse,

Spent the astonished hours, forgetful to adore.

But my paper is nearly out. As far as, 'For my garments,' p. 70,
the poem is charming; it then falls off; revives at p. 72, 'Give me
there,' p. 72 [l. 123], &c., reminds me of Dyer's 'Grongar Hill;' it
revives p. 76, toward the bottom, and concludes with sentiments

worthy of the writer, though not quite so happily expressed as other
parts of the poem. See pp. 234, 250, 'Whilst in the Muses' path I
stray;' p. 183 [*The Shepherd and the Calm*], 'The Cautious Lovers,'
p. 147, has little poetic merit, but is worth reading as characteristic
of the author. P. 80, 'Deep lines of honour,' etc., to 'maturer age.'
P. 84 [*The Change*], if shortened, would be striking; p. 67 [*Enquiry
after Peace*], characteristic; p. 57, from 'Meanwhile ye living
parent,' to the close, omitting 'Nor could we hope,' and the five
following verses; p. 111, last paragraph [*Oh, might I live, etc.*]; p.
186 [*Life's Progress*], *that* you have; pp. 136 [*Hope*], 134 [*Moral
Song*]; p. 13, was Lady W. a R. Catholic? p. 267, 'And to the clouds
proclaim thy fall;' p. 269, omit 'When scatter'd glow-worms,' and
the next couplet. I have no more room. Pray, excuse this vile scrawl.

In Mr. Grosart's edition Wordsworth's letter of May 10,
1830, is put before the one just quoted. That letter has, to
be sure, no specific date beside the postmark, 1830, but
internal evidence seems to demand that it precede the one
of May 10, for Wordsworth here, as will be seen, takes up
the subject just where he left it in the undated letter. He
writes:

My last was, for want of room, concluded so abruptly, that I
avail myself of an opportunity of sending you a few additional
words, free of postage, upon the same subject.

I observed that Lady Winchelsea was unfortunate in her models
—*Pindarics* and *Fables;* nor does it appear from her *Aristomenes*
that she would have been more successful than her contemporaries,
if she had cultivated tragedy. She had sensibility sufficient for
the tender parts of dramatic writing, but in the stormy and tumultuous she would probably have failed altogether. She seems to
have made it a moral and religious duty to control her feelings
lest they should mislead her. I have often applied two lines of
her drama (p. 355) to her affections:

Love's soft bands,
His gentle cords of hyacinths and roses,
Wove in the dewy Spring when storms are silent.

By the by, in the next page [ll. 64-5] are two impassioned lines
spoken to a person fainting:

Then let me hug and press thee into life,
And lend thee motion from my beating heart.

From the style and versification of this, so much her longest work, I conjecture that Lady Winchelsea had but a slender acquaintance with the drama of the earlier part of the preceding century. Yet her style in rhyme is often admirable, chaste, tender, and vigorous, and entirely free from sparkle, antithesis, and that over-culture, which reminds one by its broad glare, its stiffness, and heaviness, of the double daisies of the garden, compared with their modest and sensitive kindred of the fields. Perhaps I am mistaken, but I think there is a good deal of resemblance in her style and versification to that of Tickell, to whom Dr. Johnson justly assigns a high place among the minor poets, and of whom Goldsmith rightly observes, that there is a strain of ballad-thinking through all his poetry, and it is very attractive.

Mr. Dyce was much impressed by Wordsworth's minute and apt criticisms, and apparently suggested the advisability of his publishing Lady Winchilsea's poems. Wordsworth answered, in a letter from Lowther Castle, dated September 23, but without any year. The reference in the letter to a possible visit from Mr. Dyce about the "tenth December," throws doubt on even the month. Mr. Grosart suggests August, 1833. The portion of the letter referring to Lady Winchilsea thanks Mr. Dyce for his care in collecting and transmitting particulars concerning her, and concludes:

I expected to find at this place my friend, Lady Frederick Bentinck, through whom I intended to renew my request for materials, if any exist, among the Finch family, whether manuscript poems, or anything else that would be interesting; but Lady F., unluckily, is not likely to be in Westmoreland. I shall, however, write to her. Without some additional materials, I think I should scarcely feel strong enough to venture upon any species of publication connected with this very interesting woman, notwithstanding the kind things you say of the value of my critical remarks.

It is a far cry from this *Three Hours after Marriage* of Pope, Gay, and Arbuthnot to Wordsworth's *Essay* and his *Letters*, but Ardelia's fame could well afford to wait a century for so pronounced a revolution in taste. Wordsworth knew her poems minutely and sympathetically. He

dwelt upon specific excellences and defects. He was
impressed by her high qualities as a poet. He sought to
make her known. He contemplated editing her works himself. With Wordsworth begins the modern appreciation of
Ardelia, and most critics of her verse after 1815 quote the
Nocturnal Reverie and Wordsworth's comment. Only the
more significant of the nineteenth century notices of her
work demand attention here. .

Of the *Nocturnal Reverie* Christopher North (*Black-
wood's*, March, 1837) says:

Christopher   We find nothing comparable to what we have now
North   quoted in any of the effusions of the Thirty Poetesses
—let us by courtesy so call them—who flourished from the death
of Lady W. to that of Charlotte Smith.

In *Men, Women, and Books* (1847) Leigh Hunt says of
Lady Winchilsea:

Leigh Hunt   We are now come to one of the numerous loves we
possess among our grandmothers of old—or rather
not numerous, but select, and such as keep fresh with us forever,
like the miniature of his ancestress whom the Sultan took for a
living beauty. This is Anne, Countess of *Winchelsea* (now written
Winchilsea), daughter of Sir William Kingsmill, of Sidmonton, in
the county of Southampton.

He quotes the *Nocturnal Reverie* with the naive critical
method of italicizing the words and phrases he especially
likes. The celebrated *Spleen* still deserves, according to
Mr. Hunt, a place on every toilet, male and female.

Mrs. Hale's *Woman's Record* (New York, 1853), "an
invaluable manual for the parlor table," is interesting as the
first American recognition of Lady Winchilsea.
Mrs. Hale   "It should not be forgotten," Mrs. Hale says,
"that she was the first Englishwoman who attempted to
scale the Parnassian heights"—a neglect of the matchless
Orinda against which Ardelia would have been the first
to protest.

The Literary Women of England (1861) is a compilation made by Jane Williams, usually known as "Ysgafell."

Jane Williams
Miss Williams was impelled to her work by indignation that Campbell had included in his one hundred and seventy British poets but one woman, and that Dr. Johnson had admitted not one into his society of fifty-two English poets. Her commentary on Lady Winchilsea's work is unusually full and interesting:

Her verses on the *Spleen* are very poor, and ill deserve the praise lavished on them by contemporary flatterers. Her answer to half a dozen rhymed couplets, "occasioned by four verses in 'The Rape of the Lock,'" is sharp-witted and adroit, but pert and unpleasing. Her celebrated Apologue of "The Atheist and the Acorn" doubtless did good service in its day. It is also remarkable for having suggested to Hannah More another Apologue called "The Two Gardeners," and published in the Cheap Repository Tracts. . . . . Any one accustomed to contemplate rural nature under the shades of night, in stillness and in solitude, must be struck with surprise and won to sympathy by the enchanting reproduction of emotions peculiar to that hour and scene in the "Nocturnal Reverie." It is thoroughly original; a living landscape redolent of sweet tranquility, full of energy in gentlest exercise. The key-note of this most musical combination of words, thoughts, and images, seems to have been derived from Shakspeare's "Merchant of Venice," Act V., scene 1, where Lorenzo and Jessica in quiet enjoyment play upon the phrase, "In such a night." It is most true,

Soft stillness and the night
Become the touches of sweet harmony.

Every stroke of Lady Winchilsea's description is effective; and the horse, grazing leisurely and wandering at will as he crops the inviting herbage is wonderfully true to nature. The "Salisbury," whose strong and steady luster is advantageously contrasted with the pale and flickering sparkle of the glow-worm, was probably Lady Anne Tufton, second daughter of Thomas, sixth Earl of Thanet, who married in 1709, James Cecil, fifth Earl of Salisbury. Perhaps these verses were originally addressed to her, and perhaps she accompanied Lady Winchilsea in the mid-night stroll which

occasioned them. Anyhow, this allusion indicates the existence of
a friendship between the two countesses, and rescues the memory
of one from the obscurity of ancestral archives. . . . . . . Great
experimental knowledge of human life and human feeling is mani-
fested in this poem [*The Progress of Life*]; and we are induced by
it to regret our ignorance of that particular course of experience by
which Lady Winchilsea acquired the wisdom which enhanced the
power of her native genius.

Though there might be additions to this account of the
progress of Lady Winchilsea's fame, enough has probably
been quoted to show her place in critical
esteem up to the time of the publication of
Ward's *English Poets* (1880). Wordsworth was the first
man of authority to pronounce a discriminating eulogy on
Ardelia, and it is evident that his judgment impressed itself
on all succeeding criticism. But that we have any actual
knowledge of her life and poems is due to Mr. Edmund
Gosse. He introduced her to a large circle of readers by
securing for her a place in Ward's *English Poets*. Matthew
Arnold was emphatic in his expression of delight in Ardelia's
work as it stood thus revealed. The feeling of surprise and
pleasure was general, while students of the beginnings of
romanticism were stirred to the keenest interest by the
quality and significance of these poems. By his suggestive
introductory comments in *English Poets*, by a notice in his
Eighteenth Century Literature (1889), and in other ways,
did Mr. Gosse contribute to the popularity and the right
understanding of Ardelia's verse; and, finally, in *Gossip in
a Library* (1891) he made the lady herself known to us.
At his touch she emerged from the shadow-land of the past,
a charming and most real personality.

But with all this weight of high poetical and expository
authority in favor of Ardelia, there was no opportunity to
know more of her and her work than Ward's Selections and
Mr. Gosse's Essay revealed. Dyce and Wordsworth had

Edmund Gosse

contemplated an edition of her poems in 1833.   In 1876
Grosart, in his edition of Wordsworth's *Prose Works*, had
complained with regard to Lady Winchilsea: "Sad to say, a
collection of this remarkable gentlewoman's poems remains
still an unfurnished *desideratum*." In Ward's *English Poets*
Mr. Gosse, referring to possible existing collections of her
poems in MS., had said, "If these unpublished poems are still
in the possession of her family, it is highly desirable that
they should be given to the world." In his *Short History of
English Literature* (1898) Mr. Saintsbury repeats the wish.
In his finely appreciative notice, he says:

It is a pity that her poems have not been reprinted and are
difficult of access, for it is desirable to read the whole in order to
appreciate the unconscious clash of style and taste in them.

That it is, at last, possible to bring out this much-desired
complete edition of Lady Winchilsea's work is but another
portion of the debt she owes to Mr. Gosse, as will be seen in
the following account of the sources of the present volume.

The poems in this edition have been obtained from the
printed volume of 1713, from two manuscript volumes, an
octavo and a folio, and from scattered collections
**Description of
the Manuscripts** of various sorts. Of the manuscripts the octavo,
now in the possession of the Earl of Winchilsea,
is doubtless the earlier in date. Its beautiful morocco binding
and gilt edges, and the exquisitely clear and neat hand-writing
of the most of the book show that the compilation and tran-
scription of the poems was counted a matter worthy of elegant
attention.   But toward the end there is a lamentable decline
from the precise accuracy of the beginning.   The penmanship changes and is laborious and uneven, with many
erasures.   And a critical judgment seems to have passed
sentence on some of the work, for two poems have been
crossed out, letter by letter, in the most painfully effective
fashion, while several leaves have been ruthlessly excised

from the center of the volume. The title-page with its crude sketch of a cherub's wing-enfolded head, and the table of contents are the work apparently of the same untrained hand employed in copying the last poems. That the table of contents is an after-thought is shown by the fact that the excised poems are omitted, so that we do not even know their titles. There are many slight indications that the octavo is an earlier manuscript than the folio. For example, most of the interlineations and substitutions in the octavo appear in the text of the folio. "Areta," Lady Winchilsea's first-chosen pen-name, is crossed out in the octavo and "Ardelia" is written above, while in the folio, though here also an original "Areta" is sometimes changed to "Ardelia," in by far the greater number of cases, the "Ardelia" is the name first written. Then, too, no poem susceptible of a date in the octavo is later than 1689, except the last one, which is not the work of the original transcriber. This volume likewise is more intimate and personal in its general effect than the folio. The crossed-out poems that do not reappear in the folio were both personal, one being from Anne Kingsmill's maid of honor days, and one being a verse-epistle to her husband in the early days of their married life. Titles in the octavo carry out this personal impression, for they give information as to places and dates which do not reappear in the titles of the folio. For its early date, its beauty as a manuscript, and its personal character, this volume is of unique interest. It is a satisfaction to feel that after untracked wanderings the little book has at last its natural home in the library of the Earl of Winchilsea.

Of the fifty-two poems in the octavo all but five reappear in the folio, to which we therefore turn as the real storehouse of Lady Winchilsea's unpublished work. This folio manuscript is an unusually impressive volume. Its size, its heavy calf binding, its fine, strong paper, its careful arrangement, and its expert, clerkly penmanship are a distinct advance in dignity and stateliness of form over the fine-lady elegance of the earlier volume. And there was justification for this advance, for, to the contents of that volume, Ardelia is now ready to add sixty-five new poems, two long plays, an important preface, and two commendatory poems. The book was not made up from time to time as poems were written, for poems susceptible of dates do not appear in chronological order. The arrangement is rather according to subjects from the mass of poems on hand, the religious poetry making one group, the songs another, the fables a third, and the plays a fourth. The poems of general or biographical interest, however, are not so classified, but appear in different portions of the book. It is difficult to assign an exact date to this manuscript, but it probably belongs early in the eighteenth century, for it contains at least one poem, that on the death of James II., written after, and probably very soon after, 1701. This fact, together with the omission of so important a poem as the one on *The Hurricane* in 1703, would seem to date the manuscript about 1702. The title-page of this volume was not reproduced in the printed form, but is more interesting than the printed one because of the characteristic quotation from *Spenser's Shepherd's Calendar, June:*

> I never list presume to Parnass Hill
> But piping low, in shade of lowly grove
> I play to please myself, albeit ill.

A note in pencil at the foot of the page says, "Ardelia was Anne, Countess of Winchilsea. See her poems, printed by John Barber on Lambeth Hill; and sold by John Morphew, near Stationer's Hall, London, 1713." The title given is, *Miscellany Poems with two Plays by Ardelia,* neither the title nor the note being like the corresponding items on

the published title-pages. The book contains numerous
slight alterations in pencil, and since some of these notes are
in the first person, it is probable that this manuscript was
corrected by Ardelia herself.

The history of this folio is also of interest. During the
last years of the life of Heneage, fourth Earl of Winchilsea,
one of his constant companions was Mr. John Creyk, vicar
of Eastwell and the earl's private chaplain. In the letters
of the earl to Dr. Stukeley Mr. Creyk is described as "my
friend, a learned gentleman and a lover of antiquities." On
September 30, 1726, Mr. Creyk wrote to Dr. Stukeley:

> This morning at five minutes before six I performed the dole-
> ful office of closing the eyes of my dear Lord Winchilsea who died
> of the Iliac passion.

Lord Hertford, in writing to Dr. Stukeley in April, 1727,
says of Lord Winchilsea:

> By his will he left me his Medals and his Sark Antiquities ;
> what he wrote upon them is in possession of Mr. Creyk ; whether
> he will publish them or not I do not know ; he has the disposal of
> everything.

In this fashion did the folio volume of poems come into
the possession of the Creyk family, a second one of whom,
also a Mr. John Creyk, held the vicarage of Eastwell from
1742 to 1745. Birch in his *General Dictionary* (1734–1741)
said that a great number of Lady Winchilsea's poems still
continued unpublished "in the hands of the Rev. Mr.
Creake." And there they apparently remained. For a hundred and forty years the manuscript quietly outlived its
successive owners in the Creake family, till some turn of the
wheel of fortune brought their effects to public sale. Mr.
Gosse, in *Gossip in a Library*, thus describes the manner in
which the precious volume came into his possession:

> In 1884 I saw advertised, in an obscure book-list, a folio vol-
> ume of old manuscript poetry. Something excited my curiosity,

and I sent for it. It proved to be a vast collection of the poems of my beloved Anne Finch. I immediately communicated with the bookseller and asked him whence it came. He replied that it had been sold, with furniture, pictures, and books, at the dispersing of the effects of a family of the name of Creake.

The progress of the gentle lady from the sumptuous retirement of the library at Eastwell Park down the long procession of the years had been lonely and unheralded, but it was surely a gracious and benignant fate that brought her at last to the company of her peers in the library of the man who had years before constituted himself her champion. And now two hundred years after the last words were added to the book by the pen of the scribe, the poems speak for the first time from the printed page.

In 1713 Lady Winchilsea published a volume of selections from her poems. There was apparently but one edition
The Volume of this book, yet in the slow progress of publi-
of 1713 cation two title-pages were used. The one dated 1713 has, in the center of the page, a wood-cut of two flying cherubs bearing palm branches and laurel wreaths. The title reads *Miscellany Poems on Several Occasions. Written by a Lady*. The second title-page is dated 1714. It omits the cherubs. *Written by a Lady* is changed to *Written by the Right Honble Anne, Countess of Winchilsea*, a change showing probably a favorable reception of the earlier volumes, and certainly an advance in self-confidence. Of the eighty-one poems in this volume, forty-five are in neither of the manuscripts. It would not be entirely safe to assert that these new poems were all written between 1702 and 1713, but the four to which dates may be assigned do belong after 1708.

Still other poems by Lady Winchilsea are to be found scattered through various publications. In Steele's *Miscellany*, 1714, there is one poem, *To Mr. Jervas*, by the Countess

of W——, that I have not found elsewhere. Another
unsigned poem, *The Sigh*, is by her, and between these two
Other Sources poems are four unsigned poems that cannot
be certainly ascribed to Lady Winchilsea, but
that resemble her work and may be by her. Her *Lines to
Prior* appear only in Prior's *Miscellaneous Works*. *To Mr.
Pope* is found in the early collected editions of his works.
Four poems are to be found only in Birch's *General
Dictionary*. The endeavor has been to make this edition of the poems complete, but there may be fugitive
poems that have not been discovered. There is a possibility
that Birch did not quote all the new poems in the manuscript belonging to Lady Hertford, but of that manuscript,
if it is still in existence, I can get no trace. A more valuable possible discovery would be the letters of Ardelia. She
was highly esteemed as a correspondent and she wrote much
to various members of the Thynne family at Longleat, to
Lady Tufton and her daughters, to her cousin, Lady Hatton,
to her sister Dorothy, and to many others. The publication
of such letters, if there are any extant, would almost
certainly be a valuable contribution to our knowledge of the
period of William and Mary and of Anne.

III

LADY WINCHILSEA'S POEMS

What has called attention to Lady Winchilsea's work is
not so much its intrinsic worth as its place in literary
evolution. The chief attempt of the following brief study
will therefore be to show the relation of her poems to those
of other writers both before and after her day.

A minute study of Lady Winchilsea's versification is not
imperative, but some points are of considerable interest in

connection with the work of Dryden and of Pope. When Pope's *Pastorals* came out Lady Winchilsea was forty-eight years old, and by far the greater number of her poems had been written; hence her heroic couplets are to be judged by the standards of Dryden rather than by the stricter canons of Pope. Swift, for instance, boasted that his offensive triplet at the end of the *City Shower* in 1710 had killed triplets in English verse. Pope had likewise expressed his dislike for this break in the regularity of the couplet, and both Swift and Pope had made war on the Alexandrine. But Dryden, in the *Preface* to his *Æneis* (1697), had said of triplets and Alexandrines, "I regard them now as the *Magna Charta* of heroic poetry." Writing under the ægis of Dryden, Lady Winchilsea would come strongly under the condemnation of Pope, for she used these two devices for varying the couplet so frequently as sometimes almost to destroy the couplet effect for a page at a time. Again, Dryden protests vigorously against the "shock of two vowels immediately following each other." "The army" leaves, he thinks, "a horrid, ill-sounding gap betwixt the words," while "th' army" is smooth. He therefore almost invariably made use of "synalœphas," as he called elisions. Pope also disliked the hiatus but said that it was frequently to be preferred to elision, as, for example, "the old" is "smoother and less constrained" than "th' old." Lady Winchilsea holds by the canon of Dryden even when it gives rise to combinations so difficult as "t' attempt," "sh' extorts," or so broken in appearance as "th' o'r-shadowing," "t'o'r-match," but she rather inconsistently admits the hiatus sometimes when "the" is needed as filling for the verse, as

Versification

We wait on the event with ease.

In the endeavor to hold a line to ten syllables she follows the fashion of her day in preferring elisions to slurring or

the substitution of the trisyllabic foot. To modern taste
the custom of marking all metrical variations so that the
eye as well as the ear must recognize them is annoying.
The brackets that indicate triplets, and the apostrophes
with which all elisions and contractions are marked seem
to be especially in evidence in Ardelia's pages. Not only
do all preterites and past participles where the "ed" is not
to be separately pronounced have the "e" elided, but many
trisyllables with an unaccented middle vowel have this
vowel elided. Most forms of "to be" and "to have" are
contracted with pronominal subjects, contractions so difficult as "t'had," "t'have," "thou'dst," being not infrequent,
while colloquial contractions, such as "'tis," "'twas," and
"sha'nt" are much used even in serious verse. In "could"
and similar words the "l" is elided, and "does" is written
"do's," though for what reason is not apparent.

Pope also objected to expletives, but Dryden's more
rapid and freer verse did not always disdain "these fillers-
up of unnecessary syllables," while Lady Winchilsea certainly
carried the easy device so far as distinctly to enfeeble her
verse.

In one interesting point Lady Winchilsea's verse is at
variance with both the theory and the practice of Pope and
of Dryden. Dryden says in the *Preface* to his *Æneis*,

It is possible, I confess, though it rarely happens, that a verse
of monosyllables may sound harmonious, and some examples of it
I have seen. My first line of the Æneis is not harsh. . . . . It
seldom happens but a monosyllabic line turns verse to prose, and
even that prose is rugged and inharmonious. Philarchus, I
remember, taxes Balzac for placing twenty monosyllables in a file
without one dissyllable betwixt them.

And Pope says that monosyllabic lines unless "artfully
managed" are "stiff, languishing, and hard." Now, monosyllabic lines are of constant occurrence in Lady Winchilsea's
verse. In short-line stanzaic forms or in octosyllabics a

line made up of monosyllables is not unusual in the work of
any poet, but even in such cases Lady Winchilsea's use of
monosyllables is excessive.   In the second stanza of *The Wit
and the Beau* there are twenty-four monosyllables before the
first dissyllable is reached.   There are frequent octosyllabic
couplets with no dissyllables, as,

> Love when next his leave he took
> Cast on both so sweet a look.
>
> Cloath me O Fate, tho' not so gay,
> Cloath me light and fresh as May.

There are also frequent pentameter couplets with but a
single dissyllable, and some without even the one dissyllable, as,

> Thus washed in tears, as fair my soul does shew
> As the first fleece, which on the Lamb does grow.

In the *Poor Man's Lamb*, a poem of fifty-seven lines,
from which this couplet is taken, there are eight monosyllabic lines besides the couplet.   Single pentameter monosyllabic lines may be counted by the hundred.   Even
Alexandrines are sometimes monosyllabic, as,

> Urg'd him to keep his word and still he swore the same.

Though some of the monosyllabic lines have vowels and
consonants so cunningly linked, or are so placed in connection with others of different composition that the ear is not
conscious of any break in the general harmony, yet often the
recurring monosyllables give an unpleasantly staccato effect,
or they make the verse seem childish.

In a consideration of Lady Winchilsea's rhymes their correctness must, of course, be judged by the pronunciations
current in her day.   Certain variations from modern pronunciation are of especial interest.   She almost invariably, for
instance, rhymes "oi" or "oy" with "ī."   We find the following as regular rhymes: join, coin + fine; join'd, coin'd + kind;

enjoy + lie; joys, noise + devise; oyl, spoil, toil + smile;
spoil'd + wild. " Ea " and " ai " usually rhyme with " ā,"
but with interesting variations.   Meat, treat, seat and other
similar words rhyme with cate, but also sometimes with meet;
we find reveal, conceal + vale, but also + feel; said + made or
+ wed; sais (for says) + plays; again + vain or + men (in
which case it is usually written " agen "); tea and sea always
rhyme with day; but seas rhymes with ease, which in turn
rhymes with these, but easy rhymes with lazy.   We find also
pleas'd + rais'd or + seiz'd; leave + grave or + receive (but
receive, conceit, seize, and similar words apparently often had
in her poems the sound of " ā "); ceas'd, feast, east, and beast
rhyme with rest.   Divert + art, reserv'd + starv'd, wreck +
back, wreck'd + pack'd are frequent combinations. Are is frequently used with care, and were with air; wind always
rhymes with mind.   We find shew + foe or + new, been +
sin or + seen, fault (sometimes written faught) + taught.
The fact that all of these rhymes occur in Dryden and in
Pope would indicate that the pronunciation of the day
sanctioned them.

In general it may be said of Lady Winchilsea's rhymed
heroics that, according to the standard of her days they were
more than respectably correct, but that she never attained to
a conception of the couplet as the unit of verse. She has
almost no *enjambment*, but she mars the couplet effect, as
Pope conceived it, by full stops in the middle of a line or of
a couplet, by triplets and by Alexandrines, by the use of
feminine rhymes and by combinations of couplets with stanzaic effects.   Nor does she have, except faintly, the antithesis
of idea, the structural balance of line and phrase, and the
sharp, closing word that mark the couplet in its highest
development.   When her heroic verse is good its excellences
arise from vigor and ease rather than from minute finish.

Less than half of Lady Winchilsea's non-dramatic verse

is in the heroic couplet. Her dramas are in blank verse,
she makes large use of octosyllabics, her hymns and songs
show many stanzaic forms, and she has numerous pindaric
and other irregular metrical combinations. In general the
movement in all her lines is iambic, but *An Enquiry after
Peace* is a pretty good example of the catalectic trochaic
tetrameter, a line effectively combined with iambic tetrame-
ters in the *Petition for an Absolute Retreat*. Anapæstic
movement is found in *Le Passion Vaincue*, and in *The
Circuit of Apollo*, where the anapæst is lightly handled for
humorous effects.   One song in this measure, *Let the
Fool still be true*, only now and then catches the right
anapæstic dance, but the *Lines on a Punch Bowl*, a slightly
modified form of the same stanza, is a capital bit of versification. Most of the stanzas are in tetrameter lines, but
with trimeters and pentameters in frequent combinations.
At least six stanzaic forms close with an Alexandrine, the
sinuous length of which was apparently pleasing to Ardelia's
ear. The stanza of *The Sigh* is the one most often used, but
that of *Life's Progress* is more novel and used with more
smoothness and grace. In several long stanzas there are
sustained rhyme schemes that show a good deal of skill.

Of Lady Winchilsea's style not much need be said.
"Poetry requires adornment," said Dryden, "and that is not
to be had from our old Teuton monosyllables," and hence
his avowed attempt to naturalize "elegant words" from
classic authors. But Lady Winchilsea remained strangely
content with the Teuton monosyllables. Her diction has
absolutely no pedantry. She errs rather on the side of
colloquialisms, and in her humorous poems she is not afraid
of slang. She seems always to seek for the simplest, plainest
words she can find. Her sentences, too, are straightforward
and intelligible. Not even her pindarics have involutions
that really obscure the sense. She has no conceits, no

preciosity, almost no periphrases, and little poetic diction. She has surprisingly few metaphors or similes. There is no abundance or richness of descriptive epithets. It would, indeed, be difficult to find so large a body of work with less adornment. Frequently this extreme plainness of style results in long passages that are dull, commonplace, prosaic; but now and then, when Lady Winchilsea is at her best, when her ideas are based on deep and rich experience, her honesty, her reticence, her inability to say any more than just what she sees or feels, flowers out into an exact, lovely simplicity like that of the facts she records.

Among Lady Winchilsea's earliest works are her translations from the Italian. In spite of her association with

Translations Mary of Modena, she never gained more than a cursory knowledge of the Italian language, and she was obliged to make her translations through French or English versions. But it was, doubtless, while at court that she became acquainted with Tasso's *Aminta*, which so fascinated her that she at once secured a verbal translation and proceeded to turn it into verse. When, however, she had "finished the first Act extreamly to her satisfaction," and was convinced that the original "must be as soft and full of beautys as ever anything of that nature was," her conscience asserted itself, pointing out that there was nothing of "a serious morality or usefullnesse" in this soft Italian pastoral, and remanding her to the "more sollid reasonings" of her own mind. In the *Preface* to the folio she austerely recorded her repentance, and her determination to devote herself to strictly religious verse, but she is obliged to admit in a footnote that she was later beguiled into "a scene or two more," and when she selects poems for publication five "pieces" out of the *Aminta* are chosen. This translation and the tragi-comedy, *Love and Innocence*, seem to belong to the same early period of Ardelia's work. They are both marked by a soft, vague emotionalism, a hurry and abundance of detail, a luxuriance of phrase, not characteristic of later poems.

Lady Winchilsea had a competent knowledge of the French language and literature, but none of her translations from the French shows the eager delight apparent in the extracts from Tasso. Many of the earlier translations from the French read like mere exercises in versification, yet even here her choice of passages is rather significant. Mathurin Regnier caught her attention not by his clever social satire, but by the rarer, half-pensive moralizing of his occasional verse, and she reproduced his somewhat stiffly allegorical *Equipage*. So, too, in Montaigne it is not the homely common sense, the sly wit, the shrewdness, that interest her as these qualities certainly would have done later in life, but she chooses for translation the fanciful love-song of the young cannibal chieftain. From Bussy-Rabutin she selects some of the rather cynical maxims on love. Another author in whom she was interested was Madame Deshoulières, whose Idyls, especially *Les Moutons*, had gained for her the appellations of "*la Calliope Française*," "*la dixième Muse.*" She was a *Precieuse*, the leader of a brilliant salon, and at the same time " a faithful wife, tender mother, and generous friend," qualities of a sort to appeal to Ardelia. Perhaps, too, the cruel frankness with which Madame Deshoulières was advised, on the appearance of her tragedy, to *retourner a ses moutons*, touched a sympathetic chord. The most important of the translations from the French is the fragment from Racine's *Athalie*. When this play was first acted in 1691 it was far from a success. In book-form in the same year it likewise met with neglect or disapproval. Boileau alone among critics prophesied its final victory, a victory that did not come till 1716. It therefore speaks well for Lady Winchilsea's insight and independence that she should, before 1713, choose it to

translate. Probably the whole drama proved a task to which
she was unequal, but the published fragment has real merit.
The heroic couplet necessitated some padding; at any
rate she regarded her material with the freedom inculcated
by Dryden, and so did not hesitate to introduce fresh details
suggested by her knowledge of the Bible story. There is
inevitable a loss of vigor, a slight blurring of clear-cut outlines, but in general the imperious dignity, the superstitious
terror of the beautiful and wicked daughter of the painted
Jezebel is well maintained. Doubtless the scriptural theme
and the elevated tone of the drama made it especially congenial to Lady Winchilsea.

    "Our most vertuous Orinda" translated plays, hence
Ardelia feels that her own dramatic attempts cannot be altogether reprehensible. Her two plays can be
Dramas   dated with some exactness. Her account of
the writing of *Aristomenes* as given in the *Preface* definitely
puts the composition of this play very soon after 1688. In
the Epilogue she adds that it was written at "lonely God-
meersham." The Prologue commemorates the first reading
of the play to Lord Winchilsea. If this were the second
earl, the tragedy was completed before September 1689, the
date of his death. If the reference is to Charles, the young
earl—and it almost certainly is—the reading of the completed work was somewhat later, but in either case the actual
composition belongs in 1688–91. Of *Love and Innocence*
Ardelia says that it was written as an experiment to see
whether she could carry through such an attempt; hence
this play probably was written before *Aristomenes*.

    The fable of *Love and Innocence* consists of a main
plot and a sub-plot organically interwoven. The interest of suspense is well maintained, the double
Love and   denouement not occuring till within a page
Innocence   or two of the end of the play. The minor crises of each

action are clearly marked and they contribute to bring
about the catastrophe toward which each plot seems tending.   The *deus ex machina*, whereby the main plot escapes
the apparently inevitable tragic end, is an opportunely
furious storm by means of which the parted lovers are
brought together, and saved, the one from suicide, the other
from impending death.   In the sub-plot the interfering
providence is a soldier who awakens from a drunken stupor
at just the time and place to arrest the villain and save the
lady.   The villain is the center of each story.   His evil
plans, if successful, would compass the destruction of both
pairs of lovers.   Most of the crises in the story are the
forward steps of his machinations.   The drama observes the
unities of time and place.   It is indeed, for a first attempt,
a surprisingly well-knit piece of work.   Of the characteri-
zation less can be said.   Innocence is too innocent, virtue
too virtuous, villainy too villainous.   There is no shading.
Everything is marked off in black and white.   Ardelia's
"factious suttle villain" is not a success.   He is sufficiently
armed with evil deeds, but he fails to arouse interest.   There
are in his case none of the inciting, half-excusing causes
apparent in *Macbeth* or *Richard III.*, nor are we for a
moment blinded by poetic charm or over-mastering personality.   Rivalto is merely a vulgar, bad man who wishes to be
revenged on his prince for a deserved rebuke, to steal the
money of his confederates, and to kidnap a girl who detests
him.   His motto is:

> To all my senses their full pleasure give,
> I care not how reproached or scorned I live.

He has not even intellectual supremacy in his low plots.
He succeeds less through his own subtlety than through the
abnormal stupidity or credulity of his victims.   Even the
greatness of his contemplated crimes seldom raises him out
of the commonplace.   His most vigorous speech comes when

he rejoices over the probable outcome of his scheme to defame the virtuous Great Master of Rhodes:

> Think how twill feed revenge,
> To see this Saint, this praying fighting Saint,
> This child of Fame, this cloud of Holy Incence,
> Exposed a profligate, and secret sinner,
> And like an o'er spent taper stink and vanish.

Capriccio, the comic character, is elephantine in his attempted quips and cranks. The comedy scenes are not offensive like those of *Venice Preserved*, but they are crude and amateurish. Capriccio as a drunkard would never deceive the initiated. His tipsy jokes and thirsty raptures, and even his slang, have a premeditated, calculated air. There is no abandon. His best speech is the description of the bacchanalian and sensual orgy that broke out in Rhodes with most improbable celerity on the report of Aubusson's sin:

> Tis a rare world, a brave world,
> A ranting, flanting, shining world;
>
>   *   *   *   *
>
> Never such a time in Rhodes, never such an example,
> Every one quoting the Great Master,
> And trooping on to sin, under his banner,
> As if they were beating up volunteers for the Devil.

The triumph of innocence is typified by Aubusson the Great Master of Rhodes. For a nice courtesy, a delicately fastidious sense of honor, he could set the pace for Sir Charles Grandison, and in absolute, spotless, untempted virtue he walks in the footsteps of King Arthur. As a general he equals the splendid exploits of Dryden's heroes. As a ruler he is surnamed "The Just." But before an accusation of hypocrisy and secret sin he has no force, he attempts no defense. He withdraws like the traditional deer struck by the hunter's dart. He is irritatingly meek and inefficient. His plaintive, "Tell them I am not wicked," when accused,

and his triumphant, "I am not wicked," when his innocence
has been attested, are without dignity or pathos. The triumph of love is illustrated by the Queen of Cyprus and her
lover Lauredan. The women are more successfully represented than the men. There is the real play of contending
emotions in the portrayal of the Queen. Love, jealousy,
hope, suspicion, despair, claim her in turn, and one of the
most spontaneous passages in the play is expressive of her
anger and grief when she discovers the deceptions that have
induced her to banish her lover. In Blanfort we see pictured
one of the astonishingly rapid emotional developments so
frequent in contemporary tragedy. His hot-headed love for
the queen reaches its height, and declines, and the old love
for Marina reasserts itself with pristine vigor, all within
seven hours. Marina is the most interesting personality in
the play. She is a strictly romantic heroine. She would
be an appropriate Sylvia, for instance, for the Daphne of the
Aminta. She is apparently Ardelia in the stage of experience represented by the *Lines to Prior* and the translations
from Tasso. The character of Marina reminds one of
Wordsworth's conjecture that Lady Winchilsea gave up
love-poetry because she could not sufficiently temper its
transports. The chief characteristics of Marina's love are
its extravagance and self-abnegation. Her conception of
"immortal blisse" is to have "her lover stretch at her feet for
hours imprinting kisses on her hand by thousands." Soft,
modest, tender by nature, poetic, sensitive, dreamy, she lives
in her emotions, but in endurance of injuries inflicted by a
false lover she is a very patient Griselda. With none of the
dash, sparkle, and independence of Rosalind, with no abet-
tors like Celia and the Fool, Marina is driven by love to a
more strenuous enterprise than their holiday visit to the
Forest of Arden. Alone, disguised as a man, she seeks
a foreign court, consorts with rough soldiers, listens to the

raptures of her recreant lover for the Queen, and meanwhile is defenceless before the tempestuous and vulgar wooing of the villain, Rivalto. Finally, last test of the romantic heroine, she can submit to poverty and shame, can give her lover up to a rival Fair One if he so decrees, and can die with prayers for their happiness on her lips. Most of the effective passages in the play have to do with Marina. Take, for example, this description of the love-nest at Rome where Blanfort won her heart:

> The place, oh! twas most fit for the occasion,
> Secret and blooming with the verdant spring;
> A Grove of mirtles, compassed itt about,
> Which gave no more admittance to the Sun
> Then served to chear the new appearing flowers,
> And tell the birds itt was their time to sing.
> A crystal spring, stole through the tufted grasse,
> Hasting to reach a fountain which itt fed,
> But murmur'd still, when 'ere it found a stop.

The description of Marina herself is almost as charming as Marvell's lines on Maria and not unlike them:

> 'Twas here, my lord, neer to this fountain's side,
> I saw the Maid, the soft, the charming maid,
> That seemed to give the sweetness to the place,
> And in herself posseest all I've described,
> The season's youth, and freshnesse of the flowers,
> The harmony of all the tunefull birds,
> And clearness of the Spring on which she gaz'd.

Marina is, in truth, a winning and pathetic character, and it is a pity that her fidelity could not have a better reward than the regained love of the handsome, inconstant, selfish Blanfort.

The play closes with a proper distribution of rewards. Punishments are not, however, so meted out. The villain, Rivalto, is romantically, and in the grand style, forgiven, and even furnished with funds. But he takes himself off with a not altogether unintelligible distate for the abundant, self-conscious, successful virtue blooming about him.

Aristomenes follows the fashion set by Dryden, Lee, and Otway, in presenting as its hero a noted historical character.

Aristomenes Most of the events and most of the personages come with little change from the narrative of Pausanias, but Ardelia successfully manipulates dates and places in such a way as to bring the more picturesque portions of the life of Aristomenes very nearly within the compass prescribed by the unities, and that without too great sacrifice of probability or ordered sequence. The escape of Aristomenes from the cave by means of the fox, and his rescue through the assistance of Amalintha, the daughter of his enemy, are cleverly made parts of a single incident, and Amalintha's act is motived by the love she bears Aristor, the son of Aristomenes. This love is also elaborated into one of the sub-intrigues, another being the love between Demagetus, son to the Prince of Rhodes, and Herminia, daughter to Aristomenes. The play is curiously constructed, all the complications of the two subordinate love-stories having reached an apparently happy termination before the fifth act, and the hero, likewise, having succeeded in his contest with Sparta. But then a new set of circumstances brings about a tragic end. Ardelia calls this play "wholly tragical," but till near the end it certainly moves likes a tragi-comedy. The real purpose of the play is to present the character rather than the fortunes of Aristomenes. He is shown in success and in failure, in joy and in sorrow, always with the intent that he may prove himself the best of men and serve as an incitement to virtue and to wisdom. He is the Aubusson of *Love and Innocence.* We see him idolized by the soldiers, loved and reverenced by his children, adored by the people. In war he is a lion. In captivity he speaks out brave words of defiance. His wits are keen, his nerves steady, his personal resource unfailing. Just, generous, forgiving, with high spirit and passionate emotions, he yet is but an aggregation of virtues, not a man.

There are more reminisences of the heroic tragedy in this play than in *Love and Innocence*. The prison-scene between Aristor and Amalintha is not without some likeness to the wit-combats popular in Dryden's day. The long death-scene when Aristor, mortally wounded in the battle, conceals his wound from Amalintha, and Amalintha, likewise mortally wounded, conceals her wound from Aristor, until they die almost simultaneously, the promptness with which the nurse expires on seeing their dead bodies, the unanimity with which the others prepare to fall on their swords, carry us into just the air of extravagant unreality found in many of the tragic closing scenes of the heroic drama. On the stage *Aristomenes* would offer bustle and variety, with its clamor and hurry of war, its pastoral love-making, its assemblies of state, its prison-scenes, and its underground caves with spectral musicians; but it would hardly hold interest either by the plot or the characters.

Wordsworth commented on the lines:

> Love's soft bands,
> His gentle cords of Hyacinths and Roses,
> Wove in the dewy spring whem storms are silent,

as a characteristic passage, but more characteristic and quite as charming are the pathetic words of Amalintha:

> But are there none, none that do Live and Love.
> That early meet, and in the Spring of Youth,
> Uncrossed, nor troubled in the soft design,
> Set sweetly out, and travel on to age,
> In mutual joys, that with themselves expire.

Of great beauty is the lament of Aristomenes for his son Aristor:

The Sun will Keep his pace, and Time revolve,
Rough Winters pass, and Springs come smiling on ;
But thou dost talk of Never, Demagetus:
Yet ere Despair prevails, retract that word,
Whose cloudy distance bars the reach of thought.

Aristor rather subtly analyzes the process of falling in
love. He says to Amalintha:

I saw you Fair, beyond the Fame of Helen ;
But Beauty's vain, and fond of new applause,
Leaving the last Adoarer in despair
At his approach, who can but praise it better:
Whilst Love, *Narcissus*-like, courts his reflection,
And seeks itself gazing on others eyes.
When this I found in yours, it bred that passion,
Which Time, nor Age, nor Death, shall ere diminish.

Almeria in *Ardelia to Ephelia* says that Ardelia

Speaks of Otaway with such delight
As if no other pen could move or write.

and various passages emphasize her partiality for *The Orphan*
and *Venice Preserved*, which came out when she was nineteen and twenty-one years of age, at just the right time to
affect her taste and guide her efforts. Otway's tragic
death occurred while she was still in London, three or four
years before the composition of her plays. Her attention
was thus strongly directed to him, and it is not strange that
her work should betray his influence. She read Lee with
admiration, but she could not have imitated the *Rival Queens*.
Lee at his best and at his worst was out of her range. But
the tenderness and delicacy of Otway, the pathetic sweetness
of his verse, and his love of external nature, would all strike
a responsive chord in her mind and heart.

Of the songs, eighteen appear in the first manuscript.
These are copied into the folio with seven or eight additions,

Songs
but the impulse to song-writing died early, nor
did Lady Winchilsea later set much value on
this portion of her work. Her acknowledgement of indebt-

edness to Prior must refer to her conventional love-lyrics and
her few convivial songs; and so far as dates go it is not
impossible that Prior should have been influential in turning
her attention to this sort of writing, for though his songs
were not published till 1709, many of them were written as
early as 1692, and they were well-known in manuscript.
Doubtless these songs would find their way to Eastwell and
they might so have caught Ardelia's ear and attuned it to
novel melodies. The impulse must, however, have been one
quickly acted on, for Ardelia's songs are very nearly contemporary with Prior's. Beyond this suggestion or impulse,
Prior's influence on Lady Winchilsea is not apparent. She
calls him the master-singer, while she is but the bird crudely
striving to imitate his ravishing notes; but this is an overstate-
ment. Certainly where Prior is most characteristic it is
impossible that she should imitate him. She was too inflexi-
ble, too serious, too deeply conscious of realities, to reproduce
the abandon, the gayety, the dash, the moral indifference, of
Prior's captivating appeals to Chloe. *Let the Fool Still Be
True* and *If for a Woman I Would Die* have something of
Prior's spirit. But though Ardelia touches with some deft-
ness the philosophy of the butterfly lover who, inconstant
to one,

> Can each Beauty adore,
> And love all, and love all, and love all, and forever,

she much more effectively represents the dark obverse,

> Who make the hearts of men their care
> Will have their own betrayed.

Ardelia's delicately imaginative appreciation of the *Punch
Bowl* in the lines to Leslie Finch must free her from any
suspicion of a puritanic rigor hardly known in her day, but
her other poems on wine were never inspired by the god of
mirth. The riotous glee of Prior's

> 'Tis the mistress, the friend, and the bottle, old boy!

was not only outside the compass of her lyre, but typified
a bacchanalian excess that aroused her strongest disapproval.
According to her theory, which is not without a certain novel
pungency, wine makes of the heart "an inaccessible island"
to which no nymph need try to win her way.

Ardelia's best songs are not in Prior's vein at all. *The
Losse, A Sigh, The Progress of Life*, are marked by a
strain of tender, subdued melancholy as natural to Ardelia
as the flippant gayety of the conventional love-song was alien
to her. *To Grief*, a little poem inspired by the troubles of
1688, has dignity, reserve, and genuine pathos. It is in sad
little poems, the direct and simple outcome of her own experience, that her lyric impulse finds most nearly adequate
expression.

Lady Winchilsea's religious poems are nearly all direct
paraphrases from Scripture passages, or they are so saturated
Religious with biblical phraseology as to read like para-
Poems phrases. In such poems the simplicity and
literary distinction of the original must always make the
smoothest pindaric, or stanzaic, or heroic reproductions seem,
to say the least, superfluous. But aside from this objection,
Ardelia's religious poetry is of especial interest. The
delight with which she wrote it resulted in an unusual vigor
and variety of versification. And in mood and theme these
poems contribute much to a statement of her philosophy of
life. The bitter and almost contemptuous résumé of human
ambitions and attainments that characterizes the early work
of both Mary of Modena's rhyming maids of honor seems
to have been a genuine expression of opinion. The lament
of the preacher was a view of life quite natural to detached
and sober-minded observers in the reign of Charles II. But
philosophic pessimism was not to be Ardelia's permanent
mental attitude. Definite trials soon brought her face to
face with spiritual experiences of a more personal sort.

Even in her gayest days she was incapable temperamentally
of drowning grief by an acceptance of the epicurean philosophy. Her summary of this doctrine in *The Wisdom of
Solomon* is probably her best heroic verse, but the doctrine
itself is vigorously remanded to "th' industrious Devil."
It was impossible that *carpe diem* should be her motto. It
was her tendency to look before and after, and her tempta-
tion when trials came was to fall into a state of distrust and
despair. The shortness of life, the failure of the highest
hopes, the prosperity of the wicked, the affliction of the
righteous, were facts that stirred her to doubts and questionings, and the supreme religious experience commemorated
in her poems is her struggle to interpret and accept sorrow
according to the Christian ideal. She persistently describes
grief as the line by which every saint is measured, as the
furnace fire that tries the gold of true piety, as the only
"certain purifying roade" that leads to the Heavenly City.
For the earthly life Ardelia's ideal is the *via media*. According to her philosophy "all extreams to their own Ruine
haste." To walk quietly and steadily, to hold oneself in
hand, to realize that

> No Joy a Rapture must create,
> No Grief beget Despair,

in a word, to have the sources of life independent of
externals, is her creed. But in her pictures of the final
happiness of victorious saints, her eagerness and longing
find expression in phrases more nearly akin to the "enthusiasm" of Watts and the Wesleys than to the formal
morality of her own day.

In an *Ode* to Cowley Bishop Sprat said,

The
Pindaric
Odes

> Pindar has left his barbarous Greece, and thinks it just
> To be led by thee to the English shore;
> An honour to him.

Pindar was, in fact, known to the seventeenth century only

through Cowley and his imitators. But Congreve said in
his *Discourse* (*circa* 1706) that Cowley not only had not
brought Pindar to England, but had, through his "irregular
Odes," been the principal, though innocent, cause of the
great crowd of deformed poems supposedly formed on
Pindar. From this time on there was a reaction against the
more extreme licenses of the pindaric form. But the school
of Cowley held that the true pindaric marks were exalted
themes, striking and unusual figures, abrupt transitions,
impetuosity and excitement of mood, with an extreme com-
plexity and irregularity of stanzaic structure and rhyme
scheme. Lady Winchilsea's three *Odes* come between 1694
and 1703, hence they belong to the last period of Cowley's
influence and just before the reactionary period set in. She
called Cowley master, and theoretically she accepted his
pindaric conventions; but her *Odes*, while irregular, are not
markedly so, nor have they any of the "flights" of Cowley's
Odes, nor any of the conceits. Lady Winchilsea had an
inherent respect for order and coherence, and she could
never quite trust herself to the stiff gale on which the
Theban swan was supposed to stretch his wings. Hence
her pindarics seldom "toil too much the reader's ear." The
themes, moreover, are interesting. *All is Vanity* is, to be
sure, timid, and too much a versified résumé of her reading,
but it is well-knit, and its fearless outlook, its dignity and
controlled pathos, make it a promising early poem. *The
Spleen* has none of the softness and grace of *All is Vanity*.
It reads like more mature work. It is more keenly analytic,
the outlines are sharper, and the material is more frankly
based on observation and experience. The third ode, *On the
Hurricane*, written in 1703, immediately after the disas-
trous storm of November 27, 1703, is longer and much
looser in structure than the other odes. It was evidently
written in great haste and while the events of the storm

were still fresh in memory.   Its chief value is in descriptive
passages which will be spoken of later.

At the beginning of the eighteenth century there was a
new and-wide spread interest in fables.   English prose ver-

Her Fables sions of *Æsop* had held their place in popular
favor from the days of Caxton down, and the
Latin *Æsop* was in use in the schools, but it is to La Fontaine that this striking revival of interest is chiefly due.   The
first six books of his *Fables* were published in France in
1668, other parts appearing in 1671, 1678, 1679, and the
twelve books in 1694.   Their popularity in England is
shown by a remark of Addison, who, writing in 1711 in
praise of fables, says that La Fontaine " by this way of writing is come into vogue more than any other Author of our
times."   In 1692 appeared the first edition of Sir Roger
L'Estrange's collection, in which he added to the fables of
Æsop most of the new sets of fables that had been published
abroad.   In spite of the size of this extensive compilation it
quickly passed through seven editions.   L'Estrange's idio-
matic and telling prose versions of the old tales were
weighted down by "morals" and "reflexions," written
purely from the point of view of a Tory statesman.   In 1722
the ever-useful Æsop was used by the Rev. Samuel Croxall
to establish Whig doctrines.   These versions served to make
the fables widely known, but it was not till the appearance
of Gay's *Fables* in 1728 that there was any notable attempt
to follow in English the versified fable of La Fontaine, and
Gay has always been counted the progenitor of the race of
verse fable-writers in England.   It seems rather surprising
that the first quarter of the eighteenth century should not
have been a fable-writing as well as a fable-reading age.
One is led to join in Shenstone's regret that Addison did
not write fables, his purity of style, his dry humor, his easy
manner, being qualities likely to insure success.   Swift, too,

would seem to have had some natural affinities for the fable
form, but though he said there was no kind of writing he
esteemed more, he was forced to acknowledge that he had
"frequently endeavoured at it in vain." Gay agrees in
counting the fable a most difficult kind of writing, saying
that when he had completed one he was always in despair of
ever being able to find another. It is, perhaps, this real
difficulty under the apparent ease and naturalness that
warned off many writers to whom the opportunity for effective moralizing would have made the fable a seductive form.
At any rate the fact stands that before Gay, Lady Winchilsea
holds a solitary pre-eminence as an English fable-writer in
the manner of La Fontaine. But two of her fables appear
in the folio and none in the earlier manuscript. They were
probably all written between 1700 and 1713. She formed
herself almost entirely on La Fontaine, who had broken distinctly with the literary tradition of his predecessors. It
had been said that the ornament of the fable was no ornament, that brevity and conciseness were essential, that morals
must be explicitly stated. But La Fontaine deliberately
challenged this conception. He set himself to "*egayer*" the
tales, to add to them something of novelty and adornment,
to show that the fables would not resent *les graces lacédé-
moniennes*. It was to this fable convention that Lady
Winchilsea gave allegiance. She does not attempt, as did
Gay, originality of invention, but relies as frankly on La
Fontaine and L'Estrange as they had relied on their predecessors, and she follows her models with as widely varying
degrees of fidelity as did they. Sometimes her fable is a
mere translation of La Fontaine, holding as close to the
original as verse translation would allow; but in general
the material is treated with great freedom. Two lines are
expanded into as many pages; there are large omissions and
frequent condensations; details are replaced by others giv-

ing English local color; fables are broken in two; morals
are added or altered; titles are changed. But, though influ-
enced now and again by L'Estrange's racy idiom, "the easy
words," "the plain honest English" on which he prided
himself, she holds throughout to La Fontaine's ideal of
smooth, graceful, amplified narration.

Lady Winchilsea's most famous fable is *The Atheist and
the Acorn*. This poem is a brief and picturesque version of
La Fontaine's *La gland et la citrouille*. It is not an
Æsopic fable but was based on a tale found in various forms
in several sources open to La Fontaine. It excited much
attention when it first appeared in French in 1671. Lady
Winchilsea's change of the naive countryman into the
sophisticated atheist involves much loss in the way of humorous contrast. But the French Garo and the English
Atheist alike speak with scorn of the providential ordering
that could assign acorns to lordly oaks and pumpkins to
slender vines. And each, reclining under the tree in fatu-
ous self-complacency, on being hit in the eye by an acorn,
is led to justify the ways of God to man by the reflection
that had the acorn been a pumpkin, not his eye only, but his
precious brain itself would have suffered damage. Neither
La Fontaine nor Lady Winchilsea nor any of their readers
seemed to feel what Voltaire pitilessly pointed out, the
"*égoïsme comique*" of this *argumentum ad hominem*. On
the contrary, Garo and the Atheist held their own for a century as apt illustrations of the creed formulated by Pope,
"Whatever is, is best."

In spite of the fact that fables constitute one-third of
her published work, Lady Winchilsea speaks lightly of them
in general, calling them "childish Tales" by which "lazy
Triflers" seek to purchase fame. And Wordsworth regretted
that she should have spent so much time on an inferior
species of poetry. Yet in a general survey of her work the

fables are of importance for various reasons. They show her first in the field with a poetic form destined to great popularity in succeeding years; they reveal her opinions; they are vignettes of social satire; and they are interesting examples of versification.

One line of reading in which Lady Winchilsea was much interested was the critical literature of her own day. Boileau's *L'Art Poétique* (1673) had stimu- lated verse criticism in England as well as in France. The Earl of Mulgrave's *Essay on Satire* (1679), his *Essay on Poetry* (1682), Roscommon's *Essay on Trans- lated Verse* (1681), his translation of Horace's *Ars Poetica* (1680), Sir William Soame's paraphrase and adaptation of Boileau's *L'Art Poétique* (1683), were verse renderings of the critical dicta counted most authoritative by the late seventeenth century writers. All of these, with the addition of Rapin and Madame Dacier, Lady Winchilsea knew well. Horace and the Stagirite are the critical law-givers, but Mulgrave is their prophet, and she finds his *Essay on Poetry* as "delightsome" as it is instructive. But it is Dryden, she thinks, who has laid open the very mysteries of poetry and made the whole art so clear that even females should be held accountable if they transgress the rules.

Verse Criticism

Of critical work on her own account Lady Winchilsea gives us little, but that little is not without interest. Poets should "teach while they divert" is her creed. Poetry may be allowed to "stir up soft thoughts," but this must be delicately and modestly done so as to cause no blushes, and poetry most successfully responds to its divine origin when it leads men "back to the Blissful Seats Above." Yet she seems to refer with some regret to the days of Charles II, when

> Witty beggars were in fashion,
> And learning had o're-run the Nation.

The Merry Monarch, "so nice himself," and the " refin'der

sort" knew a good play when they heard it, but the literary standards of her own day are, she thinks, much coarser and less critical. *The Miser and the Poet* is a humorous arraignment of the age for its failure to give poets due recognition, a subject cleverly worked up in *Ardelia's Return Home*. In the *Critic and the Writer of Fables* she gives delightful little burlesques of the popular literary forms, the pastoral, the heroic poem, and the fable. In the closing lines of this poem, operas and panegyrics are coupled as the two forms of literature most certain of pleasing. This fling at the Italian opera is but an early expression of the critical attitude that found full statement in the *Dunciad*, and that contributed to the gusto with which *The Beggar's Opera* was received. Panegyric, though that was her own fertile vein, always awakened Ardelia's laughter. When she went to Apollo once for aid, his excuse for not loaning Pegasus was that this weary steed had been of late so spurred thick and thin in panegyric, that he could no longer endure the bit — a sarcastic reference, doubtless, since the poem was written in 1689, to the poetical tributes incident to the revolution. In comedy Lady Winchilsea preferred Etheredge and Wycherley because they had more "sense and nature" than their successors — a literary judgment enunciated, however, before Congreve had begun to write. In tragedy Dryden, Lee, and Otway, especially Otway, are her masters. It is a pity that Lady Winchilsea's critical remarks are so few, for they show considerable acumen and an unexpected cleverness in playfully sarcastic analysis.

Dr. Johnson calls *The Splendid Shilling* of Philips "a mode of writing new and unexpected," and it is probable **Fanscomb Barn** that Philips's poem, which came out in 1701, gave Lady Winchilsea the hint for her *Fanscomb Barn*, which, since this poem does not appear in either the octavo or the folio manuscript, was probably written after 1701. The novelty of Philips's poetical experiment in applying the splendid diction and elaborate sentence structure of Milton to the description of the trivial or vulgar events of ordinary life caught Lady Winchilsea's fancy, and she made use of the Miltonic blank verse to portray the tramps that congregated in Fanscomb Barn. Her poem is almost as successful a parody of Milton's style as is *The Splendid Shilling*, and the amusing contrast between the style and the subject-matter is as well sustained. But the chief importance of Lady Winchilsea's poem is in the subject-matter itself. Stropeledon and Bugeta with their "hoof-beating" compeers of the beggars' fraternity would find no worthy comrades till they could visit the ale-house of Ramsay's Maggie Johnstone, and they would not feel quite at home till they could consort with their kith and kin, the jolly beggars of Burns. Lady Winchilsea is as free as Ramsay or Burns from any display of moral censorship toward her tramps. They lie and steal and drink and brag with a self-complacency equal to that of the highwaymen and trulls of Gay's *Beggar's Opera*. Stropeledon counts mendicancy a profession with inevitable privations and hardships, but with well-earned hours of luxurious repose. He and his Bugeta grow confidential and boozy over their cups, recount their lawless deeds, and finally fall down in a drunken stupor, without a word of condemnation from their lady chronicler. A subsidiary little picture of the children drinking sugared water at Pickersdane Well is also sympathetically drawn, and approaches in effectiveness the description of the children at their sports by Shenstone in *The School-Mistress*. We can hardly say with Dr. Harris, prebendary of Rochester and rector of Winchilsea, that both Pickersdane Well and Fanscomb Barn have been "dignified" by the pen of a "notable Kentish Poetess;" but we can say what is far more significant, and that is that the notable poetess wrote the first of modern tramp-poems and gave the earliest effective modern picture of English peasant school-children, and that she was one of the first to write in blank verse of the Miltonic pattern.

During Lady Winchilsea's early maid of honor days the chief literary sensation in the court circle was Dryden's satires and the ensuing host of lampoons and libels. No personal portraits so masterly and so malicious as those by Dryden had before appeared in English literature. Nor during Lady Winchilsea's period of poetical production did any other portraits so masterly appear, but the malice remained as the possession of all the Grub-street race. There were no more great satiric poems till Pope, but there was, in the meantime, plenty of snarling and snapping. The detracting, censorious spirit was pervasive. Against this Ardelia uttered her protest. Indeed, she rather plumed herself on the fact that her own resentments had never but once lured her into personal satiric verse. And this, too, in spite of the tempting inner consciousness that she could tag rhymes in abuse of her neighbors as well as another if she would but set her hand to such business. Yet Lady Winchilsea was much more of a satirist than she was willing to admit, for besides the one satiric poem to which she confesses, there is a vein of satiric comment giving tang and pungency to many poems.

The more we study Lady Winchilsea's work, the more certain it becomes that, in her youth at least, the phrase "the gentle Ardelia," could never have been rightly applied to her. Life at Eastwell brought serenity, but her young womanhood seems to have been one of smothered revolt. Bred at court, she was yet mentally at war with contemporary social, religious, and literary ideals, and, on a surprising number of topics, she expresses herself with caustic severity.

The Fair Sex, and especially the dominant ideal concerning woman's work and woman's education, was the theme most certain to touch her pen with bitterness. In her famous *Preface* of 1703, Mary Astell says:

In the first place, Boys have much Time and Pains, Care and Cost bestowed on their education, Girls have little or none. The former are early initiated in the Sciences, are made acquainted with Antient and Modern Discoveries, they Study Books and Men, have all imaginable encouragement; not only Fame, a dry reward now-a-days, but also Title, Authority, Power, and Riches themselves which purchase all things, are the reward of their improvement. The latter are restricted, frown'd upon, beat, not *for* but *from* the Muses; Laughter and Ridicule that never-failing Scare-Crow is set up to drive them from the Tree of Knowledge. But if in spite of all difficulties Nature prevails, and they can't be kept so ignorant as their masters would have them, they are stared upon as Monsters, Censured, Envyd and every way discouraged, or at the best they have the Fate the Proverb assigns them: *Virtue is praised and starved.*

These words must have been read with secret satisfaction by Lady Winchilsea, for she had, years before, confided similar ideas to that gilt-edged, morocco-bound, diffident first manuscript of hers, and had summed up the situation in the epigrammatic phrase, "Women are Education's and not Nature's Fools." To read, to write, to think, to study— these, she indignantly exclaims, are tabooed lest they should cloud a woman's beauty, and exhaust the time more profitably spent in adorning herself for conquest. She resents the commonly received opinion that dressing and dancing, fashions and theaters, are woman's only legitimate interests. She resents with equal emphasis the ultra-domestic ideal. She frankly declares that she, at least, was never meant for "the dull manage of a servile house." Her own tastes are of the simplest. Of her table she asks little except that it be "set without her care." She can dispense with "ortolane," "treufles," and "morilia," but leisure and a free

mind are necessities. For fashion she cares not at all, and
discussions concerning brocades and laces infinitely weary
her. A new gown in spring, when the lilies and the birds
put on fresh attire, quite satisfies her ambition in the way of
apparel. Against the so-called feminine accomplishments
of her day she puts herself definitely on record. She
simply will not, she declares,

> in fading silks compose,
> Faintly, the inimitable Rose,
> Fill up an ill-drawn Bird, or paint on Glass,
> The Sovereign's blurred and undistinguished face,
> The threatening *Angel* and the Speaking *Ass*.

The courageous expression of tastes so unconventional
inevitably made Ardelia the target for ill-natured jests, and
the jests bore their natural fruit in bitterness of spirit. It
is, however, the prejudice against women authors of which
Ardelia is most acutely conscious. During her memorably
unhappy visit to London, shortly after her retirement to
Eastwell, the caustic social commentary that fell trippingly
from the gay Almeria's tongue reached its unendurable
climax when that young gossip pointed out with a sneer, "a
poetess! a woman who writes, a common jest!" Then
Ardelia's prudence and politeness give way to an indignant
sense of justice. "Why," she exclaims, "should this
poetess be a common jest? Does she make public boast of
her skill? Does she write a song so popular that the car-men
sing it, and then allow her name to be flourished above it?
Does she cause herself to be painted with a laurel wreath
and with commendatory verses encircling her picture?
Does she write lampoons?" So the badgered Ardelia, stung
by the secret knowledge of a tell-tale portfolio of rhymes
down at Eastwell, frees her mind for the nonce. But she
can never quite escape the benumbing conviction that a
woman who delights in the groves and secret springs of the
muses, who thus "deviates from the known and common

way," who dares to trace "unusual things," will be considered an intruder on the rights of men, a presumptuous
creature whom no excellence of work can justify, and in
many a dark moment she is ready to confess that "a
woman's way to charm is not by writing." But when the
splenetic mood is past she brings forth all sorts of defensive
arguments, her best weapons being always drawn from the
arsenal of the Old Testament. It was, in fact, almost
imperative to carry on the contest with Hebrew arguments,
for the foes to the advancement of women had from the out-
set massed their forces in the Garden of Eden. This sort
of discussion is well illustrated in some contemporary
anonymous letters between a certain Chloe and Urania who
are discussing woman's education. Chloe, being a repre-
sentative Fair One, cannot argue for herself, but she repeats
with pretty docility, and much apparent loss of force, the
arguments of her lover, Lysander. His reasoning is to the
effect that "in the Beginning *Woman* was created for
Obedience and *Man* for *Rule*," but that if to the beauty of
woman reason should be added, not Deity itself could maintain the order of precedence. Urania in answer merely
expresses a laconic surprise that Lysander should be so intimately in the secret counsels of the Almighty. But Mary
Astell takes up, in a minute and exhaustive manner, the texts
commonly quoted against female education, and she reaches
the comforting conclusion that the "Bible is for, and not
against us, and cannot, without great violence done to it, be
urg'd to our prejudice." And Lady Winchilsea earnestly
reminds her readers that holy virgins joined in the song
when the ark was brought back; that conquering David was
welcomed by a bright chorus of women; that Deborah led
the fainting hosts of Israel to victory, and so on through the
convincing proofs that if Ardelias wish to write pindarics
they should be given pen and ink.

This sense of injustice, this self-doubt and unrest, are the fit background for Ardelia's one confessedly satirical poem, *Ardelia's Answer to Ephelia.* It is a clever piece of work, vigorous, racy, colloquial. The portraits of the London beau and belle show that in the beautiful and witty maid of honor there had lurked a "chiel" whose note-taking was minute, keen, and even contemptuous. Ardelia's Almeria is the London woman of fashion in 1690, but, by unmistakable traits of family likeness, she betrays her kinship with heroines of a later date. She has not, to be sure, the bewildering fascination of Congreve's Millamant, nor the dazzling beauty of Pope's Belinda, but whatever in these ladies was vain, pert, flippant, and frivolous found its well-developed prototype in Almeria. She was not a whit behind Belinda, in devotion to flounces, furbelows, and feathered gowns, and in the ecstacy with which she regarded her toilet-table, and she excelled Addison's Leonora in her energetic pursuit of gewgaws and rare china. She had, furthermore, what these other fair dames had not, a carping, envious spirit, an eye keen to see all failings but her own, a tongue fluent in evil-minded gossip. Lady Winchilsea does not regard female foibles with amused tolerance. The severity of the portrait she draws does not belie her feeling. To her the Almerias of life were utterly distasteful, an insult to all true womanhood, and not to be laughed at, but scourged.

There are other slight pictures of women much in the spirit of this portrait of Almeria. *A Pastoral Dialogue,* presents two ladies, one young, vain, eager in pursuit of masculine admiration, the other old, vain, jealous, eager to recount past triumphs. The sketches of the artful coquette and the imperious wife in *The Spleen* read like studies for the *Rape of the Lock,* and *Adam Pos'd* would surely do as a text for Pope's "Most women have no characters at all."

The picture of the belles at Tunbridge in 1706 is of the most sarcastic sort. The *blasé* indifference of the men, and the too willing, too grateful reception of slight masculine attentions on the part of the maidens aroused Lady Winchilsea's indignation. The pert, shallow, forward hoydens of the fashionable watering-place were even more obnoxious to her than the trifling fops whose admiration they were courting. Especially open to Ardelia's scorn is the wife of the rich parvenu, who, without birth or breeding, displays her husband's wealth by wearing more gold and lace than a duchess. In her rooms, which are "drest anew at every Christ'ning,"

> Grinning *Malottos* in true Ermin stare,
> The best *Japan*, and clearest China-ware
> Are but as common *Delft* and English *Laquer* there.

Such is the contemptuous triplet with which Ardelia dismisses this lady's pretension to gentility. The foolish old owl in the fable is a playful but searching portrayal of many a doating mother. The wrangling woman with the "eternal clack" in *Reformation* is the typical vulgar scold and busy-body. And so on through the slight portraits which show that Ardelia, howsoever "gentle," had yet a keen eye and quick word for all that fell below her standards.

A second general topic never touched upon without severity is the *mobile*. Lady Winchilsea was an aristocrat and a royalist. She always deprecates an appeal to the public. "How can we," she exclaims,

> with their opinions join,
> Who to promote some interest would define,
> The *People's Voice* to be the *Voice Divine*.

She pities the man of sense who must be judged by a "Crowd of Fools." "The Vulgar Throng," she says, must not be cajoled or reasoned with, but governed "by stated laws." L'Estrange searched through the beast-world for

similitudes expressive of his detestation of the mob. They
are asses, and asses they will be, no matter who rides them;
they are "mungril curs" that bawl, snarl, and snap; they
are "hares that wish to secure universal parity by leveling
all beasts to their own state of weakness," and so on. With
less boldness and less contempt, Lady Winchilsea is entirely
in accord with Sir Roger's views.

"Pocket-Arguments" likewise quickly irritated Ardelia.
The man who grants

> *no* worth in anything
> But so much money as 'twill bring,

the man whose interests are in the price of corn and standing market laws, are outside the pale of her sympathies.
Marriage based on considerations of dowry or jointure is
offensive to her. In her judgment an impecunious scholar
always outranks the successful business man or even the
successful professional man. The best illustration of this
attitude is the poem to Dr. Waldron, who had given up a
fellowship at Oxford that he might make a better income
through the practice of medicine. Ardelia admits that
money, that sordid plant, does not flourish near the odor of
the bays, but she cannot understand how any hope of gain
could induce a wit to leave Oxford, "that Eden to the Fruitful Mind." Dr. Waldron's accomplishments did not extend
apparently beyond gay discourse, witty extempore effusions
in verse or prose for table-books, and an occasional poem in
some *Miscellany*, but even this *dilettante* consorting with the
muses was superior to "druggery," even though druggery
led to "glittering profit." Ardelia's satiric list is really a
long one and comprises "rallying wits," "greedy parasites,"
flatterers when they "fawn and leer," knavish lawyers, travel-
ing fops, and such social bores as buffoons, "mimmicks,"
"quoters of old saws," and retailers of second-hand jokes. Her
antipathies were lively and her insight acute, yet her satire

was seldom personal, and seldom really acrimonious.   Much
of it is in the fables and even those with the most caustic
morals are often marked in the narrative portions by a
gayety, a humorous lightness of touch, and a tolerance far
enough removed from a genuinely pessimistic view of human
nature.

The satiric poems are enlivened by many realistic details
of value to the student of social life in the years from 1680
to 1714.   Ardelia had almost as keen an eye for manners
and customs, for personal idiosyncrasy, for trifling indications of moral standards and motives, as she showed later in
her treatment of external nature.

That Lady Winchilsea, in her attitude toward external
nature, was so far in advance of her age as to be isolated

**Attitude
toward
External
Nature**
from it, is put beyond dispute by a detailed
study of her poems.   This forms, in fact, her
principal claim to the notice of posterity.

Her preference for the country and her correspondingly
strong dislike for the city find emphatic expression in
Ardelia's Answer to Ephelia, about 1690, and the *Preface*,
about 1702.   The "Almeria" of the first of these poems
belongs to the true apostolic succession of poetical heroines
who abhorred the country.   Isabella in Dryden's *Wild Gallant* says, "I cannot abide to be in the country like a wild
beast in the wilderness."   Harriet in Etheredge's *Man of
Mode* counted all beyond Hyde Park a desert, and she said
that her love of the town was so intense that she hated the
country even in tapestry and in pictures.   Sylvia in Shadwell's *Epsom Wells* assures the boor, Clodpate, the apostle
of "a pretty innocent country life," that people really live
nowhere but in London, for the "insipid dull being" of
country folk cannot be called living.   The list could be
increased indefinitely and goes far down into the eighteenth
century.   Pope's "fond virgin" whose unhappy fate com-

pelled her to seek wholesome country air, Shenstone's lady
who "could not breath anywhere else but in town," Little-
ton's fair maiden to whom country life is "supinely calm
and dully innocent," Young's Fulvia who preferred "smoke
and dust and noise and crowds" to "odious larks and nightingales," Browne's Celia who makes her banishment from
the city endurable by not giving herself up to "dull landscape" but by thinking of the country as the "town in
miniature"—these ladies represent in varying phases the
traditions of their fathers, and Almeria is legitimately of
their kin. She secretly ridicules Ardelia's "rural tastes"
and "rustic" clothes, and wonders how anyone can leave
"the beaux-monde and the dull country love," yet, "if but
an afternoon 'twould cost," she really could bring herself to
visit Ardelia in the country, "to quit the town, and for that
Time be lost." The attitude of these ladies toward the country was but the attitude of their time. Ardelia's feeling
toward city and country becomes, then, novel in the extreme.
In the midst of all the social delights Almeria can offer her,
she longs for her "groves and country walks" where "trees
blast not trees nor flow'rs envenom flow'rs," and she returns
to Eastwell with a haste and pleasure hardly to be understood by her contemporaries. The antithesis between the
town and the country was not so sharply defined by any
succeeding poet before Cowper.

The importance of Lady Winchilsea's contributions to
the poetry of external nature depends not so much on the
The Mountains number as upon the characteristics of the
and the Sea   poems that have to do with the out-door world.
In some respects these characteristics are like those of her
contemporaries. The mountains and the sea, for instance,
are treated by her in conventional fashion. She uses the
sea in similitudes where storms rage and where tides swal-
low up brooks, much in the manner of Dryden and Waller.

There are no good descriptions except, possibly, this line on the ocean in a calm,

> • For smooth it lay as if one wave made all the sea.

The treatment of mountains is equally ineffective. In her *Hymn* she does, however, address mountains as "Ye native altars of the Earth," a phrase which in the midst of utilitarian and theological objections to mountains as "huge, monstrous excrescences of nature," as mere "barriers between one sweet plain and another," as "wild, vast, undigested heaps of stone and earth," "great ruins, the result of sin," has a strangely exalted and Hebraic sound.

Dryden and his followers used storm similes with wearisome frequency and monotony, but storms themselves were **Storms** not counted poetical property till Thomson called attention to them in *The Seasons*, after which they became part of the stock in trade of every poetaster who could make the elements crash and hurtle. Lady Winchilsea's one storm is her description of the hurricane that swept over England in November, 1703, devastating the southern counties, uprooting fine old trees, unroofing palaces, destroying a third of the navy, and causing the death of fifteen hundred seamen. Eastwell was within the storm radius, and the poem is doubtless based on actual observation. This poem was subjected to much revision in the manuscript, but even in the printed form it is still unequal and disjointed. It was written too near to the event. It is marred by much that is local, personal, temporary in interest. The best passages are descriptive of external nature pure and simple, the fierce and turbulent winds, the ruined trees, the storm-beaten birds. But one point calls for especial comment here, and that is the emphasis put on the sounds of the tempest. They are so appalling and tremendous as to "wound the listening sense." They have the effect

of a battle symphony. The winds beat against solid surfaces with a drum-like resonance, they are their own fifes and clarions; each cavity and hollow tube becomes a trumpet. Crude though the poem is, it now and then has in it something of the stress and strain, something of the sweep of the storm itself.

No object in inanimate nature attracted Lady Winchilsea more strongly than trees. A charming early poem is called simply *The Tree.* The kind of tree is not **Trees** named, though it was probably an oak. But more important than botanic exactitude is the impression made by the regal personality of this tree with its imposing height and wide hospitable spread of branches. Destruction by the ax of the common workman would be degradation. Fierce winds alone are of a rank worthily to compass its fall. And the news of such an event should resound from the earth to the congregated clouds, while in the end consuming flames would be but as the funeral pyre of ancient heroes. The poem has no "unforgettable lines," but the conception of the patriarchal tree is not paralleled in kind before Christopher Smart's oak-tree in the *Immensity of the Supreme Being.*

In later poems this interest in trees is a frequent note. Ardelia's petition for an absolute retreat,

> Mongst Paths so lost and Trees so high,
> That the world may ne'er invade
> Through such windings and such shade,
> My unshaken Liberty,

was practically answered at Eastwell. During her first summer there she was so enthusiastic in her pleasure that she was constantly overtaxing her strength by long walks through the forest-like park. Its solitude and beauty gave her inexplicable joy. Her released romantic tendencies found suddenly most happy activity. The silent forest became the home of legend and myth, a realm of Spenserian enchantment. For hours at a time she wandered about alone, peopling the shades with fawns and sylvans, converting lovely nooks into the secret haunts of nymphs and fairies. Toward individual trees or groups of trees her feeling is almost as intimate as that of Lowell. She addresses them as "numerous brethren of the leafy kind," she applies the adjective "fraternal" to a clump of oaks in quite the manner of Wordsworth in his description of the yew-trees, the "fraternal four of Borrowdale." In recounting the results of the great storm, the frustrated ambitions of the beech, the oak, and the pine are sympathetically recorded along with human fatalities. The destruction of a fine old grove at Eastwell is narrated with dramatic liveliness. The winds sigh through the sentenced trees. The household awaits in dismayed silence the catastrophe it cannot avert. Even the hired clowns refuse at first to lift the ax. But when to his word of command the master adds his example by striking the first blow, all follow suit, and presently the splendid trees lie helpless in the field of their birth. This disaster occurred before Ardelia went to Eastwell, but she commemorates it with a sense of personal hurt and outrage, and one of her reasons for gratitude to Charles was that he replanted the denuded field.

Lady Winchilsea frequently "moralized" her trees, but on the way to the moral we find much excellent description, the outcome of first-hand observation. Willows, for instance, stand for youth, but we discover likewise that they are smooth of rind, straight of bough, moist of fiber, that they throw out at the top a mass of leaves, that they gather in social ranks along little streams. One forgets the moral of the dead tree in the hedge, in looking at the picture of the tree itself. Mischievous, entangling vines encompass it. Dismal-flowered night-shade, and "honesty" with its feath-

erd down curl from the topmost bough, while the honey-
suckle climbs by its dead branches to the thorn-trees above.
The oak is used as a symbol for age, but it is not the pathos
of man's declining years that stays in the memory; it is
rather the pathetic dignity of that "lonely stubborn oak"
whose

distorted trunk
Sapless branches bent and shrunk,

show the force of the imperious whirl-winds it has defied.

Lady Winchilsea's poems show a delight in flowers, but
not at all the conventional delight. Her chief pleasure in
flowers arose from their odor. That her olfac-
Flowers   tory sense was especially acute may be inferred
from the description of the physical effect of some penetrating odors, as that of the jonquil. She faints beneath
the "aromatic pain." And she is as pronounced as
Cowper in her protest against the perfume so lavishly
used by the beaux and belles of London. But of the generally diffused fragrances wafted from gardens or fields she
speaks frequently and with great pleasure. In the descriptions of the wilderness at Longleat, the entire stress was
put on the ravishing odors from woodbine, jasmine, Hesperian broom, and the Assyrian rose, which were so cunningly arranged that only by detecting their separate odors
could one find his way through the maze. She observes,
also, that odors are more powerful on hot days, especially
"piny" odors, and in the evening. The colors of flowers
did not so strongly attract her. Most of her color words
have to do with textures and gems. But even in colors she
is much richer than most of her contemporaries who describe
flowers. One of her most interesting notes is a defense of
the common white lily against the opinion of commentators
who think "that flower not gay enough" to stand in the
famous comparison of Solomon's attire to the lilies. But no

flower, she contends, "can have a greater luster than the common white lily."

On the whole, Lady Winchilsea's references to flowers are original, suggestive, and pleasing. The glowing poppy, the bright blue flowers among the standing corn, the bramble-rose on the banks of the stream, the sleepy cowslip in a sheltered nook, the foxgloves that at eventide checker the brakes with pale red, are not flowers indigenous to early eighteenth century poetry. In novelty of choice, in aptness of phrase, and in directness and simplicity of effect, these little flower pictures are of unique value in the poetry of their day.

The use of birds in Lady Winchilsea's poetry is slight, but of real significance. There is one sympathetically drawn
Birds   picture of a bird by chance imprisoned in a room. In its fright it dashes itself against the ceiling, beats with its wings on the window-panes, or flutters about in "endless circles of dismay," till some kind hand restores it to "ample space, the only heaven of birds." Equally direct and sympathetic is the description of the birds in the great storm. The picture of the "wide free sky," "where none from star to star could call the space his own," the "unentailed estate of birds," renders more effective the accompanying picture of the birds bewildered by the storm, beaten to earth by rough blasts, or tossed about by the whirlwind.

Lady Winchilsea's owl in the fable is by no means a mere reproduction of La Fontaine's. She amplifies his brief generalized description into many homely details. The curiously shaped beak, the high shoulders, the ruff around the neck, the frowsy lids, the waddling steps, the dull eye under its greenish film, are details that in the poetry of the day certainly mark an unusual attempt at minute, realistic portrayal of a bird. She speaks of an "ancient yew" that has for three hundred years belonged to "lineal Heirs" of the owl tribe, and one of the pleasing night-sounds that she records is the clear "hollowing" of the owl from a tree "famed for her delight." All of this bears the mark of first-hand and interested observation, as do likewise the two descriptions which the young rat and his dam give of the cock, in the fable *The young Rat and his Dam, the Cock and the Cat.* In *Jealousy the Rage of a Man* there is a delightfully fresh and vivid description of the courtship of two doves. The male bird puts on his most enticing airs while the female carelessly shifts her ground and indifferently pecks away at the scattered grain, but on the appearance of a rival her seeming coldness disappears, her feathers become sleek as she prepares for a fight, and in a rage she attacks the parti-colored neck of the new favorite. The dove had been long poetically relied upon as an image of cooing, conjugal content, hence this picture of a jealous, fighting dove is as original as it is effective. The observation in the little poem is strikingly exact. Wordsworth himself could not find fault with it.

The nightingale is immemorially the poet's bird. English verse has never failed to give enthusiastic, if somewhat monotonous, recognition of Philomela's claims. From Chaucer, Spenser, Sidney, Lyly, Shakespeare, Carew, Crashaw, Milton, Marvell, even Dryden, Lady Winchilsea might have compiled an anthology of nightingale poetry. From these poets the characteristics of the traditional nightingale are easily deducible, and it is interesting to discover in how far Lady Winchilsea's poem *The Nightingale* is in accord with the work of her predecessors. She is almost the only poet in the list to give no note of the time of the song, but she is at one with Lyly and Milton in mentioning spring as its season. Her nightingale apparently sang in May. The sweetness of the song is, of course, generally observed, but

Lady Winchilsea is curiously like Carew and Crashaw in
her attempt to give a more exact description of its musical
quality. As she listens to the long, pure notes, the ecstasy
of pleasure becomes almost a pain, and she implores the bird
to "let division shake her throat,"—a seventeenth century
phrase for the production of runs and trills. Carew speaks
of the bird's "sweet dividing throat," and Crashaw says that
she pours

> through the sleek passage of her open throat
> A clear unwrinkled song; then doth she point it by short diminu-
> tions.

What Mathew Arnold calls the "wild, deep-sunken, old-
world pain" of the song seldom escapes the ear or the clas-
sically trained memory of the poet. The early concrete
embodiment of this grief, a bird singing with a thorn "uptill
her breast," as given by Sir Philip Sidney, and several times
by Shakespeare, is followed by Lady Winchilsea. The new
point in Lady Winchilsea's poem is her way of listening to
the song. The traditional interpretation of the "thorn" had
always been some love-longing, but to her it is the poet's
despair in the presence of a musical perfection to which he
cannot attain. In a faint, but sweet and real way, Lady
Winchilsea's emotional experience in listening to the nightingale was like that of Shelley with the sky-lark. She traces
the song from point to point, she listens with rapture, and
has a consciousness that such strains, "taught by the forests," are beyond human skill. In none of the earlier nightingale poems does the human emotion arise thus out of the
song. The general plan is to use the song to illustrate, to
augment, or to assuage some human emotion. But Lady
Winchilsea's experience wherein the song, heard first for its
own sake, creates the emotion and suggests the human anal-
ogy, is exactly like that of Shelley with the sky-lark, Wordsworth with the daffodils, and Burns with the mouse or the
daisy.

The song of the bird in Eastwell Park seems, it must be confessed, tame, circumscribed, even thin, when compared with the rich, voluptuous, soul-enthralling notes of the nightingale that a century and a quarter later sang in the garden in Hampstead Heath and moved the poet Keats to thoughts of easeful death. But when considered in connection with its predecessors, and especially its contemporaries, Lady Winchilsea's poem becomes a remarkable production.

Of other animals than birds little is said except in the fables. Their first duty there is loyalty to the moral, and they are only secondarily independent animals, but they are often touched off with a sly, gay humor that makes some of them interesting even apart from the fable.

The traditional lover who flees to the shades to hide his mortal wound, who sees nothing in nature but rocks and **Man and Nature** thorns and other painful reminders of Sylvia's cruelty, and who, therefore, with rare good sense, goes back to the city, preferring to die by realities rather than by shadows, is described in *By Love Persu'd.* And in *Aristomenes* are examples of the subordination of nature to man, as when Climander hears Herminia utter the word "love" and exclaims:

> Oh! speak it once again, and the fond Vine
> Shall with a stricter grasp embrace the Elm,
> Whilst joyful birds shall hail it from the Branches.

This reads like a reminiscence of Tasso's *Aminta*, and is an unusual note in Lady Winchilsea's poetry. Even in the description of Marina the lover said that she *seemed* to give all the sweetness to nature, not that she did give it, and the lament of Aristomenes for his son distinctly recognizes the independence of Nature. It is especially in elegiac verse that Lady Winchilsea's conception of the relation between man and nature is shown to be widely different from the ideas then dominant. In the customary elegy, Nature is represented as "convulsed with grief" at the death of the illustrious human being. The rivulets are flooded with tears of the water-gods, brows of hills are furrowed by new streams, the heavens weep, birds droop, lilies hang their heads. Dr. Johnson characterizes such passages as "syllables of senseless dolour." Their grotesque extravagance and unreality become even more apparent when they are put side by side with the direct recognition of the truth, the daring, almost painful frankness in such lines as those in which Wordsworth declares the indifference of Nature to the death of sweet Lucy, whose body is

> Rolled round in Earth's diurnal course,
> With rocks and stones and trees.

The transition from the artificial subordination of nature to man, to the conception of nature as a vital and separate entity, was the slow process of a century. Lady Winchilsea's place in this historical sequence becomes then of especial significance, when we find in her poems not only a forecast of the modern thought, but a protest against the conventional idea. In an elegy commemorative of her relative, Sir William Twysden, she says she rejects the customary invocation to flocks and fields and flowers to join her in her grief because to her mind it is false and but a poet's dream that eternal nature is moved by man's sorrow. She is conscious that no human woe can deprive the spring of joy in her fragrant odors and purple violets. It is in vain that mourners attempt to force on inanimate things some portion of their grief. Nature, unconcerned for our sorrows, "persues her settled path, her first and steady course." That all may seem to die with the death of a friend is, she admits, true, but she insists, with the emphasis of Coleridge in the *Ode to Dejection*, that the clouds darkening over the outer world proceed only from the sad, awakened heart.

In an early poem, *The Echo*, Lady Winchilsea expressed
a quite romantic pleasure in a walk taken on a fair night to
hear a certain famous echo, but in the actual
Night experience it was not so much the mechanical
perfection of the sound that pleased her, as it was its remote,
elemental suggestiveness when associated with the loneliness
and beauty of the night. In *Democritus* one line,

> Solitary walks on starry nights,

seems to have a personal touch as if she had known such
walks. *The Hymn* strikes a somewhat deeper note in its
address to the moon as the gentle guide of

> Silent night,
> That does to solemn Praise and serious thoughts invite.

Brief though these references are, each one has a quality of
originality. But they hardly even foreshadow the perfection
of the *Nocturnal Reverie*. The fullness and delicate accuracy
of the observation in this poem have already been sufficiently
commented on. The description is doubtless the outcome of
many a fair summer night at Eastwell, but the picturesque
details are unified into a consistent whole, so that they give
the impression of a single vivid experience. The style is
simple, straightforward, unelaborated, almost bare. There
is nothing traditional or bookish. There is no ecstacy, no
emphatic statement. But in some indefinable, inevitable
fashion the little poem is suffused with the charm of the
lovely night. And not only the charm of the night, but its
significance, its message, its gift to man, find adequate
expression. The eight lines beginning, "When a sedate
content the spirit feels," present an interpretation of the
effect of nature on the heart and mind of man so exactly
Wordsworthian in substance and mood that it is hard to date
it eighty-five years before the *Lyrical Ballads*. Wordsworth's strong interest in Lady Winchilsea is justified by the
law of affinities. She is like him in that her genius needs

no strong or novel stimulus, and in this one poem, at least, she has attained to his " wise passiveness," his power of fixing an exquisite regard on the commonest facts of nature, and his ability to state these facts with fine precision, and to interpret them, not allegorically, but actually in their relation to human life.

In a faint but not at all fanciful way, Lady Winchilsea's poetical development is also comparable to that of Wordsworth. Most of the men who wrote well of nature in the eighteenth century, as Armstrong, Dyer, Thomson, Ramsay, Mickle, Bruce, Beattie, spent their youth in the country; their poetry of nature was their earliest work and was reminiscent of their country life; and the large body of their later work was didactic or dramatic. In other words they wrote their poetry of nature, before, not after, they had come into close contact with the complex and strenuous life of the city. Lady Winchilsea's experience was exactly the reverse. She first knew the court and the city; she first knew the tragic realities of life, and she first wrote dramas and satires and odes; and then at fifty years of age she wrote the *Reverie*. She was, in her spiritual history, like Wordsworth in that her chief poems on nature were not written in the flush and fervor of youth. Personal deprivations, frustrated ambitions, loss of faith in man, doubts of the providential ordering of human affairs, were the deep waters through which she was called to pass, and the end of the bitter experience found her in a state of dejection bordering on despair, a condition similar in kind though not in degree to Wordsworth's condition at the close of the experiences connected with the French revolution. The influences that led to healing in each case were human affection and the beauty and order of the external world. To her husband and to Eastwell Park Lady Winchilsea owed her restoration to her birtright of serenity and joy. But the process

was not an instantaneous one. It took time for the delicate
originality of her taste to assert itself. And she had not,
as had Wordsworth, a fund of childhood impressions on
which to draw. It was only after long and familiar contact
with nature that its full effect was apparent. But yet, season by season, year by year, new lessons were being learned,
and insensibly nature was bringing to her its normal gifts.
It is not of the sweet surprises, the novel excitements of the
early life at Eastwell of which she writes best. The adequate poem comes only after years of accumulated experience, when the loveliness of the place is known and taken for
granted, when love for it is a part of herself, when the thought
of it has mellowed and ripened. In spite of many important differences that might be insisted on, there is this one
important point of likeness between Lady Winchilsea and
Wordsworth — they both write out of the calm that follows
the storm. Their simplicity and repose grow out of the fact
that so much of life has been tested and set aside, and that
the essentials of happy living have been found to be few and
not difficult of access. In her youth Ardelia wrote an
Enquiry after Peace. It is a brief version of the world-old
vanitas vanitatum, very much in the style of Parnell's *Hymn*,
and there is a suggestion, reminding one inevitably of Dyer's
Grongar Hill, that peace may be found on some mountain-
top under the wide arch of the sky, or in some shut-away
valley. This plaintive little poem is only a fragment, but it
is beautifully rounded out and answered by the *Reverie*. The
two poems represent the extremes of the portion of Lady
Winchilsea's life best known to us — its early dissatisfactions,
questionings, rejections, its final certainties and poise.

POEMS

MERCURY AND THE ELEPHANT

A Prefatory Fable

As *Merc'ry* travell'd thro' a Wood
(Whose Errands are more Fleet than Good)
An *Elephant* before him lay,
That much encumber'd had the Way:
The Messenger, who's still in haste,
Wou'd fain have bow'd, and so have past;
When up arose th' unweildy Brute,
And wou'd repeat a late Dispute,
In which (he said) he'd gain'd the Prize
From a wild Boar of monstrous Size: 10
But Fame (quoth he) with all her Tongues,
Who Lawyers, Ladies, Soldiers wrongs,
Has, to my Disadvantage, told
An Action throughly Bright and Bold;
Has said, that I foul Play had us'd,
And with my Weight th' Opposer bruis'd;
Had laid my Trunk about his Brawn,
Before his Tushes cou'd be drawn;
Had stunn'd him with a hideous Roar,
And twenty-thousand Scandals more: 20
But I defy the Talk of Men,
Or Voice of Brutes in ev'ry Den;
Th' impartial Skies are all my Care,
And how it stands Recorded there.
Amongst you Gods, pray, What is thought?
    Quoth *Mercury*—Then have you Fought!
  Solicitous thus shou'd I be
For what's said of my Verse and Me;
Or shou'd my Friends Excuses frame,

3

And beg the Criticks not to blame   30
(Since from a Female Hand it came)
Defects in Judgment, or in Wit;
They'd but reply—Then has she Writ!

Our Vanity we more betray,
In asking what the World will say,
Than if, in trivial Things like these,
We wait on the Event with ease;
Nor make long *Prefaces*, to show
What Men are not concern'd to know:
For still untouch'd how we succeed,   40
'Tis for themselves, not us, they *Read;*
Whilst that proceeding to requite,
We own (who in the Muse delight)
'Tis for our Selves, not them, we *Write.*
Betray'd by Solitude to try
Amusements, which the Prosp'rous fly;
And only to the Press repair,
To fix our scatter'd Papers there;
Tho' whilst our Labours are preserv'd,
The Printers may, indeed, be starv'd.   50

THE INTRODUCTION

Did I, my lines intend for publick view,
How many censures, wou'd their faults persue,
Some wou'd, because such words they do affect,
Cry they're insipid, empty, uncorrect.
And many, have attain'd, dull and untaught
The name of Witt, only by finding fault.
True judges, might condemn their want of witt,
And all might say, they're by a Woman writt.
Alas! a woman that attempts the pen,
Such an intruder on the rights of men,   10

Such a presumptuous Creature, is esteem'd,
The fault, can by no vertue be redeem'd.
They tell us, we mistake our sex and way;
Good breeding, fassion, dancing, dressing, play
Are the accomplishments we shou'd desire;
To write, or read, or think, or to enquire
Wou'd cloud our beauty, and exaust our time,
And interrupt the Conquests of our prime;
Whilst the dull mannage, of a servile house
Is held by some, our outmost art, and use.   20
    Sure 'twas not ever thus, nor are we told
Fables, of Women that excell'd of old;
To whom, by the diffusive hand of Heaven
Some share of witt, and poetry was given.
On that glad day, on which the Ark return'd,
The holy pledge, for which the Land had mourn'd,
The joyfull Tribes, attend itt on the way,
The Levites do the sacred Charge convey,
Whilst various Instruments, before itt play;
Here, holy Virgins in the Concert joyn,   30
The louder notes, to soften, and refine,
And with alternate verse, compleat the Hymn Devine.
Loe! the yong Poet, after Gods own heart,
By Him inspired, and taught the Muses Art,
Return'd from Conquest, a bright Chorus meets,
That sing his slayn ten thousand in the streets.
In such loud numbers they his acts declare,
Proclaim the wonders, of his early war,
That Saul upon the vast applause does frown,
And feels, itts mighty thunder shake the Crown.   40
What, can the threat'n'd Judgment now prolong?
Half of the Kingdom is already gone;
The fairest half, whose influence guides the rest,
Have David's Empire, o're their hearts confess't.

A Woman here, leads fainting Israel on,
She fights, she wins, she tryumphs with a song,
Devout, Majestick, for the subject fitt,
And far above her arms, exalts her witt,
Then, to the peacefull, shady Palm withdraws,
And rules the rescu'd Nation, with her Laws.   50
How are we fal'n, fal'n by mistaken rules?
And Education's, more then Nature's fools,
Debarr'd from all improve-ments of the mind,
And to be dull, expected and dessigned;
And if some one, wou'd Soar above the rest,
With warmer fancy, and ambition press't,
So strong, th' opposing faction still appears,
The hopes to thrive, can ne're outweigh the fears,
Be caution'd then my Muse, and still retir'd;
Nor be dispis'd, aiming to be admir'd;   60
Conscious of wants, still with contracted wing,
To some few freinds, and to thy sorrows sing;
For groves of Lawrell, thou wert never meant;
Be dark enough thy shades, and be thou there content.

THE PREFACE

Beaumont in the beginni[n]g of a Coppy of Verses to
his freind Fletcher (upon the ill successe of his Faithfull
Shepheardesse) tells him,

I know too well! that no more, then the man
That travells throo' the burning Deserts, can
When he is beaten with the raging Sun,
Half smother'd in the dust, have power to run
From a cool River, which himself doth find,
E're he be slack'd; no more can he, whose mind
Joys in the Muses, hold from that delight,
When Nature, and his full thoughts, bid him write.

And this indeed, I not only find true by my own experience,
but have also too many wittnesses of itt against me, under
my own hand in the following Poems; which tho' never
meritting more then to be once read, and then carlessly
scatter'd or consum'd; are grown by the partiality of some
of my freinds, to the formidable appearance of a Volume;
tho' but in Manuscript, and have been solicited to a more
daring manefestation, which I shall ever resist, both from
the knowledge of their incapassity, of bearing a publick
tryal; and also, upon recalling to my memory, some of the
first lines I ever writt, which were part of an invocation of
Apollo, whose wise and limitted answer to me, I did there
suppose to be

> I grant thee no pretence to Bays,
>   Nor in bold print do thou appear;
> Nor shalt thou reatch Orinda's prayse,
>   Tho' all thy aim, be fixt on Her.

And tho' I have still avoided the confident producing anything of mine in thatt manner, yett have I come too neer itt,
and been like those imperfect penitents, who are ever relenting, and yett ever returning to the same offences. For I
have writt, and expos'd my uncorrect Rimes, and immediatly
repented; and yett have writt again, and again suffer'd them
to be seen; tho' att the expence of more uneasy reflections,
till at last (like them) wearied with uncertainty, and irreso-
lution, I rather chuse to be harden'd in an errour, then to be
still att the trouble of endeavering to over come itt: and now,
neither deny myself the pleasure of writing, or any longer
make a mistery of that to my freinds and acquaintance,
which does so little deserve itt; tho' itt is still a great satisfaction to me, that I was not so far abandon'd by my prudence, as out of a mistaken vanity, to lett any attempts of
mine in Poetry, shew themselves whilst I liv'd in such a
publick place as the Court, where every one wou'd have

made their remarks upon a Versifying Maid of Honour; and
far the greater number with prejudice, if not contempt. And
indeed, the apprehension of this, had so much wean'd me
from the practice and inclination to itt; that had nott an
utter change in my Condition, and Circumstances, remov'd
me into the solitude, & security of the Country, and the
generous kindnesse of one that possest the most delightfull
seat in itt; envited him, from whom I was inseperable, to
partake of the pleasures of itt, I think I might have stopp'd
ere it was too late, and suffer'd those few compositions I had
then by me, to have sunk into that oblivion, which I ought
to wish might be the lott of all that have succeeded them.
But when I came to Eastwell, and cou'd fix my eyes only
upon objects naturally inspiring soft and Poeticall immaginations, and found the Owner of itt, so indulgent to that Art,
so knowing in all the rules of itt, and att his pleasure, so
capable of putting them in practice; and also most obligingly
favorable to some lines of mine, that had fall'n under his
Lordship's perusal, I cou'd no longer keep within the limmitts I had prescrib'd myself, nor be wisely reserv'd, in spite
of inclination, and such powerfull temptations to the contrary.
Again I engage my self in the service of the Muses, as
eagerly as if

> From their new Worlds, I know not where,
> Their golden Indies in the air —

they cou'd have supply'd the material losses, which I had
lately sustain'd in this. And now, whenever I contemplate
all the several beautys of this Park, allow'd to be (if not of
the Universal yett) of our British World infinitely the finest,

> A pleasing wonder throo' my fancy moves,
> Smooth as her lawnes, and lofty as her Groves.
> Boundlesse my Genius seems, when my free sight,
> Finds only distant skys to stop her flight.

Like mighty Denhams, then, methinks my hand,
Might bid the Landskip, in strong numbers stand,
Fix all itts charms, with a Poetick skill,
And raise itts Fame, above his Cooper's hill.

This, I confesse, is whatt in itts self itt deserves, but the unhappy difference is, that he by being a real Poet, cou'd make that place (as he sais) a Parnassus to him; whilst I, that behold a real Parnassus here, in that lovely Hill, which in this Park bears that name, find in my self, so little of the Poet, that I am still restrain'd from attempting a description of itt in verse, tho' the agreeablenesse of the subject, has often prompted me most strongly to itt.

But now, having pleaded an irresistable impulse, as my excuse for writing, which was the cheif design of this Preface, I must also expresse my hopes of excaping all suspition of vanity, or affectation of applause from itt; since I have in my introduction, deliver'd my sincere opinion that when a Woman meddles with things of this nature,

So strong, th' opposing faction still appears,
The hopes to thrive, can ne're outweigh the fears.

And, I am besides sensible, that Poetry has been of late so explain'd, the laws of itt being putt into familiar languages, that even those of my sex, (if they will be so presumptuous as to write) are very accountable for their transgressions against them. For what rule of Aristotle, or Horace is there, that has not been given us by Rapin, Despreaux, D'acier, my Lord Roscomon, etc.? What has Mr. Dryden omitted, that may lay open the very misteries of this Art? and can there any where be found a more delightsome, or more usefull piece of Poetry, then that,

correct Essay,
Which so repairs, our old Horatian way."

If then, after the perusal of these, we fail, we cannott plead any want, but that of capacity, or care, in both of which I own myself so very defective, y⁴ whenever any things of mine, escape a censure, I allways attribute itt, to the good nature or civility of the Reader; and not to any meritt in the Poems, which I am satisfy'd are so very imperfect, and uncorrect, that I shall not attempt their justifycation.

For the subjects, I hope they are att least innofensive; tho' sometimes of Love; for keeping within those limmitts which I have observ'd, I know not why itt shou'd be more faulty, to treat of that passion, then of any other violent excursion, or transport of the mind. Tho' I must confesse, the great reservednesse of Mrs. Philips in this particular, and the prayses I have heard given her upon that account, together with my desire not to give scandal to the most severe, has often discourag'd me from making use of itt, and given me some regrett for what I had writt of that kind, and wholy prevented me from putting the Aminta of Tasso into English verse, from the verbal translation that I procured out of the Italian, after I had finish'd the first act extreamly to my satisfaction; and was convinc'd, that in the original, itt must be as soft and full of beautys, as ever anything of that nature was; but there being nothing mixt with itt, of a serious morality, or usefullnesse, I sacrafis'd the pleasure I took in itt, to the more sollid reasonings of my own mind; and hope by so doing to have made an attonement, to my gravest readers, for the two short pieces of that Pastoral, taken from the French, the Songs, and other few lighter things, which yett remain in the following sheetts.

As to Lampoons, and all sorts of abusive verses, I ever so much detested, both the underhand dealing and uncharitablenesse which accompanys them, that I never suffer'd my small talent, to be that way employ'd; tho' the facility of doing itt, is too well known to many, who can but make two words rime; and there wants not some provocation often,

either from one's own resentments, or those of others, to put
such upon itt, as are any way capable of that mean sort of
revenge. The only coppy of mine that tends towards this,
is the letter to Ephelia, in answer to an invitation to the
Town; but, as that appears to have been long written, by the
mention made of my Lord Roscommon, under the name of
Piso, given to him first, in a Panegerick, of Mr. Wallers,
before his Art of Poetry; so I do declare, that att the time
of composing itt, there was no particular person meant by
any of the disadvantageous Caracters; and the whole intention of itt, was in general to expose the Censorious humour,
foppishnesse and coquetterie that then prevail'd. And I am so
far from thinking there is any ill in this, that I wish itt oftener
done, by such hands as might sufficiently ridicule, and wean
us from those mistakes in our manners, and conversation.

Plays, were translated by our most vertuous Orinda; and
mine, tho' originals, I hope are not lesse reserv'd. The Queen
of Cyprus, I once thought to have call'd the Triumphs of
Love and Innocence; and doubted not but the latter part of the
Title, wou'd have been as aptly apply'd as the former. Aristomenes is wholy Tragicall, and, if itt answer my intention,
moral and inciting to Vertue. What they are as to the performance, I leave to the judgment of those who shall read
them; and if any one can find more faults then I think to be
in y^m; I am much mistaken. I will only add, that when
they were compos'd, itt was far from my intention ever to
own them, the first was for my own private satisfaction, only
an Essay 'wheither I cou'd go throo' with such a peice of
Poetry. The other, I was led to, by the strong impressions,
which some wonderfull circumstances in the life of Aristomenes, made upon my fancy; and cheifly the sweetnesse of
his temper, observable in itt, wrought upon me; for which
reason tho' itt may be I did not so Poetically, I chose rather
to represent him Good, then Great; and pitch'd upon such

parts of the relation, and introduc'd such additional circumstances of my own, as might most illustrate that, and shew
him to be (as declared by the Oracle) the best of Men.   I
know not what effect they will have upon others, but I must
acknowledge, that the giving some interruption to those
melancholy thoughts, which posesst me, not only for my
own, but much more for the misfortunes of those to whom
I owe all immaginable duty, and gratitude, was so great a
benefitt; that I have reason to be satisfy'd with the undertaking, be the performance never so inconsiderable.   And
indeed, an absolute solitude (which often was my lott) under
such dejection of mind, cou'd not have been supported, had
I indulg'd myself (as was too natural to me) only in the
contemplation of present and real afflictions, which I hope
will plead my excuse, for turning them for releif, upon such
as were immaginary, & relating to Persons no more in
being.   I had my end in the writing, and if they please not
those who will take the pains to peruse them, itt will be a
just accusation to my weaknesse, for letting them escape out
of their concealment; but if attended with a better successe,
the satisfaction any freind of mine, may take in them, will
make me think my time past, not so unprofitably bestowed,
as otherwise I might; and which I shall now endeavour to
redeem, by applying myself to better employments, and
when I do write to chuse, my subjects generally out of
Devinity, or from moral and serious occasions; which made
me place them last, as capable of addition; For when we
have run throo' all the amusements of life, itt will be found,
that there is but one thing necessary; and they only Wise,
who chuse the better part.   But since there must be also,
some relaxation, some entertaining of the spiritts,

> Whilst Life by Fate is lent to me,
> Whilst here below, I stay,
> Religion, my sole businesse be,
> And Poetry, my play.

THE APPOLOGY

'Tis true I write and tell me by what Rule
I am alone forbid to play the fool
To follow through the Groves a wand'ring Muse
And fain'd Idea's for my pleasures chuse
Why shou'd it in my Pen be held a fault
Whilst Mira paints her face, to paint a thought
Whilst Lamia to the manly Bumper flys
And borrow'd Spiritts sparkle in her Eyes
Why shou'd itt be in me a thing so vain
To heat with Poetry my colder Brain
But I write ill and there-fore shou'd forbear
Does Flavia cease now at her fortieth year
In ev'ry Place to lett that face be seen
Which all the Town rejected at fifteen
Each Woman has her weaknesse; mind [sic] indeed
Is still to write tho' hoplesse to succeed
Nor to the Men is this so easy found
Ev'n in most Works with which the Witts abound
(So weak are all since our first breach with Heav'n)
Ther's lesse to be Applauded then forgiven.

FRAGMENT

So here confin'd, and but to female Clay,
ARDELIA's Soul mistook the rightful Way:
Whilst the soft Breeze of Pleasure's tempting Air
Made her believe, Felicity was there;
And basking in the warmth of early Time,
To vain Amusements dedicate her Prime.
Ambition next allur'd her tow'ring Eye;
For Paradice she heard was plac'd on high,
Then thought, the Court with all its glorious Show
Was sure above the rest, and Paradice below.   10
There plac'd too soon the flaming Sword appear'd
Remov'd those Pow'rs, whom justly she rever'd,

Adher'd too in their Wreck, and in their Ruin shar'd.
Now by the Wheels inevitable Round,
With them thrown prostrate to the humble Ground,
No more she takes (instructed by that Fall)
For fix'd, or worth her thought, this rolling Ball:
Tow'rds a more certain Station she aspires,
Unshaken by Revolts, and owns no less Desires.
But all in vain are Pray'rs, extatick Thoughts,   20
Recover'd Moments, and retracted Faults,
Retirement, which the World *Moroseness* calls,
Abandon'd Pleasures in Monastick Walls:
These, but at distance, towards that purpose tend,
The lowly Means to an exalted End;
Which He must perfect, who allots her Stay,
And That, accomplish'd, will direct the way.
Pity her restless Cares, and weary Strife,
And point some Issue to escaping Life;
Which so dismiss'd, no Pen or Human Speech   30
Th' ineffable Recess can ever teach:
Th' Expanse, the Light, the Harmony, the Throng,
The Bride's Attendance, and the Bridal Song,
The numerous Mansions, and th' immortal Tree,
No Eye, unpurg'd by Death, must ever see,
Or Waves which through that wond'rous City roll.
Rest then content, my too impatient Soul;
Observe but here the easie Precepts given,
Then wait with chearful hope, till Heaven be known in Heaven.

ON MYSELFE

Good Heav'n, I thank thee, since it was design'd
I shou'd be fram'd, but of the weaker kinde,
That yet, my Soul, is rescu'd from the Love
Of all those Trifles, which their Passions move.
Pleasures, and Praise, and Plenty haúe with me

But their just value.   If allow'd they be,
Freely, and thankfully as much I tast,
As will not reason, or Religion wast.
If they're deny'd, I on my selfe can Liue,
And slight those aids, unequal chance does give.
When in the Sun, my wings can be display'd,
And in retirement, I can bless the shade.

ARDELIA TO MELANCHOLY

At last, my old inveterate foe,
No opposition shalt thou know.
Since I by struggling, can obtain
Nothing, but encrease of pain,
I will att last, no more do soe,
Tho' I confesse, I have apply'd
Sweet mirth, and musick, and have try'd
A thousand other arts beside,
To drive thee from my darken'd breast,
Thou, who hast banish'd all my rest.   10
But, though sometimes, a short repreive they gave,
Unable they, and far too weak, to save;
All arts to quell, did but augment thy force,
As rivers check'd, break with a wilder course.

Freindship, I to my heart have laid,
Freindship, th' applauded sov'rain aid,
And thought that charm so strong wou'd prove,
As to compell thee, to remove;
And to myself, I boasting said,
Now I a conqu'rer sure shall be,   20
The end of all my conflicts, see,
And noble tryumph, wait on me;
My dusky, sullen foe, will sure
N'er this united charge endure.

But leaning on this reed, ev'n whilst I spoke
It peirc'd my hand, and into peices broke.
Still, some new object, or new int'rest came
And loos'd the bonds, and quite disolv'd the claim.

These failing, I invok'd a Muse,
And Poetry wou'd often use,   30
To guard me from thy Tyrant pow'r;
And to oppose thee ev'ry hour
New troops of fancy's, did I chuse.
Alas! in vain, for all agree
To yeild me Captive up to thee,
And heav'n, alone, can sett me free.
Thou, through my life, wilt with me goe,
And make y' passage, sad, and slow.
All, that cou'd ere thy ill gott rule, invade,
Their uselesse arms, before thy feet have laid;   40
The Fort is thine, now ruin'd, all within,
Whilst by decays without, thy Conquest too, is seen.

AN INVOCATION TO SLEEP

How shall I wooe thee gentle rest,
To a sad Mind, with cares opress'd?
By what soft means, shall I invite
Thy Pow'rs into my Soul to night?
Yett, Gentle sleep, if thou wilt come,
Such darknesse shall prepare the Room,
As thy own Pallace ouerspreads,
(Thy Pallace, stor'd with peacefull Beds)
And Silence too, shall on thee waite
Deep, as in the Turkish State;   10
Whilst, still as Death, I will be found,
My arms, by one another bound;
And my dull lidds, so clos'd shall be

As if allready seal'd by thee.
Thus, I'll dispose the outward part,
Wou'd I cou'd quiet too my Heart.
But, in its overburthen'd stead
Behold I offer thee, my head;
My head, I better can com̄and,
And that, I bow beneath thy hand;   20
Nor do I think, that heretofore
Our first great Father, gaue thee more,
When, on a flow'ry bank, he lay,
And did thy strictest Laws obey:
For, to compose his louely Bride,
He yielded not alone his side,
But, if we judge by the event,
Half of his heart too, with itt went,
Which, waken'd drew him soon away
To Eve's fair bosome, where itt lay,   30
Pleas'd to admitt his rightfull claim
And tending, still, tow'rds whence itt came.
Then, gentle sleep, expect from mee
No more then I haue proffer'd thee;
For, if thou wilt not hear my Pray'rs,
Till I haue vanquish'd all my cares,
Thou 'llt stay, 'till kinder Death supplys thy place,
The surer Friend, tho' with the harsher face.

THE LOSSE

She sighd', but soon, itt mix'd with com̄on air,
Too fleet a witnesse, for her deep dispair;
She wept, but tears, no lasting greif can show,
For tears will fail, and ebb, as well as flow.
She wou'd her tongue, to the sad subject force,
But all great passions, are above discourse.
Thy heart alone, Ardelia, with itt trust,

There grave itt deep, alas! 'twill fall to dust,
Vrania is no more, to me no more,
All these combin'd, can n'er that losse deplore.

THE CONSOLATION

See, Phœbus breaking from the willing skies,
See, how the soaring Lark, does with him rise,
And through the air, is such a journy borne
As if she never thought of a return.
Now, to his noon, behold him proudly goe,
And look with scorn, on all that's great below.
A Monark he, and ruler of the day,
A fav'rite She, that in his beams does play.
Glorious, and high, but shall they ever bee,
Glorious, and high, and fixt where now we see?
No, both must fall, nor can their stations keep,
She to the Earth, and he below the Deep,
At night both fall, but the swift hand of time
Renews the morning, and again they climb,
Then lett no cloudy change, create my sorrow,
I'll think 'tis night, and I may rise to-morrow.

A SONG ON GREIFE

Sett by Mr. Estwick

Oh greif! why hast thou so much pow'r,
  Why doe the ruling Fates decree
No state shou'd e're without the[e] be,
  Why, doest thou Joys, and hopes devour,
And cloath ev'n loue him self, in thy dark livery?

Thou, and cold fear, thy close Allie,
  Do not alone on life attend,
Butt following mortalls to their end,
  Do wrack the wretches, whilst they dye;
And to eternal shades, too often, with them flye.

To thee, great Monark, I submitt,
  Thy Sables, and thy Cypresse bring,
I own thy Pow'r, I own thee King,
  Thy title, in my heart is writt,
And 'till that breaks, I ne'r shall freedom gett.

Forc'd smiles, thy rigour will allow,
  And whilst thy seat is in the soul,
  And there, all mirth thou doest controul,
Thou can'st admitt to outward show,
The smooth appearance, and disembl'd brow.

ON AFF[L]ICTION

Wellcome, what e're my tender flesh may say,
  Welcome affliction, to my reason, still;
Though hard, and ruged on that rock I lay
  A sure foundation, which if rais'd with skill,
  Shall compasse Babel's aim, and reach th' Almighty's hill.

Wellcome the rod, that does adoption shew,
  The cup, whose wholsome dregs are giv'n me here;
There is a day behind, if God be true,
    When all these Clouds shall passe, & heav'n be clear,
    When those whom most they shade, shall shine most glorious there.

Affliction is the line, which every Saint
  Is measur'd by, his stature taken right;
So much itt shrinks, as they repine or faint,
    But if their faith and Courage stand upright,
    By that is made the Crown, and the full robe of light.

A LETTER TO DAFNIS APRIL: 2D 1685

This to the Crown, and blessing of my life,
The much lov'd husband, of a happy wife.
To him, whose constant passion found the art

To win a stubborn, and ungratefull heart;
And to the World, by tend'rest proof discovers
They err, who say that husbands can't be lovers.
With such return of passion, as is due,
Daphnis I love, Daphnis my thoughts persue,
Daphnis, my hopes, my joys, are bounded all in you:
Ev'n I, for Daphnis, and my promise sake,
What I in women censure, undertake.
But this from love, not vanity, proceeds;
You know who writes; and I who 'tis that reads.
Judge not my passion, by my want of skill,
Many love well, though they express itt ill;
And I your censure cou'd with pleasure bear,
Wou'd you but soon return, and speak itt here.

TO MR. F. NOW EARL OF W.

*Who going abroad, had desired Ardelia to write some Verses upon
whatever Subject she thought fit, against his Return in the
Evening*

Written in the Year 1689

No sooner, FLAVIO, was you gone,
But, your Injunction thought upon,
    ARDELIA took the Pen;
Designing to perform the Task,
Her FLAVIO did so kindly ask,
    Ere he returned agen.

Unto *Parnassus* strait she sent,
And bid the Messenger, that went
    Unto the *Muses* Court,
Assure them, she their Aid did need,   10
And begg'd they'd use their utmost Speed,
    Because the Time was short.

The hasty Summons was allow'd;
And being well-bred, they rose and bow'd,
   And said, they'd poste away;
That well they did ARDELIA know,
And that no Female's Voice below
   They sooner wou'd obey:

That many of that rhiming Train,
On like Occasions, sought in vain   20
   Their Industry t'excite;
But for ARDELIA all they'd leave:
Thus flatt'ring can the Muse deceive,
   And wheedle us to write.

Yet, since there was such haste requir'd;
To know the Subject 'twas desir'd,
   On which they must infuse;
That they might temper Words and Rules,
And with their Counsel carry Tools,
   As Country-*Doctors* use.   30

Wherefore to cut off all Delays,
'Twas soon reply'd, a *Husband's* Praise
   (Tho' in these looser Times)
ARDELIA gladly wou'd rehearse
A *Husband's*, who indulg'd her Verse,
   And now requir'd her Rimes.

A *Husband!* eccho'd all around:
And to *Parnassus* sure that Sound
   Had never yet been sent;
Amazement in each Face was read,   40
In haste th' affrighted Sisters fled,
   And unto Council went.

Erato cry'd, since *Grizel's* Days,
Since *Troy*-Town pleas'd, and *Chivey-chace,*
    No such Design was known;
And 'twas their Bus'ness to take care,
It reach'd not to the publick Ear,
    Or got about the Town:

Nor came where Evening *Beaux* were met
O'er *Billet-doux* and *Chocolate,*   50
    Lest it destroy'd the House;
For in that Place, who cou'd dispence
(That wore his Cloaths with common Sense)
    With mention of a *Spouse?*

'Twas put unto the Vote at last,
And in the Negative it past,
    None to her Aid shou'd move;
Yet since ARDELIA was a Friend,
Excuses 'twas agreed to send,
    Which plausible might prove: 60

That *Pegasus* of late had been
So often rid thro' thick and thin,
    With neither Fear nor Wit;
In *Panegyrick* been so spurr'd,
He cou'd not from the Stall be stirr'd,
    Nor wou'd endure the Bit.

Melpomene had given a Bond,
By the new House alone to stand,
    And write of War and Strife;
Thalia, she had taken Fees,   70
And Stipends from the Patentees,
    And durst not for her Life.

Urania only lik'd the Choice;   ·
Yet not to thwart the publick Voice,
   She whisp'ring did impart:
They need no Foreign Aid invoke,
No help to draw a moving Stroke,
   Who dictate from the Heart.

Enough! the pleas'd ARDELIA cry'd;
And slighting ev'ry Muse beside,   80
   Consulting now her Breast,
Perceiv'd that ev'ry tender Thought,
Which from abroad she'd vainly sought,
   Did there in Silence rest:

And shou'd unmov'd that Post maintain,
Till in his quick Return again,   ·
   Met in some neighb'ring Grove,
(Where Vice nor Vanity appear)
Her *Flavio* them alone might hear,
   In all the Sounds of Love.   90

For since the World do's so despise
Hymen's Endearments and its Ties,
   They shou'd mysterious be;
Till We that Pleasure too possess
(Which makes their fancy'd Happiness)
   Of stollen Secrecy.

A LETTER TO THE SAME PERSON

Sure of Success, to You I boldly write
Whilst Love do's ev'ry tender Line endite; ·
Love, who is justly President of Verse,
Which all his Servants write, or else rehearse.
Phœbus (howe'er mistaken Poets dream) ·

Ne'er us'd a Verse, till Love became his Theme.
To his stray'd Son, still as his Passion rose,
He rais'd his hasty Voice in clam'rous Prose:
But when in *Daphne* he wou'd Love inspire,
He woo'd in Verse, set to his silver Lyre.   10

The *Trojan* Prince did pow'rful Numbers join
To sing of War; but Love was the Design:
And sleeping *Troy* again in Flames was drest,
To light the Fires in pitying *Dido's* Breast.

Love without Poetry's refining Aid
Is a dull Bargain, and but coarsely made;
Nor e'er cou'd Poetry successful prove,
Or touch the Soul, but when the Sense was Love.

Oh! cou'd they both in Absence now impart
Skill to my Hand, but to describe my Heart;   20
Then shou'd you see impatient of your Stay
Soft Hopes contend with Fears of sad Delay;
Love in a thousand fond Endearments there,
And lively Images of You appear.
But since the Thoughts of a Poetick Mind
Will never be to Syllables confin'd;
And whilst to fix what is conceiv'd, we try,
The purer Parts evaporate and dye:
You must perform what they want force to do,
And think what your ARDELIA thinks of you.   30
    October 21, 1690.

UPON ARDELIA'S RETURN HOME

*(After to[o] long a walk in Eastwell Park) in a water cart driven
by one of the under-keepers in his green Coat, with a Hazel-
Bough for a whip. July, 1689*

What Fate within itts Bosome carry's
For Him thats born, or Him that Marry's
Though Fate itts self does not unfold

Is by Prognosticaters told,
And some have spent their Days in terrour
Of what has sprung from canting errour
From Gypsies who their speech confounding
Have threaten'd Hanging, Horn or Drowning
In hints where doubtfull sence has hover'd
Which caus'd but laughter when discover'd.   10
  So had Ardelia sure been troubl'd
If when of piece of silver bubl'd
T' had been in broaken terms imparted
That e're her Death she shou'd be Carted.
Yett see how Time had turn'd the Story
And tun'd itt to Poetick Glory
When once reveal'd that Phœbus gave itt
And own'd the Cart and Swayne that drave itt
In his peculiar colours seen
Both whip and man array'd in Green   20
That 'twas the Engin that did bring
The water from his darling spring
Which for repose was now convey'd
Beneath a Beeche's secret shade.
When poor Ardelia weak and faint
Invades the air with this complaint
That she from Home so far had stray'd
By the aluring Muse betray'd
By Fancies light of Nymphs and Faries
Romantick Notions and figary's   30
Of Fawns and Sylvans dark abodes
Of Heroes rushing from the woods
Till length of way no strength had left her
And both of feet and breath bereft her
Who now must take for Bed and Cover
Cold earth and boughs which dangl'd over
Nor cou'd return in sheets to slumber

No more then she the stars cou'd number,
Yett loth this wretched course to follow
For once resolv'd to move Apollo.   40
Misled by Him and his vain Rabble,
To try his Curtesie and Stable
She then implor'd that for this time
And to be sure she sue'd in Rime
That he his Chariot wou'd but spare her
Which in a moment home might bear her
Scarse miss'd by him or his nine lasses.
But he reply'd she'd break the Glasses,
That late he saw such Fate attend her
And vow'd that his he n'ere wou'd lend her   50
That fitter 'twere she took the air
Like Country Doll to neighb'ring Faire
Like harvest Gill or stroling Player
For he'd not bear the World's reproaches
If Poets were allow'd their Coaches
Who spar'd on foot (with empty Purses)
Nor Prince nor Prelat in their verses
That Homer poor his spite to smother
Made fighting Fooles revile each other
Who had he but been back'd with Pelf   60
He had call'd Dogs and Rogues himself
Lampoon'd Queen Hellens well sung Flame
And giv'n Her but her coarsest Name
For which good cause and more 'twas hinted
The Tribe shou'd be kept bare and stinted
Shou'd eat by manners and good Nature
Or starve on Epigram and Satir.
She finding him thus hott proceed
Desir'd then but his winged steed
But he reply'd 'twou'd much disgrace him   70
To lett a female rider pace him

That Pegasus, what e're they fancy'd
Had ne're for them one step aduanced
Yett if that she like Quaker tir'd
But a conveniency desir'd
There shou'd from neer a verdant bush
With foot cloath matt and seat of rush
Be drawn a rev'rend grave Machine
As slow as if for Spanish Queen
As safe as Litter gently led   80
With Lady sleeping in her bed
And tho' the form some might dispise
Who view'd itt but with outward Eyes
Yett Quixotts Brancart till he built itt
A Velvett roof and richly gilt itt
With Fancy's Pencil was not braver
And with th'invention which he gave her
She might convert wou'd she not spare itt
This Roulo to tryumphant Charret
Turn wood to steel and ropes to Leather   90
And forehead bough to Ostritch Feather
Since all was as opinion made itt
Not as the Artists hand ore-laid itt.
This said, he mixt with shining Day
And left her to persue the way
Exalted high to all beholders
As Burgesse on ellecting shoulders
On totterring chair in Tumbrill's middle
And wanting but fore-running Fiddle
To guide the wond'ring Rabble right   100
And pick their Purses for the sight.

AN INVITATION TO DAFNIS

To leave his study and usual Employments, — Mathematicks
Paintings, etc. and to take the Pleasures of the feilds with
Ardelia

When such a day, blesst the Arcadian plaine,
Warm without Sun, and shady without rain,
Fann'd by an air, that scarsly bent the flowers,
Or wav'd the woodbines, on the summer bowers,
The Nymphs disorder'd beauty cou'd not fear,
Nor ruffling winds uncurl'd the Shepheards hair,
On the fresh grasse, they trod their measures light,
And a long Evening made, from noon, to night.
Come then my Dafnis, from those cares descend
Which better may the winter season spend.   10
   Come, and the pleasures of the feilds, survey,
   And throo' the groves, with your Ardelia stray.

Reading the softest Poetry, refuse,
To veiw the subjects of each rural muse;
Nor lett the busy compasses go round,
When faery Cercles better mark the ground.
Rich Colours on the Vellum cease to lay,
When ev'ry lawne much nobler can display,
When on the daz'ling poppy may be seen
A glowing red, exceeding your carmine;   20
And for the blew that o're the Sea is borne,
A brighter rises in our standing corn.
   Come then, my Dafnis, and the feilds survey,
   And throo' the groves, with your Ardelia stray.

Come, and lett Sansons World, no more engage,
Altho' he gives a Kingdom in a page;
O're all the Vniverse his lines may goe,

And not a clime, like temp'rate brittan show,
  Come then, my Dafnis, and her feilds survey,
  And throo' the groves, with your Ardelia stray.   30

Nor plead that you're immur'd, and cannot yield,
That mighty Bastions keep you from the feild,
Think not tho' lodg'd in Mons, or in Namur,
You're from my dangerous attacks secure.
No, Louis shall his falling Conquests fear,
When by succeeding Courriers he shall hear
Appollo, and the Muses, are drawn down,
To storm each fort, and take in ev'ry Town.
Vauban, the Orphean Lyre, to mind shall call,
That drew the stones to the old Theban Wall,   40
And make no doubt, if itt against him play,
They, from his works, will fly as fast away,
Which to prevent, he shall to peace persuade,
Of strong, confederate Syllables, affraid.
  Come then, my Dafnis, and the fields survey,
  And throo' the Groves, with your Ardelia stray.

Come, and attend, how as we walk along,
Each chearfull bird, shall treat us with a song,
Nott such as Fopps compose, where witt, nor art,
Nor plainer Nature, ever bear a part;   50
The Cristall springs, shall murmure as we passe,
But not like Courtiers, sinking to disgrace;
Nor, shall the louder Rivers, in their fall,
Like unpaid Saylers, or hoarse Pleaders brawle;
But all shall form a concert to delight,
And all to peace, and all to love envite.
  Come then, my Dafnis, and the feilds survey,
  And throo' the Groves, with your Ardelia stray.

As Baucis and Philemon spent their lives,
Of husbands he, the happyest she, of wives,   60
When throo' the painted meads, their way they sought,
Harmlesse in act, and unperplext in thought,
Lett us my Dafnis, rural joys persue,
And Courts, or Camps, not ev'n in fancy view.
  So, lett us throo' the Groves, my Dafnis stray,
  And so, the pleasures of the feilds, survey.

THE GOUTE AND SPIDER

A Fable

*Imitated from Mon*ʳ. de la Fontaine And Inscribed to Mr. Finch*
After his first Fitt of that Distemper

When from th' Infernal pitt two Furies rose
One foe to Flies and one to Mans repose
Seeking aboue to find a place secure
Since Hell the Goute nor Spider cou'd indure
On a rich Pallace at the first they light
Where pleas'd Arachne dazzl'd with the sight
In a conspiccuous corner of a Room
The hanging Frett work makes her active Loom.
From leaf to leaf with every line does trace,
Admires the strange convenience of the place   10
Nor can belieue those Cealings e're were made
To other end than to promote her Trade
Where prou'd and prosper'd in her finish'd work
The hungry Fiend does in close Ambush lurk
Untill some silly Insect shall repay
What from her Bowells she has spun that day.
The wiser Gout (for that's a thinking ill)
Observing how the splended chambers fill
With visitors such as abound below
Who from Hypocrates and Gallen grow   20

To some unwealthy shed resolues to fly
And there obscure and unmolested lye
But see how eithers project quickly fails
The Clown his new tormentor with him trayles
Through miry ways rough Woods and furrow'd Lands
Ne're cutts the Shooe nor propp'd on Crutches stands
With Phœbus rising stays with Cynthia out
Allows no respitt to the harrass'd Gout.

Whilst with extended Broom th' unpittying Maid
Does the transparent Laberynth invade   30
Back stroke and fore the battering Engin went
Broke euery Cord and quite unhing'd the Tent
No truce the tall Virago e're admitts
Contracted and abash'd Arachne' sitts
Then in conuenient Time the Work renews
The battering Ram again the work persues.
What's to be done?   The Gout and Spider meet,
Exchange, the Cottage this; That takes the feet
Of the rich Abbott who that Pallace kept
And 'till that time in Velvet Curtains slept   40
Now Colwort leaues and Cataplasms (thô vain)
Are hourly order'd by that griping traine.
Who blush not to Prescribe t'exhaust our Gold
For aches which incurable they hold
Whil'st stroak'd and fixt the pamper'd Gout remains
And in an easy Chair euer the Preist detains.

In a thatched Roof secure the Spider thrives,
Both mending by due place their hated liues.
From whose succeeding may this moral grow
That each his propper Station learn to know.   50

For You my Dear whom late that pain did seize,
Not rich enough to sooth the bad disease
By large expences to engage his stay

Nor yett so poor to fright the Gout away
May you but some unfrequent Visits find
To prove you patient, your Ardelia kind
Who by a tender and officious care
Will ease that Grief or her proportion bear
Since Heaven does in the Nuptial state admitt
Such cares but new endearments to begett　　60
And to allay the hard fatigues of life
Gaue the first Maid a Husband, Him a Wife.

UPON THE DEATH OF THE RIGHT HONORABLE WIL-LIAM LORD MAIDSTON

Who was a Volunteere in the Sol-bay Fight and kill'd by a Ran-dom shott, after the fight was over and the Fleets parted. On May 28th, 1672

Fate 'till the Day was ours, wou'd not dispense
With Maidston's aid, for Brittan's strong defence:
But then, least Pride, might by successe prevaile,
Threw in His losse, to poize th' unequal skale;
Giving us Sway; the Dutch a cause to boast
They'd kill'd one man, excelling all they losst.

FROM THE MUSES, AT PARNASSUS

(a hill so call'd in Eastwell Park) to the Right Honᵇˡᵉ yᵉ Ldy: Maidston on my Lord Winchilsea's Birth-day

Wonder not, Madam, that the Muses pay
Their gratefull tribute, on this happy day;
And in loud wishes, all their force employ,
That many more, like this, you may enjoy;
Since from your own Parnassus, they receive
Pleasure's, which theirs in Phocis, never gave;
And own, whilst here they reach the height of blisse,
Their forked hill, was but a type of this.
See where they come, their brows with lawrel bound,
And hear the neighbouring woods, repeat the sound,　　10

Of silver harps, and voyces that proclame
To all the expecting world, his growing fame,
Whom you, this day, presented to the earth,
Whilst Heav'n look'd down, and smil'd, upon the birth.
Hark! How they sing the Line from whence he springs,
And trace his blood, until itt mix with Kings,
That Suffolks soul, reviv'd in him is seen,
And on his face, the beautys of his Queen.
The air of youth, such as Adonis drest,
When Cytherea lodg'd him on her brest;   20
So yong, so gay, that when he haunts the groves,
The crouded shades, are throng'd with wondring Loves,
Who think him born, protector of their reign,
And boast what Conquests now they shall obtain.
They sing him Heir, to all your graces born,
And full perfections by his Father worn.
They sing him Heir, to all their shades and bow'rs,
And plead a Title to him, great as yours,
Call him their Son, their darling, their delight,
And dresse his thoughts with all that's great, and bright; 30
Their promis'd Isack, sent, when with dispair,
They saw witt old, and hopelesse of an heir.
In him, they doubt not, their lost fame to raise,
Who has out-grown allready, all their praise,
And is above what e're they can inspire,
Leaving you, Madam, nothing to desire.

UPON MY LORD WINCHILSEA'S CONVERTING THE MOUNT IN HIS GARDEN TO A TERRAS,

And other Alterations, and Improvements, In His House, Park, and Gardens

If we those Gen'rous Sons deserv'dly Praise
Who o're their Predecessours Marble raise,
And by Inscriptions, on their Deeds, and Name,

To late Posterity, convey their Fame,
What with more Admiration, shall we write,
On Him, who takes their Errours from our sight ?
And least their Judgments be in question brought,
Removes a Mountain, to remove a fault ?
Which long had stood (though threatnd oft in vain),
Concealing all the beautys of the Plaine.   10
Heedlesse when Yong, cautious in their decline,
None gone before persu'd the vast dessign,
Till ripen'd Judgment, joyn'd with Youthfull Flame,
At last but Came, and Saw, and Overcame.
And as old Rome refin'd what ere was rude,
And Civiliz'd, as fast as she subdu'd,
So lies this Hill, hew'n from itts rugged height,
Now levell'd to a Scene of smooth delight,
Where on a Terras of itts spoyles we walk,
And of the Task, and the performer talk;   20
From whose unwearied Genius Men expect
All that can farther Pollish or Protect;
To see a sheltring grove the Prospect bound,
Just rising from the same proliffick ground,
Where late itt stood, the Glory of the Seat,
Repell'd the Winter blasts, and skreen'd the Somer's heat;
So prais'd, so lov'd, that when untimely Fate,
Sadly prescrib'd itt a too early Date,
The heavy tidings cause a gen'ral Grief,
And all combine to bring a swift relief.   30
Some Plead, some Pray, some Councel, some Dispute,
Alas in vain, where Pow'r is Absolute.
Those whom Paternal Awe, forbid to speak,
Their sorrows, in their secret whispers break,
Sigh as they passe beneath the sentenc'd Trees,
Which seem to answer in a mournfull Breeze.
The very Clowns (hir'd by his dayly Pay),

Refuse to strike, nor will their Lord obey,
Till to his speech he adds a leading stroke,
And by Example does their Rage provoke.   40
Then in a moment, ev'ry arm is rear'd,
And the robb'd Palace sees, what most she fear'd,
Her lofty Grove, her ornamental shield,
Turn'd to a Desert, and forsaken Field.
So fell Persepolis, bewail'd of all
But Him, whose rash Resolve procur'd her Fall.
No longer now, we such Destructions fear,
No longer the resounding Axe we hear,
But in Exchange, behold the Fabrick stand,
Built, and Adorn'd by a supporting hand;   50
Compleat, in all itts late unequall Frame,
No Loame, and Lath, does now the Building shame,
But gracefull simetry, without is seen,
And Use, with Beauty are improv'd within.
And though our Ancestors did gravely Plott,
As if one Element they vallu'd nott,
Nor yet the pleasure of the noblest sence,
Gainst Light and Air to raise a strong defense;
Their wiser Offspring does those gifts renew,
And now we Breath[e] and now the eager View   60
Through the enlarged Windows take[s] her way,
Does beauteous Fields, and scatter'd Woods survey,
Flyes or'e th' extended Land, and sinks but in the Sea.
Or when contented with an easyer flight,
The new wrought Gardens, give a new delight,
Where ev'ry fault, that in the Old was found,
Is mended, in the well disposed Ground.
Such are th' Effects, when Wine, nor loose delights,
Devour the Day, nor waste the thoughtlesse Nights,
But gen'rous Arts, the studious Hours eugage,   70
To blesse the present, and succeeding Age.

Oh! may Eastwell, still with their aid encrease,
Plenty surround her, and within be peace.
Still may her temp'rate Air his Health maintain,
From whom she does such Strength and Beauty gain.
Florish her Trees, and may the Verdant Grasse
Again prevail, where late the plough did passe,
Still may she boast a kind and fruitfull soyle,
And still new pleasures give to crown his Toyle,
And may some one, with Admiration fill'd,   80
In just Applauses, and in Numbers skill'd,
Not with more Zeal, but more poetick heat,
Throughly Adorn, what barely we Relate.
Then, shou'd th' Elysian Groves no more be Nam'd,
Nor Tempe's Vale, be any longer Fam'd,
She shou'd the Theame, to ev'ry Verse affoard,
Until the Muse, when to advantage soar'd,
Shou'd take a nobler Aim, and dare describe her Lord.

A SONG

For my Br. Les: Finch.   Upon a Punch Bowl

From the Park, and the Play,
And Whitehall come away,
To the Punch-bowl, by far more inviting;
To the Fopps, and the Beauxs,
Leaue those dull empty shows,
And see here, what is truly delighting.

The half Globe 'tis in figure;
And wou'd itt were bigger;
Yett here's the whole Universe floating,
Here's Titles and Places,
Rich lands, and fair faces,
And all that is worthy our doating.

'Twas a World, like to this,
The hott Græcian did misse,
Of whom History's keep such a pother,
To the bottom he sunk,
And when one he had drunk
Grew maudlin, and wept for another.

THE BARGAIN

A Song in dialogue between Bacchus and Cupid

Cupid

Bacchus, to thee that turn'st the brain,
And doest o're mighty punch bowls reign,
Enthron'd upon thy lusty barrell,
I drink, to drown the ancient quarrell;
And mortalls shall no more dispute
Which of us two, is absolute.

Bacchus

I pledge thee Archer, nor disdain
To own thou over hearts doest reign,
But tears thou drink'st, drawn from low courage,
And cool'd with sighs, instead of burrage;
Were that errour once ammended,
All, might in Champaine be ended.

Cupid

I am content, so we may joyn,
To mix my waters, with thy wine;
Then henceforth farwell all defying,
And thus, we'll still be found complying,
He, that's in love, shall fly to thee,
And he thats drunk, shall reel to mee.

TO MY SISTER OGLE, DEC^BR 31, 1688

When dear Teresa, shall I be
By Heaven, again restor'd to you?
Thus, if once more your face I see,
Thus, our lost pleasures, we'll renew.

Our yesterday, when kindly past,
Shall teatch how this shou'd be enjoy'd,
And urge to morrows eager haste,
As longing, to be thus employ'd.

Time, shall pay back the years and hours,
That in our absence posted by;
Time, shall submitt to freindships pow'rs,
And as we please, shall rest, or fly.

The sun, that stood to look on War,
And lengthen'd out that fatal day,
For kindnesse, more engaging far,
Will longer sure, his fall delay.

At last, when Fate, the word shall give,
That we no longer, here below,
This soft, endearing life shall live,
In Tryumph we'll together go,

New arts to find, new joys to try,
The height of freindship to improve;
Tis' worth our pains, and fears to dye;
To learn new misteries of Love.

ARDELIA'S ANSWER TO EPHELIA,

who had invited her to come to her in town — reflecting on the
Coquetterie and detracting humour of the Age

Me, dear Ephelia, me, in vain you court
With all your pow'rfull influence, to resort
To that great Town, where Freindship can but have

The few spare hours, which meaner pleasures leave.
No! Let some shade, or your large Pallace be
Our place of meeting, love, and liberty;
To thoughts, and words, and all endearments free.
But, to those walls, excuse my slow repair;
Who have no businesse, or diversion there;
No daz'ling beauty, to attract the gaze   10
Of won'd'ring crouds to my applauded face;
Nor to my little witt, th' ill nature joyn'd,
To passe a gen'rall censure on mankind:
To call the yong, and unaffected, fools;
Dull all the grave, that live by moral rules;
To say the souldier brags, who ask'd declares
The nice escapes and dangers of his wars,
The Poet's vain, that knows his unmatch'd worth,
And dares maintain what the best Muse brings forth:
Yett, this the humour of the age is grown,   20
And only conversation of the Town.
In Satir vers'd, and sharpe detraction, bee,
And you're accomplish'd, for all company.

II

When my last visit, I to London made,
Me, to Almeria, wretched chance, betray'd;
The fair Almeria, in this art so known,
That she discerns all failings, but her own.
With a lowd welcome, and a strict embrace,
Kisses on kisses, in a publick place,
Sh' extorts a promise, that next day I dine   30
With her, who for my sight, did hourly pine;
And wonders, how so far I can remove,
From the beaux monde, and the dull country love;
Yet vows, if but an afternoon 'twoud cost
To see me there, she cou'd resolve allmost

To quitt the Town, and for that time, be lost.
  My word I keep, we dine, then rising late,
Take coach, which long had waited at the gate.
About the streets, a tedious ramble goe,
To see this Monster, or that wax work show,   40
Or any thing, that may the time bestow.
When by a Church we passe, I ask to stay,
Go in, and my devotions, humbly pay
To that great Pow'r, whom all the wise obey.
Whilst the gay thing, light as her feather'd dresse,
Flys round the Coach, and does each cusheon presse,
Through ev'ry glasse, her sev'ral graces shows,
This, does her face, and that, her shape expose,
To envying beautys, and admiring beauxs.
One stops, and as expected, all extolls,   50
Clings to the door, and on his elbow lolls,
Thrusts in his head, at once to veiw the fair,
And keep his curls from discomposing air,
Then thus proceeds —
                    My wonder itt is grown
To find Almeria here, and here alone.
Where are the Nymphs, that round you us'd to croud,
Of your long courted approbation proud,
Learning from you, how to erect their hair,
And in perfection, all their habitt wear,
To place a patch, in some peculiar way,   60
That may an unmark'd smile, to sight betray,
And the vast genius of the Sex, display?
  Pitty me then (she crys) and learn the fate
That makes me Porter to a Temple gate;
Ardelia came to Town, some weeks agoe,
Who does on books her rural hours bestow,
And is so rustick in her cloaths and meen,
'Tis with her ungenteel but to be seen,

Did not a long acquaintance plead excuse;
Besides, she likes no witt, thats now in use,   70
Dispises Courtly Vice, and plainly sais,
That sence and Nature shou'd be found in Plays,
And therefore, none will 'ere be brought to see
But those of Dryden, Etheridge, or Lee,
And some few Authors, old, and dull to me.
To her I did engage my coach and day,
And here must wait, while she within does pray.
Ere twelve was struck, she calls me from my bed,
Nor once observes how well my toilett's spread;
Then, drinks the fragrant tea contented up,   80
Without a complement upon the cup,
Tho' to the ships, for the first choice I stear'd,
Through such a storm, as the stout bargemen fear'd;
Least that a praise, which I have long engross'd
Of the best china Equipage, be lost.
Of fashions now, and colours I discours'd,
Detected shops that wou'd expose the worst,
What silks, what lace, what rubans she must have,
And by my own, an ample pattern gave;
To which, she cold, and unconcern'd reply'd,   90
I deal with one that does all these provide,
Hauing of other cares, enough beside;
And in a cheap, or an ill chosen gown,
Can vallue blood that's nobler then my own,
And therefore hope, my self not to be weigh'd
By gold, or silver, on my garments laid;
Or that my witt, or judgment shou'd be read
In an uncom̄on colour on my head.
   Stupid! and dull, the shrugging Zany crys;
When, service ended, me he moving spy's,   100
Hastes to conduct me out, and in my ear
Drops some vile praise, too low for her to hear;

Which to avoid, more then the begging throng,
I reach the coach, that swiftly rowls along,
Least to Hide park, we shou'd too late be brought,
And loose e're night, an hour of finding fault.
Arriv'd, she crys,—
      that awk'ard creature see,
A fortune born, and wou'd a beauty bee
Cou'd others but beleive, as fast as she.
Round me, I look, some Monster to discry,   110
Whose wealthy acres, must a Title buye,
Support my Lord, and be, since his have fail'd,
With the high shoulder, on his race entayl'd;
When to my sight, a lovely face appears,
Perfect in e'vry thing, but growing years;
This I defend, to do my judgment right,
Can you dispraise a skin so smooth, so white,
That blush, which o're such well turn'd cheeks does rise,
That look of youth, and those enliven'd eyes?
She soon replies,—   120
      that skin, which you admire,
Is shrunk, and sickly, cou'd you view itt nigher.
The crimson lining and uncertain light,
Reflects that blush, and paints her to the sight.
Trust me, the look, which you comend, betrays
A want of sence, more then the want of days,
And those wild eyes, that round the cercle stray,
Seem, as her witts, had but mistook their way.
As I did mine, I to my self repeat,
When by this envious side. I took my seat:
Oh! for my groves, my Country walks, and bow'rs,   130
Trees blast not trees, nor flow'rs envenom flow'rs,
As beauty here, all beautys praise devours.
But Noble Piso passes,—
       he's a witt.

As some (she sais) wou'd have itt, tho' as yett
No line he in a Lady's fan has writt,
N'ere on their dresse, in verse, soft things wou'd say,
Or with loud clamour ouer powr'd a Play,
And right or wrong, preuented the third day;
To read in publick places, is not known,
Or in his Chariot, here appears alone;   140
Bestows no hasty praise, on all that's new.
When first this Coach came out to publick veiw,
Mett in a visit, he presents his hand
And takes me out, I make a willfull stand,
Expecting, sure, this wou'd applause invite,
And often turn'd, that way, to guide his sight;
Till finding him wrapp'd in a silent thought,
I ask'd, if that the Painter well had wrought,
Who then reply'd, he 'has in the Fable err'd,
Cov'ring Adonis with a monstrous beard;   150
Made Hercules (who by his club is shewn)
A gentler fop then any of the Town,
Whilst Venus, from a bogg is rising seen,
And eyes a squint, are given to beautys queen
I had no patience, longer to attend,
And know 'tis want of witt, to discomend.
   Must Piso then! be judg'd by such as these,
Piso, who from the Latin, Virgil frees,
Who loos'd the bands, which old Sylenus bound,
And made our Albion rocks repeat the mistick sound, 160
" Whilst all he sung was present to our eyes
"And as he rais'd his verse, the Poplars seem'd to rise?"
Scarce cou'd I in my brest my thoughts contain,
Or for this folly, hide my just disdain.
When see, she says, observe my best of friends,
And through the window, half her length extends
Exalts her voyce, that all the ring may hear;

How fullsomly she oft repeats my dear,
Letts fall some doubtfull words, that we may know
There still a secret is, betwixt them two,   170
And makes a sign, the small white hand to shew.
When, Fate be prais'd, the coachman slacks the reins,
And o're my lap, no longer now she leans,
But how her choyce I like, does soon enquire?
  Can I dislike I cry, what all admire,
Discreet, and witty, civil and refin'd,
Nor, in her person fairer then her mind,
Is yong Alinda, if report be just;
For half the Caracter, my eyes I trust.
What chang'd Almeria, on a suddain cold,   180
As if I of your freind, some tale had told?
No, she replyes, but when I hear her praise,
A secret failing does my pitty raise,
Damon she loves, and 'tis my dayly care,
To keep the passion from the publick ear,
I ask, amaz'd, if this she has reveal'd,
No, 'but tis true, she crys, though much conceal'd;
I have observ'd itt long, nor wou'd betray
But to your self, what now with greif I say,
Who this, to none, but Confidents must break,   190
Nor they to others, but in whispers, speak;
I am her freind and must consult her fame.
More was she saying, when fresh objects came,
Now what's that thing, she crys, Ardelia, guesse?
A woman sure.——
                Ay and a Poetesse,
They say she writes, and 'tis a comon jest.
Then sure sh' has publickly the skill professt,
I soon reply, or makes that gift her pride,
And all the world, but scribblers, does deride;
Setts out Lampoons, where only spite is seen,   200
Not fill'd with female witt, but female spleen.

Her florish'd name, does o're a song expose,
Which through all ranks, down to the Carman, goes.
Or poetry is on her Picture found,
In which she sits, with painted lawrel crown'd.
If no such flyes, no vanity defile
The Helyconian balm, the sacred oyl,
Why shou'd we from that pleasing art be ty'd,
Or like State Pris'ners, Pen and Ink deny'd?
But see, the Sun his chariot home has driv'n   210
From the vast shining ring of spacious Heav'n,
Nor after him Celestial beautys stay,
But crou'd with sparkling wheels the milky way.
Shall we not then, the great example take
And ours below, with equal speed forsake?
When to your favours, adding this one more,
You'll stop, and leave me thank-full, att my door.
How! e're you've in the Drawing-room appear'd,
And all the follys there beheld and heard.
Since you've been absent, such intrigues are grown;   220
Such new Coquetts and Fops are to be shown,
Without their sight you must not leave the Town.
Excuse me, I reply, my eyes ne're feast
Upon a fool, tho' ne're so nicely dresst.
Nor is itt musick to my burthen'd ear
The unripe prating's of our sex to hear,
A noysy girl, who' has at fifteen talk'd more
Then Grandmother, or Mother here to fore,
In all the cautious, prudent years they bore.
Statesmen there are, (she crys) whom I can show   230
That bear the kingdoms cares, on a bent brow;
Who take the weight of politicks by grains,
And to the least, know what each scull contains,
Who's to be coach'd, who talk'd to when abroad,
Who but the smile must have, and who the nod;
And when this is the utmost of their skill,

'Tis not much wonder, if affairs go ill.
Then for the Church-men —
                        hold my lodging's here;
Nor can I longer a re-proof forbear
When sacred things nor Persons she wou'd spare.   240
  We parted thus, the night in peace I spent,
And the next day, with haste and pleasure went
To the best seat of fam'd and fertile Kent.
Where lett me live from all detraction free
Till thus the World is criticis'd by mee;
Till freind, and Foe, I treat with such dispite
May I no scorn, the worst of ills, excite.

FRIENDSHIP BETWEEN EPHELIA AND ARDELIA

   Eph.   What *Friendship* is, ARDELIA shew.
   Ard.   'Tis to love, as I love You.
   Eph.   This Account, so short (tho' kind)
           Suits not my enquiring Mind.
           Therefore farther now repeat;
           What is *Friendship* when compleat?
   Ard.   'Tis to share all Joy and Grief;
           'Tis to lend all due Relief
           From the Tongue, the Heart, the Hand;
           'Tis to mortgage House and Land;
           For a Friend be sold a Slave;
           'Tis to die upon a Grave,
           If a Friend therein do lie.
   Eph.   This indeed, tho' carry'd high,
           This, tho' more than e'er was done
           Underneath the rolling Sun,
           This has all been said before.
           Can ARDELIA say no more?
   Ard.   Words indeed no more can shew:
           But 'tis to love, as I love you.

A DESCRIPTION OF ONE OF THE PIECES OF TAPISTRY AT LONG-LEAT,

made after the famous Cartons of Raphael; *in which,* Elymas *the Sorcerer is miraculously struck blind by St.* Paul *before* Sergius Paulus, *the Proconsul of* Asia

Inscribed to the Honble Henry Thynne, *under the name of* Theanor

Thus *Tapistry* of old, the Walls adorn'd,
Ere noblest Dames the artful *Shuttle* scorn'd:
Arachne, then, with *Pallas* did contest,
And scarce th' Immortal Work was judg'd the Best.
Nor valorous Actions, then, in Books were fought;
But all the Fame, that from the Field was brought,
Employ'd the *Loom*, where the kind *Consort* wrought:
Whilst sharing in the Toil, she shar'd the Fame,
And with the *Heroes* mixt her interwoven Name.
No longer, *Females* to such Praise aspire,   10
And seldom now We rightly do admire.
So much, All Arts are by the *Men* engross'd,
And Our few Talents unimprov'd or cross'd;
Even I, who on this Subject wou'd compose,
Which the fam'd *Urbin* for his Pencil chose,
(And here, in tinctur'd Wool we now behold
Correctly follow'd in each Shade, and Fold)
Shou'd prudently from the Attempt withdraw,
But Inclination proves the stronger Law:
And tho' the Censures of the World pursue   20
These hardy Flights, whilst his *Designs* I view;
My burden'd Thoughts, which labour for a Vent,
Urge me t'explain in Verse, what by each Face is meant.

Of SERGIUS first, upon his lofty Seat,
With due Regard our Observations treat;
Who, whilst he thence on ELYMAS looks down,

Contracts his pensive Brow into a Frown,
With Looks inquisitive he seeks the Cause
Why Nature acts not still by Natures Laws.
'Twas but a Moment, since the *Sorcerer's* Sight   30
Receiv'd the Day, and blaz'd infernal Light:
Untouch'd, the Optiques in a Moment fail'd,
Their fierce Illumination quench'd, or veil'd;
Throughout th' Extention of his ample Sway,
No Fact, like this, the *Roman* cou'd survey,
Who, with spread Hands, invites Mankind to gaze,
And sympathize in the profound Amaze.
To share his Wonder every one combines,
By diff'rent Aspects shewn, and diff'rent Signs.
A comely Figure, near the Consul plac'd,   40
With serious Mildness and Instruction grac'd,
To Others seems imparting what he saw,
And shews the Wretch with reverential Awe:
Whilst a more eager Person next we find,
Viewing the Wizard with a Sceptick's Mind;
Who his fixt Eyes so near him do's apply,
We think, enliv'ning Beams might from them fly,
To re-inkindle, by so just an Aim,
The radial Sparks, but lately check'd and tame,
As Tapers new put-out will catch approaching flame. 50
But dire Surprize th' Enquiry do's succeed,
Whilst full Conviction in his Face we read,
And He, who question'd, now deplores the Deed.

To sacred PAUL a younger Figure guides,
With seeming Warmth, which still in Youth presides;
And pointing forward, Elder Men directs,
In Him, to note the Cause of these Effects;
Upon whose Brow do's evidently shine
Deputed Pow'r, t' inflict the Wrath Divine;

Whilst sad and solemn, suited to their Years,   ·   60
Each venerable Countenance appears,
Where, yet we see Astonishment reveal'd,
Tho' by the Aged often 'tis conceal'd;
Who the Emotions of their Souls disguize,   ·
Lest by admiring they shou'd seem less Wise.

But to thy Portrait, ELYMAS, we come
Whose Blindness almost strikes the Poet dumb;
And whilst *She* vainly to Describe thee seeks,
The Pen but traces, where the Pencil speaks.
Of Darkness to be *felt*, our Scriptures write,   70
Thou Darken'd seem'st, as thou would'st feel the *Light;*
And with projected Limbs, betray'st a Dread,
Of unseen Mischiefs, levell'd at thy Head.
Thro' all thy Frame such Stupefaction reigns,
As Night it self were sunk into thy Veins:
Nor by the Eyes alone thy Loss we find,
Each Lineament helps to proclaim thee Blind.
An artful Dimness far diffus'd we grant,
And failing seem all Parts through One important Want.

Oh! mighty RAPHAEL, justly sure renown'd!   80
Since in thy Works such Excellence is found;
No Wonder, if with Nature Thou'rt at strife,
Who thus can paint the Negatives of Life;
And Deprivation more expressive make,
Than the most perfect Draughts, which Others take.
Whilst to this Chiefest Figure of the Piece,
All that surround it, Heightnings do encrease:
In some, Amazement by Extreams is shewn,
Who viewing his clos'd Lids, extend their Own.
Nor can, by that, enough their Thoughts express,   90
Which op'ning Mouths seem ready to confess.

Thus stand the LICTORS gazing on a Deed,
Which do's all humane Chastisements exceed;
Enfeebl'd seem their Instruments of smart,
When keener Words can swifter Ills impart.

Thou, BARNABAS, though Last, not least our Care,
Seem'st equally employ'd in Praise, and Prayer,
Acknowledging th' Omnipotent Decree,
Yet soft Compassion in thy Face we see:
Whilst lifted Hands implore a kind Relief,   100
Tho' no Impatience animates thy Grief;
But mild Suspence and Charity benign,
Do all th' excesses of thy Looks confine.

Thus far, our slow Imagination goes:
Wou'd the more skill'd THEANOR his disclose;
Expand the Scene, and open to our Sight
What to his nicer Judgment gives Delight;
Whose soaring Mind do's to Perfections climb,
Nor owns a Relish, but for Things sublime:
Then, wou'd the Piece fresh Beauties still present,   110
Nor Length of Time wou'd leave the Eye content:
As moments, Hours; as Hours the Days wou'd seem,
Observing here, taught to observe by HIM.

GLASS

O Man! what Inspiration was thy Guide,
Who taught thee Light and Air thus to divide;
To let in all the useful Beams of Day,
Yet force, as subtil Winds, without thy Shash to stay;
T'extract from Embers by a strange Device,
Then polish fair these Flakes of solid Ice;
Which, silver'd o'er, redouble all in place,
And give thee back thy well or ill-complexion'd Face.

To Vessels blown exceed the gloomy Bowl,
Which did the Wine's full excellence controul,
These shew the Body, whilst you taste the Soul.
Its colour sparkles Motion, lets thee see,
Tho' yet th' Excess the Preacher warns to flee,
Lest Men at length as clearly soy through Thee.

THE BIRD AND THE ARRAS

By neer resemblance see that Bird betray'd
Who takes the well wrought Arras for a shade
There hopes tc pearch and with a chearfull Tune
O're-passe the scortchings of the sultry Noon.
But soon repuls'd by the obdurate scean
How swift she turns but turns alas in vain
That piece a Grove, this shews an ambient sky
Where immitated Fowl their pinnions ply
Seeming to mount in flight and aiming still more high.
All she outstrip's and with a moments pride
Their understation silent does deride
Till the dash'd Cealing strikes her to the ground
No intercepting shrub to break the fall is found
Recovering breath the window next she gaines
Nor fears a stop from the transparent Panes.

   .   .   .   .

But we degresse and leaue th' imprison'd wretch
Now sinking low now on a loftyer stretch
Flutt'ring in endlesse cercles of dismay
Till some kind hand directs the certain way
Which through the casement an escape affoards
And leads to ample space the only Heav'n of Birds.

TO THE HONORABLE THE LADY WORSLEY AT LONG-LEATE

Who had most obligingly desired my corresponding with her by Letters

If from some lonely and obscure recesse
The shunn'd retreat of solitary peace
Lost to the World and like Ardelias seat
Fitt only for the Wretch opress'd by Fate
A melancholly summons had been sent
To deal in Woe and mingle discontent
By sympathising Lines t'attempt relief
And load each Poste with sad exchange of grief
No wonder had that comon Act express'd
For still Distresse wou'd Herd with the distress'd   10
And to our Cares itt seems a short allay
To fold them close and from our selves convey.
  But that Utresia seeks to correspond
With such a dull and disproportion'd hand
Empty Replies endeavours to obtain
From secrett Cells and from a clouded Brain
Is something so unusual (thô so kind)
That scarse th' exalted motions of her mind
Or charms in Hers beyond each other Tongue
(Had we not heard Him speak from whom she sprung) 20
Cou'd more amaze us then this friendly part
That she whom all aspire but to divert
Makes itt of All her choice to sooth a sinking heart.
Utresia in her fresh and smiling bloom
With Joys incompass'd and new Joys to come
Who like the Sun in her Meridian shows
Surrounded with the Lustre she bestows
Her self dispensing by her long'd for sight
To every Place she visits full delight
For Beauty this Prerogative maintains   30

And ouer both the Sexes thus far reigns
To chear all Hearts and to suspend our pains
Who when such Eyes, so soft and bright we view
Soften our Cares and grow enlighten'd too
In sweet conformity to Things so fine
No motions feel but such as in them shine.
Cou'd but the Witt that on her paper flows
Affect my Verse and tune itt to her Prose
Through every Line a kindly warmth inspire
And raise my Art equal to my desire   40
Then shou'd my Hand snatch from the Muses store
Transporting Figures n'ere expos'd before
Somthing to Please so mouing and so new
As not our Denham or our Cowley knew.
Or shew (the harder labour to compleat)
The real splendours of our fam'd Long-leate
Which above Metaphor itts Structure reares
Thô all Enchantment to our sight appears
Magnificently Great the Eye to fill
Minut'ly finish'd for our nices[t] skill   50
Long-leate that justly has all Praise engross'd
The Strangers wonder and our Nations boast
Paint her Cascades that spread their sheets so wide
And emulate th' Italian waters pride
Her Fountains which so high their streames extend
Th' amazed Clouds now feel the Rains ascend
Whilst Phœbus as they tow'rds his Mantion flow
Graces th' attempt and marks them with his Bow.
Then shou'd my Pen (smooth as their Turf) convey
Swift Thought o're Terasses that lead the way   60
To flow'ry Groves where ev'ning Odours stray
To Lab'rinths into which, who fondly comes,
Attracted still and wilder'd with Parfumes,
Till by acquaintance he their stations knows
Here twists a Woodbine there a Jasmin grows

Next springs th' Hesperian Broom and last th' Assy-
 · rian Rose,
Shall endlesse Rove nor tread the way he went
No Thread to guide his steps, no Clue but ravish'd scent.
But Oh! Alas! cou'd we this Prospect give
And make itt in true lights and shaddows live   70
Ther's yett a Task att which 'twere vain to Strive
His Genius who th' original improv'd
To this degree that has our wonder mov'd
Too great appears and awes the trembling hand
Which can no Colours for that Draught comand
No syllables the most sublimely wrought
Can reach the loftier Immage of his thought
Whose Judgment plac'd in a superior hight
All things surveys with comprehensive sight
Then pittying us below stoops to inform us right   80
In Words which such convincing Reasons bear
We silent wish that they engraven were
And grudge those Sounds to the dispersing air.
Protect Him Heaven and long may He appear
The leading Star to his great Offspring here
Their Treasury of Council and support
Who when att last he shall attend your Court
To all his future Race the mark shall be
To stem the waves of Life's tempestuous Sea
Who from abroad shall no Examples need   90
Of men Recorded or who then Exceed
To urdge their Virtue and exalt their Fame
 · Whilest their own Weymouth stands their noblest Aime.
But we Presume, and ne're must hope to trace
His Worth profound, his Daughters matchlesse Grace
Or draw paternall Witt deriv'd into her Face
Though from his Presence and her Charms did grow
The Joys Ardelia att Long-leat did know.

So Paradice did wond'rous Things disclose
Yett surely not from them itts Name arose   100
Not from the Fruits in such profusion found
Or early Beauties of th' enammell'd Ground
Not from the Trees in their first leaves arraid
Or Birds uncurs'd that Warbl'd in their shade
Not from the streams that in new channells rol'd
O're radiant Beds of uncorrupting Gold
These might surprise but 'twas th' accomplish'd Pair
That gave the Title and that made itt fair.
All lesser Thoughts Immagination Balk
'Twas Paradice in some expanded Walk   110
To see Her motions, and attend his Talk

THE FOLLOWING LINES

occasion'd by the Marriage of Edward Herbert *Esquire, and* Mrs. Elizabet Herbert

Cupid one day ask'd his Mother,
   When she meant that he shou'd Wed?
You're too Young, my Boy, she said:
   Nor has Nature made another
   Fit to match with *Cupid's* Bed.

Cupid then her Sight directed
   To a lately Wedded Pair;
Where Himself the Match effected;
   They as Youthful, they as Fair.

Having by Example carry'd
   This first Point in the Dispute;
Worseley next he said's not Marry'd:
   Her's with *Cupid's* Charms may suit.

ON THE DEATH OF THE HONOURABLE MR. JAMES THYNNE,

Younger Son to the Right Honourable the Lord Viscount
Weymouth

Farewel, lov'd Youth! since 'twas the Will of Heaven
So soon to take, what had so late been giv'n;
And thus our Expectations to destroy,
Raising a Grief, where we had form'd a Joy;
Who once believ'd, it was the Fates Design
In Him to double an Illustrious Line,
And in a second Channel spread that Race
Where ev'ry Virtue shines, with every Grace.
But we mistook, and 'twas not here below
That this engrafted *Scion* was to grow;   10
The Seats above requir'd him, that each Sphere
Might soon the Offspring of such Parents share.
Resign him then to the supream Intent,
You, who but Flesh to that blest Spirit lent.
Again disrob'd, let him to Bliss retire,
And only bear from you, amidst that Choir,
What, Precept or Example did inspire,
A Title to Rewards, from that rich store
Of Pious Works, which you have sent before.
Then lay the fading Reliques, which remain,   20
In the still Vault (excluding farther Pain);
Where Kings and Counsellors their Progress close,
And his renowned Ancestors repose;
Where COVENTRY withdrew All but in Name,
Leaving the World his Benefits and Fame;
Where his Paternal Predecessor lies,
Once large of Thought, and rank'd among the Wise;
Whose Genius in *Long-Leat* we may behold
(A Pile, as noble as if he'd been told

By WEYMOUTH, it shou'd be in time possest,   30
And strove to suit the Mansion to the Guest.)
Nor favour'd, nor disgrac'd, there ESSEX sleeps,
Nor SOMERSET his Master's Sorrows weeps,
Who to the shelter of th' unenvy'd Grave
Convey'd the Monarch, whom he cou'd not save;
Though, *Roman*-like, his own less-valu'd Head
He proffer'd in that injur'd Martyr's stead.
Nor let that matchless *Female* 'scape my Pen,
Who their Whole Duty taught to weaker Men,
And of each Sex the Two best Gifts enjoy'd   40
The Skill to write, the Modesty to hide;
Whilst none shou'd that Performance disbelieve,
Who led the Life, might the Directions give.
With such as These, whence He deriv'd his Blood,
Great on Record, or eminently Good,
Let Him be laid, till Death's long Night shall cease,
And breaking Glory interrupt the Peace.
Mean-while, ye living Parents, ease your Grief
By Tears, allow'd as Nature's due Relief.
For when we offer to the Pow'rs above,   50
Like You, the dearest Objects of our Love;
When, with that patient Saint in Holy Writ,
We've learnt at once to Grieve, and to Submit;
When contrite Sighs, like hallow'd Incense, rise
Bearing our Anguish to th' appeased Skies;
Then may those Show'rs, which take from Sorrow birth,
And still are tending tow'rd this baleful Earth,
O'er all our deep and parching Cares diffuse,
Like *Eden's* Springs, or *Hermon's* soft'ning Dews.
But lend your Succours, ye Almighty Pow'rs,   60
For as the Wound, the Balsam too is Yours.
In vain are Numbers, or persuasive Speech,
What Poets write, or what the Pastors teach,

Till You, who make, again repair the Breach.
For when to Shades of Death our Joys are fled,
When for a loss, like This, our Tears are shed,
None can revive the Heart, but who can raise the Dead.
But yet, my Muse, if thou hadst softer Verse
Than e'er bewail'd the melancholy Herse;
If thou hadst Pow'r to dissipate the Gloom   70
Inherent to the Solitary Tomb;
To rescue thence the Memory and Air
Of what we lately saw so Fresh, so Fair;
Then shou'd this Noble Youth thy Art engage
To shew the Beauties of his blooming Age,
The pleasing Light, that from his Eyes was cast,
Like hasty Beams, too Vigorous to last;
Where the warm Soul, as on the Confines, lay
Ready for Flight, and for Eternal Day.
Gently dispos'd his Nature shou'd be shown,   80
And all the *Mother's* Sweetness made his Own.
The *Father's* Likeness was but faintly seen,
As ripen'd Fruits are figur'd by the Green.
Nor cou'd we hope, had he fulfill'd his Days,
He shou'd have reach'd WEYMOUTH'S unequal'd Praise.
Still One distinguish'd Plant each Lineage shews,
And all the rest beneath it's Stature grows.
Of *Tully's* Race but He possess'd the Tongue,
And none like *Julius* from the *Cæsars* sprung.
Next, in his harmless Sports he shou'd be drawn   90
Urging his Courser, o'er the flow'ry Lawn;
Sprightly Himself, as the enliven'd Game,
Bold in the Chace, and full of gen'rous Flame;
Yet in the Palace, Tractable and Mild,
Perfect in all the Duties of a Child;
Which fond reflection pleases, whilst it pains,
Like penetrating Notes of sad Harmonious Strains.

Selected Friendships timely he began,
And siezed in Youth that best Delight of Man,
Leaving a growing Race to mourn his End,   100
Their earliest and their Ages promis'd Friend.
But far away alas! that Prospect moves,
Lost in the Clouds, like distant Hills and Groves,
Whilst with encreasing Steps we all pursue
What Time alone can bring to nearer View,
That Future State, which Darkness yet involves,
Known but by Death, which ev'ry Doubt resolves.

TO THE PAINTER OF AN ILL-DRAWN PICTURE OF CLEONE, THE HONORABLE MRS. THYNNE

Sooner I'd praise a Cloud which Light beguiles,
Than thy rash hand which robs this Face of Smiles;
And does that sweet and pleasing Air controul,
Which to us paints the fair CLEONE's Soul.
'Tis vain to boast of Rules or labour'd Art;
I miss the Look that captivates my Heart,
Attracts my Love, and tender Thoughts inspires;
Nor can my Breast be warm'd by common Fires;
Nor can ARDELIA love but where she first admires.
Like *Jupiter's*, thy Head was sure in Pain   10
When this Virago struggl'd in thy Brain;
And strange it is, thou hast not made her wield
A mortal Dart, or penetrating Shield,
Giving that Hand of disproportion'd size
The Pow'r, of which thou hast disarm'd her Eyes:
As if, like *Amazons*, she must oppose,
And into Lovers force her vanquish'd Foes.
Had to THEANOR thus her Form been shown
To gain her Heart, he had not lost his own;
Nor, by the gentlest Bands of Human Life,   20

At once secur'd the Mistress and the Wife.
For still CLEONE's Beauties are the same,
And what first lighten'd, still upholds his Flame.
Fain his Compassion wou'd thy Works approve,
Were pitying thee consistent with his Love,
Or with the Taste which *Italy* has wrought
In his refin'd and daily heighten'd Thought,
Where Poetry, or Painting find no place,
Unless perform'd with a superior Grace.
Cou'd but my Wish some Influence infuse,   30
Ne'er shou'd the Pencil, or the Sister-Muse
Be try'd by those who easily excuse:
But strictest Censors shou'd of either judge,
Applaud the Artist, and despise the Drudge.
Then never wou'd thy Colours have debas'd
CLEONE's Features, and her Charms defac'd:
Nor had my Pen (more subject to their Laws)
Assay'd to vindicate her Beauty's Cause.
A rigid Fear had kept us both in Awe,
Nor I compos'd, nor thou presum'd to draw;   40
But in CLEONE viewing with Surprize
That Excellence, to which we ne'er cou'd rise,
By less attempts we safely might have gain'd
That humble Praise which neither has obtain'd,
Since to thy Shadowings, or my ruder Verse,
It is not giv'n to shew, or to rehearse
What Nature in CLEONE's Face has writ,
A soft Endearment, and a chearful Wit,
That all-subduing, that enliv'ning Air
By which, a sympathizing Joy we share,   50
For who forbears to smile, when smil'd on by the Fair?

TO THE RIGHT HONOURABLE THE COUNTESS OF HARTFORD,

with her volume of Poems

Of sleepless nights, and days with cares o'ercast,
Accept the fruits, tho' far beneath your taste;
Yet look with favour on Ardelia's muse,
And what your father cherish'd, still excuse.
Whenever style or fancy in them shines,
Conclude his praise gave spirit to those lines:
So deep his judgment, so acute his wit,
No critic liv'd, but did to him submit.
From his your gentle nature does proceed;
Then partial be, like him, while here you read;
Who could forgive the errors of a friend,
But knew no bounds, when prompted to commend.

UPON THE DEATH OF SIR WILLIAM TWISDEN

Cou'd Rivers weep (as somtimes Poets dream)
Cou'd neigh'bring Hills our sorrows know,
And thoughtlesse Flocks, and faiding Flowers,
Droop o're the pastures, and beneath the showers,
To sympathize with Man, and answer to his Woe;
Now, shou'd the Medway's fruitfull stream,
In broken drops, disolve away,
And pay in tears, her Tribute to the sea;
Now shou'd the Flocks, forgett to thrive,
Nor wou'd th' ensuing blasted Spring   10
One purple Violet revive,
One fragrant Odour bring;
Now, by those Eccho's, which return'd his Name
When by the loud prevailing voice
Calld to the Senate, by his Country's choice,
Twisden amongst their Rocks, and deep recesses came;

Now, shou'd by them, th' unwelcome news be spread,
O're all th' extended, mournfull Land,
O're all the coasts, o're all the Kentish strand,
That Twisden is no more, their Matchlesse Patriot's
     dead.   20

2

But oh! in vain, things void of sence, we call,
In vain, implore the murmuring sound
Of hollow groans, from underneath the ground;
Or court the loud laments, of some steep water's fall;
On things innaninate, [sic] wou'd force,
Some share of our divided greif,
Whilst Nature (unconcern'd for our relief)
Persues her settl'd path, her fixt, and steaddy course,
Leaving those ills, which Providence allows
To check our Pleasures, and contract our Brows,   30
Freely to act their uncontrouled part,
Within the center of the human breast;
There, every lighter folly, to molest,
And fill with anxious thoughts, the sad, awaken'd heart;
From whence alone proceed those gath'ring clouds
Which euery outward beauty shrouds;
From whence alone, those sad complaints ascend,
Which pittying Echo's seem to lend;
And when through weeping Eyes, the world we view,
The ancient Flood we to ourselues renew,   40
Then hasty ruine seizes all around;
All things to desolation tend,
All seems to dye, with a departed Friend,
The Earth unpeopl'd seems, and all again is drown'd,

3

Such were our thoughts, so with each Mind it far'd,
When first th' unhappy news we heard,
When told alas! that Twisden was expir'd,

Whom all lament, whom liuing, all admir'd;
For in his breast, were such perfections sown,
Such numerous excellencies plac'd,   50
That every man, with different tallents, grac'd,
Found somthing that improv'd, or answer'd to his own.
He, whose lou'd Country, was his cheifest care,
Might find her very Archives there,
Her ancient Stattutes, in their first dessign,
Prerogative, and Priviledge to joyn,
The perfect draught of all-preserving Law,
(Which, whilst unbyast hands cou'd round us draw,
Rebel, nor Tyrant, cou'd encroach,
Not that aspire, nor this extend too much;   60
None, cou'd beyond his happy Limmit goe,
Not man deprav'd, nor Demon from below
Cou'd leap the hallow'd bound, or passe the magick Line)
Well did we in our far applauded Kent,
Whilst Pious, Wise, Heroick, and refin'd,
Whilst these strong Rayes, of our old Vertue shin'd,
Make him our choice, the Whole to represent;
The worthyest pattern of the publick Mind.
Who, when alas! we more Fanatick grew,
A heavyer Immage of our Country drew   70
(Like to a fault, in every altered part)
A rough ill wrought Dessign, a work of Flemish Art.

4

Those, whom a curious search had led
Where the fam'd Tiber, from his plenteous bed
Such frequent Treasures does unfold,
As down his Streames since Cæsars days have roled
T'ubraid new Rome, with wonders of the old,
With him their great Ideas, might renew;
Enlighten'd more, and more amaz'd

Then when at first (with unexperienced view)   80
On those stupenduous Works, they (lesse assisted) **gaz'd**
With Him, who rested not alone
In Arts, that (more then did the fabl'd fire)
Give Painting breath, and do with life inspire
The new created Rock, the Man of pollish'd Stone;
But justly weigh'd (in his capacious mind)
Through ev'ry Age, her past, and present state,
What rais'd those Arts, what made Rome once so great,
And by what failing steps, now ruin'd, and declin'd;
All useful knowledge, thence he brought,   90
And 'gainst their dull, mistaken maxims, taught
(Let the constrain'd, severe Italian see)
A man dessign'd for Wisdom's last degree
Might wear an open face, with a behaviour free.

5

The soften'd Courtier, might in him discern
(What to himself, 't'had cost much pains to learn,
And was att last, but with dissembling worn)
A pleasing, and a sweet Adresse,
Beyond what Affectation, can expresse,
Good breeding lesse acquir'd, then with his temper born.
So was he vers'd, in that allusive Art   101
Which dying Israel, did the first impart,
(When he the Royal Lyon did bestow
On Him, from whom all sovereign Rule shou'd flow,
Rightly dispos'd the Wolf, and loosen'd Hind,
And Blazon'd every coat, he to each **Tribe** assign'd.)
That unto Him, all Families were known;
Their distant branches, and their wide extent,
Their Ancient rise, or more renown'd descent;
Modestly Silent, only of his own,   110
But Silence, cou'd not that Extraction wrong,
Which all besides confess'd, which Kent has born so long.

6

With Him, we the Traditions loose,
Of great, and of Illustrious Men,
Which his Discourse, reviv'd to us again.
(Their unrecorded Graces, did disclose,
Their moving Gestures, their engaging looks,
Of life, the ornamental parts;
The powerfull spells, that influence our hearts,
Their secret motives, and their apt replies,   120
Which ignorance, or brevity denies
To be at large enrowl'd, or register'd in Books)
With Him they fell, though many years before,
The World might their departed breath deplore,
'Tis now, they to Oblivion are resign'd,
Or some short page of History confin'd,
'Tis now they cease to live, and now, they are no more.
So nicely cou'd he all retain,
Of such a memory possest,
So undisturb'd might every subject rest,   130
Or range that ample store-house of the brain,
Where ancient learning early was convey'd,
The solid, and the usefull ground
Where all the modern was profusely found,
Where, what our own, or neighb'ring Witts cou'd write,
What his yett clearer thoughts, cou'd to themselves
    endite,
Was in such beauteous order iaid,
As made the Symetrie entire,
As did the whole, harmoniously inspire,
Whilst all, was in the propperest terms expresst,   140
When to our pleas'd attention still made known,
In chosen words, that best adorn'd his own,
Or in the numerous Tongues, of various Countrys
    dresst.

7

How, had we su'd so great a Life to save
From yet descending to th' unactive Grave;
How, had the loud united Prayers
Of that best Church, the object of his cares,
(The object of his still a waken'd thought,
For which so well he spoke, so well his Father wrote)
Imploring at the Throne above   150
With unresisted force, for his continnuance strove;
Had not wise Heaven (our clamours to prevent)
So secretly the fatal message sent,
(Bid the light Essense his swift wings display,
Nor his Commission to survey,
'Till passt the bounds of all th' Angellick Host,
Distant alike, from our benighted Coast,
Till sail'd into the midd'st of the Etherial way)
Least, that if either World, shou'd know
What sadly was decreed, for ours below,   160
(In favour of the happyer Skies.)
Some pious heat might grow,
Some holy strife might rise,
The Church Triumphant, to encrease her throng,
Might urge, that he had stay'd too long,
Whilst the afflicted Militant, might plead
Of such support, her more incessant need,
Repeat her passt distresse, and doubts of future woe.
Least that Himself, had in a streight been known,
Strugg'ling betwixt our Interest, and his own,   170
For whom 'twas easily resolv'd.
The better choice, to be with haste disolv'd;
Yett Charity prevailing in the strife,
For us, he might have ask'd a longer Life,
Rightly to act, in his appointed Place,
(Of Freedom mindfull, and that generous Race

Which the (too pow'full) Norman once withstood,
Beneath the covert of a moving Wood)
Unconquer'd still, 't'have kept his native Land,
Help'd to disperse her Cares, and make her fears disband.

8

Such, were His Actions; such, his just Dessigns;   181
But far too weak, are these imperfect Lines,
(Th' unskill'd attempts of an inferiour Muse)
To paint a Mind, so exquisitely bright;
To sett such Vertues, in their noblest light,
Or in our anxious greif, pathetick thoughts infuse.
   No lesse Applause, no lesse exalted Verse,
Then once adorn'd our boasted Sydney's Hearse,
Shou'd to his Caracter, do equal right;
Shou'd of this second Astrophel, endite,
"As much the Poets Friend, as much the Worlds delight."

ENQUIRY AFTER PEACE

A Fragment

Peace ! where art thou to be found?
Where, in all the spacious Round,
May thy Footsteps be pursu'd?
Where may thy calm Seats be view'd?
On some Mountain dost thou lie,
Serenely near the ambient Sky,
Smiling at the Clouds below,
Where rough Storms and Tempests grow?
Or, in some retired Plain,
Undisturb'd dost thou remain?   10
Where no angry Whirlwinds pass,
Where no Floods oppress the Grass.
High above, or deep below,

Fain I thy Retreat wou'd know.
Fain I thee *alone* wou'd find,
Balm to my o'er-weary'd Mind.
Since what here the World enjoys,
Or our Passions most employs,
Peace opposes, or destroys.
Pleasure's a tumultuous thing,   20
Busy still, and still on Wing;
Flying swift, from place to place,
Darting from each beauteous Face;
From each strongly mingled Bowl
Through th'inflam'd and restless Soul.
Sov'reign Pow'r who fondly craves,
But himself to Pomp enslaves;
Stands the Envy of Mankind,
Peace, in vain, attempts to find.
Thirst of Wealth no Quiet knows,   30
But near the Death-bed fiercer grows;
Wounding Men with secret Stings,
For Evils it on Others brings.
War who not discreetly shuns,
Thorough Life the Gauntlet runs.
Swords, and Pikes, and Waves, and Flames,
Each their Stroke against him aims.
  Love (if such a thing there be)
Is all Despair, or Extasie.
Poetry's the feav'rish Fit,   40
Th' o'erflowing of unbounded Wit. &c.

THE PETITION FOR AN ABSOLUTE RETREAT

*Inscribed to the Right Honble Catharine Countess of Thanet,
mention'd in the Poem under the Name of Arminda*

Give me O indulgent Fate!
Give me yet, before I Dye,

A sweet, but absolute Retreat,⌐
'Mongst Paths so lost, and Trees so high,
That the World may ne'er invade,
Through such Windings and such Shade,
My unshaken Liberty.

No Intruders thither come!
Who visit, but to be from home;
None who their vain Moments pass,   10
Only studious of their Glass,
News, that charm to listning Ears;
That false Alarm to Hopes and Fears;
That common Theme for every Fop,
From the Statesman to the Shop,
In those Coverts ne'er be spread,
Of who's Deceas'd, or who's to Wed,
Be no Tidings thither brought,
But Silent, as a Midnight Thought,
Where the World may ne'er invade,   20
Be those Windings, and that Shade:

Courteous Fate! afford me there
A *Table* spread without my Care,
With what the neighb'ring Fields impart,
Whose Cleanliness be all it's Art,
When, of old, the Calf was drest,
(Tho' to make an Angel's Feast)
In the plain, unstudied Sauce
Nor *Treufle*, nor *Morillia* was;
Nor cou'd the mighty Patriarch's Board   30
One far-fetch'd *Ortolane* afford.
Courteous Fate, then give me there
Only plain, and wholesome Fare.
Fruits indeed (wou'd Heaven bestow)
All, that did in *Eden* grow,

All, but the *Forbidden Tree*,
Wou'd be coveted by me;
Grapes, with Juice so crouded up,
As breaking thro' the native Cup;
Figs (yet growing) candy'd o'er,   40
By the Sun's attracting Pow'r;
Cherries, with the downy Peach,
All within my easie Reach;
Whilst creeping near the humble Ground,
Shou'd the Strawberry be found
Springing wheresoe'er I stray'd,
Thro' those Windings and that Shade.

For my *Garments;* let them be
What may with the Time agree;
Warm, when *Phœbus* does retire,   50
And is ill-supply'd by Fire:
But when he renews the Year,
And verdant all the Fields appear;
Beauty every thing resumes,
Birds have dropt their Winter-Plumes;
When the Lilly full display'd,
Stands in purer White array'd,
Than that Vest, which heretofore
The Luxurious Monarch wore,
When from *Salem's* Gates he drove,   60
To the soft Retreat of Love,
Lebanon's all burnish'd House,
And the dear *Egyptian* Spouse.
Cloath me, Fate, tho' not so Gay;
Cloath me light, and fresh as *May:*
In the Fountains let me view
All my Habit cheap and new;
Such as, when sweet *Zephyrs* fly,

With their Motions may comply;
Gently waving, to express   70
Unaffected Carelesness:
No Perfumes have there a Part,
Borrow'd from the *Chymists* Art;
But such as rise from flow'ry Beds,
Or the falling *Jasmin* Sheds!
'Twas the Odour of the Field,
Esau's rural Coat did yield,
That inspir'd his Father's Pray'r,
For Blessings of the Earth and Air:
Of Gums, or Pouders had it smelt;   80
The Supplanter, then unfelt,
Easily had been descry'd,
For One that did in Tents abide;
For some beauteous Handmaids Joy,
And his Mother's darling Boy.
Let me then no Fragrance wear,
But what the Winds from Gardens bear,
In such kind, surprizing Gales,
As gather'd from *Fidentia's* Vales,
All the Flowers that in them grew;   90
Which intermixing, as they flew,
In wreathen Garlands dropt agen,
On *Lucullus*, and his Men;
Who, chear'd by the victorious Sight,
Trebl'd Numbers put to Flight.
Let me, when I must be fine,
In such natural Colours shine;
Wove, and painted by the Sun,
Whose resplendent Rays to shun,
When they do too fiercely beat,   100
Let me find some close Retreat,
Where they have no Passage made,
Thro' those Windings, and that Shade.

Give me there (since Heaven has shown
It was not Good to be alone)
A Partner suited to my Mind,
Solitary, pleas'd and kind;
Who, partially, may something see
Preferr'd to all the World in me;
Slighting, by my humble Side,   110
Fame and Splendor, Wealth and Pride.
When but Two the Earth possest,
'Twas their happiest Days, and best;
They by Bus'ness, nor by Wars,
They by no Domestick Cares,
From each other e'er were drawn,
But in some Grove, or flow'ry Lawn,
Spent the swiftly flying Time,
Spent their own, and Nature's Prime,
In Love; that only Passion given   120
To perfect Man, whilst Friends with Heaven.
Rage, and Jealousie, and Hate,
Transports of his fallen State,
(When by *Satan's* Wiles betray'd)
Fly those Windings, and that Shade!

Thus from Crouds, and Noise remov'd,
Let each Moment be improv'd;
Every Object still produce,
Thoughts of Pleasure, and of Use:
When some River slides away,   130
To encrease the boundless Sea;
Think we then, how Time do's haste,
To grow Eternity at last,
By the Willows, on the Banks,
Gather'd into social Ranks,
Playing with the gentle Winds,

Strait the Boughs, and smooth the Rinds,
Moist each Fibre, and each Top,
Wearing a luxurious Crop,
Let the time of Youth be shown,   140
The time alas! too soon outgrown;
Whilst a lonely stubborn Oak,
Which no Breezes can provoke,
No less Gusts persuade to move,
Than those, which in a Whirlwind drove,
Spoil'd the old Fraternal Feast,
And left alive but one poor Guest;
Rivell'd the distorted Trunk,
Sapless Limbs all bent, and shrunk,
Sadly does the Time presage,   150
Of our too near approaching Age.
When a helpless Vine is found,
Unsupported on the Ground,
Careless all the Branches spread,
Subject to each haughty Tread,
Bearing neither Leaves, nor Fruit,
Living only in the Root;
Back reflecting let me say,
So the sad *Ardelia* lay;
Blasted by a Storm of Fate,   160
Felt, thro' all the *British* State;
Fall'n, neglected, lost, forgot,
Dark Oblivion all her Lot;
Faded till *Arminda's* Love,
(Guided by the Pow'rs above)
Warm'd anew her drooping Heart,
And Life diffus'd thro' every Part;
Mixing Words, in wise Discourse,
Of such Weight and wond'rous Force,
As could all her Sorrows charm,   170

And transitory Ills disarm;
Chearing the delightful Day,
When dispos'd to be more Gay,
With Wit, from an unmeasured Store,
To Woman ne'er allow'd before.
What Nature, or refining Art,
All that Fortune cou'd impart,
Heaven did to *Arminda* send;
Then gave her for *Ardelia's* Friend:
To her Cares the Cordial drop,   180
Which else had overflow'd the Cup.
So, when once the Son of *Jess*,
Every Anguish did oppress,
Hunted by all kinds of Ills,
Like a *Partridge* on the Hills;
Trains were laid to catch his Life,
Baited with a Royal Wife,
From his House, and Country torn,
Made a Heathen Prince's Scorn;
Fate, to answer all these Harms,   190
Threw a *Friend* into his Arms.
Friendship still has been design'd,
The Support of Human-kind;
The safe Delight, the useful Bliss,
The next World's Happiness, and this.
Give then, O indulgent Fate!
Give a Friend in that Retreat
(Tho' withdrawn from all the rest)
Still a Clue, to reach my Breast.
Let a Friend be still convey'd   200
Thro' those Windings, and that Shade!

    Where, may I remain secure,
Waste, in humble Joys and pure,

A Life, that can no Envy yield;
Want of Affluence my Shield.
Thus, had *Crassus* been content,
When from *Marius* Rage he went,
With the Seat that Fortune gave,
The commodious ample Cave,
Form'd, in a divided Rock, 210
By some mighty Earthquake's Shock,
Into Rooms of every Size,
Fair, as Art cou'd e'er devise,
Leaving, in the marble Roof,
('Gainst all Storms and Tempests proof)
Only Passage for the Light,
To refresh the chearful Sight,
Whilst Three Sharers in his Fate,
On th' Escape with Joy dilate,
Beds of Moss their Bodies bore, 220
Canopy'd with Ivy o'er;
Rising Springs, that round them play'd,
O'er the native Pavement stray'd;
When the Hour arriv'd to Dine,
Various Meats, and sprightly Wine,
On some neighb'ring Cliff they spy'd;
Every Day a-new supply'd
By a Friend's entrusted Care;
Had He still continu'd there,
Made that lonely wond'rous Cave 230
Both his Palace, and his Grave;
Peace and Rest he might have found,
(Peace and Rest are under Ground)
Nor have been in that Retreat,
Fam'd for a Proverbial Fate;
In pursuit of Wealth been caught,
And punish'd with a golden Draught.

Nor had He, who Crowds cou'd blind,
Whisp'ring with a snowy Hind,
Made 'em think that from above,   240
(Like the great Impostor's Dove)
Tydings to his Ears she brought,
Rules by which he march'd and fought,
After *Spain* he had o'er-run,
Cities sack'd, and Battles won,
Drove *Rome's* Consuls from the Field,
Made her darling *Pompey* yield,
At a fatal, treacherous Feast,
Felt a Dagger in his Breast;
Had he his once-pleasing Thought   250
Of Solitude to Practice brought;
Had no wild Ambition sway'd;
In those Islands had he stay'd,
Justly call'd the Seats of Rest,
Truly Fortunate, and Blest,
By the ancient Poets giv'n
As their best discover'd Heav'n.
Let me then, indulgent Fate!
Let me still, in my Retreat,
From all roving Thoughts be freed,   260
Or Aims, that may Contention breed:
Nor be my Endeavours led
By Goods, that perish with the Dead!
Fitly might the Life of Man
Be indeed esteem'd a Span,
If the present Moment were
Of Delight his only Share;
If no other Joys he knew
Than what round about him grew:
But as those, who Stars wou'd trace   270
From a subterranean Place,

Through some Engine lift their Eyes
To the outward, glorious Skies;
So th' immortal Spirit may,
When descended to our Clay,
From a rightly govern'd Frame
View the Height, from whence she came;
To her Paradise be caught,
And things unutterable taught.
Give me then, in that Retreat,   280
Give me, O indulgent Fate!
For all Pleasures left behind,
Contemplations of the Mind.
Let the Fair, the Gay, the Vain
Courtship and Applause obtain;
Let th' Ambitious rule the Earth;
Let the giddy Fool have Mirth;
Give the Epicure his Dish,
Ev'ry one their sev'ral Wish;
Whilst my Transports I employ   290
On that more extensive Joy,
When all Heaven shall be survey'd
From those Windings and that Shade.

TO THE Rᵗ HONᵇˡᵉ THE LADY C. TUFTON

*Upon Addressing to me the first letter that ever she writt at the
age of ——*

To write in Verse has been my pleasing choice
When great Arminda's kindnesse urg'd my voice
Or Madam when in softer Notes I sung
The sweet Serena beautifull and yong
Whil'st euery Muse did chearfully attend
And lent their aid Serena to commend
To speak what in that tender age became
Your blooming Beauty then your cheifest Fame.

Now to secure me from your skillfull sight
In borrow'd caracters disguis'd I write   10
Nor dare my hand or meaner stile expose
Without a Verse, aw'd by your smoother Prose.
But shelter'd in an Art unlearn'd as yett
Take this aduantage of your growing witt,
To trust to Numbers e're you know their faults
The strange delight of your Ardelia's thoughts.
When I with sweet surprise that Letter view'd
Which to myself such welcome favour shew'd
Who yett cou'd scarcely take itt for a truth
That such perfection came from so much youth   20
And that Arminda shou'd not only give
Those Graces to her Race which in her liue
But thus deriues her ornamental parts
Whil'st you inheritt her acquired Arts
And from you Madam now we look to see
Lines fine and finish'd to the same degree
As those Her favour of't conferr's on mee.
Yours too apply'd to me do also seem
To spring from the rich stock of her esteem
As if all those her wisdom condescends   30
To make her own must be Serena's Friends.
And by such gentle and engaging bands
Resign their hearts to your alluring hands.
Mine I submitt but great and louely Maid!
Remember when that Tribute I haue paid
That not your Station nor each ripen'd Charm
Th' admiring world which shall about you swarm,
The gifts of Fortune equal to your Birth,
My sinking Spirits or your prosperous Mirth,
Nor the vast distance betwixt Youth and Age,   40
Must from this happy kindnesse disengage.
So loues Arminda where she once has lou'd,

So your great Father whom her charms had mou'd
Has this to all his steadfast virtues joyn'd
That still that Loue adorns his constant mind.
Your Friendship Madam now your Pen declares
In sense and caracters beyond your years
Which first dear pledge shall in my hand remain
A lasting Honour whil'st I life retain
Whose utmost Date shall find you still possest   50
Of what those Lines haue grafted in my breast
Whil'st none that your Ardelia cou'd command
Ere fill'd my paper or employ'd my hand
To such advantage as these closing few
Owning what is so rightfully their due
My self a servant to the Tuftons name
And sharer in their Joyes for your encreasing Fame.

A POEM FOR THE BIRTH-DAY OF THE RIGHT HON^{BLE} THE LADY CATHARINE TUFTON

Occasion'd by sight of some Verses upon that Subject for the preceding Year, compos'd by no Eminent Hand

'Tis fit SERENA shou'd be sung.
High-born SERENA, Fair and Young,
Shou'd be of ev'ry Muse and Voice
The pleasing, and applauded Choice.
But as the Meanest of the Show
Do First in all Processions go:
So, let my Steps pursue that Swain
The humblest of th' inspired Train;
Whose well-meant Verse did just appear,
To lead on the preceding Year: 10
So let my Pen, the next in Fame,
Now wait on fair SERENA's Name;
The second Tribute gladly pay,
And hail this blest returning Day.

But let it not attempt to raise
Or rightly speak Serena's Praise:
Since with more ease we might declare
How Great her Predecessors were;
How Great that more distinguish'd Peer,
To whom she owes her Being here;   20
In whom our *Britain* lets us see
What once they were, and still shou'd be;
As, when the earliest Race was drown'd,
Some Patterns, from amongst them found,
Were kept to shew succeeding Times
Their Excellence without their Crimes:
More easily we might express
What Vertues do her Mother dress;
What does *her* Form and Mind adorn,
Of whom th' engaging Nymph was born;   30
What Piety, what generous Love,
Does the enlarged Bosom move
Of Her, whose Fav'rite she appears,
Who more than as a Niece endears.
Such full Perfections obvious lie,
And strike, at first, a Poet's Eye.
Deep Lines of Honour all can hit,
Or mark out a superior Wit;
Consummate Goodness all can show,
And where such Graces shine below: 40
But the more tender Strokes to trace,
T' express the Promise of a Face,
When but the Dawnings of the Mind
We from an Air unripen'd find;
Which alt'ring, as new Moments rise,
The Pen or Pencil's Art defies;
When Flesh and Blood in Youth appears,
Polish'd like what our Marble wears;

Fresh as that Shade of op'ning Green,
Which first upon our Groves is seen;   50
Enliven'd by a harmless Fire,
And brighten'd by each gay Desire;
These nicer Touches wou'd demand
A *Cowley's* or a *Waller's* Hand,
T'explain, with undisputed Art,
What 'tis affects th'enlighten'd Heart,
When ev'ry darker Thought gives way,
Whilst blooming Beauty we survey;
To shew how All, that's soft and sweet,
Does in the fair SERENA meet;   60
To tell us, with a sure Presage, .
The Charms of her maturer Age.
When *Hothfeild* shall (as heretofore
From its far-sought and virtuous Store
It Families of great Renown
Did with illustrious Hymens crown)
When *Hothfeild* shall such Treasure know,
As fair SERENA to bestow:
Then shou'd some Muse of loftier Wing
The Triumphs of that Season sing;   70
Describe the Pains, the Hopes, the Fears
Of noble Youths, th'ambitious Cares
Of Fathers, the long-fram'd Design,
To add such Splendour to their Line,
Whilst all shall strive for such a Bride
So Educated, and Ally'd.

ON THE LORD DUNDEE

It must not be; nor can the grave
Graham, your mighty acts conceal;
Oblivion, never can prevail
Against the Loyal, and the brave.

Fame, shall the gloomy Tyrant disposess,
And bear you, on her golden wings,
You, that have borne the cause of Kings
To the most distant parts, of the wide universe.
All, the yong Grecian Conquerer gain'd,
All, that his own, he e're could rate,   10
In spite of accedents, or fate,
Already is by you obtain'd.
A treacherous hand his life unty'd;
And meaner men, his world devide;
But Fame, like you, he grasp'd, and after life, retain'd.

Already, in your name, was shown
Deeds, second only to your own.
But, as if to your race 'twere due,
Due, as succession to our Kings,
Still to be made for glorious things,   20
Montrose's spirit's doubl'd upon you.
No sooner can the Nation want,
But Fate, does still a Graham grant;
And storms, and tumults seems to raise
To build them Pyramids of praise.
O Scotland! never more, be thou
A cold, unfruitfull Country nam'd,
But, be for heat, and product fam'd;
Not such as answers to the plow,
But such, as Heroes can produce,   30
For thine, and for thy Monark's use.
To nobler ends, thou doest thy heat bestow,
Not to make corn, and wine, but valiant wariers grow.

No land, but did to you impart
Dundee, what excellent she held,
To fitt you for the Court, or feild.
France, lent you all her gracefull arts,

That who e're saw you, wou'd have thought
A frame so fine, so nicely wrought,
Was only made to conquer hearts.   40
Courage, your native country gave,
With such a soul, as soon shou'd take
The best impressions Art could make:
Whilst with her sister, England joyn'd
With learning to enrich your mind.
Italy made you wise, and grave,
For Strattagem, and council fitt,
Heighten'd your conduct, and your witt,
Inspir'd her soft poetick fires,
And gave you o're the muses land   50
Such vast, such absolute command,
As suited your refin'd desires.
So was you made to be belov'd,
So born, so bred, and so improv'd,
That when Mars arm'd you, for wars fatal toile,
Venus, stood sadly by, and sweetly wept the while.

Unequal numbers, cou'd not make you fear,
Unequal numbers, might oppresse,
But cou'd not make your courage lesse.
Before your troops, thrice to your foes   60
One single life, you did expose;
Oh! had you been of that, as sure
As Fame, and Conquest to procure!
But greedy Death, envious that they,
Alone, shou'd share the glorious day,
Resolv'd, to make his part appear
In pomp, and solemn trophies drest,
Magnificent above the rest,
And make the mighty cheif, become his noble Prey.
    So great Gustavus, tho' with Conquest crown'd,   70

Had Cypresse, with his Lawrells wound,
And slept like Graham, on the field he wonn,
When the great businesse of the day, was done.

THE CHANGE

Poor *River*, now thou'rt almost dry,
What Nymph, or Swain, will near thee lie?
Since brought, alas! to sad Decay,
What Flocks, or Herds, will near thee stay?
The *Swans*, that sought thee in thy Pride,
Now on new Streams forgetful ride:
And *Fish*, that in thy Bosom lay,
Chuse in more prosp'rous Floods to play.
All leave thee, now thy Ebb appears,
To waste thy sad Remains in Tears;   10
Nor will thy mournful Murmurs heed.
Fly, wretched Stream, with all thy speed,
Amongst those solid Rocks thy Griefs bestow;
For Friends, like those alas! thou ne'er did'st know.

And thou, poor *Sun!* that sat'st on high;
But late, the Splendour of the Sky;
What Flow'r tho' by thy Influence born,
Now Clouds prevail, will tow'rds thee turn?
Now Darkness sits upon thy Brow,
What *Persian* Votary will bow?   20
What River will her Smiles reflect,
Now that no Beams thou can'st direct?
By watry Vapours overcast,
Who thinks upon thy Glories past?
If present Light, nor Heat we get,
Unheeded thou may'st rise, and set.
Not all the past can one Adorer keep,
Fall, wretched Sun, to the more faithful Deep.

Nor do thou, lofty *Structure!* boast,
Since undermin'd by Time and Frost: 30
Since thou canst no Reception give,
In untrod Meadows thou may'st live.
None from his ready Road will turn,
With thee thy wretched Change to mourn.
Not the soft Nights, or chearful Days
Thou hast bestow'd, can give thee Praise.
No lusty Tree that near thee grows,
(Tho' it beneath thy Shelter rose)
Will to thy Age a Staff become.
Fall, wretched *Building!* to thy Tomb.   40
Thou, and thy painted Roofs, in Ruin mixt,
Fall to the Earth, for That alone is fixt.

The same, poor *Man*, the same must be
Thy Fate, now *Fortune* frowns on thee.
Her Favour ev'ry one pursues,
And losing Her, thou all must lose.
No Love, sown in thy prosp'rous Days,
Can Fruit in this cold Season raise:
No Benefit, by thee conferr'd,
Can in this time of Storms be heard.   50
All from thy troubl'd Waters run;
Thy stooping Fabrick all Men shun.
All do thy clouded Looks decline,
As if thou ne'er did'st on them shine.
O wretched Man! to other World's repair;
For *Faith* and *Gratitude* are only there.

UPON THE DEATH OF KING JAMES THE SECOND

1

If the Possession of Imperial sway
Thou hads't by Death unhappy Prince resign'd

And to a mournfull successour made way
Whilst All was uncontested, All combin'd,
How had the streets, how had the Palace rung,
In praise of thy acknowledg'd Worth;
What had our num'rous Writers then broaght forth,
What melancholly Dirges had they sung,
What weeping Elegy's prepar'd,
If not from loyal grief, yett to obtain reward.   10
Thus is that Gift (which Heauen did sure bestow
To elevate the hearts of Men
And lead them to those Blissfull seats agen
Whence all harmonious Sounds and lofty Numbers
      flow)
Now, Mammon, turn'd thy slave to dig thy Mines below.

2

But Royal James though none shall pay this Verse
Bred in a Land not honour'd with thy Herse,
But Royal James who never shalt return
To cheer those Hearts which did thy sorrows mourn,
Who never shalt the Woes, the Wants, repair   20
Which for thy sake have been thy Followers share,
Though with thy latest Breath such Prospects fled
And all who saw thee Dye now wish themselves as dead,
Yett shall a free disinterested Muse
In chosen Lines perform that Task
Which does an abler Writer ask
But abler Writers will the Work refuse,
And where, alas 'twill but the Feather cost
The noblest Subjects for the Pen are lost.

3

Else how wou'd the Poetick crew,   30
Those publick Heralds of Immortal Fame
Unto the present Times renew

All which the Past did with such wonder view
And down to future Ages wou'd Proclaim
What future Ages scarse cou'd take for true
When they describ'd Thee on the Stage of War
Earlier than Cæsar far
And made Thee ere thy tenth accomplish'd year
Undaunted in the Lists appear
And martial Light'nings see and Martial Thunders
    hear   40
Which Cæsar never prov'd nor his tenth Legion knew.

4

Next had they shown Thee in the Galick Host
Performing such stupenduous Things
As influenc'd the Fates of Kings
Whil'st the best General which the World cou'd boast
Thought ready to resign his Breath
Assur'd his Troops they shou'd not feel his Death
If that Illustrious York wou'd fill th' important Post.
Thus wou'd they Thy exalted valour raise
By Turene form'd, and stamp'd with Turene's praise   50
O're Seas and Lands (as Seas and Lands have seen
Thee greatly Brave) that Fame had sounded been
Which to the skies was borne in Opdam's fiery blaze.
High o're th' Invading Fleet his vessel rose
By Thy prevailing Batteries driven
Which like a streaming Meteor dreadfull shows
Now threat'ning from th' illuminated Air
To all beneath itt Ruine and Dispair
As Heathen Witts had said to haue inkindl'd Heaven
Till down at length the Plague portended came   60
And wrought such various Deaths that some must want
    a name.
Oh mighty Prince, for here thy dark'ned Lott

Must be in this Reverse of Sight forgott
All must be Glorious whilst thy Youth we trace
Whilst shelt'ring Waves shall Brittish Shores embrace
Or whilst our Reccords shall haue place
Where thy Rewards and Attributes are such
As show noe Gratitude was thought too much
For keeping England then, superiour to the Dutch.
Whil'st These shall last no Envy shall deface   70
Of that Tryumphant Day th' Aduantage and the Grace.

5

Yett even in Youth War n'er was thy Delight
Nor Led by Thee but in the Nations right
Which well Asserted and the souldier paid
The Honour rescu'd and the gainfull Trade
The solid Buisnesse wisely done
And each who shar'd the Generous Cause
Possess'd too of the share that He had won
The warrantable Spoiles the Fauour and Applause
Again Commissions ceas'd and Arms apart were laid. 80
So good Dictators fought for ancient Rome
And brought not single Fame, but Peace and Plenty
          Home
Nor bred new Strifes to keep that ample sway
But to the Plough return'd cou'd chearfully Obey.
So had our Charles (whilst Reigning) cause to own
(The Pow'er recalled which his great Seal had shown)
The readyest subject stood the next his Throne.
Oh You who under James in fight were try'd,
Who strove successfull by that Prince's side,
Who've seen Him brave the Cannons angry breath   90
For Brittan's Interest and Renown
As if He had courted rather then her Crown
(Which was His right of birth) to merit itt by Death

Oh You who in His frequent Dangers stood
And sought to fence them at th' expence of Blood
Now lett your Teares a heavyer Tribute pay,
Give the becoming Sorrow way
Nor bring bad Paralells upon the Times
By seeking through mistaken Feares
To curb your Sighs or to conceal your Teares.   100
Twas but in Nero's dayes that Sighs and Teares were
    crimes.

6

*   *   *   *   *   *   *   *   *

(As all must do) at Death's cold feet the Crown
Him had you sure Enroll'd and justly with the Best
Then Alfred's Piety had form'd his Praise
His thoughtfull Nights compar'd and His assiduous
    Dayes.
Then had that Providential care
Which kept the Treasury full yett not the subject
    bare
Unto our frugal Henry's been preferr'd
Applauses of that Temp'rance had we heard
By whose Example had excluded been   110
What even Eliza's dayes brought in
The wasting foul Excesse miscall'd Good-natured Sin.

*   *   *   *   *   *   *   *   *

7

Weep ye Attendants who compos'd his Traine
And no Observance spent in vain
Nor ever with uneasy Feares
Contracted needful Debts and doubted your Arrears
All whom His Justice or his Bounty fed
Now gratefull weep and mix the silent Dew
(Which none will e're suspect untrue)

With your embitter'd Draughts and since diminish'd
      Bread   120
You who subordinate in Publick Cares
For his Inspection modell'd the Affaires
Remember still how easy Your Accesse
No Pleasures kept him from your sight
No late Debauch no Revel of the Night
No distant slothfull Seat e're serv'd as a Recesse.
Open to all but when the Seaman came
Known by his Face and greeted by his Name
Peculiar Smiles and Praises did impart
To all his Prowesse and Desert   130
All had his willing Hand, the Seaman had his Heart
He born an Islander by Nature knew
Her wooden walls her strength, her Guard the Naval
      Crew.

8

But draw the Vaile nor seek to paint that Grief
Which knows no Bounds nor meditates Relief
Maria weeps with unexhausted Teares
No Look that Beauteous Face but sorrow wears
And in those Eyes where Majesty was seen
To warn Admirers and Declare the Queen
Now only Reigns th' incurable Distresse   140
Which Royal James thy faithfull Consort shows
Who by Her different Grief, does too Confesse
That now alas She the Distinction knows
'Twixt Weeping for thy Losse or with Thee for thy Woes
No more the Diadem attracts Her sight
Held but by Reflection Bright
Thoughts of returning Glory move no more
Nor can She e're Receive what She Possess't before
A Grave is All She with Her James can share
And were itt not for What He left Her Care   150

How soon wou'd She Descend and be His Consort There
Pleas'd better in that Fourth and last Remove
Securely by thy unmolested side
From Life itts self an Exile to abide
Then in th' experienc'd former Three
Which yett she well sustain'd Accompanied by Thee
Strong are the Bands of Death, but stronger those of
    Love.

9

Oh Brittan take this Wish before we cease
May Rightfull Kings procure Thee lasting Peace
And having Rul'd Thee to thy Own desire   160
On thy Maternal Bosome late Expire
Clos'd in that Earth, where they had Reign'd before
Till States and Monarchies shall be no more
Since in the Day of unapealing Doom
Or King or Kingdom must Declare
What the sad Chance or weighty Causes were
That forc'd Them to Arise from out a Forrain Tomb.
Oh Brittan may Thy Days to come be fair
And All who shall intend thy Good
Be reverendly Heard and rightly Understood   170
May no Intestine Broiles thy Entrailles Tare
No Fields in Thee be fought or Nam'd anew by Blood
May all who Shield Thee due Applauses have
Whilst for my self like solitary men
Devoted only to the Pen
I but a safe Retreat amidst Thee Crave
Below th' ambitious World and just above my Grave.

VERSES

Written under the King of Sweden's Picture

Observe this Piece, which to our Sight does bring
The fittest Posture for the *Swedish* King;

(Encompass'd, as we think, with Armies round,
Tho' not express'd within this narrow Bound)
Who, whilst his warlike and extended Hand
Directs the foremost Ranks to Charge or Stand,
Reverts his Face, lest That, so Fair and Young,
Should call in doubt the Orders of his Tongue:
Whilst the excited, and embolden'd Rear
Such Youth beholding, and such Features there,
Devote their plainer Forms, and are asham'd to Fear.
Thus! ev'ry Action, ev'ry Grace of thine,
O latest Son of Fame, Son of *Gustavus* Line!
Affects thy Troops, with all that can inspire
A blooming Sweetness, and a martial Fire,
Fatal to none, but thy invading Foe.
So Lightnings, which to all their Brightness shew,
Strike but the Man alone, who has provok'd the Blow.

THE CIRCUIT OF APPOLLO

Appollo as lately a Circuit he made,
Throo' the lands of the Muses when Kent he survey'd
And saw there that Poets were not very common,
But most that pretended to Verse, were the Women
Resolv'd to encourage, the few that he found,
And she that writt best, with a wreath shou'd be crown'd.
A summons sent out, was obey'd but by four,
When Phebus, afflicted, to meet with no more,
And standing, where sadly, he now might descry,
From the banks of the Stoure the desolate Wye,   10
He lamented for Behn o're that place of her birth,
And said amongst Femens was not on the earth
Her superiour in fancy, in language, or witt,
Yett own'd that a little too loosly she writt;
Since the art of the Muse is to stirr up soft thoughts,
Yett to make all hearts beat, without blushes, or faults,

But now to proceed, and their merritts to know,
Before he on any, the Bay's wou'd bestow,
He order'd them each in their several way,
To show him their papers, to sing, or to say,   20
What 'ere they thought best, their pretention's might
          prove,
When Alinda, began, with a song upon Love.
So easy the Verse, yett compos'd with such art,
That not one expression fell short of the heart;
Apollo himself, did their influence obey,
He catch'd up his Lyre, and a part he wou'd play,
Declaring, no harmony else, cou'd be found,
Fitt to wait upon words, of so moving a sound.
The Wreath, he reach'd out, to have plac'd on her head,
If Laura not quickly a paper had read,   30
Wherin She Orinda has praised so high,
He own'd itt had reach'd him, while yett in the sky,
That he thought with himself, when itt first struck his
          ear,   •
Who e're cou'd write that, ought the Laurel to wear.
Betwixt them he stood, in a musing suspence,
Till Valeria withdrew him a little from thence,
And told him, as soon as she'd gott him aside,
Her works, by no other, but him shou'd be try'd;
Which so often he read, and with still new delight,
That Iudgment t'was thought wou'd not passe till twas
          'night;   40
Yet at length, he restor'd them, but told her withall
If she kept itt still close, he'd the Talent recall.
Ardelia, came last as expecting least praise,
Who writt for her pleasure and not for the Bays,
But yett, as occasion, or fancy should sway,
Wou'd sometimes endeavour to passe a dull day,
In composing a song, or a Scene of a Play

Not seeking for Fame, which so little does last,
That e're we can taste itt, the Pleasure is Past.
But Appollo reply'd, tho' so carelesse she seemd,   50
Yett the Bays, if her share, wou'd be highly esteem'd.

And now, he was going to make an Oration,
Had thrown by one lock, with a delicate fassion,
Upon the left foot, most genteely did stand,
Had drawn back the other, and wav'd his white hand,
When calling to mind, how the Prize alltho' given
By Paris, to her, who was fairest in Heaven,
Had pull'd on the rash, inconsiderate Boy,
The fall of his House, with the ruine of Troy,
Since in Witt, or in Beauty, itt never was heard,   60
One female cou'd yield t' have another preferr'd,
He changed his dessign, and devided his praise,
And said that they all had a right to the Bay's,
And that t'were injustice, one brow to adorn,
With a wreath, which so fittly by each might be worn.
Then smil'd to himself, and applauded his art,
Who thus nicely has acted so suttle a part,
Four Women to wheedle, but found 'em too many,
For who wou'd please all, can never please any.
In vain then, he thought itt, there longer to stay,   70
But told them, he now must go drive on the day,
Yett the case to Parnassus, shou'd soon be referr'd,
And there in a councill of Muses, be heard,
Who of their own sex, best the title might try,
Since no man upon earth, nor Himself in the sky,
Wou'd be so imprudent, so dull, or so blind,
To loose three parts in four from amongst woman kind.

AN EPISTLE

From Ardelia To Mrs. Randolph in answer to her Poem upon
Her Verses

Madam,
       till pow'rfully convinc'd by you,
I thought those Praises never were Their due,
Which I had read, or heard bestow'd by Men
On Women, that have ventur'd on the Pen.
But now must yeild (pursuaded by your stile)
That Lesbian Sapho's might all hearts beguile.
The vanquish'd Pindar, now I must beleive
Might from Corrina's Muse new Laws receive,
Since our own Age is happily possest
Of such a genius, in a Female Breast,   10
As gives us Faith for all those wonders told,
Producing New, to justify the old.
Then we'll no more submitt, but (in your name)
To Poetry renew our Ancient Claime;
Through itts retirement, we'll your worth persue,
And lead itt into Public Rule and View;
As the best Monarks, which the Romans made
Were forc'd to Thrones, from some beloved shade.
Nor, lett itt to your Verse, objected be,
That itt has stoop'd so low, to find out me,   20
Since a mean subject greater skill requires
Then one, which of itts self, high thoughts inspires.
And twas the Mantuan Poet's boasted praise,
Virgil's, who Kings and Heroes best cou'd raise,
That if to lowly Plaines, he did repair,
His Song, shou'd make 'em worth a Consull's care,
Thus, have you Madam, by your lines enhanc'd
My humble worth, and so, my fame advanc'd,
That where-so-ere that Panigerick's shown,

It stands inferiour only to your own;   30
And whilst Orinda's part you far transcend,
I proudly bear that of her glorious Friend,
Who though not equaling her lofty Witt,
Th' occasion was, of what so well she writt.
Might I the paralell yett more improve,
And gain as high a Station in your Love,
Then shou'd my Pen (directed by my heart)
Make gratefull Nature, speak the words of Art,
Since Friendship, like Devotion clears the mind,
Where every thought, is heighten'd and refin'd.   4O
Had Saul alone, upon Mount Gilboa fell,
David had sung, but had not sung so well;
Describ'd th' abandon'd Sheild, and broaken Bow,
But, to the love of Jonathan we owe
The Love, which that of Women did surpasse,
Of that sweet Elegy, the mournfull grace;
The Brother Jonathan, peirc'd deeper far
Then all the Spears of that destructive war.
Thus, may your vallu'd kindnesse, raise my sence,
Who can but treat you att your own expence,   50
Nor must, untill I in that wish succeed,
E're hope to write, what's fitt for you to read,
Since upon you, itt does alone depend
To make a Poet, when you make a Friend
                              Of Madam &c.

A PROLOGUE TO DON CARLOS

Acted by Yong Ladys, An: 1696

'Twas long debated, wheither to a Play,
So known as this, which we present to-day,
A Prologue, for the Audience shou'd be writt,
To add to all the rest, th' expence of Witt;
When in this Kingdom, 'tis so hard to find,

And from such store of Mints, so little's coin'd,
That shou'd the Muses senate, dām the old,
The new, no pleasing cōmerce cou'd uphold;
Which makes us a supply, to treat you seek
From such a Bank, as time nor chance can break;   10
And Ottaway's heroick thoughts, rehearse;
Love in his Lines, and dye in his smooth Verse.
Not tire ye, with a Farce, on powder'd Beauxs,
Who like some Trees, thrive with redoubl'd blows;
And a new crop of tawdry follys bear,
After the lash, of each satirick year;
Whom Silence mortifys the surer way,
Since Beaux, unminded, only do decay.
Nor shall we greive Ladys, with fading Graces,
By any Plott, but shewing yonger faces.   20
We'll allso spare our safe return'd cōmanders,
And be as mild, as their campagn in Flanders.
Nay, tho' we'll poyson too, the Queen of Spain,
It sha'nt be long, ere she revives again.
In our design, no secret malice lyes,
And All may 'scape, that can withstand our Eyes.
But Gentlemen, Ill tell ye, least ye say
Ye were surpris'd, and vanquish'd by foul play,
Our Eyes, for conquest, are so well prepar'd,
You'd need be warn'd to stand upon your guard.   30
The Black, with unsheath'd glances, all defying,
The softer Grey, in dang'rous Ambush lying,
And on each Cheeck, the youthfull colours flying,
Which we expect, shou'd no resistance meet,
'Till every heart, lyes beating at our feet.
Now, if you'll stay, repent itt not hereafter,
When that subdu'd, you find we give no quarter;
Nor think itt hard, we put stale witt upon you,
Who shew fresh Beauty, and excuse your mony.

A POEM, OCCASION'D BY THE SIGHT OF THE 4ᵀᴴ
EPISTLE LIB. EPIST: 1. OF HORACE

*Immitated and Inscrib'd to Richard Thornhill Esq. by Mr Rowe,
who had before sent heither, another translation from Horace*

Twice in our Solitude has now appear'd
Such verse as Rome throng'd with applauders heard,
And twice, Her Horace been to us reviv'd
As prais'd and pollish'd as to them he liv'd.
The Stuff and Workman's skill so nicely shown.
We think the Words as well as thoughts his own
And Joy to see that by relenting Fate
(Which Speech confus'd) tis given thus to translate
Whilst Babel's scatter'd streames unite again
Beneath the conduct of th' industrious Pen   10
But why shou'd such a Muse as can comend
And Paralell the Virtues of a Friend
Describe from ancient Rules with modern Art
His Copious sensce each ornamental part
Mistake the softer Buisnesse of his heart
Or ask how he the too swift Hours imploys
Who late possess'd of so long courted Joys
Flyes to some still retreate and shunn's the Citty's
          noise
As He whom Poets fein t'have rul'd above
When sway'd himself by more commanding Love   20
Left his Society and Court of Gods
To stem the Hellispont and haunt the Woods
Nor to Olimpus but some lonely shade
With untrac'd steps the beauteous Prize convey'd.
   Nor be itt thought that Tragedy has place
Within the influence of Orania's face
Not he who cou'd so well our souls comand
And toutch each string with a prevailing hand

His Belvedera's or Monimia's Fate
Cou'd 'ere haue Plotted in so bless'd a State   30
(Since 'tis from our own bosome cares that flow
The moving scenes we on the World bestow)
Yett had he liv'd Orania to have seen
His Caracters had sure more perfect been
Not such as sullied in his Plays were shown
One by anothers guilt one by her own.
Tho' for Her Charms Brothers might too contest
And the best secret quitt the closest Breast.
So bright her form for whom such Numbers strove
Till the most worthy fixt her envy'd Love   40
Whilst but to him and her own sex confin'd
Are now the soft indearments of her Mind
Inspiring Joy still chearfull and att ease
(For they are allways pleas'd who allways please)
Even I who to my Heart just bounds had sett
And in my Friendship scorn'd to be coquette
Or seem indulgent to each new Adresse
Which generall Friends in comõon terms expresse
Now (by so sweet a violence compell'd)
The amplest room to kind Orania yield   50
Then is it strange the Youth a while remains
Contemplating his Blisse on silent Plaines
Lives to Himself and the selected Fair
Nor can enough of those lov'd moments spare
(If rightly I Devine) a debt to pay
Of well writt Verse (tho' none more knows the way)
Nor hardly will affoard one sprightly Line
To crown the Health still wish'd him at the Vine
Where he returning shall sustain a part
Of heighten'd Witt and of the Critticks Art   60
With Him whose Numbers to our shades extend
And Him that stoop'd our Numbers to comēend

Whose well bred Muse found something to allow
And tho' they fail'd wou'd to the Woman bow
Happy You three! happy the Race of Men!
Born to inform or to correct the Pen
To proffitts pleasures freedom and command
Whilst we beside you but as Cyphers stand
T" increase your Numbers and to swell th' account
Of your delights which from our charms amount   **70**
And sadly are by this distinction taught
That since the Fall (by our seducement wrought)
Ours is the greater losse as ours the greater fault

AN EPILOGUE TO THE TRAGEDY OF JANE SHORE

To be spoken by Mrs. Oldfield the night before the Poet's Day

The audience seems tonight so very kind,
I fancy I may freely speak my mind,
And tell you, when the author nam'd Jane Shore,
I all her glorious history run o'er,
And thought he would have shewn her on the stage,
In the first triumphs of her blooming age;
Edward in public at her feet a slave,
The jealous Queen in private left to rave;
Yet *Jane* superior still in all the strife,
For sure that mistress leads a wretched life,   **10**
Who can't insult the Keeper and the wife.
This I concluded was his right design,
To make her lavish, careless, gay and fine;
Not bring her here to mortify and whine.
I hate such parts as we have plaid today,
Before I promis'd, had I read the play,
I wou'd have staid at home, and drank my Tea.
Then why the husband shou'd at last be brought
To hear her own and aggravate her fault,

Puzzled as much my discontented thought.   20
For were I to transgress, for all the Poet,
I'll swear no friend of mine should ever know it.
But you perhaps are pleas'd to see her mended,
And so should I; had all her charms been ended.
But whilst another lover might be had,
The woman or the Poet must be mad.
There is a season, which too fast approaches,
And every list'ning beauty nearly touches;
When handsome Ladies, falling to decay,
Pass thro' new epithets to smooth the way: 30
From *fair* and *young* transportedly confess'd,
Dwindle to *fine, well fashion'd*, and *well dress'd*.
Thence as their fortitude's extremest proof,
To *well as yet;* from *well* to *well enough;*
Till having on such weak foundation stood,
Deplorably at last they sink to *good.*
Abandon'd then, 'tis time to be retir'd,
And seen no more, when not alas! admir'd.
By men indeed a better fate is known.
The pretty fellow, that has youth outgrown,   40
Who nothing knew, but how his cloaths did sit,
Transforms to a *Free-thinker* and a *Wit;*
At Operas becomes a skill'd Musician;
Ends in a partyman and politician;
Maintains some figure, while he keeps his breath,
And is a fop of consequence till death.
And so would I have had our mistress Shore
To make a figure, till she pleas'd no more.
But if you better like her present sorrow,
Pray let me see you here again to-morrow,   50
And should the house be throng'd the Poets' day,
Whate'er he makes us women do or say,
You'll not believe, that he'll go fast and pray.

TO MR. PRIOR FROM A LADY UNKNOWN

The Nymph whose Virgin-heart thy charms have taught
To cherish Love, with secret wishes fraught,
Reserv'd at first, endeavours to conceal
What She had rather die than not reveal,
No fears the Love-sick Maid can long restrain,
None read Thy verse, or hear Thee speak in vain.
Thy melting Numbers, and polite Address,
In ev'ry Fair raise passion to excess.
In either sex You never fail, we find,
To cultivate the heart, or charm the mind,
In raptures lost. I fear not your disdain,
But own I languish to possess your vein.
As a fond bird, pleas'd with the teacher's note,
Expends his life to raise his mimic throat,
His little art, exerting all he can,
Charm'd with the tune, to imitate the man:
Rudely he chants, yet labours not in vain,
By wild essays just so much song to gain,
As tempts his master to renew the strain.
Such is my verse, with equal zeal I burn,
Too happy, shou'd I meet the same return.

THE ANSWER

[*To* Pope's *Impromptu*]

Disarm'd with so genteel an air,
  The contest I give o'er;
Yet, Alexander, have a care,
  And shock the sex no more.
We rule the world our life's whole race,
  Men but assume that right;
First slaves to ev'ry tempting face,

Then martyrs to our spite.
You of one Orpheus sure have read,
  Who would like you have writ   10
Had he in London town been bred,
  And polish'd to[o] his wit;
But he poor soul thought all was well,
  And great should be his fame,
When he had left his wife in hell,
  And birds and beasts could tame.
Yet venturing then with scoffing rhimes
  The women to incense,
Resenting Heroines of those times
  Soon punished his offence.   20
And as the Hebrus roll'd his scull,
  And harp besmear'd with blood,
They clashing as the waves grew full,
  Still harmoniz'd the flood.
But you our follies gently treat,
  And spin so fine the thread,
You need not fear his aukward fate,
  The lock wo'n't cost the head.
Our admiration you command
  For all that's gone before;   30
What next we look for at your hand
  Can only raise it more.
Yet sooth the Ladies I advise
  (As me too pride has wrought,)
We're born to wit, but to be wise
  By admonitions taught.

TO MR. POPE

The muse, of ev'ry heav'nly gift allowed
To be the chief, is public, though not proud.
Widely extensive is the poet's aim,

And in each verse he draws a bill on fame.
For none have writ (whatever they pretend)
Singly to raise a patron, or a friend;
But whatsoe'er the theme or object be,
Some commendations to themselves foresee.
Then let us find in your foregoing page,
The celebrating poems of the age;   10
Nor by injurious scruples think it fit
To hide their judgments who applaud your wit.
But let their pens to yours the heralds prove,
Who strive for you as Greece for Homer strove;
Whilst he who best your poetry asserts,
Asserts his own, by sympathy of parts.
Me panegyric verse does not inspire,
Who never well can praise what I admire;
Nor in those lofty trials dare appear,
But gently drop this counsel in your ear.   20
Go on, to gain applauses by desert,
Inform the head, whilst you dissolve the heart;
Inflame the soldier with harmonious rage,
Elate the young, and gravely warn the sage;
Allure with tender verse the female race,
And give their darling passion courtly grace;
Describe the Forest still in rural strains,
With vernal sweets fresh breathing from the plains.
Your tales be easy, natural, and gay,
Nor all the poet in that part display;   ·   30
Nor let the critic there his skill unfold,
For Boccace thus, and Chaucer tales have told.
Soothe, as you only can, each diff'ring taste,
And for the future charm as in the past.
Then should the verse of ev'ry artful hand
Before your numbers eminently stand;
In you no vanity could thence be shown,

Unless, since short in beauty of your own,
Some envious scribbler might in spite declare,
That for comparison you placed them there.   40
But envy could not against you succeed,
'Tis not from friends that write, or foes that read;
Censure or praise must from ourselves proceed.

TO A FELLOW SCRIBBLER

Prithee, friend, that hedge behold:
When all we rhiming fools grow old,
That hedge our state will represent,
Who in vain flourish life have spent;
Amidst it stands a rivall'd tree
Now representing sixty three,
And like it you and I shall be.
The bare vine round about it clings
With mischievous, intangling strings,
The night shade, with a dismal flow'r,   10
Curl's o'er it, like a Lady's tower;
Or honesty with feather'd down,
Like grizled hair deforms its crown;
Luxuriant plants that o'er it spread,
Not med'cinal for heart or head,
Which serve but to amuse the sight,
Are like the nothings that we write;
Yet still 'tis thought, that tree's well plac'd,
With beauteous Eglantine imbrac'd;
But see how false appearance proves,   20
If he that honey-suckle loves;
His love the honey-suckle scorns,
Which climbs by him to reach the thorns;
The rival thorn his age derides,
And gnaws like jealousy his sides.
Then let us cease, my friend, to sing

When ever youth is on the wing,
Unless we solidly indite,
Some good infusing while we write,
Lest with our follies hung around,   30
We like that tree and hedge be found,
Grotesque and trivial, shun'd by all,
And soon forgotten when we fall.

TO Dᴿ· WALDRON

A Fellow of All Souls Colledge in Oxford, *Who in a Letter
acknowledg'd his mistake in having lefte that Society & the
Muses to follow the Practise of Phisck*

'Tis true Mirtillo 'twas a fault
T' have been by glittering proffit wrought
To quit that seat of thoughts refined
That Eden to the fruitfull mind
Where thy well nurs'd and thriving Muse
Such sweets and plenty did diffuse
Buisnesse to court thy freedoms fane
Of Life the well nam'd Hurricane
To leave th' embraces of a Friend
Which there kind Fate did often send   10
A Miser's guilty hand to hold
And feel his Pulse, to feel his Gold
Who startles att the name of thee
And in suspence 'twixt Life and Fee
How to determine seems so loth
Till by delay, he parts with both,
Whom hadd'st thou rais'd from fainting sweats
Supporting Him had propp'd new cheats
By wealth too fatally betray'd
'Twas ill resolv'd to quitt some Maid   20
Whose blooming youth and chearfull face
Expell'd contagion from each Place

A Grand-Sires latest plaints to hear
Sick only of his nintieth year
To combat with each foul disease
That can unwholsome Nature seize
The brisker aid of sprightly wine
For Sal-volatile resign
With Druggs and their mistaken force.
'Twas ill to clogg that gay discourse   30
Which here-to-fore when unconfin'd
Remov'd all sicknesse from the Mind
Whilst Table-books were richly fraught
With Witt which cost thee scarce a thought
So swift itt from occasions rose
Extemporé in Verse or Prose
Why shou'd that Herb which cur'd our spleen
When from thy Pen so fresh so green
So soft so fragrant and so yong
It in th' inliven'd Fancy sprung   40
Grow useless by o're labour'd skill
And draining through a winding still
Why shou'd thy time and sence be lost
In saving those not worth the cost
Believe me too 'tis all in vain
Believe one of the Riming Traine
'Tis vain to strive in Fate's dispite
Numbers with mony to unite
That sordid Plant we ne're cou'd raise
Within the odour of the Bays   50
Forsake then thy ill chosen toile
Return to that abandon'd soyle
Return Mirtillo to Apollo's Rules
Return to ease and to the Muses scools
Live there a Wit leave druggery to fools

TO EDWARD JENKINSON, ESQ.

a very young Gentleman, who writ a Poem on PEACE

Fair Youth! who wish the Wars may cease,
We own you better form'd for *Peace*.
Nor *Pallas* you, nor *Mars* shou'd follow;
Your Gods are *Cupid* and *Apollo;*
Who give sweet Looks, and early Rhimes,
Bespeaking Joys, and Halcyon Times.
Your Face, which *We*, as yet, may praise,
Calls for the Myrtle, and the Bays.
The Martial Crowns Fatigues demand,
And laurell'd Heroes must be tann'd;   10
A Fate, we never can allow
Shou'd reach your pleasing, polish'd Brow.
But granting what so young you've writ,
From Nature flow'd, as well as Wit;
And that indeed you *Peace* pursue,
We must begin to *Treat* with you.
We *Females*, Sir, it is I mean:
Whilst I, like BRISTOL for the QUEEN,
For all the Ladies of your Age
As Plenipo' betimes engage;   20
And as first Article declare,
You shall be Faithful as you're Fair:
No Sighs, when you shall know their Use,
Shall be discharg'd in Love's Abuse;
Nor kindling Words shall undermine,
Till you in equal Passion join.
Nor Money be alone your Aim,
Tho' you an Over-weight may claim,
And fairly build on your Desert,
If with your Person goes your Heart.   30
But when this *Barrier* I have gain'd,

And trust it will be well maintain'd;
Who knows, but some imprudent *She*
Betraying what's secur'd by me,
Shall yield thro' Verse, or stronger Charms,
To Treat anew on easier Terms?
And I be negligently told ———
You was too *Young*, and I too *Old*,
To have our distant Maxims hold.

TO MR. JERVAS

Occasion'd by the Sight of Mrs. Chetwind's Picture

This matchless Picture, *Jervas*, hide,
  Or let it stand alone;
When one does over all preside,
  The rest are vainly shown.

The meanest Figures of the Sky,
  (Though drawn with handsome Faces,)
Are, when their Goddesses are by,
  Th' attending Nymphs and Graces.

For sure, (as Cæsar chose Renown)
  'Tis better to be reckon'd,
The *Dulcinea* of some Town,
  Than in a Court, the Second.

Then, let this new *Campaspe* go,
  Or, if thou'lt not resign,
As thou Apelles' Skill doest know,
  So, may his Heart be thine.

To praise more equal leave our Choice,
  When we thy Works survey,
Nor let each sighing Breast and Voice,
  But one Applause betray.

TO A FRIEND

In Praise of the Invention of Writing Letters

Blest be the Man! his Memory at least,
Who found the Art, thus to unfold his Breast,
And taught succeeding Times an easy way
Their secret Thoughts by *Letters* to convey;
To baffle Absence, and secure Delight,
Which, till that Time, was limited to Sight.
The parting Farewel spoke, the last Adieu,
The less'ning Distance past, then loss of View,
The Friend was gone, which some kind Moments gave,
And Absence separated, like the Grave.   10
The Wings of Love were tender too, till then
No Quill, thence pull'd, was shap'd into a Pen,
To send in Paper-sheets, from Town to Town,
Words smooth as they, and softer than his Down.
O'er such he reign'd, whom Neighbourhood had join'd,
And hopt, from Bough to Bough, supported by the Wind.
When for a Wife the youthful *Patriarch* sent,
The Camels, Jewels, and the Steward went,
A wealthy Equipage, tho' grave and slow;
But not a Line, that might the Lover shew.   20
The Rings and Bracelets woo'd her Hands and Arms;
But had she known of melting Words, the Charms
That under secret Seals in Ambush lie,
To catch the Soul, when drawn into the Eye,
The Fair *Assyrian* had not took this Guide,
Nor her soft Heart in Chains of Pearl been ty'd.

    Had these Conveyances been then in Date,
Joseph had known his wretched Father's State,
Before a Famine, which his Life pursues,
Had sent his other Sons, to tell the News.   30

Oh! might I live to see an Art arise,
As this to Thoughts, indulgent to the Eyes;
That the dark Pow'rs of distance cou'd subdue,
And make me *See*, as well as *Talk* to You;
That tedious Miles, nor Tracts of Air might prove
Bars to my Sight, and shadows to my Love!
Yet were it granted, such unbounded Things
Are wand'ring Wishes, born on Phancy's Wings,
They'd stretch themselves beyond this happy Case,
And ask an Art, to help us to Embrace.   40

CLARINDA'S INDIFFERENCE AT PARTING WITH HER BEAUTY

Now, age came on, and all the dismal traine
That fright the vitious, and afflicte the vaine.
Departing beauty, now Clarinda spies
Pale in her cheeks, and dying in her eyes;
That youthfull air, that wanders ore the face,
That undescrib'd, that unresisted grace,
Those morning beams, that strongly warm, and shine,
Which men that feel and see, can ne're define,
Now, on the wings of restlesse time, were fled,
And ev'ning shades, began to rise, and spread,   10
When thus resolv'd, and ready soon to part,
Slighting the short repreives of proffer'd art
She spake —
And what, vain beauty, didst thou 'ere atcheive,
When at thy height, that I thy fall shou'd greive,
When, did'st thou e're succesfully persue?
When, did'st thou e're th' appointed foe subdue?
'Tis vain of numbers, or of strength to boast,
In an undisciplin'd, unguided Host,
And love, that did thy mighty hopes deride,   20
Wou'd pay no sacrafice, but to thy pride.

When, did'st thou e're a pleasing rule obtain,
A glorious Empire's but a glorious pain,
Thou, art indeed, but vanity's cheife sourse,
But foyle to witt, to want of witt a curse,
For often, by thy gaudy sign's descry'd
A fool, which unobserv'd, had been untry'd,
And when thou doest such empty things adorn,
'Tis but to make them more the publick scorn.
I know thee well, but weak thy reign wou'd be   30
Did n'one adore, or prize thee more then me.
I see indeed, thy certain ruine neer,
But can't affoard one parting sigh, or tear,
Nor rail at Time, nor quarrell with my glasse,
But unconcern'd, can lett thy glories passe.

SOME PIECES OUT OF THE FIRST ACT OF THE AMINTA OF TASSO

DAPHNE'S *Answer to* SYLVIA, *declaring she should esteem all as Enemies, who should talk to her of Love*

Then, to the snowy *Ewe*, in thy esteem,
The Father of the Flock a Foe must seem,
The faithful *Turtles* to their yielding Mates.
The chearful *Spring*, which Love and Joy creates,
That reconciles the World by soft Desires,
And tender Thoughts in ev'ry Breast inspires,
To you a hateful Season must appear,
Whilst *Love* prevails, and all are *Lovers* here.
Observe the gentle Murmurs of that *Dove*,
And see, how billing she confirms her Love!
For this, the *Nightingale* displays her Throat,   10
And *Love, Love, Love*, is all her Ev'ning Note.
The very *Tygers* have their tender Hours,
And prouder *Lyons* bow beneath *Love's* Pow'rs.
Thou, prouder yet than that imperious Beast,

Alone deny'st him Shelter in thy Breast.
But why should I the Creatures only name
That Sense partake, as Owners of this Flame?
Love farther goes, nor stops his Course at these:
The *Plants* he moves, and gently bends the *Trees*.
See how those *Willows* mix their am'rous Boughs; 20
And, how that *Vine* clasps her supporting Spouse!
The silver *Firr* dotes on the stately Pine;
By Love those *Elms*, by Love those *Beeches* join.
But view that *Oak;* behold his rugged Side:
Yet that rough Bark the melting Flame do's hide.
All, by their trembling Leaves, in Sighs declare
And tell their Passions to the gath'ring Air.
Which, had but Love o'er Thee the least Command,
Thou, by their Motions, too might'st understand.

AMINTOR *being ask'd by* THIRSIS *who is the object of his Love?
speaks as follows*

Amint. THIRSIS! to Thee I mean that Name to
   show,
Which, only yet our Groves, and Fountains know:
That, when my Death shall through the Plains be
   told,
Thou with the wretched Cause may'st that unfold
To every-one, who shall my Story find
Carv'd by thy Hand, in some fair Beeches rind;
Beneath whose Shade the bleeding Body lay:
That, when by chance she shall be led that way,
O'er my sad Grave the haughty Nymph may go,
And the proud Triumph of her Beauty shew   10
To all the Swains, to Strangers as they pass;
And yet at length she may (but Oh! alas!
I fear, too high my flatt'ring Hopes do soar)
Yet she at length may my sad Fate deplore;

May weep me Dead, may o'er my Tomb recline,
And sighing, wish were he alive and Mine!
But mark me to the End—
   Thir. Go on; for well I do thy Speech attend,
Perhaps to better Ends, than yet thou know'st.
   Amint. Being now a Child, or but a Youth at most,   20
When scarce to reach the blushing Fruit I knew,
Which on the lowest bending Branches grew;
Still with the dearest, sweetest, kindest Maid
Young as myself, at childish Sports I play'd.
The Fairest, sure, of all that Lovely Kind,
Who spread their golden Tresses to the Wind;
Cydippe's Daughter, and *Montano's* Heir,
Whose Flocks and Herds so num'rous do appear;
The beauteous *Sylvia;* She, 'tis She I love,
Warmth of all Hearts, and Pride of ev'ry Grove.   30
With Her I liv'd, no Turtles e'er so fond.
Our Houses met, but more our Souls were join'd.
Together Nets for Fish, and Fowl we laid;
Together through the spacious Forest stray'd;
Pursu'd with equal Speed the flying Deer,
And of the Spoils there no Divisions were.
But whilst I from the Beasts their Freedom won,
Alas! I know not how, my Own was gone.
By unperceiv'd Degrees the Fire encreas'd,
Which fill'd, at last, each corner of my Breast;   40
As from a Root, tho' scarce discern'd so small,
A Plant may rise, that grows amazing tall.
From *Sylvia's* Presence now I could not move,
And from her Eyes took in full Draughts of Love,
Which sweetly thro' my ravish'd Mind distill'd;
Yet in the end such Bitterness wou'd yield,
That oft I sigh'd, ere yet I knew the cause,
And was a Lover, ere I dream'd I was.

But Oh! at last, too well my State I knew;
And now, will shew thee how this Passion grew.   50
Then listen, while the pleasing Tale I tell.

THIRSIS *persuades* AMINTOR *not to despair upon the Predictions of* MOPSUS *discov'ring him to be an Impostor*

Thirsis. Why dost thou still give way to such Despair!
 Amintor. Too just, alas! the weighty Causes are.
Mopsus, wise *Mopsus*, who in Art excels,
And of all Plants the secret Vertue tells,
Knows, with what healing Gifts our Springs abound,
And of each Bird explains the mystick Sound;
'Twas He, ev'n He! my wretched Fate foretold.
 Thir. Dost thou this Speech then of that *Mopsus* hold,
Who, whilst his Smiles attract the easy View,
Drops flatt'ring Words, soft as the falling Dew;   10
Whose outward Form all friendly still appears,
Tho' Fraud and Daggers in his Thoughts he wears,
And the unwary Labours to surprize
With Looks affected, and with riddling Lyes.
If He it is, that bids thy Love despair,
I hope the happier End of all thy Care.
So far from Truth his vain Predictions fall.
 Amint. If ought thou know'st, that may my Hopes
  recall,
Conceal it not; for great I've heard his Fame,
And fear'd his Words—
 Thir.   —When hither first I came,   20
And in these Shades the false Impostor met,
Like Thee I priz'd, and thought his Judgment great;
On all his study'd Speeches still rely'd,
Nor fear'd to err, whilst led by such a Guide:
When on a Day, that Bus'ness and Delight
My Steps did to the Neighb'ring Town invite,

Which stands upon that rising Mountain's side,
And from our Plains this River do's divide,
He check'd me thus — Be warn'd in time, My Son,
And that new World of painted Mischiefs shun,   30
Whose gay Inhabitants thou shalt behold
Plum'd like our Birds, and sparkling all in Gold;
Courtiers, that will thy rustick Garb despise,
And mock thy Plainness with disdainful Eyes.
But above all, that Structure see thou fly,
Where hoarded Vanities and Witchcrafts lie;
To shun that Path be thy peculiar Care.
I ask, what of that Place the Dangers are:
To which he soon replies, there shalt thou meet
Of soft Enchantresses th' Enchantments sweet,   40
Who subt'ly will thy solid Sense bereave,
And a false Gloss to ev'ry Object give.
Brass to thy Sight as polish'd Gold shall seem,
And Glass thou as the Diamond shalt esteem.
Huge Heaps of Silver to thee shall appear,
Which if approach'd, will prove but shining Air.
The very Walls by Magick Art are wrought,
And Repetition to all Speakers taught:
Not such, as from our Ecchoes we obtain,
Which only our last Words return again;   50
But Speech for Speech entirely there they give,
And often add, beyond what they receive.
There downy Couches to false Rest invite,
The Lawn is charm'd, that faintly bars the Light.
No gilded Seat, no iv'ry Board is there,
But what thou may'st for some Delusion fear:
Whilst, farther to abuse thy wond'ring Eyes,
Strange antick Shapes before them shall arise;
Fantastick Fiends, that will about thee flock,
And all they see, with Imitation mock.   60

Nor are these Ills the worst.   Thyself may'st be
Transform'd into a Flame, a Stream, a Tree;
A Tear, congeal'd by Art, thou may'st remain,
'Till by a burning Sigh dissolv'd again.
Thus spake the Wretch; but cou'd not shake my Mind.
My way I take, and soon the City find,
Where above all that lofty Fabrick stands,
Which, with one View, the Town and Plains commands.
Here was I stopt, for who cou'd quit the Ground,
That heard such Musick from those Roofs resound! 70
Musick! beyond th' enticing *Syrene's* Note;
Musick! beyond the Swan's expiring Throat;
Beyond the softest Voice, that charms the Grove,
And equal'd only by the Spheres above.
My Ear I thought too narrow for the Art,
Nor fast enough convey'd it to my Heart:
When in the Entrance of the Gate I saw
A Man Majestick, and commanding Awe;
Yet temper'd with a Carriage, so refin'd
That undetermin'd was my doubtful Mind,   80
Whether for Love, or War, that Form was most design'd.
With such a Brow, as did at once declare
A gentle Nature, and a Wit severe;
To view that Palace me he ask'd to go,
Tho' Royal He, and I Obscure and Low.
But the Delights my Senses there did meet,
No rural Tongue, no Swain can e'er repeat.
Celestial Goddesses, or Nymphs as Fair,
In unveil'd Beauties, to all Eyes appear
Sprinkl'd with Gold, as glorious to the View,   90
As young *Aurora*, deck'd with pearly Dew;
Bright Rays dispensing, as along they pass'd,
And with new Light the shining Palace grac'd.
Phœbus was there by all the Muses met,

And at his Feet was our *Elpino* set.
Ev'n humble Me their Harmony inspir'd,
My Breast expanded, and my Spirits fir'd.
Rude Past'ral now, no longer I rehearse,
But Heroes crown with my exalted Verse.
Of Arms I sung, of bold advent'rous Wars;   100
And tho' brought back by my too envious Stars,
Yet kept my Voice and Reed those lofty Strains,
And sent loud Musick through the wond'ring Plains:
Which *Mopsus* hearing, secretly malign'd,
And now to ruin Both at once design'd.
Which by his Sorceries he soon brought to pass;
And suddenly so clogg'd, and hoarse I was,
That all our Shepherds, at the Change amaz'd,
Believ'd, I on some *Ev'ning-Wolf* had gaz'd:
When He it was, my luckless Path had crost,   110
By whose dire Look, my Skill awhile was lost.
This have I told, to raise thy Hopes again,
And render, by distrust, his Malice vain.

FROM THE AMINTA OF TASSO

Tho' we, of small Proportion see
And slight the armed Golden *Bee;*
Yet if her Sting behind she leaves,
No Ease th' envenom'd Flesh receives.
Love, less to Sight than is this Fly,
In a soft *Curl* conceal'd can lie;
Under an *Eyelid's* lovely Shade,
Can form a dreadful Ambuscade;
Can the most subtil Sight beguile
Hid in the Dimples of a *Smile.*
But if from thence a Dart he throw,
How sure, how mortal is the Blow!
How helpless all the Pow'r of Art
To bind, or to restore the Heart!

FROM THE AMINTA OF TASSO

Part of the Description of the Golden Age

Then, by some Fountains flow'ry side
The Loves unarm'd, did still abide.
Then, the loos'd Quiver careless hung,
The Torch extinct, the Bow unstrung.
Then, by the Nymphs no Charms were worn,
But such as with the Nymphs were born.
The Shepherd cou'd not, then, complain,
Nor told his am'rous Tale in vain.
No Veil the Beauteous Face did hide,
Nor harmless Freedom was deny'd.
Then, Innocence and Virtue reign'd
Pure, unaffected, unconstrain'd.
Love was their Pleasure, and their Praise,
The soft Employment of their Days.

FROM THE FRENCH, OF THE 188TH SONNET OF PETRARC

When Phœbus, at declining of the day
His golden Chariot plunges in the Sea,
Leauing my Soul, and this forsaken air
With darknesse cover'd, and with black dispair,
I by the rising streaks of Cynthia's light,
My greifs bewail, and dread th' approaching night.
I to the Heav'ns, and to the Stars relate,
That hear me not, the Stories of my fate.
What wonder, if by them unheard I be,
Since all things, are insencible to me?
Fortune to me, alas! is doubly blind,
My Mistresse cruel, and the world unkind;
With these, with love, and with my self I chide,

Nor will one pleasing thought, with me abide;
Sleep, from my weary, restlesse temples flyes,
And falling tears, prevent my closing eyes.
My soul, till morning, thus her anguish shews,
When soft Aurora cheerfull light renews.
But still, behind the Cloud, my Sun remains,
'Tis she must give me light, and ease my pains.

A SONG OF THE CANIBALS

out of Mountain's Essays; done into English verse, paraphrased

The French

Coleuvre, arest toy; arest toy, Coleuvre; afin que ma
seur tire sur le patron de ta peinture, le façon, & l'ouvrage
d' un rich cordon, que je puisse donner a ma Mie. ainsi, soit
en tout temps, ta beauté, & ta disposition, preferez a touts
les autres Serpents.

The English

Lovely viper, haste not on,
Nor curl, in various folds along,
Till from that figur'd coat of thine,
Which ev'ry motion, makes more fine.
I take, as neer as art can doe,
A draught, of what I wond'ring view;
Which, in a bracelett, for my Love
Shall be with carefull mixtures wove.
So, may'st thou find thy beautys last,
As thou doest now, retarde thy haste.
So, may'st thou, above all the snakes,
That harbour, in the neigh'bring brakes,
Be honour'd; and where thou does [sic] passe
The shades be close, and fresh the grasse.

A MAXIM

For the Ladys, translated from Mon^{sr} du Bussy

From the best witt of France, receive
A maxim, he to Ladys gave.
If once with cruel love opresst
Lett secrecy concern you most,
In mistery, lett itt still be dresst,
'Tis not by Love, that you are lost,
But by the way, that 'tis expresst.

ON ABSENCE

From the maxims of Bussy Rabutin

Absence on Love effects the same
As winds oppos'd to fire
Extinguishes a feeble Flame
And blows a great one higher.

WRITTEN BEFORE A FRENCH BOOK

Entitl'd les moyens de se guerir de L'Amour

In love, who to a cure aspires,
Never felt but weak desires,
Suddain starts, of fancy'd passion,
Such, as move the Gallick nation;
Gainst which, receipts, they here compose,
Of so much Verse, to so much prose;
Whilst within our British Islands
From Pendennis, to the Highlands,
Only faces, wher'in Nature
Has not plac'd one tempting feature,
Or wrincles, that defye Pomatum
For love, are remedies probatum.

THE EQUIPAGE
Written Originally in French by L'Abbé Reigner

Since the Road of Life's so ill;
I, to pass it, use this Skill,
My frail *Carriage* driving home
To its latest Stage, the *Tomb.*
Justice first, in Harness strong,
Marches stedfastly along:
Charity, to smooth the Pace,
Fills the next adjoining Trace:
Independance leads the Way,
Whom no heavy Curb do's sway;
Truth an equal Part sustains,
All indulg'd the loosen'd Reins:
In the Box fits vig'rous *Health*,
Shunning miry Paths of Wealth:
Gaiety with easy Smiles,
Ev'ry harsher Step beguiles;
Whilst of Nature, or of Fate
Only This I wou'd intreat:
The *Equipage* might not decay,
Till the worn *Carriage* drops away.

MELINDA ON AN INSIPPID BEAUTY
In imitation of a fragment of Sapho's

You, when your body, life shall leave
Must drop entire, into the grave;
Unheeded, unregarded lye,
And all of you together dye;
Must hide that fleeting charm, that face in dust,
Or to some painted cloath, the slighted Immage trust,
Whilst my fam'd works, shall throo' all times surprise
My polish'd thoughts, my bright Ideas rise,
And to new men be known, still talking to their eyes.

PART OF THE FIFTH SCENE IN THE SECOND ACT OF *ATHALIA*, A TRAGEDY WRITTEN IN FRENCH BY MONSIEUR RACINE

Enter, as in the Temple of *Jerusalem*
ATHALIA, MATHAN, ABNER.

Mathan.

Why, to our Wonder, in this Place is seen,
Thus discompos'd, and alter'd, *Juda's* Queen?
May we demand, what Terrors seize your Breast,
Or, why your Steps are to this House addrest,
Where your unguarded Person stands expos'd
To secret Foes, within its Walls inclos'd?
Can it be thought that you remit that Hate?

Athalia.

No more! but Both observe what I relate:
Not, that I mean (recalling Times of Blood)
To make you Judges of the Paths I trod,   10
When to the empty'd Throne I boldly rose,
Treating all Intercepters as my Foes.
'Twas Heav'ns Decree, that I should thus succeed,
Whose following Favour justifies the Deed,
Extending my unlimited Command
From Sea to Sea o'er the obedient Land:
Whilst your *Jerusalem* all Peace enjoys,
Nor now the' encroaching *Philistine* destroys,
Nor wandring *Arab* his Pavilion spreads,
Near *Jordan's* Banks, nor wastes his flow'ry Meads.   20
The great *Assyrian*, Terror of your Kings,
Who bought his Friendship with their holiest Things,
Yields that a Sister, of his pow'rful Race,
Should sway these Realms, and dignify the Place.
Nor need we add the late insulting Foe,

The furious *Jehu* does this Sceptre know,
And sinks beneath the load of conscious Fears,
When in *Samaria* he my Actions hears.
Distrest by Foes, which I've against him rais'd,
He sees me unmolested, fix'd, and pleas'd;   30
At least, till now thus glorious was my State;
But something's threatned from relaxing Fate,
And the last Night, which shou'd have brought me Rest,
Has all these great Ideas dispossest.
A *Dream*, a Vision, an apparent View
Of what, methinks, does still my Steps pursue,
Hangs on my pensive Heart, and bears it down
More than the weight of an objected Crown,
My Mother (be the Name with Rev'rence spoke!)
Ere chearful Day thro' horrid Shades had broke,   40
Approach'd my Bed, magnificent her Dress,
Her Shape, her Air did *Jesabel* confess:
Nor seem'd her Face to have refus'd that Art,
Which, in despite of Age, does Youth impart,
And which she practis'd, scorning to decay,
Or to be vanquish'd ev'n in *Nature's* way.
Thus all array'd, in such defying Pride
As when th' injurious Conqu'ror she descry'd,
And did in height of Pow'r for ill-got Pow'r deride.
To me she spake, these Accents to me came: 50
"Thou worthy Daughter of my soaring Fame,
"Tho' with a more transcendent Spirit fill'd,
"Tho' struggling Pow'rs attempt thy Life to shield,
"The *Hebrew's* God (Oh, tremble at the sound!)
"Shall Thee and Them, and all their Rights confound.
A pitying Groan concludes, no Word of Aid.
My Arms I thought to throw about the Shade
Of that lov'd Parent, but my troubled Sight
No more directed them to aim aright,

Nor ought presented, but a heap of Bones,   60
For which fierce Dogs contended on the Stones,
With Flakes of mangled Flesh, that quiv'ring still
Proclaim'd the Freshness of the suffer'd Ill;
Distained with Blood the Pavement, and the Wall,
Appear'd as in that memorable Fall——

Abner.

Oh! just avenging Heaven!——[*aside.*

Mathan.

Sure, Dreams like these are for Prevention given.

LA PASSION VAINCUE

Done into ENGLISH *with Liberty*

On the Banks of the *Severn* a desperate Maid
(Whom some Shepherd, neglecting his Vows, had betray'd,)
Stood resolving to banish all Sense of the Pain,
And pursue, thro' her Death, a Revenge on the Swain.
Since the Gods, and my Passion, at once he defies;
Since his Vanity lives, whilst my Character dies;
No more (did she say) will I trifle with Fate,
But commit to the Waves both my Love and my Hate.
And now to comply with that furious Desire,
Just ready to plunge, and alone to expire,
Some Reflection on Death, and its Terrors untry'd,
Some Scorn for the Shepherd, some Flashings of Pride
At length pull'd her back, and she cry'd, Why this Strife,
Since the *Swains* are so Many, and I've but *One* Life?

AN EPISTLE FROM A GENTLEMAN TO MADAM DESHOULIERS

Returning money she had lent him at Bassette, upon the first day of their acquaintance

Translated with Liberty from the French

URANIA, whom the Town admires,
   Whose Wit and Beauty share our Praise;
This fair URANIA who inspires
   A thousand Joys a thousand ways,
She, who cou'd with a Glance convey
   Favours, that had my Hopes outdone,
Has lent me Money on that Day,
   Which our Acquaintance first begun.
Nor with the Happiness I taste,
   Let any jealous Doubts contend: 10
Her Friendship is secure to last,
   Beginning where all others end.

And thou, known Cheat! upheld by Law,
   Thou Disappointer of the craving Mind,
BASSETTE, who thy Original dost draw
   From *Venice* (by uncertain Seas confin'd);
Author of Murmurs, and of Care,
   Of pleasing Hopes, concluding in Despair:
To thee my strange Felicity I owe,
   From thy Oppression did this Succour flow. 20
Less had I gained, had'st thou propitious been,
   Who better by my Loss hast taught me how to
      Win.
Yet tell me, my transported Brain!
   (whose Pride this Benefit awakes)
Know'st thou, what on this Chance depends?
   And are we not exalted thus in vain,

Whilst we observe the Money which she lends,
   But not, alas! the Heart she takes,
The fond Engagements, and the Ties
   Her fatal Bounty does impose,   30
Who makes Reprisals, with her Eyes,
   For what her gen'rous Hand bestows?

And tho' I quickly can return
   Those useful Pieces, which she gave;
Can I again, or wou'd I have
   That which her Charms have from me borne?

Yet let us quit th' obliging Score;
And whilst we borrow'd Gold restore,
Whilst readily we own the Debt,
And Gratitude before her set   40
   In its approved and fairest Light;
Let her effectually be taught
   By that instructive, harmless Slight,
That also in *her* turn she ought
   (Repaying ev'ry tender Thought)
Kindness with Kindness to requite.

A SONG FOR A PLAY

Alcander to Melinda

More then a Sea of tears, can show,
   Or thousand sighs can prove,
Then fault'ring speech, can lett you know,
   I fair Melinda love.

You then, must to your self expresse
   The strength of my desire,
Who brings the fewel, best may guesse,
   How great must be the fire.

Think on the pow'r, that arms your eyes,
    The charms that in them shine,
Think on their aptnesse to surprise,
    And of the love in mine.

Then to my wishing looks afoard
    The heart for which they sue,
And take a longing lovers word,
    That some men can be true.

A SONG

Melinda to Alcander

Witt, as free, and unconfin'd
    As the universal air,
Was not alotted to mankind,
    Leaving us, without our share;
No, we posesse alike that fire,
And all you boast of, we inspire.

Fancy, does from beauty rise,
    Beauty, teatches you to write,
Your flames are borrow'd from our Eyes,
    You but speak, what they endite.
Then cease to boast alone, that Fame.
Witt, and love, we give and claime.

A SONG

By Love persu'd, In vain I fly
To shades, as lost and wild as I;
Cold earth my hopes, sharp thorns my cares,
Here lively paint, and urge my tears;
Fancy, makes all things bear a part,
And shews a Rock, for Sylvia's heart.

In vain, I from the object goe,
Since my own thoughts, can wound me soe;
I'll back again, and ruin'd be
By hate, by scorn, or Jealousie.
Such real ills attend us all,
Lovers, by fancy need not fall.

A SONG

Miranda, hides her from the Sun,
  Beneath those shady beaches nigh,
Whilst I, by her bright rayes undone,
  Can no where for refreshment fly.

In that fair grove, att height of noone,
  His fiercest glorys, she defies;
I have alas! such shelter, none,
  No safe umbrella, 'gainst her eyes.

Thus, does th' unequal hand of fate
  Refuse itts' favours to devide,
Giving to her, a safe retreat,
  And all ofensive arms beside.

A SONG

Whilst Thirsis, in his pride of youth
  To me alone, professt
Dessembl'd passion, dress't like truth,
  He tryumph'd in my breast.

I lodg'd him neer my yeilding heart,
  Deny'd him but my arms,
Deluded with his pleasing art,
  Transported with his charms.

The wand'rer, now I loose, or share,
　　With ev'ry lovly maid,
Who make the hearts of men their care,
　　Shall have their own, betray'd.

Our charms on them we vainly prove,
　　And boast we Conquests gain,
Where one, a victime falls to love,
　　A Thousand Tyrants reign.

A SONG

Persuade me not, there is a Grace
　　Proceeds from *Silvia's* Voice or Lute,
Against *Miranda's* charming Face
　　To make her hold the least Dispute.

Musick, which tunes the Soul for Love,
　　And stirs up all our soft Desires,
Do's but the glowing Flame improve,
　　Which pow'rful Beauty first inspires.

Thus, whilst with Art she plays, and sings
　　I to *Miranda*, standing by,
Impute the Music of the Strings,
　　And all the melting Words apply

JEALOUSY

A Song

Vain Love, why do'st thou boast of Wings,
　　That cannot help thee to retire!
When such quick Flames Suspicion brings,
　　As do the Heart about tnee fire.

Still Swift to come, but when to go
Thou shou'd'st be more—Alas! how Slow.

Lord of the World must surely be
  But thy bare Title at the most;
Since *Jealousy* is Lord of Thee,
  And makes such Havock on thy Coast,

As do's thy pleasant Land deface,
Yet binds thee faster to the Place.

A SONG

Love, thou art best of Human Joys,
  Our chiefest Happiness below;
All other Pleasures are but Toys,
Musick without Thee is but Noise,
  And Beauty but an empty Show.

Heav'n, who knew best what Man wou'd move,
  And raise his Thoughts above the Brute;
Said, Let him Be, and let him Love;
That must alone his Soul improve,
  Howe'er Philosophers dispute.

A SONG

Quickly, *Delia*, Learn my Passion,
  Lose not Pleasure, to be Proud;
Courtship draws on Observation,
  And the Whispers of the Croud.

Soon or late you'll hear a Lover,
  Nor by Time his Truth can prove;
Ages won't a Heart discover,
  Trust, and so secure my Love.

A SONG

'Tis strange, this Heart within my breast,
    Reason opposing, and her Pow'rs,
Cannot one gentle Moment rest,
    Unless it knows what's done in Yours.

In vain I ask it of your Eyes,
    Which subt'ly would my Fears controul;
For Art has taught them to disguise,
    Which Nature made t' explain the Soul.

In vain that Sound, your Voice affords,
    Flatters sometimes my easy Mind;
But of too vast Extent are Words
    In them the Jewel Truth to find.

Then let my fond Enquiries cease,
    And so let all my Troubles end:
For, sure, that Heart shall ne'er know Peace,
    Which on Anothers do's depend.

A SONG

The Nymph, in vain, bestows her pains,
That seeks to thrive, where Bacchus reigns;
In vain, are charms, or smiles, or frowns,
All Immages his torrent drowns.

Flames to the head he may impart,
But makes an Island, of the heart;
So inaccessible, and cold,
That to be his, is to be old.

A SONG

If for a Woman I wou'd dye,
  It shou'd for Gloriana be,
But lovers, you that talk so high,
Inform, whilst in the Grave I lye
  What reward can reach to me?

If, I my freedom wou'd resign,
  That freedom, she alone shou'd have,
But tell me, you that can define,
If I, by Marriage, make her mine,
  Which may be call'd the greater slave?

Then Gloriana, since 'tis plain
  Love, with these two, can n'er agree
Since death and Mariage, are his bane,
Those melancholy thoughts we'll flee,
  And chearfull Lovers, allways bee.

A SONG

Lett the fool still be true,
And one object persue,
And for ever be jealous, or dying,
Whilst he that better knows,
Will in Love, no time loose,
For that God still, that God still, that God still is
  flying.

Lett the heart that wants heat,
But with one motion, beat,
Least that flame shou'd decay, which they sever,
But we, that boast of more,
Can each Beauty adore,
And love all, and love all, and love all, and for ever.

MORAL SONG

Would we attain the happiest State,
    That is design'd us here;
No Joy a Rapture must create,
    No Grief beget Despair.
No Injury fierce Anger raise,
    No Honour tempt to Pride;
No vain Desires of empty Praise
    Must in the Soul abide.
No Charms of Youth, or Beauty move
    The constant, settl'd Breast:
Who leaves a Passage free to Love,
    Shall let in, all the rest.
In such a Heart soft Peace will live,
    Where none of these abound;
The greatest Blessing, Heav'n do's give,
    Or can on Earth be found.

HONOUR

A Song

How dear is Reputation bonght !
    When we the purchace pay
We sett the sweets of Life at nought
    And make our Joys away.

One most belou'd we often loose
    To pacify the crou'd
And even Complisance refuse
    Not to be Chast but proud.

Though Honour which the World does awe
    And makes our Sex so nice
Its self no Pedigree can draw
    But what's deriv'd from Vice.

Thus Tyrants who Usurping rise
  To fix them in that wrong
Do sharpest punishment Deuise
  For Crimes from whence they sprung.

TIMELY ADVICE TO DORINDA

Dorinda since you must decay
  Your lover now resign
As Charles that Empire gave away
  He saw wou'd soon decline

Tis better in the height of Power
  Thus with your Sway to part
Then stay till that more fatal hour
  Of his revolted heart.

For Witt but faintly will inspire
  Unless with Beauty joyn'd
And when our Eyes have lost their fire
  Tis uselesse in the Mind.

Be then advis'd and now remove
  All farther thoughts about itt.
Sinch [sic] youth we find's too short for Love
  Though Life's too long without itt.

THE PHŒNIX

A Song

A Female Friend advis'd a Swain
  (Whose Heart she wish'd at ease)
Make Love thy Pleasure, not thy Pain,
  Nor let it deeply seize.

Beauty, where Vanities abound,
  No serious Passion claims;
Then, 'till a *Phœnix* can be found,
  Do not admit the Flames.

But griev'd She finds, that his Replies
  (Since prepossess'd when Young)
Take all their Hints from *Silvia*'s Eyes,
  None from *ARDELIA*'s Tongue.

Thus, *Cupid*, of our Aim we miss,
  Who wou'd unbend thy Bow;
And each slight Nymph a *Phœnix* is,
  When Love will have it so.

HOPE

The Tree of *Knowledge* we in *Eden* prov'd;
The Tree of *Life* was thence to Heav'n remov'd:
Hope is the growth of Earth, the only Plant,
Which either Heav'n, or Paradice cou'd want.

Hell knows it not, to Us alone confin'd,
And Cordial only to the Human Mind.
Receive it then, t'expel these mortal Cares,
Nor wave a Med'cine, which thy God prepares.

LIFE'S PROGRESS

How gayly is at first begun
  Our *Life*'s uncertain Race!
Whilst yet that sprightly Morning Sun,
With which we just set out to run
  Enlightens all the Place.

How smiling the World's Prospect lies
  How tempting to go through!

Not *Canaan* to the Prophet's Eyes,
From *Pisgah* with a sweet Surprize,
  Did more inviting shew.

How promising's the Book of Fate,
  Till thoroughly understood!
Whilst partial Hopes such Lots create,
As may the youthful Fancy treat
  With all that's Great and Good.

How soft the first Ideas prove,
  Which wander through our Minds!
How full the Joys, how free the Love,
Which do's that early Season move;
  As Flow'rs the Western Winds!

Our Sighs are then but Vernal Air;
  But *April*-drops our Tears,
Which swiftly passing, all grows Fair,
Whilst Beauty compensates our Care,
  And Youth each Vapour clears.

But oh! too soon, alas, we climb;
  Scarce feeling we ascend
The gently rising Hill of *Time*,
From whence with Grief we see that Prime,
  And all its Sweetness end.

The Die now cast, our Station known,
  Fond Expectation past;
The Thorns, which former Days had sown,
To Crops of late Repentance grown,
  Thro' which we toil at last.

Whilst ev'ry Care's a driving Harm,
  That helps to bear us down;

Which faded Smiles no more can charm,
But ev'ry Tear's a Winter-Storm,
  And ev'ry Look's a Frown.

Till with succeeding Ills opprest,
  For Joys we hop'd to find;
By Age too, rumpl'd and undrest,
We gladly sinking down to rest,
  Leave following Crouds behind.

A SIGH

Gentlest Air thou breath of Lovers
  Vapour from a secret fire
Which by thee itts self discovers
  E're yett daring to aspire.

Softest Noat of whisper'd anguish .
  Harmony's refindest part
Striking whilst thou seem'st to languish
  Full upon the list'ners heart.

Safest Messenger of Passion
  Stealing through a crou'd of spys
Which constrain the outward fassion
  Close the Lips and guard the Eyes.

Shapelesse Sigh we ne're can show thee
  Form'd but to assault the Ear
Yett e're to their cost they know thee
  Ev'ry Nymph may read thee here.

CÆSAR AND BRUTUS

Though Cæsar falling, shew'd no sign of fear,
Yett Brutus, when thou did'st appear,
When thy false hand, against him came,

He vail'd his face, to hide that shame
Which did on the mistake attend,
Of having own'd thee, for his freind.

AN EPISTLE

From ALEXANDER *to* HEPHÆSTION *in His Sickness*

With such a Pulse, with such disorder'd Veins,
Such lab'ring Breath, as thy Disease constrains;
With failing Eyes, that scarce the Light endure,
(So long unclos'd, they've watch'd thy doubtful Cure)
To his *Hephæstion Alexander* writes,
To soothe thy Days, and wing thy sleepless Nights,
I send thee Love: Oh! that I could impart,
As well my vital Spirits to thy Heart!
That, when the fierce Distemper thine wou'd quell,
They might renew the Fight, and the cold Foe repel. 10
   As on *Arbela*'s Plains we turn'd the Day,
When *Persians* through our Troops had mow'd their way,
When the rough *Scythians* on the Plunder run,
And barb'rous Shouts proclaim'd the Conquest won,
   'Till o'er my Head (to stop the swift Despair)
The *Bird* of *Jove* fans the supporting Air,
Above my Plume does his broad Wings display,
And follows wheresoe'er I force my way:
Whilst *Aristander*, in his Robe of White,
Shews to the wav'ring Host th' auspicious Sight;   20
New Courage it inspires in ev'ry Breast,
And wins at once the Empire of the East.
Cou'd He, but now, some kind Presage afford,
That Health might be again to Thee restor'd;
Thou to my Wishes, to my fond Embrace;
Thy Looks the same, the same Majestick Grace,
That round thee shone, when we together went
To chear the Royal Captives in their Tent,

Where *Sysigambis*, prostrate on the Floor,
Did *Alexander* in thy Form adore;   30
Above great *Æsculapius* shou'd he stand,
Or made immortal by *Apelles* Hand.
But no reviving Hope his Art allows,
And such cold Damps invade my anxious Brows,
As, when in *Cydnus* plung'd, I dar'd the Flood
T' o'er-match the Boilings of my youthful Blood.
But *Philip* to my Aid repair'd in haste;
And whilst the proffer'd Draught I boldly taste,
As boldly He the dangerous Paper views,
Which of hid Treasons does his Fame accuse.   40
More thy Physician's Life on Thine depends,
And what he gives, his Own preserves, or ends.
If thou expir'st beneath his fruitless Care,
To *Rhadamanthus* shall the Wretch repair,
And give strict Answer for his Errors there.

Near thy Pavilion list'ning *Princes* wait,
Seeking from thine to learn their *Monarch's* State.
Submitting *Kings*, that post from Day to Day,
To keep those Crowns, which at my Feet they lay,
Forget th' ambitious Subject of their Speed,   50
And here arriv'd, only Thy Dangers heed.
The *Beauties* of the Clime, now Thou'rt away,
Droop, and retire, as if their God of Day
No more upon their early Pray'rs would shine,
Or take their Incense, at his late Decline.
Thy *Parisatis* whom I fear to name,
Lest to thy Heat it add redoubl'd Flame;
Thy lovely Wife, thy *Parisatis* weeps,
And in her Grief a solemn Silence keeps.
Stretch'd in her Tent, upon the Floor she lies,   60
So pale her Looks, so motionless her Eyes,

As when they gave thee leave at first to gaze
Upon the Charms of her unguarded Face;
When the two beauteous Sisters lowly knelt,
And su'd to those, who more than Pity felt.
To chear her now *Statira* vainly proves,
And at thy Name alone she sighs, and moves.

But why these single Griefs shou'd I expose?
The World no Mirth, no War, no Bus'ness knows,
But, hush'd with Sorrow stands, to favour thy Repose. 70
Ev'n I my boasted Title now resign,
Not *Ammon*'s Son, nor born of Race Divine,
But Mortal all, oppress'd with restless Fears,
Wild with my Cares, and Womanish in Tears.
Tho' Tears, before, I for lost *Clytus* shed,
And wept more Drops, than the old Hero bled;
Ev'n now, methinks, I see him on the Ground,
Now my dire Arms the wretched Corpse surround,
Now the fled Soul I wooe, now rave upon the Wound.
Yet He, for whom this mighty Grief did spring, 80
Not *Alexander* valu'd, but the King.
Then think, how much that Passion must transcend,
Which not a Subject raises but a Friend:
An equal Partner in the vanquished Earth,
A Brother, not impos'd upon my Birth,
Too weak a Tye unequal Thoughts to bind,
But by the gen'rous Motions of the Mind.
My Love to thee for Empire was the Test,
Since him, who from Mankind cou'd chuse the best,
The Gods thought only fit for Monarch o'er the rest. 90
Live then, my Friend; but if that must not be,
Nor Fate will with my boundless Mind agree,
Affording, at one time, the World and Thee;
To the most Worthy I'll that Sway resign,
And in *Elysium* keep *Hyphæstion* mine.

FRAGMENT AT TUNBRIDGE-WELLS

For He, that made, must new create us,
Ere *Seneca*, or *Epictetus*,
With all their serious Admonitions,
Can, for the *Spleen*, prove good Physicians.
The Heart's unruly Palpitation
Will not be laid by a Quotation;
Nor will the Spirits move the lighter
For the most celebrated Writer.
Sweats, Swoonings, and convulsive Motions
Will not be cur'd by Words, and Notions.
Then live, old *Brown!* with thy Chalybeats,
Which keep us from becoming Idiots.
At *Tunbridge* let us still be Drinking,
Though 'tis th'*Antipodes* to Thinking:
Such Hurry, whilst the Spirit's flying,
Such Stupefaction, when 'tis dying:
Yet these, and not sententious Papers,
Must brighten Life, and cure the Vapours, &c.

THE PRODIGY

A poem written at Tunbridge wells Anno 1706, on the admira-
tion that many expressed at a Gentleman's being in love,
and their endeavours to dissuade him from it, with some
advice to the young Ladies, how to main[tain] their natural
prerogative

Protect the State, and let Old England thrive,
Keep all crown'd heads this wondrous year alive ;
Preserve our palaces from wind and flame,
Safe be our fleets, and be the Scotchmen tame ;
Avert, kind fate, whate'er th' event might prove,
For here's a prodigy, a man in love !
Wasted and pale, he languishes in sight,

And spends in am'rous verse the sleepless night;
While happier youths, with colder spirits born,
View the distress with pity or with scorn,   10
And maids so long unus'd to be ador'd
Think it portends the pestilence or sword.
    How chang'd is Britain to the blooming fair,
Whom now the men no longer make their care;
But of indifference arrogantly boast,
And scarce the wine gets down some famous toast!
Not so (as still declare their works) it prov'd
When Spencer, Sydney, and when Waller lov'd,
Who with soft numbers wing'd successful darts,
Nor thought the passion lessning to their parts;   20
Then let such patterns countenance his fire,
Whom love and verse do now afresh inspire,
'Gainst all who blame or at the fate admire;
And learn the nymphs, how to regain their sway,
And make this stubborn sex once more obey;
Call back the fugitives by modest pride,
And let them fear sometimes to be deny'd;
Stay 'till their courtship may deserve that name,
And take not ev'ry look for love and flame;
To mercenary ends no charms imploy,   30
Nor stake their smiles against some rafled toy:
For every fop lay not th' insnaring train,
Nor lose the worthy to allure the vain.
Keep at due distance all attempts of bliss,
Nor let too near a whisper seem a kiss.
Be not the constant partner of a swain,
Except his long address that favor gain;
Nor be transported when some trifle's view.
Directs his giddy choice to fix on you.
Amend whatever may your charms disgrace,   40
And trust not wholly to a conquering face,

Nor be your motions rude, coquet or wild,
Shuffling or lame, as if in nursing spoil'd :
Slight not th' advantage of a graceful mein,
Tho' Paris gave the prize to beauty's Queen,
When Juno mov'd, Venus could scarce be seèn :
And if to fashions past you can't submit,
Pretend at least to some degree of wit ;
The men who fear now with it to accost
Still love the name, tho' you've the habit lost.　　50
Assert your pow'r in early days begun,
Born to undo, be not yourselves undone,
Contemn'd, and cheap, as easy to be won.
If thus, like Sov'reigns you maintain your ground,
The rebells at your feet will soon be found ;
And when with wise authority you move,
No new surprise, no prodigy will prove,
To see one man, or the whole race in love.

A PASTORAL DIALOGUE
Between Two Shepherdesses
Silvia

Pretty Nymph! within this shade,
Whilst the Flocks to rest are laid,
Whilst the World dissolves in Heat,
Take this cool, and flow'ry Seat:
And with pleasing Talk awhile
Let us two the Time beguile;
Tho' thou here no Shepherd see,
To encline his humble Knee,
Or with melancholy Lays
Sing thy dangerous Beauty's Praise.　　10

Dorinda

Nymph! with thee I here wou'd stay,
But have heard, that on this Day,

Near those Beeches, scarce in view,
All the Swains some Mirth pursue:
To whose meeting now I haste.
Solitude do's Life but waste.

Silvia

Prithee, but a Moment stay.

Dorinda

No! my Chaplet wou'd decay;
Ev'ry drooping Flow'r wou'd mourn,
And wrong the Face, they shou'd adorn. 20

Silvia

I can tell thee, tho' so Fair,
And dress'd with all that rural Care,
Most of the admiring Swains
Will be absent from the Plains.
Gay *Sylvander* in the Dance
Meeting with a shrew'd Mischance,
To his Cabin's now confin'd
By *Mopsus*, who the Strain did bind:
Damon through the Woods do's stray,
Where his Kids have lost their way: 30
Young *Narcissus* iv'ry Brow
Rac'd by a malicious Bough,
Keeps the girlish Boy from sight,
Till Time shall do his Beauty right.

Dorinda

Where's *Alexis?*

Silvia

He, alas!
Lies extended on the Grass;
Tears his Garland, raves, despairs,
Mirth and Harmony forswears;

Since he was this Morning shown,
That *Delia* must not be his Own.   40

Dorinda

Foolish Swain! such Love to place.

Silvia

On any but *Dorinda's* Face.

Dorinda

Hasty Nymph! I said not so.

Silvia

No —— but I thy Meaning know.
Ev'ry Shepherd thou wou'd'st have
Not thy Lover, but thy Slave;
To encrease thy captive Train,
Never to be lov'd again.
But, since all are now away,   50
Prithee, but a Moment stay.

Dorinda

No; the Strangers, from the Vale,
Sure will not this Meeting fail;
Graceful one, the other Fair.
He too, with the pensive Air,
Told me, ere he came this way
He was wont to look more Gay.

Silvia

See! how Pride thy Heart inclines
To think, for Thee that Shepherd pines;
When those Words, that reach'd thy Ear,
Chloe was design'd to hear;   60
Chloe, who did near thee stand,
And his more speaking Looks command.

Dorinda

Now thy Envy makes me smile.
That indeed were worth his while:
Chloe next thyself decay'd,
And no more a courted Maid.

Silvia

Next myself! Young Nymph, forbear.
Still the Swains allow me Fair,
Tho' not what I was that Day,
When *Colon* bore the Prize away;   70
When ——

Dorinda

—— Oh, hold! that Tale will last,
Till all the Evening Sports are past;
Till no Streak of Light is seen,
Nor Footstep prints the flow'ry Green.
What thou wert, I need not know,
What I am, must haste to show.
Only this I now discern
From the things, thou'd'st have me learn,
That Woman-kind's peculiar Joys
From past, or present Beauties rise.   80

THE CAUTIOUS LOVERS

Silvia, let's from the Croud retire;
    For, What to you and me
(Who but each other do desire)
    Is all that here we see?

Apart we'll live, tho' not alone;
    For, who *alone* can call
Those, who in Desarts live with One,
    If in that One they've All?

The World a vast *Meander* is,
 Where Hearts confus'dly stray;   10
Where Few do hit, whilst Thousands miss
 The happy mutual Way:

Where Hands are by stern Parents ty'd,
 Who oft, in *Cupid's* Scorn,
Do for the widow'd State provide,
 Before that Love is born:

Where some too soon themselves misplace;
 Then in Another find
The only Temper, Wit, or Face,
 That cou'd affect their Mind.   20

Others (but oh! avert that Fate!)
 A well-chose Object change:
Fly, *Silvia*, fly, ere 'tis too late;
 Fall'n Nature's prone to range.

And, tho' in heat of Love we swear
 More than perform we can;
No *Goddess*, You, but *Woman* are,
 And I no more than *Man*.

Th' impatient *Silvia* heard thus long;
 Then with a Smile reply'd: 30
Those Bands cou'd ne'er be very strong,
 Which Accidents divide.

Who e'er was mov'd yet to go down,
 By such o'er-cautious Fear;
Or for one Lover left the Town,
 Who might have Numbers here?

Your Heart, 'tis true, is worth them all,
 And still preferr'd the first;
But since confess'd so apt to fall,
 'Tis good to fear the worst.   40

In ancient History we meet
  A flying Nymph betray'd;
Who, had she kept in fruitful *Crete*,
  New Conquest might have made.

And sure, as on the *Beach* she stood,
  To view the parting Sails;
She curs'd her self, more than the Flood,
  Or the conspiring Gales.

False *Theseus*, since thy Vows are broke,
  May following Nymphs beware: 50
Methinks I hear how thus she spoke,
  And will not trust too far.

In Love, in Play, in Trade, in War
  They best themselves acquit,
Who, tho' their Inf'rests shipwreckt are,
  Keep unreprov'd their Wit.

ADAM POS'D

Cou'd our First Father, at his toilsome Plough,
Thorns in his Path, and Labour on his Brow,
Cloath'd only in a rude, unpolish'd Skin,
Cou'd he a vain Fantastick Nymph have seen,
In all her Airs, in all her antick Graces,
Her various Fashions, and more various Faces;
How had it pos'd that Skill, which late assign'd
Just Appellations to Each several Kind!
A right Idea of the Sight to frame;
T'have guest from what New Element she came;
T'have hit the wav'ring Form, or giv'n this Thing a
  Name.

RALPH'S REFLECTIONS

Upon the Anniversary of his Wedding

This day, sais Ralpho, I was free,
  'Till one unlucky hour
And some few mutter'd words by me,
  Put freedom past my pow'r.

Th' expressions I remember well,
  For better or for worse,
Till death us part, I take thee Nell,
  (That is I take a Purse.)

'Tis Gold, must make that Pill go down,
  The Priest without his Fee,
Nor simple Clerk, but for half-crown
  Would Execution see.

Rubands, and Gloves, the standers by
  To patience must encline,
Besides the hopes of a supply
  Of Bisquits, and of Wine.

The Friends that wait us to our Beds,
  (Who could no longer cross itt)
But throw our stockins at our heads,
  Or drown us with a Posset.

Oh! happy state of human life,
  If Mariage be thy best!
Poor Ralpho cry'd, yet kiss't his Wife,
  And no remorse confess't.

THE UNEQUAL FETTERS

Cou'd we stop the time that's flying
  Or recall itt when 'tis past

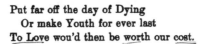

Put far off the day of Dying
  Or make Youth for ever last
To Love wou'd then be worth our cost.

But since we must loose those Graces
  Which at first your hearts have wonne
And you seek for in new Faces
  When our Spring of Life is done
It wou'd but urdge our ruine on

Free as Nature's first intention
  Was to make us, I'll be found
Nor by subtle Man's invention
  Yeild to be in Fetters bound
By one that walks a freer round.

Mariage does but slightly tye Men
  Whil'st close Pris'ners we remain
They the larger Slaves of Hymen
  Still are begging Love again
At the full length of all their chain.

ALCIDOR

While Monarchs in stern Battle strove
  For proud Imperial Sway;
Abandon'd to his milder Love,
Within a silent peaceful Grove,
  Alcidor careless lay.

Some term'd it cold, unmanly Fear;
  Some, Nicety of Sense,
That Drums and Trumpets cou'd not hear,
The sullying Blasts of Powder bear,
  Or with foul Camps dispense.   10

A patient Martyr to their Scorn,
   And each ill-fashion'd Jest;
The Youth, who but for Love was born,
Remain'd, and thought it vast Return,
   To reign in *Cloria*'s Breast.

But oh! a ruffling Soldier came
   In all the Pomp of War:
The *Gazettes* long had spoke his Fame;
Now Hautboys his Approach proclaim,
   And draw in Crouds from far.   20

Cloria unhappily wou'd gaze;
   And as he nearer drew,
The Man of Feather and of Lace
Stopp'd short, and with profound Amaze
   Took all her Charms to view.

A Bow, which from Campaigns he brought,
   And to his Holsters low,
Herself, and the Spectators taught,
That Her the fairest Nymph he thought,
   Of all that form'd the Row.   30

Next day, ere *Phœbus* cou'd be seen,
   Or any Gate unbarr'd;
At hers, upon th' adjoining Green,
From Ranks, with waving Flags between,
   Were soften'd Trumpets heard.

The Noon do's following Treats provide,
   In the Pavilion's Shade;
The Neighbourhood, and all beside,
That will attend the amorous Pride,
   Are welcom'd with the Maid.   40

Poor *Alcidor!* thy hopes are cross'd,
  Go perish on the Ground;
Thy Sighs by stronger Notes are toss'd,
Drove back, or in the Passage lost;
  Rich Wines thy Tears have drown'd.

In *Women's* Hearts, the softest Things
  Which Nature cou'd devise,
Are yet some harsh, and jarring Strings,
That, when loud Fame, or Profit rings,
  Will answer to the Noise.   50

Poor *Alcidor!* go Fight or Dye;
Let thy fond Notions cease:
Man was not made in Shades to lie,
Or his full Bliss, at ease, enjoy,
  To Live, or Love in peace.

THE CRITICK AND THE WRITER OF FABLES

Weary, at last, of the *Pindarick* way,
Thro' which advent'rously the Muse wou'd stray;
To *Fable* I descend with soft Delight,
Pleas'd to Translate, or easily Endite:
Whilst aery Fictions hastily repair
To fill my Page, and rid my Thoughts of Care,
As they to Birds and Beasts new Gifts impart,
And Teach, as Poets shou'd, whilst they Divert.

But here, the *Critick* bids me check this Vein.
Fable, he crys, tho' grown th' affected Strain,   10
But dies, as it was born, without Regard or Pain.
Whilst of his Aim the lazy Trifler fails,
Who seeks to purchase Fame by childish Tales.

Then, let my Verse, once more attempt the Skies,
The easily persuaded Poet cries,
Since meaner Works you Men of Taste despise.
The Walls of *Troy* shall be our loftier Stage,
Our mighty Theme the fierce *Achilles* Rage.
The Strength of *Hector*, and *Ulysses* Arts
Shall boast such Language, to adorn their Parts,   20
As neither *Hobbes*, nor *Chapman* cou'd bestow,
Or did from *Congreve*, or from *Dryden* flow.
Amidst her Towers, the dedicated Horse
Shall be receiv'd, big with destructive Force;
Till Men shall say, when Flames have brought her
        down.
"Troy *is no more, and* Ilium *was a Town.*

Is this the way to please the Men of Taste,
The Interrupter cries, this old Bombast?
I'm sick of *Troy*, and in as great a Fright,
When some dull Pedant wou'd her Wars recite,   30
As was soft *Paris*, when compell'd to Fight.

To Shades and Springs shall we awhile repair,
The Muse demands, and in that milder Air
Describe some gentle Swain's unhappy Smart
Whose folded Arms still press upon his Heart,
And deeper drive the two far enter'd Dart?
Whilst *Phillis* with a careless pleasure reigns
The Joy, the Grief, the Envy of the Plains;
Heightens the Beauty of the verdant Woods,
And softens all the Murmurs of the Floods.   40

Oh! stun me not with these insipid Dreams,
Th' Eternal Hush, the Lullaby of Streams.
Which still, he cries, their even Measures keep,
Till both the Writers, and the Readers sleep.

But urge thy Pen, if thou wouldst move our Thoughts,
To shew us private, or the publick Faults.
Display the Times, *High-Church* or *Low* provoke;
We'll praise the Weapon, as we like the Stroke,
And warmly sympathizing with the Spite
Apply to Thousands, what of One you write.   50

Then, must that single Stream the Town supply,
The harmless *Fable*-writer do's reply,
And all the Rest of *Helicon* be dry?
And when so many choice Productions swarm,
Must only Satire keep your Fancies warm?
Whilst even there, you praise with such Reserve,
As if you'd in the midst of Plenty starve,
Tho' ne'er so liberally we Authors carve.

Happy the Men, whom we divert with Ease,
Whom Opera's *and* Panegyricks *please.*   60

A MILLER, HIS SON, AND THEIR ASS

A Fable Translated from Monsieur de la Fontaine

Tho' to Antiquity the Praise we yield
Of pleasing Arts; and *Fable's* earli'st Field
Own to be fruitful *Greece;* yet not so clean
Those Ears were reap'd, but still there's some to glean;
And from the Lands of vast Invention come
Daily new Authors, with Discov'ries home.

This curious Piece, which I shall now impart,
Fell from *Malherbe*, a Master in his Art,
To *Racan*, fill'd with like poetick Fire,
Both tuneful Servants of *Apollo's* Choir,   10
Rivals and Heirs to the *Horatian* Lyre:
Who meeting him, one Day, free and alone,
(For still their Thoughts were to each other known)

Thus ask'd his Aid—Some useful Counsel Give,
Thou who, by living long, hast learnt to live;
Whose Observation nothing can escape;
Tell me, how I my course of Life shall shape:
To something I wou'd fix ere't be too late.
You know my Birth, my Talents, my Estate;
Shall I with these content, all Search resign,		20
And to the Country my Desires confine?
Or in the Court, or Camp, advancement gain?
The World's a mixture of Delight and Pain:
Tho' rough it seems, there's Pleasure in the Wars,
And *Hymen's* Joys are not without their Cares.
I need not ask, to what my Genius tends,
But wou'd content the World, the Court, my Friends.

Please all the World (in haste) *Malherbe* replies?
How vain th' Attempt will prove in him, that tries,
Learn from a *Fable*, I have somewhere found,		30
Before I answer all that you propound.
A *Miller* and his Son (the Father old,
The Boy about some fifteen Years had told)
Designed their *Ass* to sell, and for the Fair,
Some distance off, accordingly prepare.
But lest she in the walk should lose her Flesh,
And not appear, for Sale, so full and fresh,
Her Feet together ty'd; between them two
They heav'd her up; and on the Rusticks go:
Till those, who met them bearing thus the *Ass*,		40
Cry'd, Are these Fools about to act a Farce?
Surely the Beast (howe'er it seem to be)
Is not the greatest Ass of all the Three.
The *Miller* in their Mirth his Folly finds,
And down he sets her, and again unbinds;
And tho' her grumbling shew'd, she lik'd much more

The lazy way, she travell'd in before,
He minds her not; but up the *Boy* he sets
Upon her Back, and on the Crupper gets.
Thus on they jog, when of Three Men that pass'd, 50
The eldest thinking Age to be disgraced,
Call'd to the Youth, ho! you, young Man for shame!
Come down, lest Passengers your Manners blame,
And say, it ill becomes your tender Years
To ride before a Grandsire with grey Hairs.
Truly, the Gentlemen are in the right,
The *Miller* cries, and makes the Boy alight;
Then forward slides himself into his place,
And with a Mind content, renews his pace:
But much he had not gain'd upon his way, 60
Before a Troop of Damsels, neat and gay,
(Partial to Youth) to one another cry'd,
See, how with walking by that Dotard's side,
The *Boy* is tir'd; whilst with a Prelate's state
He rides alone, and dangling in the Seat,
Hangs like a Calf thrown up, across the Beast.
The *Miller*, thinking to have spoiled that Jest,
Reply'd, he was too Old for Veal to pass,
But after more on him, and on his Ass,
He stands convinc'd, and takes his Son again 70
To ride at ease himself, still next the Mane.
Yet ere he'd thirty Paces borne the Lad,
The next they met, cry'd—Are these Fellows mad!
Have they no Pity thus t'o'erload the Jade!
Sure, at the Fair, they for her Skin may trade.
See, how's she spent, and sinks beneath their strokes!
The *Miller*, whom this most of all provokes,
Swears by his Cap, he shews his want of Brains,
Who thus to please the World, bestows his Pains.
Howe'er we'll try, if this way't may be done; 80

And off he comes, and fetches down his Son.
Behind they walk, and now the Creature drive,
But cou'd no better in their Purpose thrive;
Nor scape a Fellow's Censure, whom they meet,
That cries, to spare the *Ass* they break their Feet;
And whilst unladen at her ease she goes,
Trudge in the Dirt, and batter out their Shooes;
As if to burthen her they were afraid,
And Men for Beasts, not Beasts for Men were made.
The Proverb right, *The Cart before the Horse.*   90
The *Miller,* finding things grow worse and worse,
Cries out, I am an Ass, it is agreed,
And so are all, who wou'd in this succeed.
Hereafter, tho' Reproof or Praise I find,
I'll neither heed, but follow my own Mind,
Take my own Counsel, how my Beast to sell.
This he resolv'd, and did it, and did well.

For you, Sir, *Follow Love, the Court, the War;*
Obtain the Crosier, or the City's Furr;
Live single all your days, or take a Wife;   100
Trust me, a Censure waits each state of Life.

THE WIT AND THE BEAU

Strephon, whose Person ev'ry Grace
  Was careful to adorn;
Thought, by the Beauties of his Face,
In *Silvia's* Love to find a place,
  And wonder'd at her Scorn.

With Bows, and Smiles he did his Part;
  But Oh! 'twas all in vain:
A Youth less Fine, a Youth of Art
Had talk'd himself into her Heart,
  And wou'd not out again.

Strephon with change of Habits press'd,
    And urg'd her to admire;
His Love alone the Other dress'd,
As Verse, or Prose became it best,
    And mov'd her soft Desire.

This found, his courtship *Strephon* ends,
    Or makes it to his Glass;
There, in himself now seeks amends,
Convinc'd, that where a *Wit* pretends,
    A *Beau* is but an Ass.

CUPID AND FOLLY

Imitated from the French

Cupid, ere depriv'd of Sight,
Young and apt for all Delight,
Met with *Folly* on the way,
As Idle and as fond of Play.
In gay Sports the time they pass;
Now run, now wrestle on the Grass;
Their painted Wings then nimbly ply,
And ev'ry way for Mast'ry try:
'Till a Contest do's arise,
Who has won th' appointed Prize.   10
Gentle *Love* refers the Case
To the next, that comes in Place;
Trusting to his flatt'ring Wiles,
And softens the Dispute with Smiles.
But *Folly*, who no Temper knows,
Words pursues with hotter Blows:
'Till the eyes of *Love* were lost,
Which has such Pain to Mortals cost.
Venus hears his mournful Crys,
And repeats 'em, in the Skys,   20

To *Jupiter* in Council set,
With Peers for the Occasion met;
In her Arms the Boy she bears,
Bathing him in falling Tears;
And whilst his want of eyes is shown,
Secures the Judges by her Own.
Folly to the Board must come,
And hear the Tryal and the Doom;
Which *Cytherea* loudly prays
May be as heavy as the Case: 30
Which, when All was justly weigh'd,
Cupid's Wings now useless made,
That a staff, his Feet must guide,
Which wou'd still be apt to slide;
This Decree at last was read,
That *Love* by *Folly* shou'd be lead.

LOVE, DEATH, AND REPUTATION

Reputation, *Love*, and *Death*,
(The Last all Bones, the First all Breath,
 The Midd'st compos'd of Restless Fire)
From each other wou'd Retire;
Thro' the World resolv'd to stray,
Every One a several Way;
Exercising, as they went,
Each such Power, as Fate had lent;
Which, if it united were,
Wretched Mortals cou'd not bear: 10
But as parting Friends do show,
To what Place they mean to go,
Correspondence to engage,
Nominate their utmost Stage;
Death declar'd he wou'd be found

Near the fatal Trumpet's sound;
Or where Pestilences reign,
And Quacks the greater Plagues maintain;
Shaking still his sandy Glass,
And mowing Human Flesh, like Grass.   20
Love, as next his Leave he took,
Cast on both so sweet a Look,
As their Tempers near disarm'd,
One relax'd, and t'other warm'd;
Shades for his Retreat he chose,
Rural Plains, and soft Repose;
Where no Dowry e'er was paid,
Where no Jointure e'er was made;
No Ill Tongue the Nymph perplex'd,
Where no Forms the Shepherd vex'd;   30
Where Himself shou'd be the Care,
Of the Fond and of the Fair:
Where that was, they soon should know,
Au Revoir! then turn'd to Go.
Reputation made a Pause,
Suiting her severer Laws;
Second Thoughts, and Third she us'd,
Weighing Consequences mus'd;
When, at length to both she cry'd:
You *Two* safely may Divide,   40
To th' *Antipodes* may fall,
And re-ascend th' encompast Ball;
Certain still to meet agen
In the Breasts of tortur'd Men;
Who by One (too far) betray'd,
Call in t'other to their Aid:
Whilst I Tender, Coy, and Nice,
Rais'd and ruin'd in a Trice,
Either fix with those I grace,

Or abandoning the Place,   50
No Return my Nature bears,
From green Youth, or hoary Hairs;
If thro' Guilt, or Chance, I sever,
I once Parting, Part for ever.

THE KING AND THE SHEPHERD

Imitated from the French

Through ev'ry Age some Tyrant Passion reigns:
Now *Love* prevails, and now *Ambition* gains
Reason's lost Throne, and sov'reign Rule maintains.
Tho' beyond Love's, Ambition's Empire goes;
For who feels Love, Ambition also knows,
And proudly still aspires to be possest
Of Her, he thinks superior to the rest.
As cou'd be prov'd, but that our plainer Task
Do's no such Toil, or Definitions ask;
But to be so rehears'd, as first 'twas told,   10
When such old Stories pleas'd in Days of old.

  A *King*, observing how a *Shepherd*'s Skill
Improv'd his Flocks, and did the Pastures fill,
That equal Care th' assaulted did defend,
And the secur'd and grazing Part attend,
Approves the Conduct, and from Sheep and Curs
Transfers the Sway, and changed his Wool to Furrs.

Lord-Keeper now, as rightly he divides
His just Decrees, and speedily decides;
When his sole Neighbour, whilst he watch'd the Fold,
A *Hermit* poor, in Contemplation old,   21
Hastes to his Ear, with safe, but lost Advice,
Tells him such Heights are levell'd in a trice,
Preferments treach'rous, and her Paths of Ice:

And that already sure 't had turn'd his Brain,
Who thought a Prince's Favour to retain.
Nor seem'd unlike, in this mistaken Rank,
The sightless Wretch who froze upon a Bank
A *Serpent* found, which for a *Staff* he took,
And us'd as such (his own but lately broke)   30
Thanking the Fates, who thus his Loss supply'd,
Nor marking one, that with amazement cry'd,
Throw quickly from thy Hand that sleeping Ill;
A *Serpent* 'tis, that when awak'd will kill.
A *Serpent* this! th' uncautioned Fool replies:
A *Staff* it feels, nor shall my want of eyes
Make me believe, I have no Senses left,
And thro' thy Malice be of this bereft;
Which Fortune to my Hand has kindly sent
To guide my Steps, and stumbling to prevent.   40
No *Staff*, the Man proceeds; but to thy harm
A *Snake* 'twill prove: The Viper, now grown warm,
Confirmed it soon, and fastened on his Arm.

Thus wilt thou find, *Shepherd* believe it true,
Some Ill, that shall this seeming Good ensue;
Thousand Distastes, t' allay thy envy'd Gains,
Unthought of, on the parcimonious Plains.
So prov'd the Event, and Whisp'rers now defame
The candid Judge, and his Proceedings blame.
By Wrongs, they say, a Palace he erects,   50
The Good oppresses, and the Bad protects.
To view this Seat the *King* himself prepares,
Where no Magnificence or Pomp appears,
But Moderation, free from each Extream,
Whilst Moderation is the Builder's Theme.
Asham'd yet still the Sycophants persist,
That Wealth he had conceal'd within a Chest,

Which but attended some convenient Day,
To face the Sun, and brighter Beams display.
The Chest unbarr'd, no radiant Gems they find,   60
No secret Sums to foreign Banks design'd,
But humble Marks of an obscure Recess,
Emblems of Care, and Instruments of Peace;
The Hook, the Scrip, and for unblam'd Delight.
The merry Bagpipe, which, ere fall of Night,
Cou'd sympathizing Birds to tuneful Notes invite.
Welcome ye Monuments of former Joys!
Welcome! to bless again your Master's Eyes,
And draw from Courts, th' instructed *Shepherd* cries.
No more dear Relicks! we no more will part,   70
You shall my Hands employ, who now revive my Heart.
No Emulations, or corrupted Times
Shall falsly blacken, or seduce to Crimes
Him, whom your honest Industry can please,
Who on the barren Down can sing from inward Ease.

How's this! the Monarch something mov'd rejoins.
With such low Thoughts, and Freedom from Designs,
What made thee leave a Life so fondly priz'd,
To be in Crouds, or envy'd, or despis'd?

Forgive me, Sir, and Humane Frailty see,   80
The Swain replies, in my past State and Me;
All peaceful that, to which I vow return.
But who alas! (tho' mine at length I mourn)
Was e'er without the Curse of some Ambition born.

THERE'S NO TO-MORROW

A Fable imitated from Sir Roger L'Estrange

Two long had Lov'd, and now the Nymph desir'd,
The Cloak of Wedlock, as the Case requir'd;
Urg'd that, the Day he wrought her to this Sorrow,

He Vow'd, that he wou'd marry her *To-Morrow.*
A'gen he Swears, to shun the present Storm,
That he, *To-Morrow,* will that Vow perform.
The *Morrows* in their due Successions came;
Impatient still on Each, the pregnant Dame
Urg'd him to keep his Word, and still he swore the same.
When tir'd at length, and meaning no Redress,   10
But yet the Lye not caring to confess,
He for his Oath this Salvo chose to borrow,
That he was Free, since there was no *To-Morrow;*
For when it comes in Place to be employ'd,
'Tis then *To-Day; To-Morrow's* ne'er enjoy'd.
The Tale's a Jest, the Moral is a Truth;
To-Morrow *and* To-Morrow, *cheat our Youth:*
In riper Age, To-Morrow *still we cry,*
Not thinking, that the present Day we Dye;
Unpractis'd all the Good we had Design'd;   20
There's No To-Morrow *to a Willing Mind*

JUPITER AND THE FARMER

When Poets gave their God in *Crete* a Birth,
Then *Jupiter* held Traffick with the Earth,
And had a Farm to Lett: the Fine was high,
For much the Treas'ry wanted a Supply,
By *Danaë's* wealthy Show'r exhausted quite, and dry.
But *Merc'ry,* who as Steward kept the Court,
So rack'd the Rent, that all who made Resort
Unsatisfy'd return'd, nor could agree
To use the Lands, or pay his secret Fee;
'Till one poor Clown (thought subt'ler than the rest,   10
Thro' various Projects rolling in his Breast)
Consents to take it, if at his Desire
All Weathers tow'rds his Harvest may conspire;
The Frost to kill the Worm, the brooding Snow,

The filling Rains may come, and *Phœbus* glow.
The Terms accepted, sign'd and seal'd the Lease,
His Neighbours Grounds afford their due Encrease
The Care of Heav'n; the Owner's Cares may cease.
Whilst the new Tenant, anxious in his Mind,
Now asks a Show'r, now craves a rustling Wind   20
To raise what That had lodg'd, that he the Sheaves may
     bind.
The Sun, th'o'er-shadowing Clouds, the moistning Dews
He with such Contrariety does chuse;
So often and so oddly shifts the Scene,
Whilst others Load, he scarce has what to Glean.

O *Jupiter!* with Famine pinch'd he cries,
No more will I direct th' unerring Skies;
No more my Substance on a Project lay,
No more a sullen Doubt I will betray,
Let me but live to Reap, do Thou appoint the way.   30

FOR THE BETTER

Imitated from Sir Roger L'Estrange

A *Quack*, to no true Skill in Physick bred,
With frequent visits cursed his Patient's Bed;
Enquiring, how he did his Broths digest,
How chim'd his Pulse, and how he took his Rest:
If shudd'ring Cold by Burnings was pursu'd,
And at what time the Aguish Fit renew'd.
The waining Wretch, each day become more faint,
In like proportion doubles his Complaint;
Now swooning Sweats he begs him to allay,
Now give his Lungs more liberty to play,   10
And take from empty'd Veins these scorching Heats
     away:

Or if he saw the Danger did increase,
To warn him fair, and let him part in Peace.
My Life for yours, no Hazard in your Case
The *Quack* replies; your Voice, your Pulse, your
   Face,
Good Signs afford, and what you seem to feel
Proceeds from Vapours, which we'll help with Steel.
With kindled Rage, more than Distemper, burns
The suff'ring Man, who thus in haste returns:
No more of Vapours, your belov'd Disease,   20
Your Ignorance's Skreen, your *What-you-please*,
With which you cheat poor Females of their Lives,
Whilst Men dispute not, so it rid their Wives.
For me, I'll speak free as I've paid my Fees;
My Flesh consumes, I perish by degrees:
And as thro' weary Nights I count my Pains,
No Rest is left me, and no Strength remains.
All for the Better, Sir, the *Quack* rejoins:
Exceeding promising are all these Signs.
Falling-away, your Nurses can confirm,   30
Was ne'er in Sickness thought a Mark of Harm.
The want of Strength is *for the Better* still;
Since Men of Vigour Fevers soonest kill.
Ev'n with this Gust of *Passion* I am pleas'd;
For they're most *Patient* who the most are seiz'd.
But let me see! here's that which all repels:
Then shakes, as he some formal Story tells,
The *Treacle-water*, mixt with powder'd *Shells*.
My Stomach's gone (what d'you infer from thence?)
Nor will with the least Sustenance dispense.   40
The Better; for, where appetite endures,
Meats intermingle, and no Med'cine cures.
The Stomach, you must know, Sir, is a Part——
But, sure, I feel Death's Pangs about my Heart.

Nay then Farewell! I need no more attend
The *Quack* replies. A sad approaching Friend
Questions the Sick, why he retires so fast;
Who says, because of Fees I've paid the Last,
And, whilst all Symptoms tow'rd my Cure agree,
Am, *for the Better*, Dying as you see.   50

THE JESTER AND THE LITTLE FISHES

A FABLE

Immitated from the French

Far, from Societies where I haue place
Be all half Witts, and Acters of grimace;
Buffoons, and Mimmicks, quoters of old saws,
The easy purchasers of dull Applause;
Still, plagues to men of true, but modest sence,
Who, must not take, though Jestors give offence;
Nor, yett, oppose the Laughers, and the cry,
And but by Silence, their assent deny.

A Jester, was the man, of whom we treate
Though now, more Innocent was his conceit   10
And, not for mischeif utter'd but for meat.
Receiv'd a Guest, at such a plenteous Board
As did of Fish, all rarities affoard,
It griev'd him sore, that next to him were plac'd
By chance, or malice, but the worst and least,
Whilst, at the upper end, his greedy Eye
Survey'd such Fish, as Killigrew might buy;
A Smelt at length, from out his slender cheer
He draws, and seems to whisper in itts ear;
Does then another, and another, take,   20
And with them all, in private, feigns to speak,
The luckyer feeders, for a moment ceas'd,

To penetrate the meaning of the jest;
No jest, he cries, but forreign news I try
To learn, by conuersation with the Fry,
A Scott, my Friend, some Akers had of Land,
Which, since no Corn, nor Tree wou'd on them stand,
He turn'd to pounds, and thought his fortune made
By joyning in the Caledonian Trade;
So, cross'd the waves, but now, sad rumours come   30
Th' unhappy youth, abroad has found his Doom;
To know the truth, and sett my thoughts att ease,
I question'd with these Pigmies of the Seas,
Who modestly reply, with loosen'd tongue,
For Dariens Istmus they were far too yong,
Nor from the Shoar, a League cou'd hard'ly keep;
But, send me, to those Monsters of the Deep,
Which round the World a yearly course maintain
Till now, here dress'd, they swim in sawce again,
Cou'd I, but speak, with one of those full-grown,   40
My Friend's disaster might be thoroughly known;
Whether, detain'd by Death, by want, or wind,
The Project broke, he stayes so long behind?
None, need demand, if his invention took,
Who for his teeth, thus made his tongue the hook.
A Jest, well tim'd, though from a worthless Man
Often obtains, more then true merit can.

THE ATHEIST AND THE ACORN

Methinks this World is oddly made,
      And ev'ry thing's amiss,
A dull presuming Atheist said,
As stretch'd he lay beneath a Shade;
      And instanced in this:

Behold, quoth he, that mighty thing,
      A *Pumpkin*, large and round,

Is held but by a little String,
Which upwards cannot make it spring,
    Or bear it from the Ground.

Whilst on this *Oak*, a Fruit so small,
    So disproportion'd, grows;
That, who with Sence surveys this *All*,
This universal Casual Ball,
    Its ill Contrivance knows.

My better Judgment wou'd have hung
    That Weight upon a Tree,
And left this Mast, thus slightly strung,
'Mongst things which on the Surface sprung,
    And small and feeble be.

No more the Caviller cou'd say,
    Nor farther Faults descry;
For, as he upwards gazing lay,
An *Acorn*, loosen'd from the Stay,
    Fell down upon his Eye.

Th' offended Part with Tears ran o'er,
    As punish'd for the Sin:
Fool! had that Bough a *Pumpkin* bore,
Thy Whimseys must have work'd no more,
    Nor Scull had kept them in.

THE PREVALENCE OF CUSTOM

A Female, to a Drunkard marry'd,
When all her other Arts miscarry'd,
Had yet one Stratagem to prove him,
And from good Fellowship remove him;
Finding him overcome with Tipple,
And weak, as Infant at the Nipple,

She to a Vault transports the Lumber,
And *there expects* his breaking Slumber.
A Table she with Meat provided,
And rob'd in Black, stood just beside it;   10
Seen only, by one glim'ring Taper,
That blewly burnt thro' misty Vapor.
At length he wakes, his Wine digested,
And of her Phantomship requested,
To learn the Name of that close Dwelling,
And what offends his Sight and Smelling;
And of what Land she was the Creature,
With outspread Hair, and ghastly Feature?
Mortal, quoth she, (to Darkness hurry'd)
Know, that thou art both Dead and Bury'd;   20
Convey'd, last Night, from noisie Tavern,
To this thy still, and dreary Cavern.
What strikes thy Nose, springs from the Shatters
Of Bodies kill'd with Cordial Waters,
Stronger than other Scents and quicker,
As urg'd by more spirituous Liquor.
My self attend on the Deceas'd,
When all their Earthly Train's releas'd;
And in this Place of endless Quiet,
My Bus'ness is, to find them Diet;   30
To shew all sorts of Meats, and Salades,
Till I'm acquainted with their Palates;
But that once known, then less suffices.
Quoth he (and on his Crupper rises)
Thou Guardian of these lower Regions,
Thou Providor for countless Legions,
Thou dark, but charitable Crony,
Far kinder than my *Tisiphony*,
Who of our Victuals thus art Thinking,
If thou hast Care too of our Drinking,   40

A *Bumper* fetch: Quoth she, a *Halter*
Since nothing less thy Tone can alter,
Or break this Habit thou'st been getting,
To keep thy Throat in constant wetting.

THE MUSSULMAN'S DREAM OF THE VIZIER AND DERVIS

Where is that World, to which the Fancy flies,
When Sleep excludes the Present from our Eyes;
Whose Map no Voyager cou'd e'er design,
Nor to Description its wild Parts confine?
Yet such a Land of Dreams We must allow,
Who nightly trace it, tho' we know not how:
Unfetter'd by the Days obtruded Rules,
We All enjoy that Paradise of Fools;
And find a Sorrow, in resuming Sense,
Which breaks some free Delight, and snatches us
    from thence.   10

Thus! in a Dream, a *Mussulman* was shown
A *Vizir*, whom he formerly had known,
When at the *Port* he bore deputed Sway,
And made the Nations with a Nod obey.
Now all serene, and splendid was his Brow,
Whilst ready Waiters to his Orders bow;
His Residence, an artful Garden seem'd,
Adorn'd with all, that pleasant he esteem'd;
Full of Reward, his glorious Lot appear'd,
As with the Sight, our Dreamer's Mind was chear'd;
But turning, next he saw a dreadful Sight,   21
Which fill'd his Soul with Wonder and Affright,
Pursu'd by Fiends, a wretched *Dervis* fled
Through scorching Plains, which to wide Distance
    spread;

Whilst every Torture, gloomy Poets paint,
Was there prepar'd for the reputed Saint.
Amaz'd at this, the sleeping *Turk* enquires,
Why He that liv'd above, in soft Attires,
Now roll'd in Bliss, while t'other roll'd in Fires?
We're taught the Suff'rings of this Future State, 30
Th' Excess of Courts is likeliest to create;
Whilst solitary Cells, o'ergrown with Shade,
The readiest way to Paradise is made.
True, quoth the Phantom (which he dream'd reply'd)
The lonely Path is still the surest Guide,
Nor is it by these Instances deny'd.
For, know my Friend, whatever Fame report,
The *Vizier* to Retirements wou'd Resort,
Th' ambitious *Dervis* wou'd frequent the Court.

THE SHEPHERD PIPING TO THE FISHES

A Shepherd seeking with his Lass
    To shun the Heat of Day;
Was seated on the shadow'd Grass,
Near which a flowing Stream did pass,
    And Fish within it play.

To *Phillis* he an Angle gave,
    And bid her toss the Line;
For sure, quoth he, each Fish must have,
Who do's not seek to be thy Slave,
    A harder Heart than mine.

Assemble here you watry Race,
    Transportedly he cries;
And if, when you behold her Face,
You e'er desire to quit the Place,
    You see not with my Eyes.

But you, perhaps, are by the Ear,
  More easie to be caught;
If so, I have my Bagpipe here,
The only Musick that's not dear,
  Nor in great Cities bought.

So sprightly was the Tune he chose,
  And often did repeat;
That *Phillis*, tho' not up she rose,
Kept time with every thrilling Close,
  And jigg'd upon her Seat.

But not a Fish wou'd nearer draw,
  No Harmony or Charms,
Their frozen Blood, it seems, cou'd thaw,
Nor all they heard, nor all they saw
  Cou'd woo them to such Terms.

The angry Shepherd in a Pett,
  Gives o'er his wheedling Arts,
And from his Shoulder throws the Net,
Resolv'd he wou'd a Supper get
  By Force, if not by Parts.

Thus stated Laws are always best
  To rule the vulgar Throng,
Who grow more Stubborn when Carest,
Or with soft Rhetorick addrest,
  If taking Measures wrong.

THE DECISION OF FORTUNE

A Fable

Fortune well Pictured on a rolling Globe,
With waving Locks, and thin transparent Robe,
A Man beholding, to his Neighbour cry'd,

Whoe'er would catch this Dame, must swiftly ride.
Mark, how she seems to Fly, and with her bears,
All that is worth a busie Mortal's Cares:
The gilded Air about her Statue shines,
As if the Earth had lent it all her Mines;
At random Here a Diadem she flings,
And There a scarlet Hat with dangling Strings,   10
And to ten Thousand Fools ten Thousand glorious
   Things.
Shall I then stay at Home, Dull and Content
With Quarter-Days, and hard extorted Rent?
No, I'll to Horse, to Sea, to utmost Isles,
But I'll encounter her propitious Smiles:
Whilst you in slothful Ease may chuse to Sleep,
And scarce the few Paternal Acres keep.
Farewel, reply'd his Friend, may you advance,
And grow the Darling of this Lady *Chance:*
Whilst I indeed, not courting of her Grace,   20
Shall dwell content, in this my Native Place,
Hoping I still shall for your Friend be known:
But if too big for such Acquaintance grown,
I shan't be such a fond mistaken Sot,
To think Remembrance should become my Lot;
When you Exalted, have your self Forgot.
Nor me Ambitious ever shall you find,
Or hunting Fortune, who, they say, is Blind:
But if her Want of Sight shou'd make her Stray,
She shou'd be Welcome, if she came this Way.   30
'Tis very like (the Undertaker cry'd)
That she her Steps to these lost Paths shou'd guide:
But I lose Time, whilst I such Thoughts deride.
Away he goes, with Expectation chear'd,
But when his Course he round the World had steer'd,
And much had borne, and much had hop'd and fear'd,

Yet cou'd not be inform'd where he might find
This fickle Mistress of all Human-kind:
He quits at length the Chace of flying Game,
And back as to his Neighbor's House he came,   40
He there encounters the uncertain Dame;
Who lighting from her gaudy Coach in haste,
To him her eager Speeches thus addrest.
Fortune behold, who has been long pursu'd,
Whilst all the Men, that have my Splendors view'd,
Madly enamour'd, have such Flatt'ries forg'd,
And with such Lies their vain Pretensions urg'd,
That Hither I am fled to shun their Suits,
And by free Choice conclude their vain Disputes;
Whilst I the Owner of this Mansion bless,   50
And he unseeking *Fortune* shall possess.
Tho' rightly charg'd as something Dark of Sight,
Yet Merit, when 'tis found, is my Delight;
To Knaves and Fools, when I've some Grace allow'd,
'T has been like scattering Money in a Croud,
To make me Sport, as I beheld them strive,
And some observ'd (thro' Age) but Half-Alive;
Scrambling amongst the Vigorous and Young,
One proves his Sword, and One his wheedling Tongue,
All striving to obtain me right or wrong: 60
Whilst Crowns, and Crosiers in the Contest hurl'd,
Shew'd me a Farce in the contending World.
Thou wert deluded, whilst with Ship, or Steed,
Thou lately didst attempt to reach my Speed,
And by laborious Toil, and endless Pains,
Didst sell thy Quiet for my doubtful Gains:
Whilst He alone my real Fav'rite rises,
Who every Thing to its just Value prizes,
And neither courts, nor yet my Gifts despises.

THE BRASS-POT, AND STONE-JUGG
A Fable

A Brazen *Pot*, by scouring vext,
With Beef and Pudding still perplext,
Resolv'd t' attempt a nobler Life,
Urging the *Jugg* to share the Strife:
Brother, quoth he, (Love to endear)
Why shou'd We Two continue here,
To serve and cook such homely Cheer?
Who tho' we move with awkward pace,
Your stony Bowels, and my Face,
Abroad can't miss of Wealth and Place.   10
Then let us instantly be going,
And see what in the World is Doing.
The bloated *Jugg*, supine and lazy,
Who made no Wish, but to be easy,
Nor, like it's Owner, e'er did think
Of ought, but to be fill'd with Drink;
Yet something mov'd by this fine Story,
And frothing higher with Vain-glory,
Reply'd, he never wanted Metal,
But had not Sides, like sturdy *Kettle*,   20
That in a Croud cou'd shove and bustle,
And to Preferment bear the Justle;
When the first Knock would break *His* Measures,
And stop his Rise to Place and Treasures.
Sure (quoth the *Pot*) thy Scull is thicker,
Than ever was thy muddiest Liquor:
Go I not with thee, for thy Guard,
To take off Blows, and Dangers ward?
And hast thou never heard, that Cully
Is borne thro' all by daring Bully?   30
Your self (reply'd the Drink-conveigher)

May be my Ruin and Betrayer:
A Superiority you boast,
And dress the *Meat,* I but the *Toast:*
Than mine your Constitution's stronger
And in Fatigues can hold out longer;
And shou'd one Bang from you be taken,
I into Nothing shou'd be shaken.
A *d'autre* cry'd the *Pot* in scorn,
Dost think, there's such a Villain born,   40
That, when he proffers Aid and Shelter,
Will rudely fall to Helter-Skelter?
No more, but follow to the Road,
Where Each now drags his pond'rous Load,
And up the Hill were almost clamber'd,
When (may it ever be remember'd!)
Down rolls the *Jugg,* and after rattles
The most perfidious of all Kettles;
At every Molehill gives a Jump,
Nor rests, till by obdurate Thump,   50
The Pot of Stone, to shivers broken,
Sends each misguided Fool a Token:
To show them, by this fatal Test,
That Equal Company is best,
Where none Oppress, nor are Opprest.

THE OWL DESCRIBING HER YOUNG ONES

Why was that baleful Creature made,
Which seeks our Quiet to invade,
And screams ill Omens through the Shade?

'Twas, sure, for every Mortals good,
When, by wrong painting of her Brood,
She doom'd them for the Eagle's Food:

Who proffer'd Safety to her Tribe,
Wou'd she but shew them or describe,
And serving him, his Favour bribe.

When thus she did his Highness tell;   10
In Looks my Young do all excel,
Nor Nightingales can sing so well.

You'd joy to see the pretty Souls,
With wadling Steps and frowzy Poles,
Come creeping from their secret Holes.

But I ne'er let them take the Air,
The Fortune-hunters do so stare;
And Heiresses indeed they are.

This ancient Yew three hundred Years,
Has been possess'd by Lineal Heirs: 20
The Males extinct, now All is Theirs.

I hope I've done their Beauties right,
Whose Eyes outshine the Stars by Night;
Their Muffs and Tippets too are White.

The King of *Cedars* wav'd his Power,
And swore he'd fast ev'n from that Hour,
Ere he'd such Lady Birds devour.

Th' Agreement seal'd, on either part,
The Owl now promis'd, from her Heart
All his Night-Dangers to divert;   30

As Centinel to stand and Whoop,
If single Fowl, or Shoal, or Troop
Should at his Palace aim or stoop.

But home, one Evening without Meat,
The Eagle comes, and takes his Seat,
Where they did these Conditions treat.

The Mother-Owl was prol'd away,
To seek abroad for needful Prey,
And forth the Misses came to play.

What's here! the hungry Monarch cry'd, 40
When near him living Flesh he spy'd,
With which he hop'd to be supply'd.

But recollecting, 'twas the Place,
Where he'd so lately promis'd Grace
To an enchanting, beauteous Race;

He paus'd a while, and kept his Maw,
With sober Temperance, in awe,
Till all their Lineaments he saw.

What are these Things, and of what Sex,
At length he cry'd, with Vultur's Becks, 50
And Shoulders higher than their Necks?

These wear no *Palatines*, nor Muffs,
Italian Silks, or *Doyley* Stuffs,
But motley Callicoes, and Ruffs.

Nor Brightness in their Eyes is seen,
But through the Film a dusky Green,
And like old *Margery* is their Mien.

Then for my Supper they're designed,
Nor can be of that lovely Kind,
To whom my Pity was inclin'd. 60

No more Delays; as soon as spoke,
The Plumes are stripped, the Grisles broke,
And near the Feeder was to choak.

When now return'd the grizly Dame,
(Whose Family was out of Frame)
Against League-Breakers does exclaim.

How! quoth the Lord of soaring Fowls,
(Whilst horribly she wails and howls)
Were then your Progeny but Owls?

I thought some *Phœnix* was their Sire,   70
Who did those charming Looks inspire,
That you'd prepar'd me to admire.

Upon your self the Blame be laid;
My Talons you've to Blood betray'd,
And ly'd in every Word you said.

Faces or Books, beyond their Worth extoll'd,
Are censur'd most, and thus to pieces pull'd.

THE PHILOSOPHER, THE YOUNG MAN, AND HIS STATUE

A Fond *Athenian* Mother brought
A *Sculptor* to indulge her Thought,
    And carve her Only Son;
Who to such strange perfection wrought,
That every Eye the Statue caught
    Nor ought was left undone.

A youthful Smile adorn'd the Face,
The polish gave that Smile a Grace;
    And through the Marble reigns
(Which well the Artist's Skill cou'd trace,
And in their due Positions place)
    A Thread of purple Veins.

The Parasites about it came,
(Whose Praises were too large to name)
    And to each other said;
The Man so well had reach'd his Aim,
Th' Original cou'd o'er it claim
    Only a native Red.

Mean while a Sage, amidst the Croud,
Thus, with a Precept wise and loud,
   Check'd the Vain-glorious Boy;
By telling him, who now grew proud,
That tho' with Beauty 'twas endow'd,
   The Figure was a Toy:

Of no Advantage to the State,
'Twou'd neither combate, nor debate,
   But idly stand alone;
Bids him beware, whilst Men create
In Stone thus his Resemblance great,
   He prove not like the stone.

THE HOG, THE SHEEP, AND GOAT, CARRYING TO A FAIR

Who does not wish, ever to judge aright,
   And, in the Course of Life's Affairs,
To have a quick, and far extended Sight,
   Tho' it too often multiplies his Cares?
And who has greater Sense, but greater Sorrow shares?

This felt the *Swine*, now carrying to the Knife;
   And whilst the *Lamb* and silent *Goat*
In the same fatal Cart lay void of Strife,
   He widely stretches his foreboding Throat,
Deaf'ning the easy Crew with his outragious Note.

The angry *Driver* chides th'unruly Beast,
   And bids him all this Noise forbear;
Nor be more loud, nor clamorous than the rest,
   Who with him travel'd to the neighb'ring *Fair*.
And quickly shou'd arrive, and be unfetter'd there.

This, quoth the *Swine*, I do believe, is true,
   And see we're very near the Town;

Whilst these poor Fools of short, and bounded View,
    Think 'twill be well, when you have set them down,
And eas'd One of her Milk, the Other of her Gown.

But all the dreadful Butchers in a Row,
    To my far-searching Thoughts appear,
Who know indeed, we to the Shambles go,
    Whilst I, whom none but *Belzebub* wou'd shear,
Nor but his Dam wou'd milk, must for my Carcase fear.

But tell me then, will it prevent thy Fate?
    The rude unpitying Farmer cries;
If not, the Wretch who tastes his suff'rings late,
    Not He, who thro' th'unhappy Future prys,
Must of the Two be held most Fortunate and Wise.

THE SHEPHERD AND THE CALM

Soothing his Passions with a warb'ling Sound,
A Shepherd-Swain lay stretch'd upon the Ground;
Whilst all were mov'd, who their Attention lent,
Or with the Harmony in Chorus went,
To something less than Joy, yet more than dull Content.
(Between which two Extreams true Pleasure lies,
O'er-run by *Fools*, unreach'd-at by the *Wife*)
But yet, a fatal Prospect to the Sea
Wou'd often draw his greedy Sight away.
He saw the Barques unlading on the Shore,   10
And guess'd their Wealth, then scorn'd his little Store.
Then wou'd that Little lose, or else wou'd make it more.
To Merchandize converted is the Fold,
The Bag, the Bottle, and the Hurdles fold;
The Dog was chang'd away, the pretty *Skell*
Whom he had fed, and taught, and lov'd so well.
In vain the *Phillis* wept, which heretofore

Receiv'd his Presents, and his Garlands wore.
False and upbraided, he forsakes the Downs,
Nor courts her Smiles, nor fears the Ocean's Frowns. 20
For smooth it lay, as if one single Wave
Made all the Sea, nor Winds that Sea cou'd heave;
Which blew no more than might his Sails supply:
Clear was the Air below, and *Phœbus* laugh'd on high.
With this Advent'rer ev'ry thing combines,
And Gold to Gold his happy Voyage joins;
But not so prosp'rous was the next Essay,
For rugged Blasts encounter'd on the way,
Scarce cou'd the Men escape, the Deep had all their
        Prey.
Our broken Merchant in the Wreck was thrown   30
Upon those Lands, which once had been his own;
Where other Flocks now pastur'd on the Grass,
And other *Corydons* had woo'd his Lass.
A Servant, for small Profits, there he turns,
Yet thrives again, and less and less he mourns;
Re-purchases in time th'abandon'd Sheep,
Which sad Experience taught him now to keep.
When from that very Bank, one Halcyon Day,
On which he lean'd, when tempted to the Sea,
He notes a Calm; the Winds and Waves were still, 40
And promis'd what the Winds nor Waves fulfill,
A settl'd Quiet, and Conveyance sure,
To him that Wealth, by Traffick, wou'd procure.
But the rough part the Shepherd now performs,
Reviles the Cheat, and at the Flatt'ry storms.
Ev'n thus (quoth he) you seem'd all Rest and Ease,
You sleeping Tempests, you untroubl'd Seas,
That ne'er to be forgot, that luckless Hour,
In which I put my Fortunes in your Pow'r;
Quitting my slender, but secure Estate,   50

My undisturb'd Repose, my sweet Retreat,
For Treasures which you ravish'd in a Day,
But swept my Folly, with my Goods, away.
Then smile no more, nor these false Shews employ,
Thou momentary Calm, thou fleeting Joy;
No more on me shall these fair Signs prevail,
Some other Novice may be won to Sail,
Give me a certain Fate in the obscurest Vale.

THE LORD AND THE BRAMBLE

To view his stately Walks and Groves,
  A Man of Pow'r and Place
Was hast'ning on; but as he roves,
His Foe the slighted *Bramble* proves,
  And stops his eager Pace.

That Shrub was qualify'd to Bite;
  And now there went a Tale,
That this injurious partial Wight
Had bid his Gard'ner rid it quite,
  And throw it o'er the Pail.

Often the *Bry'r* had wish'd to speak,
  That this might not be done;
But from the Abject and the Weak,
Who no important Figure make,
  What Statesman does not run?

But clinging now about his Waste,
  Ere he had time to fly,
My Lord (quoth he) for all your haste,
I'll know why I must be displac'd,
  And 'mongst the Rubbish lie.

Must none but buffle-headed Trees
  Within your Ground be seen?

Or tap'ring Yews here court the Breeze,
That, like some *Beaux* whom Time does freeze,
  At once look Old and Green?

I snarl, 'tis true, and sometimes scratch
  A tender-footed Squire;
Who does a rugged *Tartar* catch,
When me he thinks to over-match,
  And jeers for my Attire.

As to Yourself, who 'gainst me fret,
  E'en give this Project o'er:
For know, where'er my Root is set,
These rambling Twigs will Passage get,
  And vex you more and more.

No Wants, no Threatnings, nor the Jail
  Will curb an angry Wit:
Then think not to chastise, or rail;
Appease the Man, if you'd prevail,
  Who some sharp Satire writ.

THE HOUSE OF SOCRATES

For *Socrates* a House was built,
  Of but inferiour Size;
Not highly Arch'd, nor Carv'd, nor Gilt;
  The Man, 'tis said, was Wise.

But *Mob* despis'd the little Cell,
  That struck them with no Fear;
Whilst Others thought, there should not dwell
  So great a Person there.

How shou'd a due Recourse be made
  To One, so much Admir'd?
Where shou'd the spacious Cloth be laid,
  Or where the Guests retir'd?

Believe me, quoth the list'ning Sage,
   'Twas not to save the Charge;
That in this over-building Age,
   My House was not more large.

But this for faithful Friends, and kind,
   Was only meant by me;
Who fear that what too streight you find,
   Must yet contracted be.

THE YOUNG RAT AND HIS DAM, THE COCK AND THE CAT

No Cautions of a Matron, Old and Sage,
Young Rattlehead to Prudence cou'd engage;
But forth the Offspring of her Bed wou'd go,
Nor reason gave, but that he *wou'd* do so.
Much Counsel was, at parting, thrown away,
Ev'n all, that Mother-Rat to Son cou'd say;
Who follow'd him with utmost reach of Sight,
Then, lost in Tears, and in abandon'd Plight,
Turn'd to her mournful Cell, and bid the World Good
   Night.
But *Fortune*, kinder than her boding Thought,   10
In little time the Vagrant homewards brought,
Rais'd in his Mind, and mended in his Dress,
Who the *Bel-air* did every way confess,
Had learnt to flow'r his Wigg, nor brusht away
The falling Meal, that on his Shoulders lay;
And from a Nutshell, wimbl'd by a Worm,
Took Snuff, and cou'd the Government reform.
The Mother, weeping from Maternal Love,
To see him thus prodigiously improve,
Expected mighty Changes too, within,   20
And Wisdom to avoid the Cat, and Gin.

Whom did you chiefly note, Sweetheart, quoth she,
Of all the Strangers you abroad did see?
Who grac'd you most, or did your Fancy take?
The younger Rat than curs'd a noisy Rake,
That barr'd the best Acquaintance he cou'd make;
And fear'd him so, he trembl'd ev'ry Part;
Nor to describe him, scarce cou'd have the Heart.
High on his Feet (quoth he) himself he bore,
And terribly, in his own Language, swore;   30
A feather'd Arm came out from either Side,
Which loud he clapp'd, and Combatants defy'd,
And to each Leg a Bayonette was ty'd:
And certainly his Head with Wounds was sore;
For That, and both his Cheeks a Sanguine Colour wore.
Near Him there lay the Creature I admir'd,
And for a Friend by Sympathy desir'd:
His Make, like Ours, as far as Tail and Feet,
With Coat of Furr in parallel do meet;
Yet seeming of a more exalted Race,   40
Tho' humble Meekness beautify'd his Face:
A purring Sound compos'd his gentle Mind,
Whilst frequent Slumbers did his Eye-lids bind;
Whose soft, contracted Paw lay calmly still,
As if unus'd to prejudice, or kill.
I paus'd a while, to meditate a Speech,
And now was stepping just within his reach;
When that rude Clown began his hect'ring Cry,
And made me for my Life, and from th' Attempt to fly.
Indeed 'twas Time, the shiv'ring Beldam said,   50
To scour the Plain, and be of Life afraid.
Thou base, degen'rate Seed of injur'd Rats,
Thou veriest Fool (she cry'd) of all my Brats;
Would'st thou have shaken Hands with hostile Cats,
And dost not yet thine Own, and Country's Foe,

At this expence of Time, and Travel know?
Alas! that swearing, staring, bullying Thing,
That tore his Throat, and blustered with his Wing,
Was but some paltry, Dunghill, Craven Cock,
Who serves the early Household for a Clock.   60
And We his Oats, and Barley often steal,
Nor fear, he shou'd revenge the pilfer'd Meal:
Whilst that demure, and seeming harmless Puss
Herself, and mewing Chits regales with Us.
If then, of useful sense thou'st gain'd no more,
Than ere thou'dst past the Threshold of my Door;
Be here, my Son, content to Dress and Dine,
Steeping the List of Beauties in thy Wine,
And neighb'ring Vermin with false Gloss outshine.
   Amongst Mankind a Thousand *Fops* we see,   70
Who in their Rambles learn no more than Thee;
Cross o'er the *Alpes*, and make the *Tour* of *France*
To learn a paltry Song, or antick Dance;
Bringing their Noddles, and Valizes pack'd
With Mysteries, from Shops and Taylors wreck'd:
But what may prejudice their Native Land;
Whose Troops are raising, or whose Fleet is mann'd,
Ne'er moves their Thoughts, nor do they understand.
Thou, my dear Rattlehead, and such as These
Might keep at home, and brood on Sloth and Ease;   80
Whilst Others, more adapted to the Age,
May vig'rously in Warlike Feats engage,
And live on foreign Spoils, or dying thin the Stage.

THE EXECUTOR

A Greedy *Heir* long waited to fulfill,
As his Executor, a *Kinsman*'s Will;
And to himself his Age repeated o'er,
To his Infirmities still adding more;

And nicely kept th' Account of the expected Store:
When *Death*, at last, to either gave Release,
Making One's Pains, the Other's Longings cease;
Who to the Grave must decently convey,
Ere he Possession takes the kindred Clay,
Which in a Coach was plac'd, wherein he rides,   10
And so no Hearse, or following Train provides;
Rejecting *Russel*, who wou'd make the Charge
Of one dull tedious Day, so vastly Large.
When, at his Death the humble Man declar'd,
He wished thus privately to be Interr'd.
And now, the Luggage moves in solemn State,
And what it wants in Number, gains in Weight.
The happy *Heir* can scarce contain his Joy,
Whilst sundry Musings do his Thoughts employ,
How he shalt act, now Every thing's his Own,   20
Where his Revenge, or Favour shall be shown;
Then recollecting, draws a counterfeited Groan.
The Avenues, and Gardens shall be chang'd,
Already he the Furniture has ranged.
To ransack secret Draw'rs his Phancy flies,
Nor can th' appearing Wealth his Mind suffice.
Thus he an Age runs o'er betwixt the Porch
Of his Friend's House, and the adjacent Church:
Whilst the slow Driver, who no reck'ning kept
Of what was left, indulging Nature, slept;   30
Till on a Bank, so high, the Wheel was borne
That in a Moment All must overturn:
Whilst the rich *Heir* now finds the giving Dead
Less weighty in his Gold, than in his Lead;
Which falling just on his contriving Breast,
Expell'd the Soul, leaving the corpse to rest
In the same Grave, intended for his Friend.
Then why shou'd We our Days in Wishes spend,
Which, ere we see fulfill'd, are often at an End?

A TALE OF THE MISER AND THE POET

Written about the Year 1709

A Wit, transported with Inditing,
Unpay'd, unprais'd, yet ever Writing;
Who, for all Fights and Fav'rite Friends,
Had Poems at his Finger Ends;
For new Events was still providing;
Yet now desirous to be riding,
He pack'd-up ev'ry *Ode* and *Ditty*
And in Vacation left the City;
So rapt with Figures, and Allusions,
With secret Passions, sweet Confusions;   10
With Sentences from Plays well-known,
And thousand Couplets of his own;
That ev'n the chalky Road look'd gay,
And seem'd to him the *Milky Way.*
But *Fortune*, who the Ball is tossing,
And *Poets* ever will be crossing,
Misled the Steed, which ill he guided,
Where several gloomy Paths divided.
The steepest in Descent he followed,
Enclos'd by Rocks, which Time had hollow'd;   20
Till, he believed, alive and booted,
He'd reach'd the Shades by *Homer* quoted.
But all, that he cou'd there discover,
Was, in a Pit with Thorns grown over,

Old *Mammon* digging, straining, sweating,
As Bags of Gold he thence was getting;
Who, when reproved for such Dejections
By him, who lived on high Reflections,
Reply'd; Brave Sir, your Time is ended,
And *Poetry* no more befriended.   30

I hid this Coin, when *Charles* was swaying;
When all was Riot, Masking, Playing;
When witty Beggars were in fashion,
And Learning had o'er-run the Nation,
But, since Mankind is so much wiser,
That none is valued like the *Miser*,
I draw it hence, and now these Sums
In proper Soil grow up to *Plumbs;*
Which gather'd once, from that rich Minute
We rule the World, and all that's in it.   40

But, quoth the *Poet*, can you raise,
As well as Plumb-trees, Groves of Bays?
Where you, which I wou'd chuse much rather,
May Fruits of Reputation gather?
Will Men of Quality, and Spirit,
Regard you for intrinsick Merit?
And seek you out, before your Betters,
For Conversation, Wit, and Letters?

Fool, quoth the Churl, who knew no Breeding;
Have these been Times for such Proceeding?   50
Instead of Honour'd and Rewarded,
Are you not Slighted, or Discarded?
What have you met with, but Disgraces?
Your PRIOR cou'd not keep in Places;
And your VAN-BRUG had found no quarter,
But for his dabbling in the Morter.
ROWE no Advantages cou'd hit on,
Till Verse he left, to write *North-Briton.*
PHILIPS, who's by the *Shilling* known,
Ne'er saw a Shilling of his own.   60
Meets PHILOMELA, in the Town
Her due Proportion of Renown?
What Pref'rence has ARDELIA seen,

T'expel, tho' she cou'd write the *Spleen?*
Of Coach, or Tables, can you brag,
Or better Cloaths than Poet RAG?
Do wealthy Kindred, when they meet you,
With Kindness, or Distinction, greet you?
Or have your lately flatter'd Heroes
Enrich'd you like the Roman *Maroes?*　　　70

　No—quoth the Man of broken Slumbers:
Yet we have Patrons for our Numbers;
There are *Mecœnas's* among 'em.

　Quoth *Mammon*, pray Sir, do not wrong 'em;
But in your Censures use a Conscience,
Nor charge Great Men with thriftless Nonsense:
Since they, as your own Poets sing,
Now grant *no Worth in any thing*
But so much Money as 'twill bring.
Then, never more from your Endeavours　　　80
Expect Preferment, or less Favours.
But if you'll 'scape Contempt, or worse,
Be sure, put Money in your Purse;
Money! which only can relieve you
When Fame and Friendship will deceive you.

　Sir, (quoth the *Poet* humbly bowing,
And all that he had said allowing)
Behold me and my airy Fancies
Subdu'd, like Giants in Romances.
I here submit to your Discourses;　　　90
Which since Experience too enforces,
I, in that solitary Pit,
Your Gold withdrawn, will hide my Wit:
Till Time, which hastily advances,
And gives to all new Turns and Chances,

Again may bring it into use;
Roscommons may again produce;
New *Augustean* Days revive,
When *Wit* shall please, and *Poets* thrive.
Till when, let those converse in private,   100
Who taste what others don't arrive at;
Yielding that Mammonists surpass us;
And let the *Bank* out-swell *Parnassus*.

THE TRADESMAN AND THE SCHOLAR

A Citizen of mighty Pelf,
But much a Blockhead, in himself
Disdain'd a Man of shining Parts,
Master of Sciences and Arts,
Who left his Book scarce once a day
For sober Coffee, Smoak, or Tea;
Nor spent more Money in the Town
Than bought, when need requir'd, a Gown;
Which way of Living much offends
The *Alderman*, who gets and spends,   10
And grudges him the Vital Air,
Who drives no Trade, and takes no Care.
Why *Bookworm!* to him once he cry'd,
Why, setting thus the World aside,
Dost thou thy useless Time consume,
Enclos'd within a lonely Room,
And poring damnify thy Wit,
'Till not for Men or Manners fit?
Hop'st thou, with urging of thy Vein,
To spin a Fortune from thy Brain?   20
Or gain a Patron, that shall raise
Thy solid State, for empty Praise?
No; trust not to your Soothings vile,

Receiv'd per me's the only Stile.
Your Book's but frown'd on by My Lord;
If Mine's uncross'd, I reach his Board.
In slighting Yours, he shuts his Hand;
Protracting Mine, devolves the Land.
Then let Advantage be the Test,
Which of us Two ev'n Writes the best.   30
Besides, I often Scarlet wear,
And strut to Church, just next the *Mayor*.
Whilst rusty Black, with Inch of Band,
Is all the Dress you understand;
Who in the Pulpit thresh to Please,
Whilst I below can snore at Ease.
Yet, if you prove me there a Sinner,
I let you go without a Dinner.
This Prate was so beneath the Sence
Of One, who Wisdom cou'd dispense,   40
Unheard, or unreturn'd it past:
But War now lays the City waste,
And plunder'd Goods profusely fell
By length of Pike, not length of Ell.
Abroad th' Inhabitants are forc'd,
From Shops, and Trade, and Wealth divorc'd.
The Student leaving but his Book,
The Tumult of the Place forsook.
In Foreign Parts, One tells his Tale,
How Rich he'd been, how quick his Sale,   50
Which do's for scanty Alms prevail.
The Chance of War whilst he deplores,
And dines at Charitable Doors;
The Man of Letters, known by Fame,
Was welcom'd, wheresoe'er he came.
Still, Potentates entreat his Stay,
Whose Coaches meet him on the Way:

And Universities contest
Which shall exceed, or use him best.
Amaz'd the *Burgomaster* sees   60
On Foot, and scorn'd such Turns as these;
And sighing, now deplores too late
His cumb'rous Trash, and shallow Pate:
Since loaded but with double Chest
Of learned Head, and honest Breast,
The *Scholar* moves from Place to Place,
And finds in every Climate Grace.

    Wit and the Arts, on that Foundation rais'd,
    (*Howe'er the Vulgar are with Shows amaz'd*)
      Is all that recommends, or can be justly prais'd. 70

MAN'S INJUSTICE TOWARDS PROVIDENCE

A Thriving *Merchant*, who no Loss sustained,
In little time a mighty Fortune gain'd.
No Pyrate seiz'd his still returning Freight;
Nor foundring Vessel sunk with its own Weight:
No Ruin enter'd through dissever'd Planks;
No Wreck at Sea, nor in the Publick Banks.
Aloft he sails, above the Reach of Chance,
And do's in Pride, as fast as Wealth, advance.
His Wife too, had her Town and Country-Seat,
And rich in Purse, concludes her Person Great.   10
A Dutchess wears not so much Gold and Lace;
Then 'tis with Her an undisputed Case,
The finest Petticoat must take the Place.
Her Rooms, anew at ev'ry Christ'ning drest,
Put down the Court, and vex the City-Guest.
Grinning *Malottos* in true Ermin stare;
The best *Japan*, and clearest *China* Ware
Are but as common *Delft* and *English Laquar* there.

No Luxury's by either unenjoy'd,
Or cost withheld, tho' awkardly employ'd.   20
How comes this Wealth? a Country Friend demands,
Who scarce cou'd live on Product of his Lands,
How is it that, when Trading is so bad
That some are Broke, and some with Fears run Mad,
You can in better State yourself maintain,
And your Effects still unimpair'd remain!
My *Industry*, he cries, is all the Cause;
Sometimes I interlope, and slight the Laws;
I wiser Measures, than my Neighbours, take,
And better speed, who better Bargains make.   30
I knew, the *Smyrna*-Fleet wou'd fall a Prey,
And therefore sent no Vessel out that way:
My busy Factors prudently I chuse,
And in streight Bonds their Friends and Kindred noose:
At Home, I to the Publick Sums advance,
Whilst, under-hand in Fee with hostile *France*,
I care not for your *Tourvills*, or *Du-Barts*,
No more than for the Rocks, and Shelves in Charts:
My own sufficiency creates my Gain,
Rais'd, and secur'd by this unfailing Brain.   40
This idle Vaunt had scarcely past his Lips,
When Tydings came, his ill-provided Ships
Some thro' the want of Skill, and some of Care,
Were lost, or back return'd without their Fare.
From bad to worse, each Day his State declin'd,
'Till leaving Town, and Wife, and Debts behind,
To his Acquaintance at the Rural Seat   .
He Sculks, and humbly sues for a Retreat.
Whence comes this Change, has Wisdom left that Head,
(His Friend demands) where such right Schemes were
        bred?   50
What Phrenzy, what Delirium mars the Scull,

Which fill'd the Chests, and was it self so full?
Here interrupting, sadly he Reply'd,
In Me's no Change, but Fate must all Things guide;
To *Providence* I attribute my Loss.

Vain-glorious Man do's thus the Praise engross,
When Prosp'rous Days around him spread their
    Beams:
But, if revolv'd to opposite Extreams,
Still his own Sence he fondly will prefer,
And Providence, not He, in his Affairs must Err! 60

THE EAGLE, THE SOW, AND THE CAT

The Queen of Birds, t'encrease the Regal Stock,
Had hatch'd her young Ones in a stately Oak,
Whose Middle-part was by a *Cat* possest,
And near the Root with Litter warmly drest,
A teeming *Sow* had made her peaceful Nest.
(Thus Palaces are cramm'd from Roof to Ground,
And Animals, as various, in them found.)
When to the *Sow,* who no Misfortune fear'd,
Puss with her fawning Compliments appear'd,
Rejoicing much at her Deliv'ry past,   10
And that she 'scap'd so well, who bred so fast.
Then every little *Piglin* she commends,
And likens them to all their swinish Friends;
Bestows good Wishes, but with Sighs implies,
That some dark Fears do in her Bosom rise.
Such Tempting Flesh, she cries, will *Eagles* spare?
Methinks, good Neighbour, you should live in Care:
Since I, who bring not forth such dainty Bits,
Tremble for my unpalatable Chits;
And had I but foreseen, the *Eagle's* Bed   20
Was in this fatal Tree to have been spread;

I sooner would have kitten'd in the Road,
Than made this Place of Danger my abode.
I heard her young Ones lately cry for *Pig*,
And pity'd you, that were so near, and big.
In Friendship this I secretly reveal,
Lest Pettitoes shou'd make th' ensuing Meal;
Or else, perhaps, Yourself may be their aim,
For a *Sow's Paps* has been a Dish of Fame.
No more the sad, affrighted Mother hears,   30
But overturning all with boist'rous Fears,
She from her helpless Young in haste departs,
Whilst *Puss* ascends, to practice farther Arts.
The Anti-chamber pass'd, she scratch'd the Door;
The *Eagle*, ne'er alarum'd so before,
Bids her come in, and look the Cause be great,
That makes her thus disturb the Royal Seat;
Nor think, of Mice and Rats some pest'ring Tale
Shall, in excuse of Insolence, prevail.
Alas! my Gracious Lady, quoth the *Cat*,   40
I think not of such Vermin; Mouse, or Rat
To me are tasteless grown; nor dare I stir
To use my Phangs, or to expose my Fur.
A Foe intestine threatens all around,
And ev'n this lofty Structure will confound;
A Pestilential *Sow*, a meazl'd Pork
On the Foundation has been long at work,
Help'd by a Rabble, issu'd from her Womb,
Which she has foster'd in that lower Room;
Who now for Acorns are so madly bent,   50
That soon this Tree must fall, for their Content.
I wou'd have fetch'd some for th' unruly Elves;
But 'tis the Mob's delight to help Themselves:
Whilst your high Brood must with the meanest drop,
And steeper be their Fall, as next the Top;

Unless you soon to *Jupiter* repair,
And let him know, the Case demands his Care.
Oh! may the Trunk but stand, 'till you come back!
But hark! already sure, I hear it crack.
Away, away—The *Eagle*, all agast,   60
Soars to the Sky, nor falters in her haste:
Whilst crafty *Puss*, now o'er the Eyry reigns,
Replenishing her Maw with treach'rous Gains.
The *Sow* she plunders next, and lives alone;
The *Pigs*, the *Eaglets*, and the *House* her own.

Curs'd Sycophants! *How wretched is the Fate*
Of those, who know you not, till 'tis too late!

THE MAN BITTEN BY FLEAS

A Peevish Fellow laid his Head
    On Pillows stuff'd with Down;
But was no sooner warm in bed,
    With hopes to rest his Crown,

But Animals of slender size,
    That feast on humane Gore,
From secret Ambushes arise,
    Nor suffer him to snore;

Who starts, and scrubs, and frets, and swears,
    'Till, finding all in vain,
He for Relief employs his Pray'rs
    In this old Heathen strain.

Great *Jupiter!* thy Thunder send
    From out the pitchy Clouds,
And give these Foes a dreadful End,
    That lurk in Midnight Shrouds:

Or *Hercules* might with a Blow,
　If once together brought,
This Crew of Monsters overthrow,
　By which such Harms are wrought.

The Strife, ye Gods! is worthy You,
　Since it our Blood has cost;
And scorching Fevers must ensue,
　When cooling Sleep is lost.

Strange *Revolutions* wou'd abound,
　Did Men ne'er close their Eyes;
Whilst those, who wrought them would be found
　At length more Mad, than Wise.

Passive Obedience must be us'd,
　If this cannot be Cur'd;
But whilst One *Flea* is slowly bruis'd,
　Thousands must be endur'd.

Confusion, Slav'ry, Death and Wreck
　Will on the Nation seize,
If, whilst you keep your Thunders back,
　We're massacred by *Fleas*.

Why, prithee, shatter-headed Fop,
　The laughing Gods reply;
Hast thou forgot thy Broom, and Mop,
　And Wormwood growing nigh?

Go sweep, and wash, and strew thy Floor,
　As all good Housewives teach;
And do not thus for Thunders roar,
　To make some fatal Breach:

Which You, nor your succeeding Heir,
　Nor yet a long Descent
Shall find out Methods to repair,
　Tho' Prudence may prevent.

For Club, and Bolts, a Nation *call'd of late,*
Nor wou'd be eas'd by Engines of less Weight:
But whether lighter had not done as well,
Let their Great-Grandsons, or their Grandsons
    tell.

REFORMATION

A Gentleman, most wretched in his Lot,
A wrangling and reproving *Wife* had got,
Who, tho' she curb'd his Pleasures, and his Food,
Call'd him *My Dear*, and did it for his Good,
Ills to prevent ; She of all Ills the worst,
So wisely Froward, and so kindly Curst.
The Servants too experiment her Lungs,
And find they've Breath to serve a thousand Tongues.
Nothing went on ; for her eternal Clack
Still rectifying, set all Matters back ;   10
Nor Town, nor Neighbours, nor the Court cou'd please,
But furnish'd Matter for her sharp Disease.
To distant Plains at length he gets her down,
With no Affairs to manage of her own ;
Hoping from that unactive State to find
A calmer Habit, grown upon her Mind:
But soon return'd he hears her at his Door,
As noisy and tempestuous as before;
Yet mildly ask'd, How she her Days had spent
Amidst the Quiet of a sweet Content,   20
Where Shepherds 'tend their Flocks, and Maids their
    Pails,
And no harsh Mistress domineers, or rails?
Not rail! she cries —— Why, I that had no share
In their Concerns, cou'd not the Trollops spare;
But told 'em, they were Sluts —— And for the Swains,
My Name a Terror to them still remains;

So often I reprov'd their slothful Faults,
And with such Freedom told 'em all my Thoughts,
That I no more amongst them cou'd reside.
Has then, alas! the Gentleman reply'd,   30
One single Month so much their patience try'd?
Where you by Day, and but at Seasons due,
Cou'd with your Clamours their Defects pursue;
How had they shrunk, and justly been afraid,
Had they with me one Curtain Lecture heard!
Yet enter *Madam*, and resume your Sway;
Who can't Command, must silently Obey.
In secret here let endless Faults be found,
Till, like Reformers who in States abound,
You all to Ruin bring, and ev'ry Part confound.   40

THE LYON AND THE GNAT

To the still Covert of a Wood,
    About the prime of Day,
A *Lyon*, satiated with Food,
With stately Pace, and sullen Mood,
    Now took his lazy way.

To Rest he there himself compos'd,
    And in his Mind revolv'd,
How Great a Person it enclos'd,
How free from Danger he repos'd,
    Though now in Ease dissolv'd!

Who Guard, nor Centinel did need,
    Despising as a Jest
All whom the Forest else did feed,
As Creatures of an abject Breed,
    Who durst not him molest.

But in the Air a Sound he heard,
　　That gave him some dislike;
At which he shook his grisly Beard,
Enough to make the Woods affeard,
　　And stretch'd his Paw to strike.

When on his lifted Nose there fell
　　A Creature, slight of Wing,
Who neither fear'd his Grin, nor Yell,
Nor Strength, that in his Jaws did dwell,
　　But gores him with her Sting.

Transported with th' Affront and Pain,
　　He terribly exclaims,
Protesting, if it comes again,
Its guilty Blood the Grass shall stain.
　　And to surprize it aims.

The scoffing *Gnat* now laugh'd aloud,
　　And bids him upwards view
The *Jupiter* within the Cloud,
That humbl'd him, who was so proud,
　　And this sharp Thunder threw.

That Taunt no *Lyon's* Heart cou'd bear;
　　And now much more he raves,
Whilst this new *Perseus* in the Air
Do's War and Strife again declare,
　　And all his Terrour braves.

Upon his haughty Neck she rides,
　　Then on his lashing Tail;
(Which need not now provoke his Sides)
Where she her slender Weapon guides,
　　And makes all Patience fail.

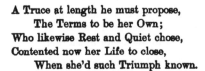

A Truce at length he must propose,
 The Terms to be her Own;
Who likewise Rest and Quiet chose,
Contented now her Life to close,
 When she'd such Triumph known.

You mighty Men, who meaner ones despise,
Learn from this Fable to become more Wise;
You see the Lyon *may be vext with* Flies.

THE MAN AND HIS HORSE

Within a Meadow, on the way,
A sordid Churl resolv'd to stay,
 And give his *Horse* a Bite;
Purloining so his Neighbours Hay,
That at the Inn he might not pay
 For Forage all the Night.

With Heart's content th' unloaded Steed
Began to neigh, and frisk, and feed;
 For nothing more he car'd,
Since none of all his Master's breed
E'er found such Pasture, at their need,
 Or half so well had far'd.

When, in the turning of a Hand,
Out comes the Owner of the Land,
 And do's the Trespass eye;
Which puts poor *Bayard* to a Stand,
For now his Master do's command
 Him to return and fly.

But Hunger quick'ning up his Wit,
And Grass being sweeter than the Bit,
 He to the Clown reply'd:

Shall I for you this Dinner quit,
Who to my Back hard Burdens fit,
  And to the Death wou'd ride?

No; shou'd I as a Stray be found,
And seiz'd upon forbidden Ground,
  I'll on this Spot stand still;
For tho' new Riders shou'd abound,
(Or did Mankind this Field surround)
  They cou'd but use me ill.

Urge no Man to despair; lest in the Fit
He with some Counterblow thy Head may hit.

THE DOG AND HIS MASTER

No better *Dog* e'er kept his Master's Door
Than honest *Snarl*, who spar'd nor Rich nor Poor;
But gave the Alarm, when any one drew nigh
Nor let pretended Friends pass fearless by:
For which reprov'd, as better Fed than Taught,
He rightly thus expostulates the Fault.

 To keep the House from Rascals was my Charge;
The Task was great, and the Commission large.
Nor did your *Worship* e'er declare your Mind,
That to the begging Crew it was confin'd;   10
Who shrink an Arm, or prop an able Knee,
Or turn up Eyes, till they're not seen, nor see.
To Thieves, who know the Penalty of Stealth,
And fairly stake their Necks against your Wealth,
These are the known Delinquents of the Times,
And Whips and *Tyburn* testify their Crimes.
But since to Me there was by Nature lent
An exquisite Discerning by the Scent;
I trace a Flatt'rer, when he fawns and leers,

A rallying Wit, when he commends and jeers: 20
The greedy Parasite I grudging note,
Who praises the good Bits, that oil his Throat;
I mark the Lady, you so fondly toast,
That plays your Gold, when all her own is lost:
The Knave, who fences your Estate by Law,
Yet still reserves an undermining Flaw.
These and a thousand more, which I cou'd tell,
Provoke my Growling, and offend my Smell.

THE BATTLE BETWEEN THE RATS AND THE WEAZLES

In dire Contest the *Rats* and *Weazles* met,
And Foot to Foot, and Point to Point was set:
An ancient Quarrel had such Hatred wrought,
That for Revenge, as for Renown, they fought.
Now bloody was the Day, and hard the Strife,
Wherein bold Warriors lost neglected Life:
But as, some Errors still we must commit,
Nor Valour always ballanc'd is by Wit;
Among the *Rats* some Officers appear'd,
With lofty Plumage on their Foreheads rear'd,
Unthinking they, and ruin'd by their Pride:
For when the *Weazles* prov'd the stronger Side,
A gen'ral Rout befell, and a Retreat,
Was by the Vanquish'd now implor'd of Fate;
To slender Crannies all repair'd in haste,
Where easily the undress'd Vulgar past:
But when the *Rats* of Figure wou'd have fled,
So wide those branching Marks of Honour spread,
The Feather in the Cap was fatal to the Head.

DEMOCRITUS AND HIS NEIGHBOURS
Imitated from Fontaine

In Vulgar Minds what Errors do arise!
How diff'ring are the Notions, they possess,
  From theirs, whom better Sense do's bless,
Who justly are enroll'd amongst the Learn'd and Wise!
Democritus, whilst he all Science taught,
  Was by his foolish Neighbours thought
    Distracted in his Wits;
  Who call his speculative Flights,
  His solitary Walks in starry Nights,
    But wild and frantick Fits.   10
Bless me, each cries, from such a working Brain!
  And to *Hippocrates* they send
  The Sage's long-acquainted Friend,
To put in Tune his jarring Mind again,
    And Pericranium mend.
Away the Skilful *Doctor* comes
  Of Recipes and Med'cines full,
To check the giddy Whirl of Nature's Fires,
  If so th' unruly Case requires;
Or with his Cobweb-cleansing Brooms   20
To sweep and clear the over-crouded Scull,
If settl'd Spirits flag, and make the Patient dull.
  But asking what the Symptoms were,
  That made 'em think he was so bad?
  The Man indeed, they cry'd, is wond'rous Mad.
You, at this Distance, may behold him there
  Beneath that Tree in open Air,
Surrounded with the Engines of his Fate,
  The Gimcracks of a broken Pate.
    Those *Hoops* a Sphere he calls,   30
    That *Ball* the Earth;

And when into his raving Fit he falls,
'Twou'd move at once your Pity, and your Mirth,
  To hear him, as you will do soon,
Declaring, there's a Kingdom in the Moon;
  And that each Star, for ought he knows,
  May some Inhabitants enclose:
Philosophers, he says, may there abound,
Such Jugglers as himself be in them found;
Which if there be, the World may well turn round; 40
  At least to those, whose Whimsies are so strange,
  That, whilst they're fixt to one peculiar Place,
  Pretend to measure far extended Space,
  And 'mongst the Planets range.
  Behold him now contemplating that Head,
From which long-since both Flesh, and Brains are fled;
Questioning, if that empty, hollow Bowl
Did not ere while contain the Human Soul:
Then starts a Doubt, if 't were not to the Heart
That Nature rather did that Gift impart.   50
Good Sir, employ the utmost of your Skill,
To make him Wiser, tho' against his Will;
Who thinks, that he already All exceeds,
And laughs at our most solemn Words and Deeds:
Tho' once amongst us he wou'd try a Cause,
  And Bus'ness of the Town discuss,
  Knowing as well as one of us,
The Price of Corn, and standing Market-Laws;
  Wou'd bear an Office in his Turn,
For which good Purposes all Men were born;   60
Not to be making Circles in the Sand,
And scaling Heav'n, till they have sold their Land;
Or, when unstock'd below their Pasture lies,
To find out Bulls and Rams, amidst the Skies.
From these Mistakes his Madness we conclude;

And hearing, you was with much Skill endu'd,
Your Aid we sought. *Hippocrates* amaz'd,
Now on the Sage, now on the Rabble gaz'd;
And whilst he needless finds his artful Rules,
Pities a Man of Sense, judg'd by a Croud of Fools. 70
Then how can we with their Opinions join,
Who, to promote some Inf'rest, wou'd define
The Peoples *Voice to be the Voice* Divine?

FANSCOMB BARN

In Imitation of MILTON

In *Fanscomb Barn* (who knows not *Fanscomb* Barn?)
Seated between the sides of rising Hills,
Whose airy Tops o'erlook the *Gallick* Seas,
Whilst, gentle *Stower*, thy Waters near them flow,
To beautify the Seats that crown thy Banks.
              — In this *Retreat*
Through Ages pass'd consign'd for Harbour meet,
And Place of sweet Repose to Wand'rers poor,
The weary *Strolepedon* felt that Ease,
Which many a dangerous Borough had deny'd   10
To him, and his *Budgeta* lov'd Compeer;
Nor Food was wanting to the happy Pair,
Who with meek Aspect, and precarious Tone,
Well suited to their Hunger and Degree,
Had mov'd the Hearts of hospitable Dames,
To furnish such Repast as Nature crav'd.
Whilst more to please the swarthy Bowl appears,
Replete with Liquor, globulous to fight,
And threat'ning Inundation o'er the Brim;
Yet, ere it to the longing Lips was rais'd   20
Of him who held it at its due Desert,
And more than all entreated Bounty priz'd,

Into the strong Profundity he throws
The floating Healths of Females, blith and young,
Who there had rendezvouz'd in past Delight,
And to stol'n Plenty added clamorous Mirth,
With Song and Dance, and every jovial Prank
Befitting buxom Crew, untied by Forms:
Whilst kind *Budgeta* nam'd such sturdy Youths,
As next into her tender Thoughts revolv'd,　　　30
And now were straggling *East*, and *West*, and *South*,
Hoof-beating, and at large, as Chance directs,
Still shifting Paths, lest Men (tho' stil'd of Peace)
Should urge their calmer Thoughts to Iron War,
Or force them to promote coercive Laws,
Beating that Hemp which oft entraps their Lives;
Or into Cordage pleated, and amass'd,
Deprives unruly Flesh of tempting Skin.
Thus kind Remembrance brought the Absent near
And hasten'd the Return of either's Pledge:　　　40
Brown were the Toasts, but not unsav'ry found
To Fancies clear'd by Exercise and Air,
Which the spirituous Nectar still improves,
And gliding now thro' every cherish'd Vein,
New Warmth diffused, new Cogitations bred,
With Self-conceit of Person, and of Parts.
When *Strolepedon* (late distorted Wight,
Limb-wanting to the View, and all mis-shap'd)
Permits a pinion'd Arm to fill the sleeve,
Erst pendant, void, and waving with the Wind,　　　50
The Timber-Leg obsequiously withdraws,
And gives to that of Bone Precedence due.
Thus undisguis'd that Form again he wears,
Which Damsel fond had drawn from houshold Toils,
And strict Behests of Parents, old and scorn'd;
Whilst farther yet his Intellects confess

The bouzy Spell dilated and inhans'd,
Ripe for Description, and sett Turns of Speech,
Which to Conjugal Spouse were thus addrest.
My Wife (acknowledg'd such thro' maunding Tribes,
As long as mutual Love, the only Law,   61
Of Hedge or Barn, can bind our easy Faiths)
Be thou observant of thy Husband's Voice,
Sole Auditor of Flights and Figures bold;
Know, that the Valley which we hence descry
Richly adorn'd, is *Fanscomb-Bottom* call'd:
But whether from these Walls it takes the Name,
Or they from that, let Antiquaries tell,
And Men, well-read in Stories obsolete,
Whilst such Denomination either claims,   70
As speaks Affinity contiguous ——
Thence let thy scatter'd Sight, and oft-griev'd Smell
Engulf the Sweets, and Colours free dispos'd
To Flowers promiscuous, and redundant Plants.
And (if the drouzy Vapour will admit,
Which from the Bowl soon triumphs o'er thy Lidds,
And Thee the weaker Vessel still denotes)
With Looks erect observe the verdant Slope
Of graceful Hills, fertile in Bush and Brake,
Whose Height attain'd, th' expatiated Downs   80
Shall wider Scenes display of rural Glee;
Where banner'd Lords, and fair escutcheon'd Knights,
With gentle Squires, and the Staff-griping Clown,
Pursue the trembling Prey impetuous;
Which yet escaping, when the Night returns,
And downy Beds enfold their careless Limbs,
More wakeful *Trundle* (Knapsack-bearing Cur)
Follows the Scent untrac'd by nobler Hounds,
And brings to us the Fruit of all their Toil.

Thus sung the Bard, whom potent Liquor rais'd, 90
Nor so contented, wish'd sublimer Aid.
Ye Wits! (he cry'd) ye Poets! (Loiterers vain,
Who like to us, in Idleness and Want
Consume fantastick Hours) hither repair,
And tell to list'ning *Mendicants* the Cause
Of Wonders, here observ'd but not discuss'd:
Where, the *White Sparrow* never soil'd her Plumes,
Nor the dull Russet cloaths the *Snowy Mouse*.
To *Helicon* you might the *Spring* compare,
That flows near *Pickersdane* renowned Stream, 100
Which, for Disport and Play, the Youths frequent,
Who, train'd in Learned School of ancient *Wye*,
First at this Fount suck in the Muses Lore,
When mixt with Product of the *Indian* Cane,
They drink delicious Draughts, and part inspir'd,
Fit for the Banks of *Isis*, or of *Cham*,
(For *Cham* and *Isis* to the *Bard* were known,
A *Servitor*, when young in *College-Hall*,
Tho' vagrant Liberty he early chose,
Who yet, when Drunk, retain'd Poetick Phrase.) 110
Nor shou'd (quoth he) that *Well*, o'erhung with shade,
Amidst those neighb'ring Trees of dateless growth,
Be left unfathom'd by your nicer Skill
Who thence cou'd extricate a thousand Charms,
Or to oblivious *Lethe* might convert
The stagnant Waters of the sleepy Pool.
But most unhappy was that *Morphean* Sound
For lull'd *Budgeta*, who had long desir'd
Dismission fair from Tales, not throughly scann'd,
Thinking her Love a Sympathy confest, 120
When the Word *Sleepy* parted from his Lips,
Sunk affable and easy to that Rest,
Which Straw affords to Minds, unvex'd with Cares.

PSALM THE 137TH PARAPHRAS'D TO THE 7TH VERSE

Proud *Babylon!* Thou saw'st us weep;
   Euphrates, as he pass'd along,
Saw, on his Banks, the Sacred Throng
   A heavy, solemn Mourning keep.
Sad Captives to thy Sons, and Thee,
When nothing but our Tears were Free!

A Song of *Sion* they require,
   And from the neighb'ring Trees to take
Each Man his dumb, neglected Lyre,
   And chearful Sounds on them awake:
But chearful Sounds the Strings refuse,
Nor will their Masters Griefs abuse.

How can We, Lord, thy Praise proclaim,
   Here, in a strange unhallow'd Land!
Lest we provoke them to Blaspheme
   A Name, they do not understand;
And with rent Garments, that deplore
Above whate'er we felt before.

But, Thou, *Jerusalem*, so Dear!
   If thy lov'd Image e'er depart,
Or I forget thy Suff'rings here;
   Let my right Hand forget her Art;
My Tongue her vocal Gift resign,
   And Sacred Verse no more be mine!

A PREPARATION TO PRAYER

Lett no bold Pray'r, presume to rise,
   Lett no unhallow'd Incense. goe
A fruitlesse progresse, throo' the skyes,

Whilst here thy heart remains below,
Thy heart, adorn'd in all its best desires,
The Father kindly courts, thy awful God requires.

Think, with what reverence, and state,
 Thy Maker is ador'd above,
What mighty Beings, round him waite,
 And pay their Worship, and their Love.
That Cherubims, are in his sight afraid,
And with enfolded wings their glorious faces shade.

How must that Guardian Angel greive,
 That to attend thy soul is sent,
Such cold petitions to receive,
 As his warm zeal, can n'ere present?
How must he greive, thy empty forms to see,
In spirit, and in truth, his God must worship'd bee?

How will itt swell thy final cares,
 How, will it all thy hopes defeat,
To see thy Sins, encreas't by Pray'rs,
 Which only cou'd their force abate?
How can'st thou hope, t' escape those forrain harms,
Who thus against thy self, turn'st thy defensive
 arms?

A PASTORAL

*Between Menalcus and Damon, on the Appearance of the Angels
to the Shepheards on Our Saviour's Birth Day*

Menalc:

Damon, whilst thus, we nightly watches keep,
Breaking the gentle bands of downy sleep,
Least to the greedy woolves, that hungry stray,
Our wand'ring flocks, become an easy Prey,
Do thou, for song renown'd, some one recite,

To charm the season, and deceive the night.
   Whether, thou Sampson's nervous strength willt chuse,
And in bold numbers, exercise thy Muse?
Or if to tender subjects more enclin'd,
That move soft pitty, and dissolve the mind,   10
Thou Joseph's story, rather wilt rehearse,
And weep o're Benjamin, in melting Verse,
Begin, whilst list'ning to thy voyce, we lye,
Nor mind the whist'ling winds, that o're us fly.
So! Jesse's Son, upon these plaines, when yong,
Watch'd ore his flocks, and so, the Shepheard sung.

Dam:

So, rais'd indeed, that youth, his voyce devine,
Fir'd with the promis'd glorys of his Line,
As if, on Heavens high Mount himself had trod,
And seen his Seed, ascend the seat of God.   20
   Oh! had he lately, on our pastures been,
And heard the tydings, and the Vision seen,
When Heav'nly Spirits, cloath'd in Robes of light,
Broke the thick Shaddows, and expell'd the Night,
Proclaiming Peace below, and Praise above,
And op'ning all the misteries of Love,
How had he then, above all others skill'd,
In raptures sung, of Prophecys fullfill'd?
Our gath'ring flocks, upon the splendour gaz'd,—
The weary slept not, nor the hungry graz'd,   30
Their leaders, by them stood, delighted, and amazed.
A pleasing wonder, tho' allay'd with fear,
Fill'd every breast, and open'd every ear,
When thus began the Messengers of Heaven;
   To you a Child is born, to you a Son is giv'n,
Prayses they gave, and titles did encrease,
Wonderfull! Councellour! and Prince of Peace!

Long since Emanuel, by the Prophett stil'd,
Now, God with us! They call'd the glorious Child.
" But hold, a Shepheard while his flock does feed, 40
" Must chuse a subject suited to his Reed,
Nor with mistaken strength, attempt the Sky,
But o're the Plaines, with easy motion fly.
Enough by us, Menalcus may be said,
Of the first Shepheards, and that lovely Maid
Whose eyes, cou'd seven years servitude allay,
And make them doubl'd seem but as a day.

Now, to the silver streams their flock they led,
Now, where the friendly beech his arms had spread
Wide open, to envite 'em to his shade,   50
Behold the happy pair, securely lay'd.
Oh Israel! how did Heav'n thy joys approve,
Who plac'd thy profitt, where itt plac'd thy Love?
This, be my subject, while with reverend awe
My words, from what they cannot reach, withdraw.
Begin my Muse, begin the tender song,
The season sha'nt be cold, nor shall the Night be long,

Menalc :

As much this Song (att other times approv'd)
Wou'd grate thy hearers, with those wonders mov'd,
As if wild gourds were offer'd to the taste,   60
When the full Vine with purple fruit was grac't.

As if, Dametas shou'd to sing encline,
And raise his voyce, when we expected thine.

But lett thy Muse attempt that Nobler song,
The season sha'nt be cold, nor shall the night be long.

Dam :

Then be itt so, tho' much I fear to try
The lofty measures of a flight so high:
The fallen Moon, had now her beams withdrawn,

And left the Skyes, 'ere morning light cou'd dawn.
The Swaynes were silent, and the flocks were still,   70
The rappid stream, that flows from yonder hill,
Did by itts winding banks so softly stray,
As if itt meant unseen, to steal away.
A general darknesse o're the world was spread,
And not one Star, wou'd show his trembling head,
Conscious no doubt, (their dwellings being so nigh)
Of greater Glory, breaking from the sky.
   And loe! itt came.   Th' Etherial Princes came,
Gently reclin'd on hills of harmlesse flame,
Upon the Winds officious Wings they flew,   80
And fairer seem'd, still as they neerer drew.
Misterious wreaths upon their heads, they wore,
And in their hands, the smiling Olive bore,
Emblems no doubt, of what they came to move,
For all their words were Peace, and all their looks were
   love.
But ne're by me, the Vision be expresst
By the Suns rising, from the radiant East.
But ne're by me, their voyces be compar'd
To Pans own notes, when on the mountains heard.
But ne're by me, be that transcendent show,   90
Liken'd to ought we glorious call, below.
Night, in her sable mantle wrapt her head,
And with unusual haste, to lower Worlds she fled.
   Fear, that att distance, had our hearts possesst,
To softer passions, yeilded ev'ry breast,
When thus began the Messengers of Heav'n,
To you a Child is born, to you a Son is given.
   Such joy, as ends the harvests happy toyle,
Such joy, as when the Victors, part the spoyl,
Upon your ransom'd heads, shall ever smile.   100
   When to full Stature, and perfection grown

Possess'd of holy Davids sacred Throne,
He shall, th' Immortal and tryumphant Boy,
Th' Infernal Powers, and all their rule destroy,
The cursed Serpent's head, his weight shall feel,
And threaten'd vengance, for his brused heel.
The flaming Cherub, shall his guard remitt,
And Paradice, again be open sett.
Angels and God, shall dwell with men below,
And men releas'd, to God, and Angels go.   110
Peace, to the troubl'd World he shall restore,
And bloody discord, shall prevail no more,
The Lamb, his side by the tam'd Wolff shall lay,
And o're the Aspicks den, the child shall play.
Contending Elements, his Pow'r shall own,
The Winds, shall att his word their rage lay down,
And the chaf't billows, shall forbear to frown.
Th' untun'd Creation (by the fall of man)
Shall move harmoniously as itt began.
The fruitfull Autumn, and the gaudy Spring,   120
Shall sure returns, of sweets, and plenty bring,
And thorough every Grove, the holy swaynes shall sing
Of weighty truths, preserv'd in sacred Rimes,
T' instruct the Pastors of succeeding times,
In the soft rules, of Charity and Love,
Goodwill to men, and praise to Heaven above.
And thou, poor Bethlehem, enclos'd with shade,
Shalt throo' all ages, be illustrious made,
Since in thy bosome, the Redeemer's layd;
Thousands in Juda, did thy state dispise,   130
Thousands in Juda now, thy lott shall prise.
Now Beor's Son, the Star by thee foretold,
Newly adorn'd, in pointed Rays of Gold,
Call's from thy learned East, th' adoring Kings,
And ev'ry one, a several Tribute brings,

Sabean odours, and Arabian ore,
Shall now be offer'd from their choicest store,
Go with them, Shepheards go, and with like faith adore.
    But see! whilst in these pleasing paths I stray,
Night, has resign'd her rule to rising day,   140
Behind those Eastern hills, the sun appears,
And the gay Horizon, about him chears.
Our joyfull flocks, the chearfull morning view,
And from their fleeces, shake the orient dew.
No more, Menalcus, we, no more, must sing,
But now our sheep to the fresh pastures bring.

Menalc:

Oh! happy shepheard, favour'd with that sight,
That can when but repeated, thus delight.
    Not flow'ry Garlands, in the pride of May,
Nor rural presents, can thy meritts pay.   150
Not our first Lambs, or choices[t] fruits that grow,
Enough, alas! our gratitude can show!
There shall a Bowl, of antique date, be thine,
And Joseph's 'twas, by which he did devine;
Upon the sides, is carv'd in works of gold
The mystick sense, of what thou doest unfold,
Clusters of grapes, about itts borders twine,
That seem when fill'd, to have produc'd the wine.
To me, by long inheritance, itt came,
Now thy reward, and witnesse to thy fame.   160
    When night returns, repeat again this song,
The Season sha'nt be cold, nor shall itt then, be long.

ON EASTER DAY

Hark! sure I hear Vrania play,
    I hear her tune the heavenly strings,
    Some wondrous tidings, sure she brings,

O now! methinks, I hear her say,
The Sun of Righteousnesse today,
Must break, must rise, must come away,
   With healing in his wings.

'Tis done, behold the God appear,
   Fulfilling all that he has said;
   Captivity, is Captive led,
Death, of his old invenom'd spear
Behold disarm'd, and Conquer'd here;
The Grave, no more the Members fear,
   Since risen in the Head.

In vain the silly Rabbins strove,
   A Strattagem of force to find,
   The Lord Omnipotent to bind.
Too weak, to stop Almighty love,
Their guard, their stone, their seal must prove,
The trembling Earth, does all remove
   Like dust before the wind.

Lett ransom'd men in praises vye,
   Lett ev'ry faithfull Soul, rejoyce,
   And tune to Angels notes, his voyce.
Hail! Son of David, lett them cry,
Hail! Thou that livest, and didst dye,
That left'st thy glorious Seat, on high,
   And Sufferings mad'st thy choyce.

Unfold, ye Everlasting Gates,
   That guard the great Jehova's Towers,
   Those sacred, mystick leaves of yours,
The King of Glory for you waites;
   Receive him, oh! ye blissfull Bowers,
   Ye Thrones, Dominions, Scepter'd Powers,
   He Comes! accomplish'd are the hours,
Appointed by the Fates.

Be now, thy foes, thy footstool made,
  Exalted high, on God's right hand,
  A Preist for ever may'st thou stand,
Thy dear Redeeming blood, to plead,
Th' imperfect Sacrafice, to aid,
 Which is, by wretched man convey'd
  And never must be scann'd.

HALLELUJAH

Seraphick sound! Eternal Praise!
Upon whose wings, my Soul I raise,
Till Heaven is reach'd by heavenly Layes.

Our Hallelujah's hence, that fly,
Repose not, till they meet on high
With those, the Church tryumphant cry.

This Sacred Musick, in my ear,
I cry, transported, God is here,
Such tastes of Glory, doe appear.

Before the dread Jehovah's seat,
Glad Cherubims, this praise repeat,
Whilst miriads, worship att his feet.

Mongst whom, my searching Faith can see
A voyce, and Lyre, bestow'd shall be,
And Hallelujah's sung by mee.

My soul, which hungars here, for Grace,
Attending Spirits, there, shall place,
To see th' Eternal, face to face.

This hope makes all afflictions light,
Directs my heart, and actions right,
My cloud by day, my fire by night.

Thy Saints, throo' hopes refreshment, shall
With hourly Hallelujah's fall,
Untill the great Arcangell's call.

Which hasten Lord, thy Chosen Pray,
Th' Elect, all languish for that day,
Oh come! Lord Jesus, come away!

SOME REFLECTIONS

*In a Dialogue Between TERESA and ARDELIA. On the 2nd
and 3rd Verses of ye 73rd Psalm*

My feet were allmost gone, my treadings had well nigh
slipped; and why, I was greived att the wicked, I doe also
see the Vngodly in such prosperity.

Teresa

Heither, Ardelia, I your stepps persue,
No solitude shou'd e're exclude a freind,
Your greifs I see, and as to freindship due,
   Demand the cause, to which these sorrows tend,
   What their beginnings were, and what may be their
     end?

Ardelia

Alas! Ardelia is not vainly sad,
Nor to the clouds, that shade my carefull brow,
Can fancys, dark and false suggestions add,
   But my Teresa, since you wish to know,
   I all my cares will tell, and all my greifs will show. 10

How, I my God, and his just laws adore,
How I have serv'd him, with my early years,
How I have lov'd his Name, and fear'd his Pow'r,
   Wittnesse his Temples, where my falling teares,
   Have follow'd still my faults, and usher'd in my
     fears.

But oh! this God, the Glorious Architect
  Of this fair world, of this large Globe we see,
Seems those who trust him most, most to neglect,
  Else my Teresa, else, how could itt be,
That all his storms attend, and tempests fall on me.   20

The Proud he hates, yett me he does expose
  Empty of all things, naked to their scorn.
His world, on them he liberally bestows,
  Theirs are his Vines, his feilds, his flocks, his corn,
  And all that can sustain, and all that can adorn.

These are the men, posses the mighty store,
  Compasse the Earth, and with the boundlesse Deep
All they bestow, receive again, with more;
  Whilst I, in fears to loose, and cares to keep,
  Obtain but daily bread, with interrupted sleep.   30

          Teresa

Ardelia hold, if more thou hast to say
  On this pernitious subject, lett it dye;
The subtill Fiend, that leads thy soul astray,
  Thou doest not in this hour of sin, descry,
  Oh! if we wander once, how soon the serpent's nigh.

Art thou content, to have thy portion here,
  The Tyrian purple, and the costly fare,
The purchase waits thee, but will cost thee dear,
  For mighty sums of Vice, thou must not spare,
  Do, as the wicked does, and thou, with him may'st
    share?   40

Canst thou repine, that Earth is not thy lott,
  And in that want, thy bounteous God distrust,
Confining all his mercys to that spott?
  Others of weight, acknowledge sure, we must,
  Or be to truth oppos'd, and Providence unjust.

Who, seals thy forehead, when the Plague is nigh,
    Ere the destroying Angel can descend?
Who, guides th' avenging shafts, that o're thee fly?
    When thou didst yett upon the breast depend,
    Who was thy Father then, and who was then thy
        freind?   50

Who gave his blood, when thine could not suffice
    To pay thy debt, who for thee sigh'd and wept,
And bought that Glory, att a wondrous price,
    Which is to future Ages for thee kept,
    Unlesse thou chuse this world, and that to come,
        neglect?

Who leads thee throo' this Vale of tears below,
    To bring thee to thy Country, safe att last?
Who in the way, does all thou want'st below,
    For more than this, his sacred word n'ere passt,
    And all thou truly want'st, assuredly thou hast?   60

What if to prove thee, when the billows rise,
    He from thy danger turns, and seems to sleep,
Wilt thou to murmures, strait convert thy crys,
    The crowd we see, the shoar may safely keep,
    Whilst the distinguish'd twelve are threatn'd by the
        deep?

Ardelia

Teresa, from my guilty dream, I wake,
    The truth has reach'd me, and my fault I find,
Forgive me God, forgive the short mistake,
    How cou'd itt enter my deluded mind,
    That all, both Worlds cou'd give, was for one Wretch
        design'd?   70

I saw the Mighty, and began to slide,
    My feet were gone, but I return again,

And wou'd not with them here, the spoyles devide;
  Nor look'd I att the end of Glorious men,
  Nor thought how lost they were, nor how abandon'd
    then.

A while, the Servant of Elisha, soe
  Altho' his Master's pow'r with Heav'n he knew,
His faith forgoes, surrounded with the foe,
  Till by the Prophett's pray'r, the Vaile withdrew
  And show'd the doubted aid of Providence in view. 80

THE 10TH PART OF THE 119TH PSALM PARAPHRASED

In the manner of a Prayer from the 1st to ye 6th Verse

Thy workmanship, O Lord, I am,
  Thy hands have moulded, and designed,
And for thy Glory, rais'd this frame,
  Which is to thee, again resigned.

O thou ! who did'st create the whole,
  Cheifly regard the nobler part,
With understanding cloath my Soul,
  And plant thy doctrine in my heart.

Then shall the Pious and the Just,
  Beholding me, their hopes improve,
Then shall my full rewarded trust,
  Assure their faith, and fix their love.

'Tis of thy mercy, Lord I know
  That I afflictions have sustain'd ;
Afflictions, from thy mercy flow,
  By which we are from sin restrain'd.

O ! Lett that mercy, still to me
  (According to thy gracious word)
A just proportion'd Cordial be,
  When thou these tryals doest affoard.

That I may live, thy mercy send,
From thence, my vital breath I draw,
My life does on thy love depend,
And all my love, is on thy law.

THE 146TH PSALM PARAPHRAS'D

Oh! praise the Lord, and lett his fame be told,
Oh! now my Soul, thy best affections raise,
To him, who gave, and does thy being hold,
Return thy gratefull Hymns, and thy loud songs of Praise.

In man, in Princes, who the Scepter's sway,
Can there be faith repos'd, can there be trust?
Their promises, alas! are vain as they,
Their promises are air, and they alas! are dust.

The breath of man, shall certainly expire,
His Soul forsake him, and his thoughts shall dye,
His body, to the lowly Grave retire,
Who then can trust on man, who, can on man relye.

He only can be safe, he only blest,
Above the reach of falsehood, or decay,
His hopes at Anchor, and his fears att rest,
Whose trust is in the Lord, whose God, is all his stay.

He who the Heavens, and Air, and Earth, the Deep
With all therein, created by his word,
His word to all Eternity shall keep ;
His Will is sacred truth, and Power, is with the Lord.

Mercy, and Justice, still with him remain,
That feeds the hungry, this th' oprest releives ;
Mercy, dissolves th' afflicted Pris'ner's chain,
To long benighted Eyes, mercy the light retreives.

The Righteous, are the Lord's peculiar care,
  To him, for refuge, the poor Widdows come,
The Fatherlesse, is God's adopted Heir,
  The stranger too, in God, is sure to find an home.

Those that are fallen, he again erects,
  The wicked, that persue ungodly ways,
He searches out, he frustrates, and detects,
  He ruines their designs, and on them builds his praise.

Thy Lord, O Sion! this, thy Lord, is King;
  Throughout all ages, shall his reign endure,
Thou, Everlasting praise, may'st to him sing,
  And ever may'st thou rest, beneath his love, secure.

GOLD IS TRY'D IN THE FIRE, AND ACCEPTABLE MEN IN THE TIME OF ADVERSITY

If all th' appointed days of man were fair,
    And his few hours, mov'd o're him, like a breeze,
    That gently plays among the trees,
Soft, and smooth, and void of care,
As infants balmy slumber are,
    How, shou'd we then assured bee,
    That even temper, we might see,
    Were Vertue, not prosperity.

Not so, th' Almighty wisdom has design'd,
    We shou'd in ease, and luxury remain,
    Untry'd by sorrow, or by pain.
No, the searcher of the mind,
Unshaken vertue, there must find,
    Tho' low, as to the dunghill brought,
    With him, whose sifted patience taught,
    He serv'd for Duty, else for naught.

We see the wealthyest ore the earth does hide,
  Is not receav'd or pass'd for currant gold,
  Nor by the greedy Miser, told,
Till by the cleansing furnace try'd,
It does the sevenfold test, abide;
  So must the path of greif, be trod,
  (That certain, purifying roade)
  By all th' accepted sons of God.

Who in this method, to our needs, has bow'd,
  Nor is itt reason guides, when we complain,
  Favours, alas! but fall in vain,
And the good things, that are allow'd,
Instead of happy, make us proud,
  Lett us not then refuse this part,
  But wisely learn, the saving art,
  Our tears, to comforts to convert.

THE POOR MAN'S LAMB

*Or, Nathan's Parable to David after the Murder of Uriah, and
his Marriage with Bathsheba
Turn'd into Verse and Paraphras'd*

Now spent the alter'd King, in am'rous Cares,
The Hours of sacred Hymns and solemn Pray'rs:
In vain the Altar waits his slow returns,
Where unattended Incense faintly burns:
In vain the whisp'ring Priests their Fears express,
And of the Change a thousand Causes guess.
Heedless of all their Censures He retires,
And in his Palace feeds his secret Fires;
Impatient, till from *Rabbah* Tydings tell,
That near those Walls the poor *Uriah* fell,   10
Led to the Onset by a Chosen Few,
Who at the treacherous Signal, soon withdrew;

Nor to his Rescue e'er return'd again,
Till by fierce *Ammon's* Sword they saw the Victim slain.
'Tis pass'd, 'tis done! the holy Marriage-Knot,
Too strong to be unty'd, at last is cut.
And now to *Bathsheba* the King declares,
That with his Heart, the Kingdom too is hers;
That *Israel's* Throne, and longing Monarch's Arms
Are to be fill'd but with her widow'd Charms.   20
Nor must the Days of formal Tears exceed,
To cross the Living, and abuse the Dead.
This she denies; and signs of Grief are worn;
But mourns no more than may her Face adorn,
Give to those Eyes, which Love and Empire fir'd,
A melting softness more to be desir'd;
Till the fixt Time, tho' hard to be endur'd,
Was pass'd, and a sad Consort's Name procur'd:
When, with the Pomp that suits a Prince's Thought,
By Passion sway'd, and glorious Woman taught,   30
A *Queen* she's made, than *Michal* seated higher,
Whilst light unusual Airs prophane the hallow'd *Lyre*.

Where art thou *Nathan?* where's that Spirit now,
Giv'n to brave Vice, tho' on a Prince's Brow?
In what low Cave, or on what Desert Coast,
Now Virtue wants it, is thy Presence lost?

But lo! he comes, the Rev'rend *Bard* appears,
Defil'd with Dust his awful silver Hairs,
And his rough Garment, wet with falling Tears.
The King this mark'd, and conscious wou'd have fled,   40
The healing Balm which for his Wounds was shed:
Till the more wary Priest the Serpents Art,
Join'd to the Dove-like Temper of his Heart,
And thus retards the Prince just ready now to part.
Hear me, the Cause betwixt two Neighbours hear,

Thou, who for Justice doth the Sceptre bear:
Help the Opprest, nor let me weep alone
For him, that calls for Succour from the Throne.
Good Princes for Protection are Ador'd,
And Greater by the *Shield* than by the *Sword.*   50
This clears the Doubt, and now no more he fears
The Cause his Own, and therefore stays and hears:
When thus the *Prophet:*——
                    —In a flow'ry Plain
A King-like Man does in full Plenty reign;
Casts round his Eyes, in vain, to reach the Bound,
Which *Jordan's* Flood sets to his fertile Ground:
Countless his Flocks, whilst *Lebanon* contains
A Herd as large, kept by his numerous Swains,
That fill with morning Bellowings the cool Air,
And to the Cedar's shade at scorching Noon repair.   60
Near to this Wood a lowly *Cottage* stands,
Built by the humble Owner's painful Hands;
Fenc'd by a Stubble-roof, from Rain and Heat,
Secur'd without, within all Plain and Neat.
A Field of small Extent surrounds the place,
In which One single *Ewe* did sport and graze:
This his whole Stock, till in full time there came,
To bless his utmost Hopes, a snowy *Lamb*;
Which, lest the Season yet too Cold might prove,
And Northern Blasts annoy it from the Grove,   70
Or tow'ring Fowl on the weak Prey might sieze,
(For with his Store his *Fears* must too increase)
He brings it Home, and lays it by his Side,
At once his Wealth, his Pleasure and his Pride;
Still bars the Door, by Labour call'd away,
And, when returning at the Close of Day,
With One small Mess himself, and that sustains,
And half his Dish it shares, and half his slender Gains.

When to the great Man's table now there comes
A *Lord* as great, follow'd by hungry Grooms: 80
For these must be provided sundry Meats,
The best for Some, for Others coarser Cates.
One Servant, diligent above the rest
To help his Master to contrive the Feast,
Extols the Lamb was nourished with such Care,
So fed, so lodg'd, it must be Princely Fare;
And having this, my Lord his own may spare.
In haste he sends, led by no Law, but Will,
Not to entreat, or purchase, but to Kill.
The Messenger's arriv'd: the harmless Spoil,   90
Unus'd to fly, runs Bleating to the Toil:
Whilst for the Innocent the Owner fear'd,
And, sure wou'd move, cou'd Poverty be heard.
Oh spare (he cries) *the Product of my Cares,*
My Stock's Encrease, the Blessing on my Pray'rs;
My growing Hope, and Treasure of my Life!
More was he speaking, when the murd'ring Knife
Shew'd him, his Suit, tho' just, must be deny'd,
And the white Fleece in its own Scarlet dy'd;
Whilst the poor helpless Wretch stands weeping by,   100
And lifts his Hands for Justice to the Sky.
  Which he shall find, th' incensed *King* replies,
When for the proud Offence th' Oppressor dies.
O *Nathan!* by the *Holy* Name I swear,
Our Land such Wrongs unpunished shall not bear.
If, with the Fault, th' Offender thou declare.
  To whom the *Prophet*, closing with the Time,
Thou art the Man replies, and thine th' ill-natur'd Crime.
Nor think, against thy Place, or State, I err;
A Pow'r above thee does this Charge prefer;   110
Urg'd by whose *Spirit*, hither am I brought
T'' expostulate his *Goodness* and thy *Fault;*

To lead thee back to those forgotten Years,
In Labour spent, and lowly Rustick Cares,
When in the Wilderness thy Flocks but few
Thou didst the Shepherd's simple Art pursue
Thro' crusting Frosts, and penetrating Dew:
Till wondring *Jesse* saw six Brothers past,
And Thou Elected, Thou the Least and Last;
A Sceptre to thy Rural Hand convey'd,   120
And in thy Bosom Royal Beauties laid;
A lovely Princess made thy Prize that Day,
When on the shaken Ground the *Giant* lay
Stupid in Death, beyond the Reach of Cries
That bore thy shouted Fame to list'ning Skies,
And drove the flying Foe as fast away,
As Winds, of old, *Locusts* to *Egypt's* Sea.
Thy Heart with Love, thy Temples with Renown,
Th' All-giving Hand of Heav'n did largely crown,
Whilst yet thy Cheek was spread with youthful Down.   130
What more cou'd craving Man of God implore?
Or what for favour'd Man cou'd God do more?
Yet cou'd not these, nor *Israel's* Throne, suffice
Intemp'rate Wishes, drawn thro' wand'ring Eyes.
One Beauty (not thy own) and seen by chance,
Melts down the Work of Grace with an alluring Glance;
Chafes the Spirit, fed by sacred Art,
And blots the Title AFTER GOD'S OWN HEART;
Black Murder breeds to level at *his* Head,
Who boasts so fair a Part'ner of his Bed,   140
Nor longer must possess those envy'd Charms,
The single Treasure of his House, and Arms:
Giving, by this thy Fall, cause to Blaspheme
To all the Heathen the *Almighty* Name.
For which the *Sword* shall still thy Race pursue,
And, in revolted *Israel's* scornful View,

Thy captiv'd Wives shall be in Triumph led
Unto a bold Usurper's shameful Bed;
Who from thy Bowels sprung shall seize thy Throne,
And scourge thee by a Sin beyond thy own.   150
Thou hast thy Fault in secret Darkness done;
But this the World shall see before the Noonday's Sun.

Enough! the King, enough! the *Saint* replies,
And pours his swift Repentance from his Eyes;
Falls on the Ground and tears the Nuptial Vest,
By which his Crime's Completion was exprest:
Then with a Sigh blasting to Carnal Love,
Drawn deep as Hell, and piercing Heaven, above
Let *Me* (he cries) let *Me* attend his Rod,
For *I* have sinn'd, for *I* have lost my God.   160

Hold! (says the *Prophet*) of that Speech beware,
God ne'er was lost, unless by Man's Despair.
The Wound that is thus willingly reveal'd,
Th' Almighty is as willing should be heal'd.
Thus wash'd in Tears, thy Soul as fair does show
As the first Fleece, which on the Lamb does grow,
Or on the Mountain's top the lately fallen Snow.
Yet to the World that Justice may appear
Acting her Part impartial, and severe,
The *Offspring* of thy Sin shall soon resign   170
That Life, for which thou must not once repine;
But with submissive Grief his Fate deplore,
And bless the Hand, that does inflict no more.

Shall I then pay but Part, and owe the Whole?
My Body's Fruit, for my offending Soul?
Shall I no more endure (the King demands)
And 'scape thus lightly his offended Hands?
Oh! let him All resume, my Crown, my Fame;

Reduce me to the Nothing, whence I came;
Call back his Favours, faster than he gave;   180
And, if but Pardon'd, strip me to my Grave:

Since (tho' he seems to *Lose*) He surely *Wins*,
Who gives but earthly Comforts for his Sins.

THE SECOND CHAPTER OF THE WISDOM OF SOLOMON PARAPHRASED

The first twelve Verses, being an Introduction

How weak is man, that wou'd himself persuade
Out of his Int'rest, and his Tempter aid;
Mislead by present joys, and human pride,
Wou'd gladly lay his future hopes aside.
Uncloath himself, of all he holds Devine,
And to the Earth, his ashes wou'd confine;
Consent his Soul, all pains on itt to spare,
Shou'd vanish, like the soft, and silent air;
This Doctrine, which in ancient times was penn'd,
Th' industrious Devil, took care shou'd still descend, 10
And we by Atheists now, the same are told,
Which Israel's wisest Prince, describes of old.

THE CHAPTER BEGINS

Thus reason'd they, said he, but not aright,
Deluded, by the charms of vain delight.
Tho' life be short, how tedious is the day,
Which some new pleasure, does not drive away?
Death, hastens on, all human things to seize,
And there's no remedy, for that desease;
None from the Grave return, not Moses' Laws,
Have seen him come, to vindicate their cause.   20
Chance made the World, and the same hand of Chance

Does blindly man, into that World advance;
And when the date of certain years expires,
As he had never been, he back retires:
That active fire, which annimat's the heart,
And thence, all life, and motion does impart,
By some contending Element oppresst,
Extinguish't fails, and quitts the darken'd brest,
The Vapour, in our nostrills, stealls away,
And all that now remains is common clay.   30
Time, preys upon our memory, and name,
And deep oblivion, swallows up our fame;
Like a swift cloud, we passe unheeded by,
No track is left, no mark where itt did fly,
Nor shall itt e're return, to shade the sky.
Since past, and future, we att distance see,
And present time, can only usefull bee,
Voluptuous, and in pleasures lett us live,
And freely spend, what moments we receive.
Still, lett us gay, and warm affections hold,   40
And when in Age, forgett thatt we are old.
Roses, about our youthful tresses tye,
Roses, shall when they fall, their place supply.
The chearfull spring, shall round our temples twine,
And our full bowls, flow with Autumnal Wine.
The pollish'd skin, with ointments shall be gay,
Circling perfumes, shall usher on the way,
And soft harmonious airs, about us play.
Diffusing as we passe, luxuriant Bliss,
This, is our Portion, and our Lott, is this,   50
    Justice, shall lay aside her uselesse scales,
And force, shall justice be, when force prevailes;
No Law shall govern, no dull Rule take place,
The Widdow, nor the hoary head find grace;
Oppression, shall the righteous man devour,

Fassion'd by Conscience, for the Tyrant's pow'r,
Who meekly yeilds to wrong, or vile disgrace,
Yett, from th' Immortal God derives his Race;
And by himself, is arrogantly stil'd
Of Him he worships, the apparent Child.   60
Him, lett us wait for, that upbraids us still,
With breach of Laws, and Education ill;
That but at distance, views our loose delight,
And blasts our mirth, with his reproachfull sight;
Who, not like us, his youth to pleasure gives,
But singular, and solitary lives;
And, does his Eyes on distant prospects bend,   ·
Saying, the Just is blessed in his end;
That lett us hasten, and his patience prove,
And his cool temper, with rough usage move;   70
If Son to Him, whom he Almighty calls,
He sure will save, when in our hands he falls,
Let us in shame, and tortures make him dye,
And so his truth, and his Protectour try.

Full place, did such immaginations find
With men in mists of Sin, and errour blind:
That knew not God, nor did his Laws regard,
Undmindfull of the Work, or the Reward
That shall on blameless Souls, here-after rest,
When with Eternity of Pleasures blesst.   80
God, stamp'd His Immage, on created Earth,
And made itt so, Immortal in itts birth;
And tho' th' infernal Fiend (with envy fill'd)
Brought Death into the world, and some has kill'd,
Yett, only those, that do his part embrace,
Shall fall to Him, and his appointed place.

JEALOUSIE IS THE RAGE OF A MAN

Whilst with his falling wings, the courtly Dove
Sweeps the low earth, and singles out his Love,
Now murmurs soft, then with a rowling note
Extends his crop, and fills his am'rous throate,
On ev'ry side accosts the charming Fair,
Turns round, and bows with an inticing ayre,
She, carelessly neglecting all his pain,
Or shifts her ground, or pecks the scatter'd grain.
But if he cease, and through the flight wou'd range,
(For though renown'd for truth, e'vn Doves will change)
The mildnesse of her nature laid aside,
The seeming coldnesse, and the carelesse pride,
On the next Rival, in a rage she flies;
Smooth, ev'ry clinging plume, with anger lies,
Employs in feeble fight her tender beck,
And shakes the Favrites, parti-colour'd neck.
Thus, jealousy, through ev'ry species moves;
And if so furious, in the gallesse Doves,
No wonder, that th' experienc'd Hebrew sage,
Of Man, pronounc'd itt the extremest Rage.

ALL IS VANITY

I

How vain is *Life!* which rightly we compare
  To flying *Posts*, that haste away;
To *Plants*, that fade with the declining Day;
  To *Clouds*, that sail amidst the yielding Air;
Till by Extention into that they flow,
  Or, scatt'ring on the World below,
Are lost and gone, ere we can say they were;
  To *Autumn-Leaves*, which every Wind can chace;

To rising *Bubbles*, on the Waters Face;
  To fleeting *Dreams*, that will not stay,   10
Nor in th' abused Fancy dance,
  When the returning Rays of Light,
Resuming their alternate Right,
Break on th' ill-order'd Scene on the fantastick Trance:
As weak is *Man*, whilst Tenant to the Earth;
As frail and as uncertain all his Ways,
From the first moment of his weeping Birth,
Down to the last and best of his few restless Days;
  When to the Land of Darkness he retires
From disappointed Hopes, and frustrated Desires;   20
  Reaping no other Fruit of all his Pain
Bestow'd whilst in the vale of Tears below,
  But this unhappy Truth, at last to know,
That Vanity's our Lot, and all Mankind is Vain.

II

If past the hazard of his tendrest Years,
  Neither in thoughtless Sleep opprest,
  Nor poison'd with a tainted Breast,
Loos'd from the infant Bands and female Cares,
  A *studious Boy*, advanc'd beyond his Age,
Wastes the dim Lamp, and turns the restless Page;   30
  For some lov'd Book prevents the rising Day,
  And on it, stoln aside, bestows the Hours of Play;
Him the observing Master do's design
For search of darkned Truths and Mysteries Divine;
  Bids him with unremitted Labour trace
The Rise of Empires, and their various Fates,
The several Tyrants o'er the several States,
  To *Babel's* lofty Towers, and warlike *Nimrod's* Race;
Bids him in Paradice the Bank survey,
  Where Man, new-moulded from the temper'd Clay,   40

(Till fir'd with Breath Divine) a helpless Figure lay:
  Could he be led thus far — What were the Boast,
  What the Reward of all the Toil it cost,
What from that Land of ever-blooming Spring,
  For our Instruction could he bring,
Unless, that having Humane Nature found
Unseparated from its Parent Ground,
  (Howe'er we vaunt our Elevated Birth)
  The Epicure in soft Array,
  The lothsome Beggar, that before   50
His rude unhospitable Door,
  Unpity'd but by Brutes, a broken Carcass lay,
Were both alike deriv'd from the same common Earth?
  But ere the Child can to these Heights attain,
  Ere he can in the Learned Sphere arise;
  A guiding Star, attracting to the Skies,
A fever, seizing the o'er-labour'd Brain,
  Sends him, perhaps, to Death's concealing Shade;
Where, in the Marble Tomb now silent laid,
  He better do's that useful Doctrine show,   60
  (Which all the sad Assistants ought to know,
  Who round the Grave his short continuance mourn)
That first from Dust we came, and must to Dust return.

III

A *bolder Youth*, grown capable of Arms,
Bellona courts with her prevailing Charms;
  Bids th' inchanting Trumpet sound,
  Loud as Triumph, soft as Love,
  Striking now the Poles above,
  Then descending from the Skies,
  Soften every falling Note;   70
As the harmonious *Lark* that sings and flies,
When near the Earth, contracts her narrow Throat,

And warbles on the Ground:
Shews the proud Steed, impatient of the Check,
  'Gainst the loudest Terrors Proof,
Pawing the Valley with his steeled Hoof,
With Lightning arm'd his Eyes, with Thunder cloth'd
    his Neck;
  Who on th' advanced Foe, (the Signal giv'n)
Flies, like a rushing Storm by mighty Whirlwinds
    driv'n;
  Lays open the Records of Fame,   80
No glorious Deed omits, no Man of mighty Name;
  Their Stratagems, their Tempers she'll repeat,
  From *Alexander's*, (truly stil'd the GREAT)
  From *Cæsar's* on the World's Imperial Seat,
  To *Turenne's* Conduct, and to *Conde's* Heat.
'Tis done! and now th' ambitious Youth disdains
  The safe, but harder Labours of the Gown,
  The softer pleasures of the Courtly Town,
The once lov'd rural Sports, and Chaces on the Plains;
  Does with the Soldier's Life the Garb assume,   90
  The gold Embroid'ries, and the graceful Plume;
  Walks haughty in a Coat of Scarlet Die,
  A Colour well contrived to cheat the Eye,
Where richer Blood, alas! may undistinguisht lye.
  And oh! too near that wretched Fate attends;
  Hear it ye Parents, all ye weeping Friends!
  Thou fonder Maid! won by those gaudy Charms,
  (The destin'd Prize of his Victorious Arms)
  Now fainting Dye upon the mournful Sound,
That speaks his hasty Death, and paints the fatal
      Wound!   100
  Trail all your Pikes, dispirit every Drum,
  March in a slow Procession from afar,
  Ye silent, ye dejected Men of War!

Be still the Hautboys, and the Flute be dumb!
Display no more, in vain, the lofty Banner;
For see! where on the Bier before ye lies
The pale, the fall'n, th' untimely Sacrifice
To your mistaken Shrine, to your false Idol Honour!

IV

As Vain is *Beauty*, and as short her Power;
Tho' in its proud, and transitory Sway,   110
The coldest Hearts and wisest Heads obey
That gay fantastick Tyrant of an Hour.
On *Beauty*'s Charms, (altho' a Father's Right,
Tho' grave *Seleucus!* to thy Royal Side
By holy Vows fair *Stratonice* be ty'd)
With anxious Joy, with dangerous Delight,
Too often gazes thy unwary Son,
Till past all Hopes, expiring and undone,
A speaking Pulse the secret Cause impart;
The only time, when the Physician's Art   120
Could ease that lab'ring Grief, or heal a Lover's Smart.
See Great *Antonius* now impatient stand,
        Expecting, with mistaken Pride,
On *Cydnus* crowded Shore, on *Cydnus* fatal Strand,
A *Queen*, at his Tribunal to be try'd,
A *Queen* that arm'd in Beauty, shall deride
His feeble Rage, and his whole Fate command:
O'er the still Waves her burnisht Galley moves,
Row'd by the Graces, whilst officious Loves
To silken Cords their busie Hands apply,   130
Or gathering all the gentle Gales that fly,
To their fair Mistress with those Spoils repair,
And from their purple Wings disperse the balmy Air.
Hov'ring Perfumes ascend in od'rous Clouds,
Curl o'er the Barque, and play among the Shrouds;

Whilst gently dashing every Silver Oar,
  Guided by the Rules of Art,
  With tuneful Instruments design'd
To soften, and subdue the stubborn Mind,
A strangely pleasing and harmonious Part   140
  In equal Measures bore.
Like a new *Venus* on her native Sea,
  In midst of the transporting Scene,
(Which Pen or Pencil imitates in vain)
On a resplendent and conspicuous Bed,
With all the Pride of *Persia* loosely spread,
  The lovely *Syrene* lay.
  Which but discern'd from the yet distant Shore,
  Th' amazed Emperor could hate no more;
  No more a baffled Vengeance could pursue;   150
  But yielding still, still as she nearer drew,
  When *Cleopatra* anchor'd in the Bay,
  Where every Charm cou'd all its Force display,
Like his own *Statue* stood, and gaz'd the *World* away.
  Where ends alas! this Pageantry and State;
  Where end the Triumphs of this conqu'ring Face,
Envy'd of *Roman* Wives, and all the Female Race?
  Oh swift Vicissitude of Beauty's Fate!
  Now in her Tomb withdrawn from publick Sight,
    From near Captivity and Shame,   160
    The Vanquish'd, the abandon'd Dame
Proffers the Arm, that held another's Right,
To the destructive Snake's more just Embrace,
And courts deforming *Death*, to mend his Leaden Pace.

V

But *Wit* shall last (the vaunting *Poët* cries)
Th' immortal Streams that from *Parnassus* flow,
Shall make his never-fading Lawrels grow,

Above this mouldring Earth to flourish in the Skies:
"And when his Body falls in Funeral Fire
 When late revolving Ages shall consume   170
 The very Pillars, that support his Tomb,
"His name shall live, and his best Part aspire.
 Deluded Wretch! grasping at future Praise,
  Now planting, with mistaken Care,
 Round thy enchanted Palace in the Air,
 A Grove, which in thy Fancy time shall raise,
 A Grove of soaring Palms, and ever-lasting Bays;
 Could'st Thou alas! to such Renown arrive,
 As thy Imaginations wou'd contrive;
 Should numerous Cities, in a vain contest,   180
  Struggle for thy famous Birth;
 Should the sole Monarch of the conquer'd Earth,
  His wreathed Head upon thy Volume rest;
    Like *Maro*, could'st thou justly claim,
    Amongst th' inspired tuneful Race,
 The highest Room, the undisputed Place;
 And after near Two Thousand Years of Fame,
 Have thy proud Work to a new People shown;
  Th' unequal'd Poems made their own,
 In such a Dress, in such a perfect Stile   190
 As on his Labours *Dryden* now bestows,
 As now from *Dryden's* just Improvement flows,
In every polish'd Verse throughout the *British* Isle;
  What Benefit alas! would to thee grow?
  What Sense of Pleasure wou'dst thou know?
  What swelling Joy? what Pride? what Glory have,
  When in the Darkness of the abject Grave,
  Insensible, and *Stupid* laid below,
  No Atom of thy Heap, no Dust wou'd move,
For all the Airy Breath that form'd thy Praise
  above?   200

VI

True, says the Man to *Luxury* inclin'd;
Without the Study of uncertain Art,
    Without much Labour of the Mind,
Meer uninstructed Nature will impart,
That Life too swiftly flies, and leaves all good behind.
    Sieze then, my Friends, (he cries) the present Hour;
        The Pleasure which to that belongs,
    The Feasts, th' o'erflowing Bowls, the Mirth, the Songs,
    The Orange-Bloom, that with such Sweetness blows,
        Anacreon's celebrated Rose,   210
The Hyacinth, with every beateous Flower,
Which just this happy Moment shall disclose,
Are out of Fortune's reach, and all within our Power.
Such costly Garments let our Slaves prepare,
As for the gay *Demetrius* were design'd;
Where a new Sun of radiant Diamonds shin'd,
Where the enamel'd Earth, and scarce-discerned Air,
    With a transparent Sea were seen,
A Sea composed of the Em'rald's Green,
And with a golden Shore encompass'd round;   220
Where every Orient Shell, of wondrous shape was found.
    The whole Creation on his Shoulders hung,
    The whole Creation with his wish comply'd,
Did swiftly, for each Appetite provide,
        And fed them all when Young.
    No less, th' *Assyrian* Prince enjoy'd,
Of Bliss too soon depriv'd, but never cloy'd,
    Whose Counsel let us still pursue,
Whose Monument, did this Inscription shew
    To every Passenger, that trod the way,   230
Where, with a slighting Hand, and scornful Smile
The proud Effigies, on th' instructive Pile,

A great Example lay.
I, here Entomb'd, did mighty Kingdoms sway,
Two Cities rais'd in one prodigious Day:
Thou wand'ring Traveller, no longer gaze,
No longer dwell upon this useless Place;
Go Feed, and Drink, in Sports consume thy Life;
For All that else we gain's not worth a Moment's Strife.
Thus! talks the Fool, whom no Restraint can bound,
When now the Glass has gone a frequent round; 241
When soaring Fancy lightly swims,
Fancy, that keeps above, and dances o'er the Brims;
Whilst weighty Reason sinks, and in the bot-
tom's drown'd:
Adds to his Own, an artificial Fire,
Doubling ev'ry hot Desire,
Till th' auxiliary Spirits, in a Flame,
The Stomach's Magazine defy,
That standing Pool, that helpless Moisture nigh
Thro' every Vital part impetuous fly,   250
And quite consume the Frame;
When to the Under-world despis'd he goes,
A pamper'd Carcase on the Worms bestows,
Who rioting on the unusual Chear,
As good a Life enjoy, as he could boast of here.

VII

But hold my Muse! thy farther Flight restrain,
Exhaust not thy declining Force,
Nor in a long, pursu'd, and breathless Course,
Attempt, with slacken'd speed, to run
Through ev'ry Vanity beneath the Sun,   260
Lest thy o'erweary'd Reader, should complain,
That of all Vanities beside,

.   Which thine, or his Experience e'er have try'd,
Thou art, too tedious Muse, most frivolous and vain;
   Yet, tell the Man, of an aspiring Thought,
    Of an ambitious, restless Mind,
   That can no Ease, no Satisfaction find,
   Till neighb'ring States are to Subjection brought,
Till Universal Awe, enslav'd Mankind is taught;
   That, should he lead an Army to the Field,   270
    For whose still necessary Use,
   Th' extended Earth cou'd not enough produce,
   Nor Rivers to their Thirst a full Contentment yield;
   Yet, must their dark Reverse of Fate
   Roll round, within that Course of Years,
   Within the short, the swift, and fleeting Date
   Prescrib'd by *Xerxes*, when his falling Tears
   Bewail'd those Numbers, which his Sword employ'd,
And false, *Hyena*-like, lamented and destroy'd.
   Tell Him, that does some stately Building raise, 280
    A *Windsor* or *Versailles* erect,
   And thorough all Posterity expect,
With its unshaken Base, a firm unshaken Praise;
   Tell Him, *Judea's* Temple is no more,
   Upon whose Splendour, Thousands heretofore
Spent the astonish'd Hours, forgetful to adore:
   Tell him, into the Earth agen is hurl'd,
   That most stupendious Wonder of the World,
   Justly presiding o'er the boasted Seven,
   By humane Art and Industry design'd,   290
   This! the rich Draught of the Immortal Mind,
    The Architect of Heaven.
   Remember then, to fix thy Aim on High,
   Project, and build on t'other side the Sky,
   For, after all thy vain Expence below,
   Thou canst no Fame, no lasting Pleasure know;

No Good, that shall not thy Embraces fly,   .
Or thou from that be in a Moment caught,
Thy Spirit to new Claims, new Int'rests brought,
Whilst unconcern'd thy secret Ashes lye,   300
Or stray about the Globe, *O Man ordain'd to Dye!*

THE SPLEEN

A Pindarik Poem

What art thou, *SPLEEN*, which ev'ry thing dost ape?
  Thou *Proteus* to abus'd Mankind,
  Who never yet thy real Cause cou'd find,
Or fix thee to remain in one continued Shape.
  Still varying thy perplexing Form,
  Now a Dead Sea thou'lt represent,
  A Calm of stupid Discontent,
Then, dashing on the Rocks wilt rage into a Storm.
  Trembling sometimes thou dost appear,
  Dissolved into a Panick Fear;   10
  On Sleep intruding dost thy Shadows spread,
  Thy gloomy Terrours round the silent Bed,
And croud with boading Dreams the Melancholy
      Head;
  Or, when the Midnight Hour is told,
  And drooping Lids thou still dost waking hold,
  Thy fond Delusions cheat the Eyes,
  Before them antick Spectres dance,
Unusual Fires their pointed Heads advance,
  And airy Phantoms rise.
  Such was the monstrous *Vision* seen,   20
When *Brutus* (now beneath his Cares opprest,
And all *Rome's* Fortunes rolling in his Breast,
  Before *Philippi's* latest Field,
Before his Fate did to *Octavius* lead)
  Was vanquish'd by the *Spleen*.

Falsly, the Mortal Part we blame
Of our deprest, and pond'rous Frame,
Which, till the First degrading Sin
Let Thee, its dull Attendant, in,
Still with the Other did comply,   30
Nor clogg'd the Active Soul, dispos'd to fly,
And range the Mansions of it's native Sky.
 Nor, whilst in his own Heaven he dwelt,
 Whilst Man his Paradice possest,
His fertile Garden in the fragrant East,
 And all united Odours smelt,
 No armed Sweets, until thy Reign,
 Cou'd shock the Sense, or in the Face
 A flusht, unhandsom Colour place.
Now the *Jonquille* o'ercomes the feeble Brain;   40
We faint beneath the Aromatick Pain,
Till some offensive Scent thy Pow'rs appease,
And Pleasure we resign for short, and nauseous Ease.

 In ev'ry One thou dost possess,
 New are thy Motions, and thy Dress:
 Now in some Grove a list'ning Friend
 Thy false Suggestions must attend,
Thy whisper'd Griefs, thy fancy'd Sorrows hear,
Breath'd in a Sigh, and witness'd by a Tear;
 Whilst in the light, and vulgar Croud,   50
 Thy Slaves, more clamorous and loud,
By Laughters unprovok'd, thy Influence too confess.
In the Imperious *Wife* thou Vapours art,
 Which from o'erheated Passions rise
 In Clouds to the attractive Brain,
 Until descending thence again,
 Thro' the o'er-cast, and show'ring Eyes,
 Upon her Husband's soften'd Heart,

He the disputed Point must yield,
Something resign of the contested Field;   60
Till Lordly *Man*, born to Imperial Sway,
Compounds for Peace, to make that Right away,
And *Woman*, arm'd with *Spleen*, do's servilely Obey.

The *Fool*, to imitate the Wits,
Complains of thy pretended Fits,
And Dulness, born with him, wou'd lay
Upon thy accidental Sway;
Because, sometimes, thou dost presume
Into the ablest Heads to come:
That, often, Men of Thoughts refin'd,   70
Impatient of unequal Sence,
Such slow Returns, where they so much dispense,
Retiring from the Crond, are to thy Shades inclin'd:
O'er me alas! thou dost too much prevail:
I feel thy Force, whilst I against thee rail;
I feel my Verse decay, and my crampt Numbers fail.
Thro' thy black Jaundice I all Objects see,
As Dark, and Terrible as Thee,
My Lines decry'd, and my Employment thought
An useless Folly, or presumptuous Fault: 80
Whilst in the *Muses* Paths I stray,
Whilst in their Groves, and by their secret Springs
My Hand delights to trace unusual Things,
And deviates from the known, and common way;
Nor will in fading Silks compose
Faintly th' inimitable *Rose*,
Fill up an ill-drawn *Bird*, or paint on Glass
The *Sov'reign's* blurr'd and undistinguish'd Face,
The threatning *Angel*, and the speaking *Ass*.

Patron thou art to ev'ry gross Abuse,   90
The sullen *Husband's* feign'd Excuse,

When the ill Humour with his Wife he spends,
And bears recruited Wit, and Spirits to his Friends.
    The Son of *Bacchus* pleads thy Pow'r,
    As to the Glass he still repairs,
    Pretends but to remove thy Cares,
Snatch from thy Shades one gay, and smiling Hour,
And drown thy Kingdom in a purple Show'r.
When the *Coquette*, whom ev'ry Fool admires,
    Wou'd in Variety be Fair,   100
    And, changing hastily the Scene
    From Light, Impertinent, and Vain,
    Assumes a soft, a melancholy Air,
    And of her Eyes rebates the wand'ring Fires,
    The careless Posture, and the Head reclin'd,
      The thoughtful, and composed Face,
    Proclaiming the withdrawn, the absent Mind,
    Allows the Fop more liberty to gaze,
    Who gently for the tender Cause inquires;
    The Cause, indeed, is a Defect in Sense,   110
Yet is the *Spleen* alledg'd, and still the dull Pretence.
    But these are thy fantastic Harms,
    The Tricks of thy pernicious Stage,
    Which do the weaker Sort engage;
    Worse are the dire Effects of thy more pow'rful Charms.
    By Thee *Religion*, all we know,
    That shou'd enlighten here below,
    Is veil'd in Darkness, and perplext
    With anxious Doubts, with endless Scruples vext,
And some Restraint imply'd from each perverted Text.
    Whilst *Touch* not, *Taste* not, what is freely giv'n, 121
Is but thy niggard Voice, disgracing bounteous Heav'n.
    From Speech restrain'd, by thy Deceits abus'd,
    To Deserts banish'd, or in Cells reclus'd,
    Mistaken Vot'ries to the Pow'rs Divine,

Whilst they a purer Sacrifice design,
Do but the *Spleen* obey, and worship at thy Shrine.
   In vain to chase thee ev'ry Art we try,
     In vain all Remedies apply,
     In vain the *Indian* Leaf infuse,   130
     Or the parch'd *Eastern* Berry bruise;
Some pass, in vain, those Bounds, and nobler Liquors use.
     Now *Harmony*, in vain, we bring,
     Inspire the Flute, and touch the String.
     From Harmony no help is had;
Musick but soothes thee, if too sweetly sad,
And if too light, but turns thee gayly Mad.
     Tho' the Physicians greatest Gains,
     Altho' his growing Wealth he sees
     Daily increas'd by Ladies Fees,   140
   Yet doft thou baffle all his studious Pains.
   Not skilful *Lower* thy Source cou'd find,
   Or thro' the well-dissected Body trace
   The secret, the mysterious ways,
By which thou dost surprise, and prey upon the Mind.
   Tho' in the Search, too deep for Humane Thought,
     With unsuccessful Toil he wrought,
     'Till thinking Thee to've catch'd, Himself by thee
       was caught,
     Retain'd thy Pris'ner, thy acknowledg'd Slave,
And sunk beneath thy Chain to a lamented Grave. 150

A PINDARICK POEM

Upon the Hurricane in November 1703, referring to this Text in
Psalm 148. ver. 8. Winds and Storms fulfilling his Word.

With a Hymn compos'd of the 148th Psalm Paraphras'd

You have obey'd, you WINDS, that must fulfill
   The Great Disposer's righteous Will;
Throughout the Land, unlimited you flew,

Nor sought, as heretofore, with Friendly Aid
  Only, new Motion to bestow
Upon the sluggish Vapours, bred below,
Condensing into Mists, and melancholy Shade.
  No more such gentle Methods you pursue,
  But marching now in terrible Array,
    Undistinguish'd was your Prey: 10
  In vain the *Shrubs*, with lowly Bent,
  Sought their Destruction to prevent;
  The *Beech* in vain, with out-stretch'd Arms,
  Deprecates th'approaching Harms;
  In vain the *Oak* (so often storm'd)
  Rely'd upon that native Force,
  By which already was perform'd
  So much of his appointed Course,
  As made him, fearless of Decay,
    Wait but the accomplish'd Time   20
  Of his long-wish'd and useful Prime,
To be remov'd, with Honor, to the Sea.
  The strait and ornamental *Pine*
  Did in the like Ambition joyn,
  And thought his Fame shou'd ever last,
When in some Royal Ship he stood the planted Mast;
  And shou'd again his Length of Timber rear,
  And new engrafted Branches wear
  Of fibrous Cordage and impending Shrouds,
Still trimm'd with human Care, and water'd by the
        Clouds.   30
  But oh, you *Trees!* who solitary stood;
    Or you, whose Numbers form'd a Wood;
    You, who on Mountains chose to rise,
    And drew them nearer to the Skies;
    Or you, whom Valleys late did hold
    In flexible and lighter Mould;

You num'rous Brethren of the Leafy Kind,
    To whatsoever Use design'd,
    Now, vain you found it to contend
With not, alas! one Element; your Friend   40
Your Mother Earth, thro' long preceding Rains,
    (Which undermining sink below)
No more her wonted Strength retains;
Nor you so fix'd within her Bosom grow,
That for your sakes she can resolve to bear
    These furious Shocks of hurrying Air;
But finding All your Ruin did conspire,
She soon her beauteous Progeny resign'd
To this destructive, this imperious Wind,
That check'd your nobler Aims, and gives you to the
        Fire.   50

    Thus! have thy Cedars, *Libanus*, been struck
      As the lythe Oziers twisted round;
    Thus! *Cadez*, has thy Wilderness been shook,
    When the appalling, and tremendous Sound
      Of rattl'ing Tempests o'er you broke,
      And made your stubborn Glories bow,
    When in such Whirlwinds the *Almighty* spoke,
Warning *Judea* then, as our *Britannia* now.
      Yet these were the remoter Harms,
Foreign the Care, and distant the Alarms: 60
      Whilst but sheltring Trees alone,
      Master'd soon, and soon o'erthrown,
      Felt those Gusts, which since prevail,
      And loftier Palaces assail;
      Whose shaken Turrets now give way,
With vain Inscriptions, which the Freeze has borne
Through Ages past, t'extol and to adorn,
      And to our latter Times convey;

Who did the Structures deep Foundation lay,
Forcing his Praise upon the gazing Croud,   70
And, whilst he moulders in a scanty Shroud,
Telling both Earth and Skies, he when alive was proud.
Now down at once comes the superfluous Load,
     The costly Fret-work with it yields,
Whose imitated Fruits and Flow'rs are strew'd,
Like those of real Growth o'er the Autumnal Fields.
     The present Owner lifts his Eyes,
And the swift Change with sad Affrightment spies:
The Cieling gone, that late the Roof conceal'd;
The Roof untyl'd, thro' which the Heav'ns reveal'd, 80
Exposes now his Head, when all Defence has fail'd.

     What alas, is to be done!
Those, who in Cities wou'd from Dangers run,
     Do but encreasing Dangers meet,
And Death, in various shapes, attending in the Street;
     While some, too tardy in their Flight,
     O'ertaken by a worse Mischance,
     Their upward Parts do scarce advance,
When on their following Limbs th' extending Ruins light.
One half's interr'd, the other yet survives,   90
And for Release with fainting Vigour strives;
Implores the Aid of absent Friends in vain;
With fault'ring Speech, and dying Wishes calls
Those, whom perhaps, their own Domestick Walls
By parallel Distress, or swifter Death retains.

     O *Wells!* thy Bishop's Mansion we lament,
So tragical the Fall, so dire th'Event!
     But let no daring Thought presume
To point a Cause for that oppressive Doom.
Yet strictly pious KEN! had'st Thou been there,   100
This Fate, we think, had not become thy share;

Nor had that awful Fabrick bow'd,
Sliding from its loosen'd Bands;
Nor yielding Timbers been allow'd
To crush thy ever-lifted Hands,
   Or interrupt thy Pray'r.
Those Orizons, that nightly Watches keep,
Had call'd thee from thy Bed, or there secur'd thy Sleep.
  Whilst you, bold Winds and Storms! his Word obey'd,
  Whilst you his Scourge the Great *Jehova* made,   110
And into ruin'd Heaps our Edifices laid.
You *South* and *West* the Tragedy began,
As, with disorder'd haste, you o'er the Surface ran;
   Forgetting, that you were design'd
  (Chiefly thou *Zephyrus*, thou softest Wind!)
Only our Heats, when sultry, to allay,
And chase the od'rous Gums by your dispersing Play.
   Now, by new Orders and Decrees,
   For our Chastisement issu'd forth,
You on his Confines the alarmed *North*   120
    With equal Fury sees,
   And summons swiftly to his Aid
   Eurus, his Confederate made,
His eager Second in th'opposing Fight,
That even the Winds may keep the Balance right,
Nor yield increase of Sway to arbitrary Might.
   Meeting now, they all contend,
   Those assail, while These defend;
   Fierce and turbulent the War,
   And in the loud tumultuous Jar   130
   Winds their own Fifes, and Clarions are.
Each Cavity, which Art or Nature leaves,
Their Inspiration hastily receives;
   Whence, from their various Forms and Size,
   As various Symphonies arise,

Their Trumpet ev'ry hollow Tube is made,
And, when more solid Bodies they invade
   Enrag'd, they can no farther come,
The beaten Flatt, whilst it repels the Noise,
Resembles but with more outrageous Voice   140
     The Soldier's threatning Drum:
And when they compass thus our World around,
   When they our Rocks and Mountains rend,
When they our Sacred Piles to their Foundations send,
   No wonder if our ecchoing Caves rebound;
   No wonder if our list'ning Sense they wound,
When arm'd with so much Force, and usher'd with such
     Sound.

Nor scarce, amidst the Terrors of that Night,
When you, fierce Winds, such Desolations wrought,
When you from out his Stores the Great Commander
     brought,   150
   Cou'd the most Righteous stand upright;
   Scarcely the Holiest Man performs
   The Service, that becomes it best,
By ardent Vows, or solemn Pray'rs addrest;
Nor finds the Calm, so usual to his Breast,
     Full Proof against such Storms.
   How shou'd the Guilty then be found,
The Men in Wine, or looser Pleasures drown'd,
To fix a stedfast Hope, or to maintain their Ground!
   When at his Glass the late Companion feels,   160
That Giddy, like himself, the tott'ring Mansion reels!
     The Miser, who with many a Chest
     His gloomy Tenement opprest,
     Now fears the over-burthen'd Floor,
And trembles for his Life, but for his Treasure more.
   What shall he do, or to what Pow'rs apply?

To those, which threaten from on High,
By him ne'er call'd upon before,
Who also will suggest th' impossible Restore?
No; *Mammon*, to thy Laws he will be true,   170
And, rather than his Wealth, will bid the World adieu.
The Rafters sink, and bury'd with his Coin
That Fate does with his living Thoughts combine;
For still his Heart's inclos'd within a Golden Mine.

Contention with its angry Brawls
By Storms o'er-clamour'd, shrinks and falls;
Nor WHIG, nor TORY now the rash Contender calls.
Those, who but Vanity allow'd,
Nor thought, it reach'd the Name of Sin,
To be of their Perfections proud,   180
Too much adorn'd without, or too much rais'd within,
Now find, that even the lightest Things,
As the minuter parts of Air,
When Number to their Weight addition brings,
Can, like the small, but numerous Insects Stings,
Can, like th' assembl'd Winds, urge Ruin and Despair.

Thus You've obey'd, you Winds, that must fulfill
The Great disposer's Righteous Will:
Thus did your Breath a strict Enquiry make,
Thus did you our most secret Sins awake,   190
And thus chastis'd their Ill.

Whilst vainly Those, of a rapacious Mind,
Fields to other Fields had laid,
By Force, or by injurious Bargains join'd,
With Fences for their Guard impenetrable made;
The juster Tempest mocks the wrong,
And sweeps, in its directed Flight,
Th' Inclosures of another's Right,

Driving at once the Bounds, and licens'd Herds along.
  The Earth agen one general Scene appears;   200
    No regular distinction now,
  Betwixt the Grounds for Pasture, or the Plough,
    The Face of Nature wears.

Free as the Men, who wild Confusion love,
    And lawless Liberty approve,
    Their Fellow-Brutes pursue their way,
  To their own Loss, and disadvantage stray,
As wretched in their Choice, as unadvis'd as They.
  The tim'rous *Deer*, whilst he forsakes the Park,
  And wanders on, in the misguiding Dark,   210
  Believes, a Foe from ev'ry unknown Bush
    Will on his trembling Body rush,
  Taking the Winds, that vary in their Notes,
For hot pursuing Hounds with deeply bellowing Throats.
  Th' awaken'd *Birds*, shook from their nightly Seats,
    Their unavailing Pinions ply,
    Repuls'd, as they attempt to fly
In hopes they might attain to more secure Retreats.
  But, Where ye wilder'd Fowls wou'd You repair?
    When this your happy Portion given,   220
  Your upward Lot, your Firmament of Heaven,
  Your unentail'd, your undivided Air,
  Where no Proprietor was ever known,
  Where no litigious Suits have ever grown,
Whilst none from Star to Star cou'd call the space his Own;
  When this no more your middle Flights can bear,
  But some rough Blast too far above conveighs,
Or to unquitted Earth confines your weak Essays.
  Nor You, nor wiser Man cou'd find Repose,
    Nor cou'd our Industry produce   230
    Expedients of the smallest Use,

To ward our greater Cares, or mitigate your Woes.
 Ye *Clouds!* that pity'd our Distress,
  And by your pacifying Showers
 (The soft and usual methods of Success)
 Kindly assay'd to make this Tempest less;
 Vainly your Aid was now alas! employ'd,
In vain you wept o'er those destructive Hours,
 In which the Winds full Tyranny enjoy'd,
  Nor wou'd allow you to prevail,   240
But drove your scorn'd, and scatter'd Tears to wail
  The Land that lay destroy'd.

 Whilst You obey'd, you Winds! that must fulfill
  The just Disposer's Righteous Will;
 Whilst not the Earth alone, you disarray,
But to more ruin'd Seas wing'd your impetuous Way.

 Which to foreshew, the still portentous *Sun*
 Beamless, and pale of late, his Race begun,
 Quenching the Rays, he had no Joy to keep,
 In the obscure, and sadly threaten'd Deep. 250
 Farther than we, that Eye of Heaven discerns,
 And nearer plac'd to our malignant Stars,
Our brooding Tempests, and approaching Wars
   Anticipating learns.
  When now, too soon the dark Event
  Shews what that faded Planet meant;
 Whilst more the liquid Empire undergoes,
 More she resigns of her entrusted Stores,
 The Wealth, the Strength, the Pride of diff'rent Shores
 In one Devoted, one Recorded Night, 260
 Than Years had known destroy'd by generous Fight,
  Or Privateering Foes.
  All Rules of Conduct laid aside,
  No more the baffl'd *Pilot* steers,

Or knows an Art, when it each moment veers,
To vary with the Winds, or stem th'unusual Tide.
   Dispers'd and loose, the shatter'd Vessels stray,
     Some perish within sight of Shore,
   Some, happier thought, obtain a wider Sea,
But never to return, or cast an Anchor more!   270
   Some on the *Northern* Coasts are thrown,
And by congealing Surges compass'd round,
   To fixt and certain Ruin bound,
    Immoveable are grown:
The fatal *Goodwin* swallows All that come
Within the Limits of that dangerous Sand,
Amphibious in its kind, nor Sea nor Land;
Yet kin to both, a false and faithless Strand,
Known only to our Cost for a devouring Tomb.
   Nor seemed the HURRICANE content,   280
Whilst only Ships were wreckt, and Tackle rent;
   The Sailors too must fall a Prey,
Those that Command, with those that did Obey;
The best Supporters of thy pompous Stile,
Thou far Renown'd, thou pow'rful BRITISH Isle!
Foremost in Naval Strength, and Sov'reign of the Sea!
   These from thy Aid that wrathful Night divides,
   Plung'd in those Waves, o'er which this Title rides.
   What art Thou, envy'd *Greatness*, at the best,
    In thy deluding Splendors drest?   290
   What are thy glorious Titles, and thy Forms?
   Which cannot give Security, or Rest
   To favour'd Men, or Kingdoms that contest
With Popular Assaults, or Providential Storms!
   Whilst on th'Omnipotent our Fate depends,
And They are only safe, whom He alone defends.
   Then let to Heaven our general Praise be sent,
Which did our farther Loss, our total Wreck prevent.

And as our Aspirations do ascend,
Let every Thing be summon'd to attend;   300
And let the Poet *after God's own Heart*
Direct our Skill in that sublimer part,
  And our weak Numbers mend!

THE HYMN

To the Almighty on his radiant Throne,
  Let endless Hallelujas rise!
Praise Him, ye wondrous Heights to us unknown,
Praise Him, ye Heavens unreach'd by mortal Eyes,
Praise Him, in your degree, ye sublunary Skies!

Praise Him, you Angels that before him bow,
  You Creatures of Celestial frame,
Our Guests of old, our wakeful Guardians now,
Praise Him, and with like Zeal our Hearts enflame,
Transporting then our Praise to Seats from whence you
      came!

Praise Him, thou Sun in thy Meridian Force;
  Exalt Him, all ye Stars and Light!
Praise Him, thou Moon in thy revolving Course,
Praise Him, thou gentler Guide of silent Night,
Which do's to solemn Praise, and serious Thoughts invite.

Praise Him, ye humid Vapours, which remain
  Unfrozen by the sharper Air;
Praise Him, as you return in Show'rs again,
To bless the Earth and make her Pastures fair:
Praise Him, ye climbing Fires, the Emblems of our
      Pray'r.

Praise Him, ye Waters petrify'd above,
  Ye shredded Clouds that fall in Snow,

Praise Him, for that you so divided move;
Ye Hailstones, that you do no larger grow,
Nor, in one solid Mass, oppress the World below.

Praise Him, ye soaring Fowls, still as you fly,
And on gay Plumes your Bodies raise;
You Insects. which in dark Recesses lie,
Altho' th' extremest Distances you try,
Be reconcil'd in This, to offer mutual Praise.

Praise Him, thou Earth, with thy unbounded Store;
Ye Depths which to the Center tend:
Praise Him ye Beasts which in the Forests roar;
Praise Him ye Serpents, tho' you downwards bend,
Who made your bruised Head our Ladder to ascend.

Praise Him, ye Men whom youthful Vigour warms;
Ye Children, hast'ning to your Prime;
Praise Him, ye Virgins of unsullied Charms,
With beauteous Lips becoming sacred Rhime:
You Aged, give Him Praise for your encrease of Time.

Praise Him, ye Monarchs in supreme Command,
By Anthems, like the *Hebrew* Kings;
Then with enlarged Zeal throughout the Land
Reform the Numbers, and reclaim the Strings,
Converting to His Praise, the most Harmonious Things.

Ye Senators presiding by our Choice,
And You Hereditary Peers!
Praise Him by Union, both in Heart and Voice;
Praise Him, who your agreeing Council steers,
Producing sweeter Sounds than the according Spheres.

Praise Him, ye native Altars of the Earth!
Ye Mountains of stupendious size!

Praise Him, ye Trees and Fruits which there have birth,
Praise Him, ye Flames that from their Bowels rise,
All fitted for the use of grateful Sacrifice.

He spake the Word; and from the Chaos rose
   The Forms and Species of each Kind:
He spake the Word, which did their Law compose,
   And all, with never ceasing Order join'd,
Till ruffl'd for our Sins by his chastising Wind.

But now, you Storms, that have your Fury spent,
   As you his Dictates did obey,
Let now your loud and threatning Notes relent,
   Tune all your Murmurs to a softer Key,
And bless that Gracious Hand, that did your Progress stay.

From my contemn'd Retreat, obscure and low,
   As Grots from whence the Winds disperse,
May this His Praise as far extended flow;
   And if that future Times shall read my Verse,
Tho' worthless in it self, let them his Praise rehearse.

TO THE ECCHO

In a clear night upon Astrop walks

Say lovely Nymph, where dost thou dwell?
Where is that secret Sylvan seat,
That melancholy, sweet retreat,
From whence, thou doest these notes repell,
And moving Syllables repeat?
Oh lovely Nymph, our joys to swell,
Thy hollow, leafy mantion tell,
Or if thou only charm'st the ear,
And never wilt to sight, appear,
But doest alone in voyce excell,   10
Still with itt, fix us here.

Where Cynthia, lends her gentle light,
Whilst the appeas'd, expanded air,
A passage for thee, does prepare,
And Strephon's tunefull voyce, invite,
Thine, a soft part with him to bear.
Oh pleasure! when thou'dst take a flight,
Beyond thy comon, mortal height,
When to thy sphere above, thou'dst presse,
And men, like Angels, thou woud'st blesse,   20
Thy season, be like this, fair Night,
And Harmony thy dresse.

THE BIRD

Kind bird, thy praises I design,
Thy praises, like thy plumes, shou'd shine;
Thy praises, shou'd thy life outlive,
Cou'd I the fame I wish thee, give.
Thou, my domestick musick art,
And dearest trifle of my heart.
Soft, in thy notes, and in thy dresse,
Softer, then numbers can expresse,
Softer then love, softer then light
When just escaping from the night,   10
When first she rises, unaray'd,
And steals a passage through the shade.
Softer then air, or flying clouds
Which Phœbus glory, thinly shrouds,
Gay as the spring, gay as the flowers,
When lightly strew'd with pearly showers,
Ne'r to the woods shalt thou return,
Nor thy wild freedom, shalt thou mourn,
Thou, to my bosome shalt repair,
And find a safer shelter there;   20
There shalt thou watch, and shou'd I sleep,

My heart, thy charge, securely keep.
Love, who a stranger is to me,
Must by thy wings be kin to thee;
So painted o're, so seeming fair,
So soft, his first adresses are,
Thy guard, he n'er can passe, unseen;
Thou, surely thou hast often been,
Whilst yett a wand'rer in the grove,
A false accomplice, with this Love;   30
In the same shade, hast thou not sate,
And seen him work some wretches fate?
Hast thou not sooth'd him in the wrong;
And grac'd the mischeif, with a song,
Tuning thy loud conspiring voyce,
O're falling lovers, to rejoyce?
If so, thy wicked faults redeem,
In league with me, no truce with him
Do thou admitt, but warn my heart,
And all his sly designs impart,   40
Least to that breast, by craft he gett,
Which has defy'd and brav'd him yett.

THE TREE

Fair *Tree!* for thy delightful Shade
'Tis just that some Return be made;
Sure, some Return is due from me
To thy cool Shadows, and to thee.
When thou to *Birds* do'st Shelter give,
Thou Musick do'st from them receive;
If *Travellers* beneath thee stay,
Till Storms have worn themselves away,
That Time in praising thee they spend,
And thy protecting Pow'r commend: 10

The *Shepherd* here, from Scorching freed,
Tunes to thy dancing Leaves his Reed;
Whilst his lov'd Nymph, in Thanks, bestows
Her flow'ry Chaplets on thy Boughs.
Shall I then only Silent be,
And no Return be made by me?
No; let this Wish upon thee wait,
And still to flourish be thy Fate,
To future Ages may'st thou stand
Untouch'd by the rash Workman's hand;   20
'Till that large Stock of Sap is spent,
Which gives thy Summer's Ornament;
'Till the fierce Winds, that vainly strive
To shock thy Greatness whilst alive,
Shall on thy lifeless Hour attend,
Prevent the Axe, and grace thy End;
Their scatter'd Strength together call,
And to the Clouds proclaim thy Fall;
Who then their Ev'ning-Dews may spare,
When thou no longer art their Care;   30
But shalt, like ancient Heroes, burn,
And some bright Hearth be made thy Urn.

TO THE NIGHTINGALE

Exert thy Voice, sweet Harbinger of Spring!
    This Moment is thy Time to sing,
    This Moment I attend to Praise,
And set my Numbers to thy Layes.
    Free as thine shall be my Song;
    As thy Musick, short, or long.
Poets, wild as thee, were born,
    Pleasing best when unconfin'd,
    When to Please is least design'd,
Soothing but their Cares to rest;   10

Cares do still their Thoughts molest,
  And still th' unhappy Poet's Breast,
Like thine, when best he sings, is plac'd against a Thorn.
She begins, Let all be still!
  Muse, thy Promise now fulfill!
Sweet, oh! sweet, still sweeter yet
Can thy Words such Accents fit,
Canst thou Syllables refine,
Melt a Sense that shall retain
Still some Spirit of the Brain,   20
Till with Sounds like these it join.
  'Twill not be! then change thy Note;
  Let division shake thy Throat.
Hark! Division now she tries;
Yet as far the Muse outflies.
  Cease then, prithee, cease thy Tune;
  Trifler, wilt thou sing till *June?*
Till thy Bus'ness all lies waste,
And the Time of Building's past!
  Thus we Poets that have Speech,   30
Unlike what thy Forests teach,
  If a fluent Vein be shown
  That's transcendent to our own,
Criticize, reform, or preach,
Or censure what we cannot reach.

A NOCTURNAL REVERIE

In such a *Night*, when every louder Wind
Is to its distant Cavern safe confin'd;
And only gentle *Zephyr* fans his Wings,
And lonely *Philomel*, still waking, sings;
Or from some Tree, fam'd for the *Owl's* delight,
She, hollowing clear, directs the Wand'rer right:
In such a *Night*, when passing Clouds give place,

Or thinly vail the Heav'ns mysterious Face;
When in some River, overhung with Green,
The waving Moon and trembling Leaves are seen;   10
When freshen'd Grass now bears it self upright,
And makes cool Banks to pleasing Rest invite,
Whence springs the *Woodbind*, and the *Bramble*-Rose,
And where the sleepy *Cowslip* shelter'd grows;
Whilst now a paler Hue the *Foxglove* takes,
Yet checquers still with Red the dusky brakes
When scatter'd *Glow-worms*, but in Twilight fine,
Shew trivial Beauties watch their Hour to shine;
Whilst *Salisb'ry* stands the Test of every Light,
In perfect Charms, and perfect Virtue bright: 20
When Odours, which declin'd repelling Day,
Thro' temp'rate Air uninterrupted stray;
When darken'd Groves their softest Shadows wear,
And falling Waters we distinctly hear;
When thro' the Gloom more venerable shows
Some ancient Fabrick, awful in Repose,
While Sunburnt Hills their swarthy Looks conceal,
And swelling Haycocks thicken up the Vale:
When the loos'd *Horse* now, as his Pasture leads,
Comes slowly grazing thro' th' adjoining Meads,   30
Whose stealing Pace, and lengthen'd Shade we fear,
Till torn up Forage in his Teeth we hear:
When nibbling *Sheep* at large pursue their Food,
And unmolested Kine rechew the Cud;
When *Curlews* cry beneath the Village-walls,
And to her straggling Brood the *Partridge* calls;
Their shortliv'd Jubilee the Creatures keep,
Which but endures, whilst Tyrant-*Man* do's sleep;
When a sedate Content the Spirit feels,
And no fierce Light disturb, whilst it reveals;   40
But silent Musings urge the Mind to seek

Something, too high for Syllables to speak;
Till the free Soul to a compos'dness charm'd,
Finding the Elements of Rage disarm'd,
O'er all below a solemn Quiet grown,
Joys in th' inferiour World, and thinks it like her Own:
In such a *Night* let Me abroad remain,
Till Morning breaks, and All's confus'd again;
Our Cares, our Toils, our Clamours are renew'd,
Or Pleasures, seldom reach'd, again pursu'd.   50

———

TO DEATH [1]

O King of Terrors, whose unbounded Sway
All that have Life, must certainly Obey;
The King, the Priest, the Prophet, all are Thine,
Nor wou'd ev'n *God* (in Flesh) thy Stroke decline.
My Name is on thy Roll, and sure I must
Encrease thy gloomy Kingdom in the Dust.
My soul at this no Apprehension feels,
But trembles at thy Swords, thy Racks, thy Wheels;
Thy scorching Fevers, which distract the Sense,
And snatch us raving, unprepar'd from hence;
At thy contagious Darts, that wound the Heads
Of weeping Friends, who wait at dying Beds.
Spare these, and let thy Time be when it will;
My Bus'ness is to Dye, and Thine to Kill.
Gently thy fatal Sceptre on me lay,
And take to thy cold Arms, insensibly, thy Prey.

[1] This poem was accidentally misplaced. It belongs with the group of religious poems beginning on p. 214.

THE TRIVMPHS OF LOVE AND INNOCENCE
A TRAGECOMEDY
AN ADVERTISEMENT

Having seen (out of the love of novelty) many Plays brought upon the stage, wh^th have been as indifferent as these two of mine, and not being able, longer then my own life, to protect either of them,·from the same fate, of being expos'd, censured, and condemn'd, I prefix these few lines, which will accompany them as long as they are to have a being, to assure all that shall peruse them, that a more terrible injury cannot be offer'd me, then to occasion, or permitt them ever to be represented. I have both private, as well as declar'd reasons for this, and did I not hope by my entreaty, to be secure of prevailing in this particular, I wou'd assure myself of itt, by a total suppression, of what I have suffer'd to be coppy'd, only for the entertainment of some particular persons; but since they are to passe (if they live till hereafter) only throo' the hands of Relations, and such as have professt some esteem for me, I will not disquiett myself, with any fears, or distrusts of the honour or generosity of them, who can in nothing so much oblige me, as in being strict (against any importunitys whatsoever) to the observation of this earnest request of . . . .   Ardelia.

THE NAMES AND CARACTERS OF THE PERSONS
THE MEN

Aubusson, Great Master of Rhodes.

Lauredan, General of Cyprus for the reigning queen Catherine Cornare, and Ambassadour from the State of Venice.

Blanfort, A yong French nobleman, nephew to Aubusson, in love with the true Queen of Cyprus, formerly contracted to Marina.

Rivalto,
Villmarin, } Knights of Rhodes, and factious against Aubusson.
Linnian,

Riccio, A Cyprian Lord, Counsellour to the exil'd queen.

Capriccio, A merry drinking Captain of the Guards, something exceptious.

Monthaleon, An honest knight of Rhodes, friend to Aubusson, and Blanfort.

THE WOMEN

Queen of Cypress, Expell'd and come to Rhodes for refuge.
Marina, Contracted to and forsaken by Blanfort, now disguis'd,
   and under the name of Carino, serves as page to Aubusson.
Clarilla, Favorite, and confident to the Queen.

Guards and Attendants on the Great Master, and on the Generall,
   and Women and Attendants on the Queen.

The General Scene is the Great Masters Pallace in the Isle of
   Rhodes.

THE FIRST ACT: THE FIRST SCENE

The Queen's Apartment

*At the drawing up of the Curtain, a sound of Hautbois, Trum-
   petts, and other naval musick is heard as from the Sea*

Enter Riccio and Clarilla.

   Ric. Clarilla, where's the Queen?
Knows she the news, that Lauredan is landing?
   Clar. Who is alive in Rhodes, and does not know itt?
So loud his trumpetts eccho round the Shoar,
And usher in the pomp, with which he sails;
The sound, to all that love the Queen, is hatefull,
Since to his arm alone, she owes her ruine,
Who fix'd the bold Vsurper on her throne,
And now maintains his Widdowe in that wrong,
The proud Cornara, whom he serves with passion.   10
   Ric. Nay! more Clarilla, all his businesse here
Is to remove our Queen, from this retreat,
And at the best, confine her close for ever.
   Clar. He cant be cruel sure to that degree,
Fame gives itt out, he has some noble thoughts,
And pitty too (as I have been inform'd)
For our great Mistresse, in her change of fortune;
Which cannot, sure, consist with such harsh usage.
   Ric. Compassion, oh! 'tis deaf, when intrest moves.

Did itt not plead, d'you think, with all itts arts   20
To Agamemnon, for his Daughter's life?
Did itt not tell him, she was fair, and Yong,
Guiltlesse, as Nymphs that haunt the fountains side
Far from th' infected air of Towns, and Courts?
Did not soft pitty, whisper to his soul
That 'twas himself, that he must wound in her,
And the dear mother's part, which more he pris'd?
Yet, ouer all these tender bounds he passt
And sees her to the Temple brought, at last.
The People groan, and he himself appears   30
Like a full cloud, just breaking into tears.
The Priest too wept, but int'rest had decreed
Int'rest the god of all, that she shou'd bleed;
For int'rest, now she's on the altar laid,
And but a pow'r devine cou'd save the maid.
   Clar. Good Riccio, speak no more such moving things;
Our present ills, have made my heart so apt
For sad impressions —
That I can weep, at hearing but a fable.
And tell me then, if pitty cannot do itt,   40
What may be thought on, to preserve the Queen?
   Ric. We sail, indeed, amid'st a world of dangers,
Some Ports we haue, but many winds against us.
Venice,that bred Cornara in her bosome,
Wou'd still maintain her, in the height she's grown to,
And 'tis from them, the Genral's now commission'd
To make the attempt I told you, on our freedom.
Rivalto's Suttle, and the Master's foe,
And link'd in that, with Villmarin and Linian,
Who still oppose the interests of our Queen.   50
These shou'd be soothed and flatter'd into freindship;
But Blanfort's love, oh! thats our Southern gale,
Which if improv'd, we shou'd not want a harbour.

These things you may insinuate to the Queen,
Who has no hopes, but in the help of freinds.
  Clar. Oh! name not freindship, 'tis a weak supporter;
And in this base and most degenerat age,
Fitt only to erect a Som̄er bower,
And bear the curling top of some light vine;
But if a torn, and tempest beaten oak,   60
Falling, shou'd lean upon itts boasted aid,
Twou'd faintly shrink from the stupendious weight,
And leave itt to embrace the humble dust.
Nor can she flatter, she, who is the Sun
To which those earthy vapours shou'd ascend,
Will n'ere decline her beams, to court the foggs.
For Blanfort's love, she shuns itt with such care,
That yett, 't has ne're been told her, but by blushes.
But 'tis the Prince, 'tis Aubusson, the just
That must protect us, to preserve that title.   70
  Ric. So may itt prove, and since the Queen is private
I will return, and listen to the news.
Do you attend her still, and chear her spiritts,
Perhaps, our fears present our dangers double,
There is no Hydra, like uncertain trouble.
                        [Exeunt severally

     The Scene changes to a Room of State.
              Florish.

Enter at one door Aubusson, Blanfort Carino, Monthaleon, Capric-
    cio, &c., *at the other,* Lauredan, Rivalto, Villmarin, Linnian,
    and Lauredan's *traine.*

  Aub. Brave Lauredan, the Isle of Rhodes salutes you.
And hauing told you, in her warlike voyce
Of drums and trumpetts, and the Canon's thunder
That you are welcome to her crouded shoares,
Does now by me, her father and her freind,
In the soft sounds of peace, again confirm itt;

And from the State of Venice, what you bring,
We stand prepar'd, with these our Knights to hear.
   Laur. Then, from that Citty, thus I'm bid to say,
To Aubusson, the Prince of conq'uring Rhodes,   10
The Christians Bullwork, and the Turks confusion,
That much she seeks the freindship of that State
Whose piety, and strictnesse to their vows,
Can bring down Heav'n to blesse their brave attempts,
And send their Fame, to be recorded there.
All love she offers, and all kind accesse,
Succours in war, and trade in fertile peace,
With what shall farther be by you requir'd
To knitt the bands, of this most wish'd for league.
   Aub. Proceed my lord, to tell us her demands,   20
For, if they are as gentle, as these proffers,
Beleive me, Rhodes and Venice, shall be twinns,
So much her wisdom; and her love we vallue.
   Laur. Oh! they are gentler far, and of no tryal,
No charge, or weighty burthen to the Isle,
No nice requests, that ask a long debate
And keep the sever'd Councill in suspence;
This is the whole, that you resign to me
To be conducted, where they have decree'd
The person of the refug'd Cyprian Queen.   30
A confused murm'ring of approbation arises among the faction,
   then Rivalto *speaks.*
   Riv. It is most fitt.
   Lin. We cannot buy it cheaper.
   Vil. He is no friend to Rhodes, that likes not this.
   Aub. My lord, you call'd her refug'd in you⌈r⌉ speech,
Sure you did ill to mix that sacred word
With those, that urge to violate the trust.
Indeed, she came into our arms, for safety,
And stak'd her royal life, upon our truth.

Here too, sh' has slept without her train of fears.
Only because we said she might dismisse them   40
And when she talk'd of seizing and confinement,
We bid her think herself as free as air;
And shall we now, to that, convert our words,
Making them lighter then the chaff itt plays with
Oh no! my Lord, she is, she shall be free.

   Laur. She shall, and curs'd be he that wou'd opose itt,
She shall be free, on me repose that trust.

   Aub. 'Tis lodg'd in us, and when we give itt up,
Our honour, at that moment we resign.
And think my Lord, what we have done for honour,   50
Who when th' Imperial Turk came proudly on,
Follow'd by numbers, countlesse as the stars,
T' exact a shamefull tribute worse then death,
With handfulls, in that cause, repuls'd the Tyrant
And struck him, in his Tent, with such dispair,
As made his Soul, a sacrafice to peace,
That long had trembl'd, underneath his fury.
Oh! Lauredan, lett Venice still remember
'Twas honour, made us stem that high wrought tide,
And force an ebb on that prodigious Sea.   60
And since 'tis in this cause as much engag'd,
Tell 'em, that with like vigour wee'll maintain it.

   Laur. My Lord I've done, but cou'd me thinks have wisht,
That ere you'd urg'd so fully your refusall,
The reasons might have been at large discuss'd,
On which the Senate built this fair request.

                                   [*To Aub*

   Vil. The reasons, ought to have been heard, my Lord.
   Lin. We're all concern'd, and tis no private cause.
   Rivalt. 'Tis fitt, that Venice who bestows that Crown,
Shou'd in her pow'r, haue all that are pretenders;   70
We are not to decide whose right itt is.

Blanf. Nor are you call'd Rivalto to that task,
What our Great Master has return'd in answer,
Will please the good, the gen'rous, and the just,
And I so fully joyn in that decree,
That this, and life shall leave me e're 'tis chang'd.

[Laying his hand on his sword

Laur. So yong! so handsome! and so much concern'd?
It strikes me deeper then my last dessign,
For sure in that, ther's something more then honour.

Aub. Blanfort, as neerest me in blood and duty, *[Aside.* 80
I first command you silence, and respect;
Next, know Rivalto, Vilmarin, and Linian,
That you shall thrive no better, in this strife,
Then when ye poorly from the Town retir'd,
And drew your troops from off the Citty's guard,
Because your clamorous councill to resign itt
Was over rul'd, by all the freinds to honour.
That, I forgave, but will not still be cross'd,
Nor yeild my pow'r, and place, to bold intruders,
Capriccio, see your guards perform their duty, 90
And silence all that dare to interrupt us.

*[Linian *offers to speak,* Rivalto *speaks to him aside*

Riv. No more, 'tis not a time to urge him farther,
Leave itt to me, to fell this soaring pride,
When things are ripen'd, which I have in working.

Aub. Think not my Lord, because you hear dissension
That 'tis my arbitrary will prevails
But know, that ere your vessel loos'd from Venice,
Fame, with her thousand tongues, had told your purpose.
And 'twas the states, th' assembl'd states decree,
That it shou'd instantly be thus rejected 100
Least, that a secret, and obscure debate

Might make itt thought, we were dispos'd to yeild,
And only held our honour at a price
Above, what your commission was to offer.
Therefore my Lord, here end this vain request,
Whilst thus again, I take you to my arms.

                                 [*Embracing him.*

And to our love, repeat you are most welcome.
    Laur. To charm the person, whilst you blast his hopes,
Is sure my Lord, particular to you.
Yett grant me this att least, to see the Queen.   110
In private but to see, and to discourse her,
My last demand, I fix upon this point;
Which if obtain'd, shall still my discontents,
And make me think myself not unsuccesfull.
    Aub. If she consents my lord itt shall be so,
There let itt rest.——
Whilst Rhodes shall tryumph that within her walls
She lodges such a Souldier as your self.
Lead on before, and lett our trumpetts tell
How much we glory in our warlike guest.   120

[*Exeunt* Aub. *with* Laur. *follow'd by all but* Rivalto, *who stays
    and lays hold on* Carino, *who seems to endeavour to get from
    him.*]
    Riv. Why, strive you to avoid me thus Marina,
Am I become of late, so dreadfull to you?
    Car. Oh! good Rivalto, lett the voyce be low
That speaks a name, which I must own with blushes
You only know, I am not what I seem,
And when you wrought me to assume this shape,
Upon your Order, solemnly you swore,
Ne're to reveal, without my free consent,
That itt conceal'd a poor, unhappy woman.
    Riv. Nor have I, though your frequent scorns have urg'd
    itt   .   130

Beyond the patience of all hearts, but mine.
O! yett relent, fair, charming Maid relent,
And pleasure, with her best supporter, wealth,
Shall still be handmaids, to your matchlesse beauty.
    Car. Name 'em no more, to her that's lost to both,
Wealth I abandon'd, when I left my father,
And fled his house, a vagabond for love.
And as for pleasure, oh! Rivalto, know,
Tis so confin'd, with all its sweet attractions,
To the dear person, of my faithlesse Blanfort,   140
That since he's false, tis not in Fortune's pow'r
To tempt my soul, with the deluding proffer.
    Riv. Do all your joys, depend then on his truth.
    Car. Yes, were he mine, as holy vows oblige him,
And lay unmindfull of the fleeting hours,
'Stretch'd at my feet, 'till Phœbus left the skye,
Breathing out sighs, soft as the southern winds,
And printing on my hands, a thousand kisses,
Then, cou'd I tell my soul in full delight,
That this was pleasure, fitt for the immortals.   150
But oh! they're past, those eager joys are past,
And all extreams, to their own ruine haste.
    Riv. No more! Marina, I will hear no more,
By all the stars, that crosse my hopes, I will not.
Why, shou'd you speak such fond, and moving things,
And not for me, who know I best deserve them?
Weigh but my services, against his youth,
And when the beauty of his form persuades,
Be just, and sett the dangers I have run
To bring you here, from all your pow'rfull freinds   160
Against that gaudy trifle of an hour.
    Car. Vrge not those dangers, which you fondly sought
To gratify your own, and not my passion.
Oh! had I known in Rome, your true dessign,

Ne'ere had I listen'd to those fair pretences.
Which drew me thence, to misery, and Rhodes.
To see my Lord, doat on another face,
Whilst not one feature here, he doth suspect
To be the same he lov'd in poor Marina.
Oh why Rivalto, why, would you deceive me,   170
Why wou'd you work all this, why wou'd you love?
   Riv. Why, wou'd you lett me know that you cou'd love
And talk, above the rate of other women?
Why wou'd you rob me of a safe belief
(The only guard against enticing beauty,)
That all your sex, were foolish, vain, inconstant,
Form'd of a rib, beneath the heart of man.
The seat of noble, and exalted passions,
·And only made pertakers of his spleen,
By which they laugh, and weep, and love, and hate,   180·
And steer the course of their uncertain souls,
Why did you let me see, to my undoing,
You was not thus, and charm me from my refuge?
   Car. Think on your order and your vow Rivalto,
Oh! think of that, and leave to urge me more,
For what, you shou'd not take, if itt were granted
   Riv. When itt was made, war was my soverain passion,
And Faith, I swore, to that my native cheif,
But love prevailing ore my alter'd heart,
Tells me to love, I only owe obedience;   190
Therfore to you, the Pow'r that sways my soul,
Upon my knees, again I will repeat them,
And on this altar, white as Parian marble,
Seal and confirm, th' irrevocable oath.
                                  [*Offers to take her hand.*
   Car.   Oh! hear me first, what I intend to swear,
                                      [*Shee kneels.*
Tis now my turn, you've done itt once already.
   By all the hearts, that bleed without return,

By all the Virgins, that in secret mourn,
By all the tender and aluring things,
Writt by soft pens, drawn from yong Cupids wings,   200
By love himself, and by his mothers smiles,
By ev'ry thing, that flatters and beguiles
I swear to man, I n'ere will listen more —

[*She pauses and sighs.*

Unlesse to him, who broak all vows before.
Riv. Ten thousand curses, tear him from the earth,
And furies (such as prey upon my soul)
Be still th' attendants of his anxious hours.
And as for you, Marina —
Cruel, ungratefull, obstinate Marina,
Know, that I will not whine, and be despis'd,   210
Nor dye dispairing, and yett blesse the cause.
    No, from this hour, itt is resolv'd, your charms
    Shall be embrac'd, or crush'd between these arms.

[*She goes out att one door, he going meets at the other door,* Vilmarin *and* Linnian, *and returns with them.*]

    Vil. You're tame Rivalto, and have made us so;
Restrain'd the gen'rous heat, we shou'd have shewn,
Before the Great, and strict observing General,
Who may report itt, that he saw us baffl'd,
Rated like boys, and slander'd with reproach
Of base dessigns, to haue betray'd our Country.
    Riv. It was no slander that, we wou'd have done itt.   220
And tho his pow'r o'recame, and made us yeild,
Yett, were itt to be try'd again I'de tempt itt:
And to the Turk, the Tartar, or the Fiend
Give up my Country, Kinsmen, Laws, Religion,
Rather then see them bow beneath the sway
Of this adoar'd, insulting Aubusson.
    Lin. Why did you stop me then, when I was fir'd,

And would have urg'd it, loudly to the croud,
That his proceedings were tyrannical.
   Riv. Yes, to have bred their sport —   230
When Captain puff, had stopt your tongue,
And haled ye to confinement.
No, no, revenge shall take a surer course,
And when my thunder darts, with full comission,
It shall not leave, to this aspiring Cedar,
One lofty branch, to kisse the passe [*sic*] clouds,
Or tell the world that once itt rul'd the grove.
   Vil. If 'tis his life you mean, when thus you threat'n,
Th' attempting that, perhaps may cost our own.
   Riv. It might indeed.—   240
Think therefore, how t'would please ye, to destroy
What more then life, he euer has esteem'd,
And yett be safe, to see, and to rejoyce in 't.
   Lin. How itt wou'd please, is sure, not to be told;
But he's so fenc'd about with fame, and freinds,
With fortune, and the fawning of the world,
That, to my eye, no part appears unguarded,
Where we may fix a wound that wou'd be fatal.
   Riv. To shew you that, must be my part, my freinds,
But this is not a time, or place for secrets.   250
Only thus much, think how 'twill feed revenge,
To see this Saint, this praying fighting Saint,
This child of Fame, this cloud of holy Incence,
Expos'd a profligate, and secret sinner,
And like an orespent taper, stink, and vanish.
   Lin. Oh! 'twill be rare, but tell me, is he thus?
For though I wish itt, I can scarce beleive itt.
   Riv. You shall beleive, and both be actors in itt,
For shou'd I undertake the task alone,
It might appeare, season'd with too much malice,   260
For, since he from the Treasury, thrust me out,

With publick scandal of abuses there,
The world's too well acquainted how I hate him;
Anon we'll meet, at his, or at your lodgings,
And all shall be reveal'd, till when, farewell.
 Lin. I long to hear itt, till that time we'll part.
 Vil. The lesse we're seen together, 'tis the better.
              [*Exeunt.*
     Enter Blanfort *and* Monthaleon.

 Blan. 'Tis true, the very mention of itt, shook me,
And call'd up all the anger of my soul.
Oh! think how Rhodes wou'd look if she were absent, 270
How dull, how solitary, 'twoud appear,
Did not her smiles, that tryumph o're her sorrows,
Chear, and enliven, all the glad beholders.
 Month. My Lord, you speak as if we all were lovers,
To you indeed, I grant it may be so.
 Blan. To me indeed, I do confesse Monthaleon
The Sun n'ere rises, but with new delight
I think 'twill bring again, some happy hour
When I may gaze upon a brighter beauty.
And folded in, by night's returning shades, 280
I blesse 'em not, for silence, or for rest,
But for the softer slumbers, that present
The lovely Queen, in all her charms of wonder.
 Month. As honour'd with the title of you[r] freind,
I shou'd be greiv'd to hear this mighty passion,
Did I not hope, your most indulgent kinsman
Wou'd both allow, and urge itt with the Queen;
Who, may for shelter, from the present storm,
Be glad to find a haven in your arms,
And so, be more secure, of our protection. 290
 Blan. The proposition, warms me into raptures,
But oh! I wou'd not owe itt to her fears,
My passion is too nice (tho' ne'r so famist)

To feed on ought, but what's prepared by love;
Therefore, I'll tell her first, how I adore her,
And hope to be more blest in my endeavours,
To find a time, when I may own my flame,
Then heitherto, my fortune has affoarded,
Since first I languish't in this soft desire;
Till that is done, forbear to urge the Master.   300
   Month. May you succeed, and when you shall com̄and
       me,
I'll do my part, pray loose no time my lord.
   Blan. Oh! fear me not, this moment I'll about itt.
   To urge me on to haste, as vain wou'd prove,
   As to give speed to time, or wings to love.
                           [*Exeunt.*

          Enter Riccio *alone.*

   Ricc. To see and to discourse with her in private
That's his request, and Aubusson allows itt
Perhaps, the Queen will give itt her permission,
If not deterr'd by my severer council,
Which shall be urg'd most strongly, to prevent itt,   310
Nor, will I stick to aggravate his speech.
And put such harshnesse on his late demands
As shall create a new displeasure for him.
His hate to me, I hear he has profess'd,
For that, I won my Queen, to fly from Cyprus,
And not to trust the false and flatt'ring speeches,
With which, he subtly strove to have detain'd her
Wherefore, I must be ware of his revenge,
And not allow, (tho' twou'd restore her Crown)
That he shou'd 'ere conferr with her, in private,   320
Least something might be urg'd, to work my ruine.
   For yet the World has n'ere that Statesman known,
   Who for his Princes int'rest, wav'd his own.   [*Exit.*

ACT II SCENE I
A Room of State
Enter the Queen, *talking with* Riccio

Queen. Is he so earnest then, to urge my fetters,
And seems his barb'rous tryumph uncompleat,
Unlesse, a Princesse grace itt, with her presence.
The meanest wretch, to liberty is born,
And 'tis a tyrant's work, to force 'em from it.
The forest claims itt, for her savage traine;
And chearfull birds, that feel itt in the air,
Sing to that happy state, their softest carolls.
And, wou'd he rob me, of this comon blessing?
Oh! 'tis most cruel, most inhuman Riccio,   10
Did none reply, and tell him 'twas inhuman?
Or was he sooth'd with flatt'ry of the croud,
Who still believe, the last heard tale, is best?

Ricc. It prov'd so here indeed, the faction murmur'd,
And call'd his bold request, a just demand;
Cheifly, Rivalto seconded his speech,
Till yong Lord Blanfort, like another Perseus
In the fair cause of Innocence opresst,
Rush'd on the Monster, with such gen'rous fury,
As struck him into silent rage, and blushes,   20
At which the haughty Gen'ral, sternly frown'd,
And utter'd something, lost to me by distance.

Queen. I much disire to know, by what comission,
He undertakes, to be my publick Champion?
On his great kinsman, I repose my fortunes,
Nor will a weaker Atlas, 'ere support 'em.
But Riccio, go, and give the Prince of Rhodes,
That answer to his message, I deliver'd,
For by your reasons, urg'd to me within,
I am determin'd not to see the General.   30

Ricc. Your wise comands, I'll instantly obey,
And soon return, to lett you know th' event.
   Queen. Do so, I with impatience, shall expect itt.
                                         [*Exit* Ricc.
Will loue be caught, with gazing but an hour,
If so, itt is not safe to look abroad,
And women's eyes, by flatt'rers call'd so dreadfull,
Will only prove of danger to themselves?
I ne'er beheld this Lauredan, but once,
And 'twas that fatal day, which crush'd my fortunes,
Yett, is his form, still present to my sight,   40
And such methinks, as I cou'd wish the mans
Whom fate wou'd chuse, to give me back my Crown.
And that he's brave, I know, by having lost itt.
Nor did he seem to me so rudely feirce,
So full of terrour, as they now describe him;
His speech was gentle and his looks were sad,
My sighs he eccho'd, and to stop my tears,
Told me, if that I left not yett the shore,
He wou'd retreive the fortune of the day,
And give me back my Kingdom for a smile;   50
But Riccio sais, he loves my Throne's possessour,
And now to fix her, urges my confinement,
Else, all his wrongs, I cou'd methinks forgive,
That hours soft treatment, pleads so strongly for him.
  [*As she walks upon the stage, enter* Blanfort, *and talks to himself,*
              whilest her face is from him.]
   Blan. I've sent Capriccio, to engage her women,
Carino too, that us'd to interrupt me
As certainly as if he had design'd itt,
Is playing out a game, which I begun,
And cannot rob me of this happy moment.
   Queen. He has surpris'd me, which I still avoided,   60
                            [*Aside seeing him.*

And once Clarilla, has forgot my orders,
I must not lett him manage the discourse.

If I may guesse, my Lord, what brings you here;
To seek me out, before the publick hour,
Tis to describe some splendid entertainment,
Some Mask design'd, or musick, to devert
The stranger, lately landed on your shoars.
   Blan. Had you but guest more right, or durst I speak itt.
Then, Madam, wou'd the cause that brings me here,
Appear as much above those comon trifles,   70
As, you excell all others, in perfection.
   Queen. If 'tis my Lord so dang'rous to be told,
Still to conceal itt, is the way to safety.
   Blan. Oh! rather say to death, and to dispair;
So long, allready, have I trod the path,
The solitary path of silent wishes,
That rather than I still will wander there,
I'll boldly leap the precipice before me,
And perish in attempting to be free.
See! Madam, at your feet, to rise no more,   [*He kneels.* 80
If you deny his suit, the wretched'st slave
That ere submitted to the pow'r of ——

           [*Seeing* Carino *enter the* Queen *interrupts* Blan.

   Queen. My Lord you are observ'd, but if to me,
You've anything of moment to impart,
Riccio, my wise, and faithfull Councellour,
Will best receive, and bring itt to my knowledge.
His coming, just to stop the word, I fear'd,

           [*Aside as she walks from him.*

Was as I cou'd have wish'd itt.
   Blan. Who sins in love in love shall still be curs'd,

                 [*Aside.*

Else, sure this boy, cou'd n'er have crosst me now.   90
How is itt, thou hast left the play, Carino,   [*To* Car.
I trusted thee to manage, in my absence.
   Car. Indeed, my Lord, since I have been in Rhodes,
I'm seiz'd sometimes, with such a sudden passion,
Such quick disorder'd beatings at my heart,
As nothing but the air and motion cures.
Forgive me, that when now I felt itt coming
I left with Linnian, what you gave to me,
And know, he better will perform the task.
   Blan. I do forgive thee, but I must be plain,   100
And tell thee, I wou'd entertain the Queen
Without a witnesse, therefore now retire,
Before she turns, and may perhaps detain thee.
   Car. My Lord, I'll passe that way, and find her women.
                    [*Pointing to y*ᵉ *door where the* Queen *stands.*

   Blan. Thou't be observ'd.
   Car. I'll steal so gently by,
I must retire, since he so plainly bids itt,   [*Aside.* .
But I've one strattagem, Love make it prosper.

[*Seems to steal by y*ᵉ Queen, *pulling a handerchief out of her
      pockett, a paper falls out in sight of the* Queen.

   Queen. What paper's this, comes itt from you, Carino?
   Blan. The trifler has undone my dear dessign.   110
                                        [*Aside.*
And robb'd me, of this long sought hour of blisse.
   Car. Forgive me, Madam, that my carelesse action
                              [*Taking up the paper.*
Has made it fall, so neer your royal feet
   Queen. Is't not a song, confesse the truth Carino,
Come I will see itt, or be much displeas'd
Who waits? call in Phelinda, she shall sing itt.
                              [*Enter* Phelinda.]

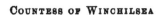

THE SONG

All your sighs, to air are turning,
  All your vows, will soon be lost,
Quench'd those flames, which ne're left burning,
  'Till they had my freedom cost.   120

Yett, remember whilst denying,
  How you strove to change my mind,
Men are lost, but by complying,
  Women lou'd but 'till they're kind.

Queen. Indeed 'tis well, extreamly well Carino.
But this complaint, shou'd not be made by you.

Enter Riccio

Blan. More interruption, then 'tis vain to hope,   [*Aside.*
And opertunity's as coy as beauty.
  Queen. With the great Master Riccio have you been?
  Blan. I find he comes with buisnesse, to the Queen   130
·And must retire——

          But oh! 'tis death to goe,
          And not the fortune of my passion knowe.

                              [*Exit, followed by* Carino.

Ricc. Great Aubusson, entreats your Royal presence,
Who waits with some selected from the Council,
For conference with you, on this great occasion.
But Madam, for the reasons lately urg'd
I wou'd advise, that still you shou'd resolve
To stand unmov'd, in what I now have told you.
  Queen. Fear not my Lord, that I will see the Generall,
                              [*Going out.*
Who pleads for nothing, but my certain ruine.   140
                              [*Exeunt.*

The Scene changes to an outward room in the Queen's *apartment,*
Blanfort *passing through it with* Carino

   Blan. Thou knowst I love, and cannot chide thee long;
But prithee, be more carefull for the future,
Not to prevent, my conference with the Queen,
Since I have told thee, that my life depends on 't.

As they are going off Capriccio *peeps out att the contrary door,
and in a low voyce calls to* Blanfort.

   Cap. My Lord, my Lord, may I not be releas't,
I've done an hour's hard duty here, to serve you,
Another such, wou'd wear me to a shaddow?
   Blan. Well, take thy liberty, itt is enough.

                                 [Capriccio *enters.*

Prythee, what is't has made thee so impatient,
Their conversation, cou'd not tire thee, sure.   10
   Cap. Their prating did, I know not what you call itt.
   Blan. Well, their discourse, how did they entertain thee?
   Cap. Why, alltogether, and ev'ry one, as much as she
      cou'd.
Sing us a song, good Captain, says one.

                               [*Imitating their voyces.*

No, no, says another, tell us a story of the Turks;
Oh! but was you never in love, says a third.
Yes, yes, says I, most inhumanely,
And then I looked leeringly thus, upon my Lady Clarilla,
That she might think itt was with her.
But was you never drunk, says another,   20
A notable pert wench, that,
And came home to me, i' faith;
But says I, what in my face betrays itt?
Nay, nothing says she,
For a red nose, may be caught with standing
Too long in the sun, and at that,

They all sett up a laugh, tee, hee, ha, ha, a,
Which lasted a full quarter of an hour,
Without any interruption; but I was glad of that,
For itt gave me time to study an answer.   30
   Car. And 'twas a good one, sure, lett's hear itt Captain?
   Cap. Why, I told em, so many tongues
Was too much for one pair of ears,
And that, if itt was not for somebody's sake,
More then their own, they shou'd have talk'd
To themselves for me.
And that a man was a man, and a nose was a nose,
Lett it look of what colour it wou'd.
   Blan. 'Twas smart indeed,
But you did ill, to let them anger you,   40
Twas that, which bred their mirth,
No more of this, for our great Master comes.

Enter as from Council with the Queen, Aubusson, Monthaleon,
Vilmarin, Linian, &c.

   Aub. Not, that I fear a war with the Venetians,
Or to have bought their freindship, with dishonour,
Did I endeavour to persuade the Queen
To some complyance with the Gen'ralls wishes;
But in that Prince, there lives a soul so noble,
So great, so gen'rous, and so truly valiant,
That much it greives me, he shou'd part from Rhodes
(Which boasts herself the nurse of all these vertues)   50
With such a hard repulse as here he meets.
   Month. Indeed, my lord, I think t' have given him
     audience,
Had been an act of prudence, in the Queen,
Nor were the reasons Riccio urg'd against itt,
Of weight enough, to give him satisfaction,
And 'tis most sure, we've drawn a war upon us.

Blan. Why, let itt come, we have no other buisnesse,
Tis the foundation of our sacred order.
And though 'twas cheifly meant against the Turks,
Yett he that asks us, what we shou'd not grant,   60
By that, becomes as much our Country's foe.
The war, the war, I'm for the war, and scorn the proposition.
   Aub. Carino says not so, the mention of itt
Has chang'd the colour, from his youthfull cheeks.
   Car. I hope I should not shun itt, out of fear.
   Aub. What then Carino, care to keep thy beauty?

        [*Laying his hand on her head and stroaking her face.*

Thou art indeed, too handsome for the field,
And 'twas such features, cross'd great Pompey's fortune,
Loosing him at Pharsalia, half the world,
Which till that time, he held in spite of Cæsar.   70
   Vil. So, so, soft and gentle, a lovely woman truly,

        [*Aside to* Lin.

What fools were we, not to perceive it sooner.
   Blanf. Was then my lord, that battle lost by beauty
   Aub. O! yes itt was,
For Juluis, marking how their troops came on,
(Repelling with their beams, the sun's bright lustre,
A golden army, and a feather'd war,
Where ev'ry youth, to his complexion, match'd
Colours, that best adorn'd and set it off)
Call'd to his Vetterans, deform'd with scarrs,   80
And bid 'em mark those faces, like their own;
The stern command, as roughly was obey'd;
And now, assaulted in that seat of charms,
Sooner they chose, to show the foe their backs,
Then not before their Mistresse [s], appear
With those sweet looks, that drew their parting tears.
But we loose time,
Follow me Blanfort, and Monthaleon too,

That we may think, what terms will best become,
And soften, what the Gen'rall must be told. 90
   Blan. Where shall I meet with thee again, Carino? [*Aside.*
   Car. I'll waite you in the Grove, that fronts the Pallace,
A Lute, and voyce, shall tell the place directly.

Exeunt Aub: Month: Blan: Car.

   Lin. Lett's seek Rivalto,
Since what we've mark'd our selves,
I long for more discourse, upon the subject.   [*Exeunt.*

Enter Rivalto

   Riv. They're now engag'd, both in my dark contrivance;
What I have next to doe;
Will be to fleece 'em of the wealth I want:
And then lett Fortune, as they're fools, befreind 'em. 100
The rest of my dessigns, come bravely on,
Already, has the General been treated
Just as I meant he shou'd, when by forg'd letters
I wrought on Riccio, to oppose his purpose,
Which, may, provoke the State, he stands concern'd for
And breed new troubles, to our haughty Master.
For Blanfort too, something I must contrive,
Which may, without my hand, cut off a Rival.
And when I have expos'd Marina's fame,
Making that use on't, my revenge exacts, 110
I'll take her, humbl'd by the world's contempt,
And flying to some far, some sweet retreat,
Shake off these Vows, that manacle my Soul,
And taste the joys, of liberty, and Love.
   Tis luxury, not honour, I desire,
   The real warmth, and not the painted fire;
   To all my senses, their full pleasures give
   I care not how reproach'd or scorn'd I live.

[*Enter to him a Gentleman, with a letter.*]

Gent. Receive this, Sir, sent to you from the General,
Who with itt, bids me tell you, on his honour,　　　　120
Noe harm shall reach you, if itt meets complyance.
Since all his ends are fair, as time shall prove them,
And that he chose this way, to shun suspition,
Which might have risen from a private conference.

Riv. I'm proud, in anything to be commanded
By that great man, whom here we treat so slightly,
Oh! we are bravely govern'd, but no more.

　Nay, then, if fates as [*sic*] work, as fast as I　[*Reads aside.*
　It must go well.
Sir, tell the Gen'ral, what he here desires　　　　130
Falls in the compasse of my pow'r and will,
And, when the proper hour of night, arrives,
I'll wait upon him and secure his purpose
This and all honour to him.　　　　　　　[*Exeunt.*

　　　[*The scene changes to a Grove*, Carino *alone.*]

Car. I am resolv'd, at last, to tempt my fortune,
And by some tender policy, renew
The dear remembrance of his once fond passion;
And if one spark of all that fire remains,
　I'll own myself, and try to urge itt higher,
　Or else in silence, and dispair, expire.

　　　　　　　　　　　[*Enter one with a Lute.*

Oh! here's the tunefull guide, I said, shou'd lead him,
'Tis well you're come, pray sing the song I sent you,
And, lett your musick soften, what's too harsh.

A SONG

　　Love, give thy traine of slaves away,　　　　10
　　　To those whose Pleasure is their pride,
　　To me, a gentle sigh convey,
　　　Unheard by all the world beside.

A soft and secret falling tear,
   A tender thought but half expresst,
Whilst am'rous looks, allay'd with fear,
   And glowing blushes, speak the rest.

Oh! still to me, addresse such fires,
   As were beneath the Mirtles known,
E're men had learn'd to feign desires,   20
   Or Women, proud, or false, were grown.

For since to Courts, and Cittys come,
   Wealth, thy declining pow'r invades,
And Vanity usurps thy room,
   Unknown to Innocence and shades.

Car. See, itt has brought him   [*Aside.*
Now you may retire.   [*Exit musician.*

           Enter Blanfort

Blan. I come, Carino, drawn by thy sweet notes,
Which through the grove, take their harmonious way,
Whilst hov'ring Cupids hang upon the air,   30
And catch the feathered sounds, to wing their arrows.
But tell me, Youth, why doest thou seek retirement?
The dark, and gloomy corners of the world,
Were only made, for sad, and sighing lovers.
Of these, thou art not one, I hope thou art not,
For in that name, all misery's compris'd.   [*He sighs.*
   Car. Alas! my lord, I grieve to hear you sigh,
For one, that does the precious breath dispise,
And thinks her shrine, too glorious for such incense.
But, did you never Love, my Lord, till now,   40
Nor taste the pleasing part, of that sweet passion?
Methinks, this place to confidence invites.
And I cou'd here unfold my secrett thoughts,
Were but your bosome, willing to receive them,

And I might hope a sutable return;
Shall I begin my lord, or ask your pardon
For having thus presum'd, to seek an honour,
Which you may think me too unworthy of.
   Blan. No, I dare trust thee,
And if thy tale be love, mine shall be soe;   50
Do thou begin, and then I will unfold
Who won my heart, before I saw the Queen;
Here we'll lye down, and on this bank of flow'rs
Discourse of love, and all itt's pleasing powers.
                [*They sett down leaning agaynst y*ᵉ *bank.*
   Car. Keep off intruders, Fortune, for this moment,
And all my life, shall be at thy dispose.   [*Aside.*
   Blan. Why doest thou pause, if love 'ere toutch'd thy
      breast,
Begin, and tell the time,
With ev'ry circumstance, that bred thy passion?
   Car. The time, my lord, when I began to love,   60
And yielded, to this Tyrant of my peace,
Was that, which brought your last deceased Master
With all his traine, of warlike knights to Rome,
To clear himself, before the holy chair
Of foul aspersions, cast upon his honour;
Sure you was there my Lord; I think you was.
Do you remember nothing of that time?
   Blan. O! yes I doe, and if that was the season,
Ther's something, sure, of Sympathy betwixt us.
Go on, and make me know as well the place.   70
   Car. The place, oh! 'twas most fitt for the occasion,
Secret, and blooming, with the verdant spring;
A Grove of mirtles, compass'd itt about,
Which gave no more admittance to the Sun
Then serv'd to chear the new appearing flowers,
And tell the birds, itt was their time to sing

A cristal spring, stole through the tufted grasse,
Hasting, to reach a fountain, which itt fed,
And murmur'd still, when 'ere itt found a stop.

[*She pauses.*

   Blan. As I shall do, if thou doest not proceed,   80
What then Carino?
   Car. I must be vain, and now describe myself
As he, then told me, I appear'd to him.   [*Aside.*
'Twas here, my lord, neer to this fountains side
I saw the Maid, the soft, the charming Maid,
That seem'd to give the sweetnesse to the place,
And in her self, posesst all I've describ'd,
The season's youth, and freshnesse of the flow'rs,
The harmony of all the tunefull birds,
And clearnesse of the Spring, on which she gaz'd.   90
   Blan. 'Tis wond'rous sweet,
What doest thou call this Paradice of pleasure?
   Car. The Gardens, to the Duke of Mantua's Pallace.
   Blan. Ha! tis yett more strange, but hast'n to the rest,
For night, I think begins to steal upon us
   Car. At my approach, she left her mossy seat,
And from her arm, a scarfe, an azure scarfe
Fell to the ground, which hastily I seiz'd on,
And by that pledge, stopt her intended flight,
She stood endeav'ring to regain the favour,   100
And I, transported, gazing on her charms,
Blessing the chance, but what I said I know not;
Yett, sure if words are coppy'd from the heart,
'Twas something, that expresst a sweet amaze,
A mighty rapture, and a new born passion.
My Lord, you seem as if you markt me not,
A thoughtfull air, has disposess'd the smiles
With which you bid me to repeat my passion.
   Blan. Tell me Carino, where thou hadst this story?

[*Rising in disorder*

By my past love, and future hopes 'tis mine;   110
The time, the place, all circumstances mine;
The very scarfe, which thus thou hast describ'd,
Is now within my Cabinett lockt up.
Unfold this riddle, for I will be told
If she, whom once I trusted with my soul,
And all the infant follys, of my love
Has lightly, made itt a discourse, for boys?

[*He coming up to her, looks earnestly on her, then turns aside
and speaks.*

Oh! I have found a secret that distracts me,
Dull as I was, 'ere this not to perceive itt.

    Car. I dare not speak, nor turn my eyes that way, [*Aside.*
I know I've but too well explain'd myself,   121
And have procur'd instead of what I hop'd for,
Only his hate, which this last transport shews me.

             [*Enter* Capriccio *throwing up his cap and singing.*

    Capr. Tell not me of the killing,
        The wild, and the willing
           In faith, I shou'd chuse the much rather,
             I'll have one that shall come,
             At the beat of my Drum,
           Or the tossing up of my feather.

Such Chios! such Cypresse! such daring, dancing, delicate
    liquors!   130
Such ragouts! to quicken the pallate; such mirth! such
    madnesse!
Such firing! such hurra's! such healths!

    Blan. Hey, where's all this.
Such hungry, thirsty raptures, I never heard of.

    Capr. No, nor never will, if you lye whining,
And sighing, and singing, under an old rotten tree.
Till the Caterpillars breed nests, in your dainty locks.
But come away to your great Vnkle

That sends for you, who makes to-night
For the renown'd General, a most magnificent supper,   140
A supper! such a supper! butt I'll say no more on't
Till I see itt
My Lord, he told me he was in haste,
Therefore if you'll come, you'll come.
If you won't, tell him so your self.
    I'll lose no time, the table fills apace,
      And the glad Preist, has huddl'd o're his grace.   [*Exit.*
    Blan. Half drunk already, thou'lt be dead e're midnight.
Carino, oh Carino, be discreet,
Else what thou'st told, may prove a fatal story.   150
I cannot stay, to reason with thee farther,
But know that Death, and nothing else shall part me
From the persuit of the fair Cypprian Queen.   [*Exit.*
    Car. I will not Hinder itt, I will not Blanfort,
Too well alas! Marina loves thee still,
Perjur'd, ungratefull, cruel as thou art,
To hang upon thy soft, and chearfull soul,
Her load of greifs, and break thy growing pleasures;
Nor, will I longer struggle with my fate,
But casting off this most unlucky garb,   160
And putting on to-night, my virgin dresse,
    I'll to some holy, secret Cell remove,
      And sigh and Pray, till I've outweary'd Love;
    Then to the Grave, this hated body give,
      And dye contented, that he so may live.   [*Exit.*

ACT III SCENE 1ˢᵗ

A Room of State, the Queen *and* Clarilla *appear in a balcony that
looks down into itt*

    Clar. This curtain, safely will conceal you Madam,
Yett being made transparent, does allow
That you may see, and hear them as you please;

Nor will itt now be long 'ere they arrive,
For I was told they're risen from the table.

   Queen.   Then goe, Clarilla, and secure the door,
That none surprise me 'till I find thee there.   [*Exit* Clar.
I wou'd be free, to hate him as I ought,
His comon theam, as Riccio has inform'd me,
Is on my Rival, and her labour'd praises,   10
The better, to insinnuate to the world
Things, less'ning to my person, and my title.
Oh! may he urge itt now, and work my cure;
For still in spite of all the wrongs I bear,
Ther's something in my soul, too partial tow'rds him.
But here they come, resentment, help me now.

Enter as from supper, Aubusson, Lauredan, Blanfort, Monthaleon
         Rivalto, Vilmarin, Linnian, Capriccio, *etc.*

   Aub.   With you, my Lord, we must divide that honour,
For whil'st by Land, we gained the prize we fought for,
Your winged Vessels, flew before the wind,
And oretook Conquest on the watry world.   20
But now, of War no more — bring in some wine,
A Lady's health, shall soften the rough sound,
Conclude the night, and give us peacefull slumbers.
                [*Wine brought in,* Aub. *drinks.*
Health to the Queen of Cyprus,
I know, my Lord, you are too much a Courtier
To take offence, at this our civil custome,
Tho' you, and she are not the freinds I wish yee.
                [Laur. *takes the glass and kneels.*
   Laur.   A Royal health, methinks, comands the knee.
   Blan.   A health like this, my Lord, comands the heart.
   Laur.   Then with my heart, health to the lovely Queen,   30
The peace of Angells, and the pow'r of Kings,
The joys of Love, and wealth of both the Indies,
Still crown her life, and wait upon her fortunes.

Cap. A rare smooth health, how itt skim'd over the glasse,
Like a duck and a drake over a smiling river
Twill come at last to me, I have itt right. [*Aside.*
  Blan. Dissembler! vile dissembler!
                     [*Aside whilst* Laur. *drinks.*
I'll grate his soul through with a wish lesse sounding.
Health to the Queen, and may she rule in Cyprus.
  Ric. My Lord, this complement exacts our thanks. 40
               [*To* Laur. *while the health goes round.*
  Laur. Away, I did not do't to gain thy favour. [*Scornfully.*
  Ric. So scornful still, oh! I have acted wisely. [*Aside.*
[Capr., *the health being come to him, falls down on both knees.*
  Capr. Health to the Queen of Cyprus,
May she be still in peace with all the angels,
In love with Kings, and sent to both the Indies.
        [*They laugh, he rises in a rage and breaks the glasse.*
Hang your new coin'd healths, that if a man misse but a
word, setts you all a laughing at him thus. I know well
enough, I shou'd have brought in wealth if I cou'd, but
what has a soldier to do with money. If I live till to-mor-
row, some shall hear 'ont; Kings, and Pow'rs and Angels,
and the Devil and all; keep 'em to your selves gentlemen
for me, I'll, I'll e'en go sleep, and think on't.
                     [*Exit very drunk.*
  Aub. My Lord forgive him, he is truly honest,
But has this mighty fault, that he will drink,
And then be most exceptious as you see.
But long, I will not lett him keep this custome.
The night grows late, kind sleep my lord attend you.
  Laur. My Lord good night, good night to all,
No ceremony, pray.
  Aub. Permitt 'em to attend you 'tis their duty. 60
[*Exeunt on one side,* Aub: Blan: Month: *on the other* Laur Riv:
  Vil: Lin:

[*Re enter as from waiting on the General* Riv: Vil: & Lin.

Lin. A woman! and so near his holy person,
Oh! hypocrite, not to be match'd in story.
But we already have in part unmask'd him,
By secret whispers, scatter'd round the court,
Had you but seen the fondnesse of this day,
Oh! such sweet words, and looks, such nautious praises,
Of her youth and features, and amorous strokings
Of her wanton cheeks, you wou'd I think have blush'd,
Tho' joy'd to see.—

Riv. Alas! I've seen much more my friends,   70
Dotage, beyond expression,
Such fondnesse, that I think his heart must break,
In that last pang, that shall devide her from him.

Vil. Oh! Fate give wings to that perplexing moment,
When I shall see him stand confus'd and sad,
Blushing for shame, for what's already past,
Yett, madly raving, 'cause 'twill last no longer.
Oh! devil, devil, with an Angel's semblance,
How riggidly still has he check'd our pleasures,
And punish'd ev'ry fault that lookt tow'rds woman.   80
Oh! I'm impatient for the full discovery.

Riv. Lett us about it then;
You know to-night 'tis I that keep the watch
And if in walking of the midnight round,
I can find out deeds, as dark, and close as that,
Be neer att hand, to hunt the game I spring yee,
Till then farwell.

Lin: We will not fayle, and so good night dear mischeif.
[*Exeunt* Lin: & Vil:

Riv. Farewell dear fools, whom I but trust by halves,
Yett make such use of, as occasion calls for.   90
They must not know, how far my self
And Blanfort are concern'd.

Least if they found itt had a false foundation,
They shou'd not urge the plott on Aubusson.
Nor will she in the midst of her disgrace
Declare the truth,
For fear her lover, shou'd yett more detest her.
Tho' if she shou'd, 'twere easy to posesse
The censuring world, that 'twas contrived still
To secure the Master, his nephew only   100
Took itt to himself.—
And to keep off all proofs of former love,
I've stole the contract, and all other pledges
Which they might have produc'd to gain beleif.
But 'tis the time that Lauredan expects me,
Whose harmlesse purpose too, shall serve my ends,
    And may the projects of this fatal night,
    On those I hate, in blood, & ruine light.   [*Exit.*

The scene changes to the Queen's *dressing-Room, a toilett spread,*
Enter the Queen *and* Clarilla

    Queen. The hour is come in which I us'd to rest,
But rest is not so forward as the hour.
Leave me awhile to think away my sorrows,
And when that's done, I will again recall thee.   [*Exit* Clar.
He wish'd me peace,
But to posesse itt, I must n'er have seen him.
He wish'd me pow'r, yett knew not at that moment,
But I might have employ'd itt to his ruine.
He nam'd the joys, the mighty joys of love,
And oh! me thought, that word so well became him,   10
I cou'd have stood to hear him speak itt ever.
Why, did I fondly wish again to see him,
And hope a cure, from what first bred my pain?
Oh! I have done, as hasty gamesters use,
Who having lost part of their shining store,
Sett all the rest, on one adventurous cast,

And leap into the ruine, they wou'd fly from.
Ha! What noyse is that?   [*She hears a noyse.*
The night's far spent, and ev'ry sound breeds horrour,
Again!   20
[*Two men appear att the door in disguise, one speaks to the other,*
   & then retires.
   First. I'll keep 'em from their posts till you return,
Come boldly back, and fear no opposition.
                    [*He goes off & the other comes just within the door.*
   Queen. Protect me heav'n, from farther acts of treason,
My life alone, is all the past have left me.
          [*As she is going to the contrary door, he kneels & speaks.*
   Second. Oh! fly not madam, fly not from your safety,
From him, who wears his life but to preserve you;
Can there be terrour, in this humble posture,
These arms thus folded, and this awfull distance?
Lett reason tell you, that if I were wicked,
And dark intents, had brought me on thus far,   30
Your inmost room, your Closset cou'd not save you,
But prove a fitter scene, for acts of mischeif.
   Queen. 'Tis true, who 'ere he is, I'm in his pow'r.
                    [*Aside, stopping at the extremity of the stage.*
Therefore, had better humour this respect,
Till I can search into his secret purpose
Which may not be so bad, as fear presents itt.
Keep then that distance still, and I will stay,   [*To him.*
And trust, so much, to what you have deliver'd,
As to demand the cause, for which you came?
   Second. To putt into your hands, your beauteous hands, 40
Your people's homage, and your Rival's fate,
The Gen'rall's life, that once oppos'd your right,
And all the Royal dignity you've lost.
   Queen. The Gen'rall's life, oh! then I must discover,
                                        [*Aside.*

And prevent him.
Such sounds as these, indeed com̄and attention,   [*To him.*
And tho', they like the Syrens, led to ruine,
Yett, wou'd I listen to the soft enchantment.
                              [*She comes towards him.*
And thus discarding all my woman's fears,
Will boldly ask, in whom the power is lodg'd   50
To work these miracles, you have declar'd.
                    [*He discovers himself to be* Lauredan.

  Laur. 'Tis all in Lauredan, and he in yours.
  Queen. Ha! Lauredan, nay then again I fear. [*She starts.*
  Laur. So, starts the passenger, who in his way
Meets a yong Lyon, arm'd with pow'r to kill,
And in that moment of his fear, forgetts,
That nature, bids the royal savage tremble
Before the awfull form, of Godlike man,
As I do now in presence of your charms.
Oh! do not wrong them, Madam, by distrust,   60
Or think your self lesse safe, thus arm'd in beauty,
Then the yong Grecian, with his phalanx bound,
Who stood unmov'd, the shock of all the persians.
  Queen. This flattery my lord, breeds more suspicion,
But curiosity, our sexes frailty
Will yett prevail, to make me hear you farther,
If you will rise, if not, I must retire.
                              [*He rises, she goes on.*
Pray rise my lord, why shou'd you kneel to me,
Alas! you best can tell I am no Queen?
Think on that day my Lord, I ever shall,   70
When all the room I cou'd com̄and in Cyprus,
Where I had liv'd in peace, and rul'd in love,
And been my self, the Genious of the place,
Was but one poor appartment in my pallace,
Which had its deep foundations in the sea;

Some few attendants my ill fate had left,
Who told with me, each shout the people gave,
As their new Lord, passed throo' the crowded streets,
And now, so neer, the horrid tumult came,
That in dispair, leaning on Riccio's arm,   80
I bid him lead me, to my last dominion,
A poor frail bark, that danc'd upon the waves,
And yett me thought, was steddyer then my Island,
When you my Lord came in.
   Laur. When I came in!
And saw more beauty breaking throo' your tears,
Then rose with Venus, when she left the deep;
When I came in!
A wretched Conqu'rer, in the Tyrant's cause,
Which then, I did beleive to have been just,   90
But oh! your eyes soon punish'd the mistake,
And cast such lightning, as destroy'd my laurells,
D'you bid me Madam, think upon that day,
In all th' account of time, I know no other:
The part of life I spent, ere that arriv'd,
Like a dull, empty scene, is all discard'd:
And since 'tis past, my thoughts have had no buisnesse,
But to preserve, and represent itt to me.
And, madam, since so nicely you recount itt,
Oh! Lett me speak, what I endur'd that day,   100
I saw, ador'd, and dy'd for you that day,
And yett, that fatal day, provoked and lost you.
   Queen. My lord, you take occasion from my fortunes
To speak such things, as else you wou'd not offer.
Yett, make them true, oh Love, and I'll adore thee.   [*Aside.*
   Laur. Be witnesse Love, and all thy gentle pow'rs,
If one presumptuous thought, inhabitts here.
                          [*Pointing to his breast.*
Yett I do love, beyond what words can utter;

Fortune be witnesse, and the Crown I part with,
If Lauredan grows giddy with successe.   110
Hear Madam! what your subjects have decreed,
And what is too, confirm'd by the Venetians,
Whose pow'rs expell'd and keep you from the throne,
First, that Cornara, whom att last they find
Too weak to hold itt, quitt the Sov'rain sway,
Then that the Crown shall be confirm'd on me,
And all my race, to wear itt by succession,
Some lessening offers to your self they make,
Not fitt for you to hear, or me to mention.

    Queen. D'you come my Lord, for my consent to this? 120
    Laur. Oh! hear me out, another frown like that
Wou'd strike me speechlesse,
Hear 'ere it kills, what Love and I decree,
What Heaven decrees,
Who has inspired my army with one soul,
And made that plyant, only to my wishes.
You are their Queen, and mine.
Again we will replace you on the throne,
And bound the uttmost height of our ambition,
To be the guard, still of your crown, and Person.   130
    Queen. 'Tis highly gen'rous this, I must acknowledge;
Yett let me ask, why with this fair dessign,
You here have made such rough, such harsh demands,
As aimed more to confine then reinthrone me.
    Laur. Indeed th' occasion forc'd me to be secret,
And keep my real purpose unreveal'd,
The power of Venice is att sea so mighty,
That I cou'd ne'er have seen you safe att Cyprus,
Had I not won them with a fein'd pretence,
That 'twould more firmly fix me in the throne,   140
If in my pow'r, I held the true pretender.
And so, procur'd them, 'ere I was declar'd,

To give me means, to compasse my dessign.
Yett, lett me kneel, for seeming to offend,
And breaking thus, upon your private hours,
Which I had shunn'd, but that deny'd your presence,
I cou'd not serve you, but by this intrusion.
   Queen. I'm satisfy'd, my Lord, pray kneel no more.
   Laur. No, lett me kneel,
And if there were a posture more submissive,   **150**
Low as the grave, and humble as my hopes,
Twoud now become, what I must speak or perish.
   Queen. Proceed my Lord,
And think, you cannot easily ofend me.
   Laur. Then, lett me ask, since 'tis my heart's concern,
When I have compass'd, what my life has toyl'd for,
And plac'd you uncontrol'd in sov'raine pow'r,
If Blanfort, shall not enter on my labours,
And reap the dear rewards, I dare not think of.
   Queen. My Lord, you wrong me much, if you suppose itt,
Lett that suffice, and urge your fears no farther.   **161**
All you have said, this night, I will reflect on,
And in the morning, give you private notice
How I shall act in such a great concern.
Pray rise my lord.   *[He rises.*
   Laur. Oh! Give not all the night to thoughts of buisnesse,
If I had n'er admitted softer cares,
You'd now had no occasion for them, Madam.
   Queen. My Lord, good night, I wish you safe retir'd
   Laur. Permitt this honour first, that I'll take care of. 170
                                [Leading her within the scene.
        Enter at the other end of the stage Blanfort
   Blan. A letter thrown just now in at my window
Tells me, that one alone, and in disguise
Enter'd a while agoe, the Queen's apartment.
                    [Laur. returns from the Queen.

Tis true indeed, and Lauredan's the man.

Laur. So late, and Blanfort here, amazment strikes me.

[*Aside.*

Blan. My Lord, this visit being out of season,
In the great Masters name, I must demand
For what occasion, at this hour you gave itt.

Laur. I wou'd not fight in hearing of the Queen. [*Aside.*
Come you from him my lord with this commission,   180
If so, to-morrow I'll inform him of itt,
If not, give way, I own no other power.

Blan. No, stay my Lord, 'tis from myself I ask itt,
And will be bold, or this shall force an answer.   [*Draws.*

Laur. Take then the best reply, that this can make you.

[*They fight, and* Blanfort *falls.*

Enter the Queen, Clar. *&* Ric, *who supports* Blan.

Queen. Oh dire misfortune, call more help Clarilla,
Look up my Lord, oh! speak and say you live,
He's dead he's dead, else wou'd my voyce
Have wak'd him —
I know att least, itt wou'd have forc'd one sigh,   190
If he had breath enough to have supply'd itt.

[Laur. *observes the* Queen *all this while.*

Laur. Oh! mortal sound, wou'd I were in his place.
Yett hear me Madam, hear me, but a moment.

[*She weeps by* Blan,

Queen. Twas hearing you my Lord, drew on this ruine,
Oh! do not urge itt now, but leave the place,
This fatal place, and 'ere the morning passe,
I'll yett send to you. ——

Laur. I know not how to understand this rightly,
But will have patience, till I hear her answer.   [*Exit* Laur.

[*Enter Servants and Chirurgeon.*

Queen. Oh! Aubusson, when thou shalt hear of this,   200
How will it greive thee, to have harbour'd mé,

That (though unwilling) is the wretched cause
Of his sad fate, and thy perpettual mourning.
   Surg. Madam, he breathes, we'll bear him to his lodgings,
I think the wound is in no mortal part,
Take him up gently, and convey him hence.
                                     [Ex. Surg. with Blan., *etc.*
   Queen. You stand amaz'd, and seem to wonder Riccio,
The General and I have had this meeting.
But his intentions are not what you think 'em,
Come in with me, for I have much to tell you,   210
And ne'r I think, have wanted more your councill.
Oh! Blanfort live, that greif sitts here so heavy,
Twill not affoard room for one pleasing thought,
Tho' that remov'd, I've all I'd ask of fortune.
                              [Ex. Queen, Clar. & Ric.
                  Enter Rivalto
   Riv. The letter, which I threw in att his window,
Had the desir'd effect, I saw 'em fight,
And Blanfort sure is kill'd.
Marina too, as I cou'd have contriv'd itt,
Is weeping by a taper in her Chamber,
Dresst in her female garb, Ho! Vilmarin Linian,   220
I'll make 'em go that way, to call the Master,
And tell him of these accidents have happen'd,
Who when he hears the noyse, will be drawn theither,
And being caught by them, with her alone,
Will seem to all, as guilty as I've made him.
They come not, yett I bid 'em be att hand
Curse on their neglegence, all may be lost by 't
Butt I must go find em ——   *[Exitt.*
   The scene changes to Aub⁵ *ante chamber. He in his night-
gown, talking with* Monthaleon.
   Aub. I will correct itt, I will indeed Monthaleon,
And tho' the war, as 'tis itts banefull custom,

Has sown amongst us, the foul seeds of vice,
They shall not thrive, or bear their fruits in Rhodes.
   Month. My lord, you take the best, and surest method,
By setting such a pattern as your conduct,
Who lead, before your forty 'th year's arriv'd,
A life, that aged Hermitts cannot reach to.
   Aub. I wou'd do so, but speak of that no more.
This night, I talk'd to Vilmarin and Linian,   10
And freindly counsail'd them, to leave their vices,
At which they smil'd and said they'd be more secret.
My Confessour too, 'ere he left my Clossett,
Pour'd out a flood of tears, and cry'd beware,
Beware hypocrisy, that sin of Devills.
It something troubles me to know the meaning,
But I have trespass'd on thy rest too long,
Only remember this, to tell Capriccio,
When next he's drunk, I'll have him sleep
Without his Souldiers office.   20
Good-night Monthaleon.
   Mont. Good-night my Lord, and rest compose your
      thoughts.   [*Exeunt severally.*

ACT IV SCENE I

Marina's Chamber. She appears drest in her Woman's habbitt

   Mar. I've wept enough, and now farwell, for ever,
Farwell my good, my great, my gen'rous Master
Farwell these walls, where I have felt more sorrow
Than all the stones can count, that make the pile.
Farwell Rivalto, Auther of my ruine;
The world farwell, and, all itts vain delusions.
Yett, there's one farwell more, cou'd I but speak itt,
But oh! 'twere vain, to say farwell false Blanfort,
Since in my heart, I bear him with me still,

But I must go, before the day appears,   10
Kind night conceal my blushes, and my fears.

*[She goes with a key in her hand, to the door. A violent calling
and knocking is heard from the other side of itt.*

Vil. Ho! Carino, open the door, Carino,
We must immediately speak with the great Master;
Ho! Carino.

Mar. Oh! I am ruin'd, whether shall I run,
How 'scape their sight, how answer them
How stay them?

Lin. Ho! rise Carino, rise and lett us through.

Mar. I must speak to 'em, why d'ye call thus loud,
Your haste and noyse, has made me loose the key?   20
I cannot lett ye in, why come ye this way,
The other's free, I cannot lett ye in.

Lin. No, Vilmarin was there, and 'tis barr'd up,
Break down the door.

Mar. What shall I do, that's the great Master's chamber.

[Pointing to the other door.

Yett in this danger I must try to 'scape
By stealing down that way, to gain the street.

[She going to that door. Enter Aub: *in his night gown, his sword
in his hand.*

Aub. There's sure some mutiny they call so loud,

[Seeing her.

Ha! What art thou, thou dreadfull apparition.

[She covers her face with her handkercheif.

Mar. Oh! I am nothing, nothing but confusion.   30

[They beat down the other door. Enter Mont: Riv. Vil: Lin: Capr.

Month. What do I see!
My sight sure plays me false,
And night has rais'd a Vision to distract me.

*[Aub. *stands amazd saying nothing.*

Vil. Your arms my Lord are needlesse, we'll retire,
Nor did we mean to interrupt your pleasures.

Riv. Indeed I wou'd have led them t'other way,
Knowing this was your scene of private joys.

Lin. Be not concern'd my lord we'll keep the secret,
Alas! you know, this way, we've all our failings.

       [Aub. *leans upon* Month, *seeming weak and dispirited.*

Aub. Come heither freind, if yett thou'lt own that title, 40
I did not ask to be supported thus,
When with one bold Hungarian by my side,
I fac'd the Turks, and bore against their army,
Till ours that fled, return'd to fame and conquest.

                      [*Throws away his sword.*

Lye there my sword, for I am yett a Christian,
Else wou'd I put thee to a braver use,
And wash this stain from my polluted honour,
With blood as noble, as an ancient Romans.
Oh! that I cou'd convince thee my Monthaleon;
Yett, when thy Master's lay'd in humble dust,   50
Try to persuade the world, I was not wicked,
Not that vile wretch,
Which this foul chance, wou'd speak me.

       [Marina *all this time weeping and leaning against the scene.*

Mont. My lord, I've kept my eyes still on the Maid.
And 'tis your Boy, Carino in disguise.
Be comforted, 'tis nothing but a Trick,
I know itt is a trick, and we'll revenge itt.

       [Lin. *pulls aside her garment and discovers her neck.*

Lin. This neck, methinks is counterfitted well,
And breasts like these, do much disguise a boy.

Mont. Itt is Carino, but itt is a woman,   [*Aside*
I know not what to think, and stand confounded.   61

Aub. Oh! take her hence, remove her from my sight,

I care not who she is, nor why she came.
All leave the room, all, but Monthaleon leave me,
Nor will I bribe your foul and blister'd tongues,
To hide this scandal, from the babling world.
'Tis Heavn's concern, that Innocence like mine
Shou'd stand upright, without such vile supporters.
   Lin. Shall we not tell him of his nephew's hurt.
                           [*Aside to* Monthal.
   Mont. Not for your life, he bears too much already.   70
   Riv. Be still secure, and happy if you please.
               [*Aside to* Mar. *offering to lead her.*
   Mar. Stand off base wretch, stand off, and do not touch me,
I'll put myself into Capriccio's hands,
And fly from thee, and from thy brace of furies.
   Capr. The Master's Mistresse, under my custody,
                              [*Aside.*
See how preferment comes sometimes unlookt for.
Give me your hand Lady, and this shall still protect you.
               [*Exeunt all but* Aub. *and* Month.
   Month. My lord, I beg you wou'd again retire,
And seek to rest—
Leaving itt to your freinds, and cheifly me,   80
To sound the depth, of this most vile contrivance.
   Aub. Oh! They have strook me in the tend'rest part
The subtle villains, exquisite in mischeif,
Knew this would wound me, deeper then their daggers;
My life, I cou'd have yielded them, Monthaleon,
Wou'd they had taken't, when my fame was clear,
Then had I sett, like the declining Sun,
With all my glorious beams, about my head,
And left the world, repining at my fall.
But oh! to horrid darknesse, now I goe,   90
Wrapt in those deeds, that seemingly are soe.
                   [*Ex: leaning on* Month.

The Scene changes to the Queen's *Apartment,* Ricc: *alone*

Ric. It was my master peice, and hard I wrought itt,
How I was forc'd to swear that to my knowledge
Those proffers, were but baits, to catch her freedom;
That all his army, was dispers'd and broken,
His int'rest quite declin'd with both the states,
And that he had no means again to raise itt,
But by obliging 'em, with her full ruine.
Yett all prevail'd not, till at last I urg'd
That still he languish'd for the proud Usurper,
And sent from hence, as I assur'dly knew,   10
Expresses to her, charg'd with love, and duty;
This stirr'd that passion in her I desir'd,
And so, procur'd a message to my wishes,
Which lost not of itt's force, by my delivery,
But he's by this time gone,
And all my fears, and cares, are vanish'd with him.
Better be here, depending still a[t] Rhodes,
Then under his dominion, though in Cyprus.

Enter Clarilla

Ric. Clarilla, is the Queen yett to be spoke with?
Clar. She is not Riccio, but has sent her orders   20
That you shou'd lett me know the Gen'rall's answer,
Or send it written, if he so commanded.

Ric. I thought to have conceal'd the papers from her,
                                                    [*Aside.*
But if she shou'd hereafter come to know itt,
That, yett may prove of greater danger to me,
Besides he's gone, and I'm resolv'd to venture.
Then tell her, that I found him all alone,
Expecting as he told me, her comands,
And from my lipps, no sooner were they fall'n,
But he retir'd, and wrote in haste this letter,   30
Which sure, I think, encloses more within itt.

Then call'd an Officer, that waited neer,
And bid his Anchors instantly be weigh'd,
For that he wou'd immediatly on board.
The other, vainly urg'd a storm was risen
Which might endanger him, and all the fleet,
For he persisted still, to have itt done.
Then gave me this, and fluug out of my presence.
I know no more — But how the Queen resents itt,
And what's contain'd, in all this pacquett here,　　　40
Shall hope to hear from you.—　　　*[Is going but returns.*
I had allmost forgot, tell her
That Blanfort's wound is of no danger,
Nor such, as to confine him to his bed.
Th' expence of spirits, in his mighty passion
Being the cheif cause, that sence, and motion left him,
As I came back, I mett this information.　*[Exeunt severally.*

Enter Capriccio *drunk*

　Cap. 'Tis a rare world, a brave world,
A ranting, flanting, shining world;
Not a tavern in the town but's in a blaze,　　　50
Not a pretended sister, cosen, or other civil Relation,
That is not publickly own'd,
For an errant, tory rory strumpett.
Linnian leads up a couple, Vilmarin a couple more,
Only that rogue Rivalto,
Has the impudence, to sin in secret, now 'tis out of fassion,
But I'll discover his haunts,
Or beat him till he owns 'em,
Never such a time in Rhodes, never such an example.
Every one quoting the Great Master,　　　60
And trooping on to sin, under his banner,
As if they were beating up Volonteers for the Devil.
I'll ee'n away, and be drunk with the best of 'em
And then, as an honest man shou'd,

Go soberly home, and look to my charge,
A rare time, there's not one now—
                                But will come,
                At the beat of my drum,
                Or the tossing up of my feather.
                                [*Exit singing.*

The Scene drawn, discovers Blanfort *lying upon a couch,* Month:
                sitting by him

Blan. It is indeed a melancholy story,
But will he leave us, does he say Monthaleon?
    Mon. He does my Lord,
For having heard the riots of the Town,
And how they ground em all on his example,
It strikes him so, together with the thoughts
That he must n'er attempt to stop itts fury,
And that 'tis now their int'rest to maintain
His seeming Vice, to guild their own the better,
That he resolves, some more successful arm,   10
Shall take that task, and bear the publick sway,
Whilst he retires, to secrecy, and prayers.
Blan. Oh! thou art wretched Blanfort,   [*Aside*
What said the Maid,
For such I sure beleive her.
    Month. No word she uttered, yet her silence spoke,
Att least to me, that so did understand it,
And said, that she was wrong'd, was wrong'd, and guiltlesse.
And more I must observe to clear her farther,
That since she as a youth, has served the Master,   20
Not all his gentle chidings, cou'd prevail
To make her once attend him in his chamber.
    Blan. How look'd she freind, in such a sad surprise?
    Month. Modest, and lovely Blanfort,
As looks the fair, and gentle rising morning,
When watry vapours, half conceal her blushes.

Blan. Tis I that ought to blush, poor, poor Marina. [*Aside.*
Has she since nothing told of who she is,
Or what induc'd her to assume this shape.   ·

   Month. Nothing, but only sais she is a wretch,   30
And urges to be sent into a Convent,
Which is deferr'd, in hopes of some discovery.

   Blan. Oh! gen'rous Maid, what does she not deserve?
I'll try to find her out, that we may meet,
And weep att least, over our mutual sorrows.   [*Aside.*
Where is she lodg'd, who has her now in charge?

   Month. Cappriccio has dispos'd her neer this place,
Her lodging joyns close to the Pallace wall,
And has a door, that us'd to lett into itt.

   Blan. No more of this,   40
To Lauredan, what's happen'd since our quarrel.

   Month. He's gone on board, and toss'd with such a storm,
Tis thought he'll perish 'ere he leaves the Port.
But certain 'tis, the Queen of Cyprus loves him.
Her present fears, have told itt to her women,
And they (as women use) to all the world.

   Blan. This does not move me, as I should have thought,
My guilt, has fill'd my mind, with so much horrour. [*Aside.*
I will go rest upon my bed Monthaleon,
This posture to my wound is most uneasy,   50
And oh! to my afflicted kinsman, say
That I would dye, to sett his fame as clear
As in th' all seeing eye of Heav'n, itt stands.

                [*Exeunt, he leaning on* Month.
              [*Enter* Rivalto, Vilmarin *and* Linnian

   Lin. To search our houses, for the state's lost jewels,
I ne'r yett knew of any of them missing,
They're so remarkable, 'twere vain to steal them.
'Tis but a trick—
To give us some disturbance, in revenge.

Riv. It may be so, but still ye have done well
To send in all your wealth, that that may 'scape them.   60
I've lodg'd it safely, safely as my own,
And when this search is past, you'll call it back.

Vil. Oh! yes, itt shall but trouble you till then.

Riv. To serve my freinds, I n'er yett thought a trouble,
But since I stand the foremost in their hate,
And I am sure, they mean the search I tell ye,
Not knowing, but they may extend it farther,
And under that pretence, secure my person,
I am resolv'd, that I'll awhile withdraw,
What think ye of itt, will itt not do well.   70

Lin. Do as you will, when shall we hear of you.

Riv. Before three days are past, assure your selves,
Therefore, 'till then make no enquiry for me,
Another thing, I had almost forgott,
The Master sends this night a private Convoy
To bear his Damzell to a distant Convent,
And when she's gone, what'ere reports ye hear,
Know that's the truth, now lett us part,
For we're suspected, if but seen together.

Vil. But for three days, you say, you shall be absent,   80

Riv. Not an hour more.

Lin. Then till that time, farwell.   [*Exeunt* Vil *and* Lin.

Riv. Thus far 'tis right, I've all their wealth on board,
And now tis mine, in spite of all our freindship.
For he, whose aim at mighty mischeif tends,
Must own no gratitude, nor know no freinds.   [*Exit.*

The *Scene changes to the* Queen's *antichamber.*
Riccio *alone.*

Ric. Blow on ye winds, and swell the seas so high
That ore his fleet, your proud insulting waves,
May ride in tryumph, sinking all beneath ye.
I long to hear the temper of the Queen,

But here Clarilla comes, in time to tell me.

　　　　　　　　　　　　　　　　　　　　[*Enter* Clar.

How fares it with our great, and Royal Mistresse?

　Clar. Oh! Riccio, I want words to let you know itt,
But fear the fatal papers which you brought,
Will finish, what the tempest has begun,
And rob us of her most unhappy life.　　　　　　　　10

　Ric. Explain your self, what saw she in those papers?

　Clar. That she has lost the most auspitious moment
That 'ere was influenc'd, by a gentle planett.
Two writings sign'd,
By all the Lords of Cyprus, and of Venice
Declare the Gen'ral King, with one consent,
And that our Queen, but by espousing him,
Must ne'r again, expect to rule in Cyprus.
But oh! his letter, calls this, such presumption,
As he wou'd ne'r have offer'd to her sight,　　　　　20
Were itt not to convince her, e're his death,
That itt was love, not int'rest urg'd him on
To seek her here, and offer at her feet
That Crown, he might have worn without her favour.
Then makes itt plain, what he allready proffer'd,
That 'twas his full intention to restore her
By his own power, 'ere this had reach'd her knowledge,
And to herself have left it, to dispose
Of him, and all his fortunes, at her pleasure.

　Ric. You much surprise me, was there nothing more,　30
Fool that I was to lett her see those papers.　　　[*Aside.*

　Clar. Nothing, but sad complaints, and soft expressions
Jealous mistakes, that 'twas her love to Blanfort
That repuls'd him.——
And how he greiv'd, his sword had peirct his bosome,
Since she had in itt, treasur'd up her heart,
But that itt shou'd procure her speedy vengeance,

By bringing on that death, he went to seek for.
But whilst I'm here, all this repeating to you,
Dispair may seize too deeply on her soul,   40
Go in my Lord, and try to bring her comfort.
　Ric. I go Clarilla, follow, and assist me.
How neer was I to see him in the throne,
Had not his foolish modesty and love,
Prevented itt, and so secur'd my safety.   [*Aside.*
I must now meet, and try to lay this passion.
Her greifs are easyer calm'd then his revenge   [*Exit.*
　Clar. I must stay here, to free my tears awhile
Which in her presence, I wou'd fain keep back.
Oh! would this tempest yett but be appeas'd,   50
We might again see happynesse, and Cyprus.
But here she comes, alas, who can behold her,
　So Dido saw the Trojan navy part,
　With looks so wild, and such a breaking heart.

[*Enter* Queen, *disordered, in all the transports of a violent pas-
　　sion,* Riccio *follows endeavouring to speak to her.*

　Queen. Preach to the winds, thou dull, thou doating
　　statesman,
Go to that storm, that plays with all my hopes,
And try if thou can'st calm itt with a speech,
Tell itt of inter'est, politicks, and caution,
And if for these, 'twill bate one angry billow,
Then may'st thou hope to talk me into patience.   60
Fool that I was, to list'n to thy counsell,
To knitt my brow, when love and fortune smil'd
Because thy coward fears, cry'd out be carefull.
　Ric. Yett, hear me Madam.
　Queen. Away, away, and leave me to my self
To this soft counseller, that breaks with greif,
　　　　　　　　　　　　　　[*Pointing to her breast.*
Because it was not harken'd to in season.   [*Exit* Ric.

A noyse as of a ship, striking against the shoar follow'd by
repeated crys from within of many voyces.

From w^{th}in. The Admiral's splitt, send out more boats.

                        [The Queen *sinks into* Clarilla's *arms.*

Queen. Take me Clarilla, take me to thy bosome,
And tell those freinds, which fortune yett has left me.   70
The Gen'rals too (if they vouchsafe to hear thee)
Tell 'em, that I forgave him all my wrongs,
Tell 'em Clarilla, that I mourn'd his fall,
Nay tell 'em (since in death, there's no dissembling)
I loved him, more, then liberty or Empire.

    Clar. Talk not of dying, since he still may live,
And 'tis but prudence to support this greif,
At least, till we can hear our fears are certain.

    Queen. Wou'dst thou then have me stand upon the shoar,
And wait, like sad Alcyone of old,   80
'Till some huge billow, cast him at my feet,
A breathlesse trunk, a pale, and livid corse,
Oh! no, it is too much, too much to think itt;
And 'ere the angry sea, returns his body,
I'll meet his soul in the blest seats above,
And free my self, from that new scene of sorrow. *[She faints.*

    Clar. Oh! help, the Queen expires, she dyes, she dyes.

[Enter the rest of her women, whilst they are busy about her
enters Lauredan, *his dagger in his hand and speaks entering.*

    Laur. I'll do itt in her sight, the storm was kind
To spare my life, for had I perish'd there,
My eyes cou'd not have told my curious soul   '   90
How she receiv'd the off'ring, fate had made her.

                        [He sees her fainted.

Ha!
Yett hold my heart, Clarilla how came this?
Is Blanfort dead, else what cou'd kill the Queen?

[*He puts the dagger within his cloathes and kneels down by the Queen.*

Rest here awhile, thou sure, thou active Cordial,
That I may pray, as sacraficers use,
Before I strike to earth, the ready victime.
O! lovely ruine, beautyfull destruction,   [*Takes her hand.*
To touch this hand whilst life had lent it warmth,
Had been to mine, thats so, transporting pleasure   100
Perhaps 'twill be the same, when both are cold.
  Therefore I'll haste, th' experiment to try
  'Tis death to live, and why not life to dye.

                    [*Going to stab himself with his other hand.*
  Clar. Hold, hold my lord, she breaths again, she breaths,
Oh! hold and rather help us to support her.

                        [*He throws away his dagger, and helps.*
  Laur. More gladly, then I'd prop the sinking world,
If fate, had left that task, to my sole arm.

                            [*She comes a little to herself.*
  Queen. Where have I been, sure itt was Neptune's court,
For Lauredan was newly there arriv'd,
And held a Trydent, for his staff of battel.   110
I heard his voyce, but oh! his looks were chang'd
And still methought, he told the list'ning Nymphs
That 'twas the Queen of Cyprus, sent him theither.

                                [*She struggles.*
But I will follow him, I will, I will,
Love that could drive Leander o're the deep,
Shall dive with me, throo' all the silver waves,
Till I can find, and tell him I repent.
But Riccio shall not go, he shall not goe,
Least he should urge me still to scorn him there,
And force him to attempt some unknown ruine.   120
  Laur. Oh! harmony, beyond the Thracian Lyre
No words e're fell so soft, or peirc'd so deep.

Clar. My Lord, I must entreat you to retire,
My fear and care, made me forgett my duty,
And prudence tells me now, you must retire.

> [*He holds the* Q. *still in his arms.*

Laur. Talk not of prudence, in this happy season.
It must not, nay itt shall not here intrude;
When in the feild, I'll make itt rule o're thousands,
And in the Counsell, pleading for my Queen,
Permitt itt to direct each word, and gesture,   130
But Love, that only waits to catch those hours,
Those few soft Hours, that fall in her wish'd absence,
Must not be forc'd to quit the hard gain'd treasure.

> [*The* Q. *looking amaz'dly round.*

Queen. Why am I thus, and tell me who are these?
My heart, and thoughts, are full of wild disorder,
Heav'n grant no word has 'scap'd my troubl'd tongue,
To make me wish, I ne'r had known itts use.

Clar. Pray be not seen, my lord, 'twill much disturb her,
You've learnt already that which most concerns you,
And for the future, trust to be inform'd   140
Of what may make you still become more happy.

> [*He gives the* Queen *into her arms.*

Laur. So, quitts the dying Miser, that rich store
Which cruell fate, will lett him grasp no more,
Promis'd, alike from present joys we move,
To be in future paid our wealth, and Love,
But 'tis necessity, not choice, prevails,
And hopes n'er please, but when possession fails.   [*Exit.*

Clar. Now gently raise, and lead her to her bed,
'Tis rest alone, that must restore her spirits.

> [*They convey her out.*

ACT V SCENE I

The Scene drawn discovers Marina *upon a couch, with a book in her hand.*

Mar. I've try'd by reading to appease my greifs
Till my sad eyes, grown heavy as my heart,
Will serve no longer to pursue the story,
I'll seek to rest,
  —Kind sleep afoard thy charms,
To her that knows no peace, but in thy arms.
  [*She falls asleep.*

[Blanfort *brought in a chair to the door, turns and speaks to them that brought him, then leaning on his sword comes weakly on.*

Blan. Wait there, till I return —   [*He sees her asleep.*
She sleeps, poor injured innocence, she sleeps,
And in this balmy slumber, looks so lovely,
That now the Queen of Cypress, seems not fairer,
Nor wears the Goddesse of that place more sweetnesse   10
Why tore I from my heart, these fruitfull charms,
  [*He kneels by her.*
To give itt up to others, most ungratfull?
But I againe will plant them deeper there,
Though misery, is all they now can grow to.
And oh! methinks, I sighing hear her say
When I have told her we must meet no more,
That Blanfort (tho' repenting) was her ruine.   [*She wakes.*
Mar. Oh! who names Blanfort, who upbraids my love,
Who says 'twas he that ruin'd poor Marina
Who says alas, that we must meet no more.   20
Blan. 'Tis base Rivalto, with his vile confederates,
Who o're thy virgin fame have drawn a cloud
So dark, 'twould loose us both, if there encount'ring,
Else, when my sighs, had blown away my faults

And, kneeling thus, I'd woo thee to a pardon.
Our time to come shou'd all have passt in love,
And joys as soft, and melting as this bosome,
Marina, oh Marina, must we part?
By this embrace, and this, I swear we will not.

                     [*She strives and he quitts his hold.*

Again thy charms, o'recome my ravish'd sence,   30
And empty honour shall not take thee hence.

                     [*Going to embrace her.*

  Mar. Forbear, my lord, forbear, this must not bee,
And if again such libertys you take,
I shall beleive, you think me what they say,
Pray rise—
Alas, you're weak, you stagger, lett me help you.

                     [*He rises and sits down by her.*

Now lett us talk awhile, before we sever,
For they have much to say who part for ever.
Since first I listen'd to your vows, my lord,
How I have lov'd you, lett my ruine speak,   40
That but for you, I priz'd my blooming Youth,
And what your passion call'd some share of beauty,
Lett my concealing itt from all the world
When once you slighted itt, bear witnesse for me.
That now I love you, more then Misers wealth,
Then women courtship, or then Tyrant's pow'r,
Lett this persuade, this last, this tend'rest proof,
That I will leave you, to secure your fame,
Though woo'd to stay, by all your moving arts,
And death must waite upon the seperation.   50

  Blan. If we must seperate, to dye is best,
But lett me know Marina thy retreat,
That fame, when charg'd with tidings of my fate,
May not mistake ye way, and misse thy mantion.

  Mar. Oh! n'ere believe that she will stoop so low

To seek those shades, where I intend to goe,
For tho' employ'd, still in adorning Tombs,
Within the Grave, her splendour never comes,
There Love and Fame, their pains and pleasures cease,
And nothing will remain with us, but peace.   60

[A noise within.

I hear some steps, and fear a new surprize,
Lett me but take this look, for 'tis my last,
Farewell, my lord, this night devides us ever,
Now lett my eyes begin their work assign'd,   *[She weeps.*
Till death shall close, or tears shall weep them blind.

  Blan. Will thou forsake me then, to-night my love,
This fatal night, oh! stay but till to-morrow,
Stay but untill she's wearing towards the dawn
And lett me make thee yett one visit more
In that soft hour, of secrecy, and love.   70
I have not told thee half what I've to say,
Not on these hands, enough renew'd my vows,
Nor warm'd 'em, with my dear repenting tears,
I must return, I must return, Marina,
And then again, we'll thus, and thus, take leave.

    [Eagerly kissing her hand; Capriccio calls from within.

  Cap. Charge, charge, where are you,
Come let me take care of you quickly,
Or I shall fall asleep.

  Mar. Away my lord, that noysy fellow's coming,
Like the loud roar of some o're swelling flood,   80
To break the gentle murmurs of our parting,
Farwell to all thats dear — a long and last farwell.

    [She goes slowly off, he looking after till she's out of sight.

  Blan. Oh! do not speak itt, nor so swiftly move
But take by such degrees, that object from me,
That till tis past, I scarce may feel my ruine,

So gazes on the low descending Sun,
The traveller, whose journeys yett not done,
Follows the latest beam, with eager sight,
That gone, persue's his way, sad, as prevailing night.
                                    [*Exit, the scene shutts.*
      Lauredan, *enter to him* Clarilla

  Laur. Oh! you are come most happily Clarilla,
For grown impatient of a longer stay
My love had urg'd me to some new attempt,
Again to seek the presence of my Queen.
Tell me, had I offended in my zeal,
For ore our strongest hopes, still fears will rise,
And claim their turn, to sway the Lover's bosome.
  Clar. I think my lord 'twas better you forbore,
And still, you must support a longer absence,
  Laur. Oh! say not so, repeat itt not Clarilla.   10
Is this, the promis'd happynesse, you bring,
For which I gave up pleasures in possession,
Dearer then life, and high, as Love cou'd make them.
Or was itt but a dream, and now awak'd,
The Queen, the lovely Queen, recalls those hopes,
And says, that reason did not guide her speeches.
  Clar. Nothing of this, she's still the same my Lord,
And sure to tell you more then that were needlesse
But 'ere she will determin in your favour,
Or readmitt you to her wish'd for presence,   20
Resolves the Prince of Rhodes, her friend, her refuge,
Her better father, as she justly stiles him,
Shall be acquainted with the whole design,
And she, and that, submitted to his liking.
  Laur. I fly Clarilla, to obtain his aid
And whilst these hours of form, passe slowly by,
Oh lett my love, still dwell upon thy tongue,
And plead in gentle terms, for my recalling.

Clar. My lord, be sure of all my pow'r to serve you.
[*Exeunt.*

The Scene drawn discovers a Bedchamber, and Marina *alone.*

Mar. I heard his voyce, when in the outward room,
And in that closett, when I call'd Capriccio
Me thoughts from hence again he answer'd me,
But here he is not, and I want his aid,
T'assist me in my most unhappy flight.
For now tis death to go, since Blanfort's true
And bid to him, and love a last adiew.

Enter Rivalto *who locks the door, then overtakes her endeavor-*
ing to gain the other, he locks that also and puts the keys in
his pockett.

Mar. Oh! I am ruin'd, ruin'd past redemption,
Who can asist me now, or hear my crys?

Riv. No one alive, therefore no more repeat them.   10
Hear me, for I'll be short, tho' sure as fate,
How I have lov'd you, need not be repeated,
But that I will posesse you, is as certain,
And if your ruine, which I therefore wrought,
As well as to revenge me on the Master,
Has made you wise enough to yield to this,
We may be happy both, beyond expression.
To night, I leave this hated place for ever,
A vessel waits me at the haven's mouth,
Laden with wealth, enough to feed our riots,   20
Take part with me, retire, and be my wife,
Or, if that name, beares to much of constraint,
Be free, and lett our pleasures be so too,
Give me your answer, positive and speedy.

Mar. Then take itt thus, I'll dye within these walls,
Before I'll yeild, to live with such a monster.

Riv. If your in earnest, here's the way to do itt,
[*Drawing a dagger.*

Nor can you hope but by consent t' avoid itt,
No, when I told you of my wealth, and purpose,
'Twas not to lett you 'scape, and so prevent me,   30
Therefore once more, I sett the choice before you.
                              [*She weeps and trembles.*

  Mar. Then I will go, leave me an hour but to prepare my
    self,
And I will go, when you return again.
  Riv. Oh! fine request, no, I have laid things better,
A private door behind that loose hung arras,
Leads down a pare of stairs into the sea,
A cover'd boat, now waits there to receive us.
Give me your hand, without one farther thought,
Else here I'll leave you dead, and 'scape that way myself.
Your hand Marina.—   40
  Mar. I'll dye e're give my hand to such a villain.
Thou canst not, darest not, wilt not be so wicked.
              [*He going to stab her, she runs towards the bed.*
  Riv. Then take that just revenge of all thy pride,
I've sworn to reach thy heart, and now I'll do itt.
  Mar. Oh! murther, murther,
Some unseen pow'r, protect me from this murther.

[Capriccio *starting from the bed, lays hold on* Rivalto's *dagger
    hand. Whilst they strive the key falls out of* Rivalto's *pock-
    ett, she takes itt and runs out crying murther.*

  Cap. That pow'r am I, oh! rogue, assault a woman,
  Mar. Oh! help, some help to catch a villain.   [*Exit.*
  Capr. I have itt now, but twas a plaguy tugg
                              [*Cap. gets yͤ dagger.*
Ha! what more work,   50
[Rivalto *gets out his sword and endeavours to passe by him he
    draws.*

Then this must stop your course.
                    [*Enter* Blan: *leaning upon his sword.*

Blan. It was Marina's voyce, and I'll obey itt,
I cannot sure, want strength, when she's in danger.
But see, Capriccio has disarmed Rivalto,
What is itt, Gentlemen, has bred your quarrel.

     [Capr. *with both swords stands between* Riv. *and the door.*

Cap. Nay ask him, how he, and my charge came to fall
    out
I was quietly asleep, 'till she cry'd murther,
And then up I got, and have done as you see.

    Riv. Curse on my fortune,
Give me butt my dagger, and I'll secure ye   60
From further trouble.

       [*Enter* Month: *and guards with* Vil: *and* Lin: *seized.*

    Month. Oh! see 'tis true, and he's disarm'd and taken,
These two were well secured, till time shall show,
How far they stand concern'd in all his plotts.
Bring 'em away, all to the Queens apartment,
Theither the rescu'd trembling Virgin fled,
And has declared, that 'tis by him confess'd,
He cast the scandal on our worthy Master,
To compasse his revenge, att once and Love.
That Princesse, therefore makes itt her request   70
That all may be examin'd, in her presence
And she may be partaker of his joy,
You'll go my lord

    Blan. Yes, with your help I will,
Tis my concern, more then you yett immagin.

[*The Prisoners are carry'd out, by the guards.* Blanf. *follows
leaning on* Month.

The Scene changes to the Queen's *Apartment. The* Queen, Aub:
Laur: Marin: Clar: Rice:

    Aub. If I have serv'd you Madam, with such zeal,

                 [*To the* Queen.

As now to do me honour, you acknowledge,
Permitt me to compleat, and urge it farther,
By off'ring to your Love, this generous man,
By Birth a Prince, a sou'dier by profession,
To fight your battels, and support your Crown.
And bear the weight, whilst you but know the lustre.

 Queen. My lord, I still have prosper'd by your councills,
And lett my gratitude prevent my blushes,
If to your much deserving friend, I own   10
I n'er comply'd more willingly then now.
        [Laur. *kneels and kisses her hand.*

 Lau. Oh! thou hast paid me love, for all my sorrows,
Prepaid 'em all, by this transporting moment,
And when I seek a Crown, but at these feet,
May'st thou forsake, and make me great, and wretched.

  [*Enter* Blan. *supported by* Month. Capr. *guard & prisoners.*

 Aub. I have not seen you Nephew, since your hurt,
Welcome to life and mee.
 Laur. Can you forgive the wound, your self occasion'd?
 Blan. My Lord, I ask your pardon, and the Queens,
For that rude combat, thus end all our quarrels. 20
          [*Embracing him.*

 Aub. Now, lett my Joys return, my fame be clear'd,
And virtue sink no more beneath my scandall,
Before this Royal presence, speak Rivalto
All that thou know'st,
Relating to this lady, and my self.
 Riv. Shall I be free, be favoured and rewarded,
Without all these, I ask not to be pardon'd,
If I do speak, and answer your desires.
 Aub. I tell thee no,
If what thou say'st exposes thee a Villain,   30
Nor will I flatter Vice, for vertue's service.

Riv. Then lett the world beleive as now they do.
I will not speak, tho' you cou'd take my life.

    Aub. Oh! harden'd impudence,—search him for papers.

    Riv. Forbear but that, and I will speak the truth.

    Aub. Nay then it is of weight, proceed Capriccio.

                  [Riccio *seems all the while speaking to* Laur·

    Laur. I do not ask, what urg'd you to oppose me,
But I will make itt now, so much your interest,
N'er more to do itt, that I will beleive you.

    Capr. Here are my lord, two papers nothing more.   40

    Aub. What's this, come heither Blanfort,

                 [*Looking on one of* y^e *papers.*

Know you this caracter —

    Blan. 'Tis mine my lord, and when some points are
      clear'd,
I shall be both asham'd, and proud to own itt.

    Aub. That nothing here may seem to passe in private,
Behold a contract, sign'd and seal'd by Blanfort,
Unto the Duke of Mantua's, yongest Daughter.
How did this fall into your hands, Rivalto?

    Riv. From her, herself, whom there you see, I stole itt,
Spare yett the other, and I'll tell you more.   50

    Aub. The superscription's odd—

      " If in three days, I'm not again in Rhodes,
        Deliver this to Vilmarin or Linain."

The boatman I suppose, that bore him off,
Was to be charg'd with this at parting from him,
Read itt Monthaleon.   [*He reads.*

It is not fitt that freinds shou'd part without some
remembrance, and that I may keep you two ever in my mind,
I have taken wth me, never to return, the wealth which you
putt into my hands, to secure; but that I may not be altogether ungratefull, I must putt you upon a right foundation,
either to persue the Plott, or come of from itt as you think

best.   Know then, that the Great Master is wholy innocent
of what's suppos'd, and never knew Marina was a woman,
'till drawn by me that night into her Chamber, the maid
was Blanforts right, contracted to him, tho' here not known
by him to be her self, she's mine att present, having lov'd her
long, and now farwell, and may your next adventure prove
more lucky."

Vil. Robb'd of our witts, and of our wealth att once, 70
[To Lin.

Lin. 'Tis vain to talk, we are both fool'd and ruin'd.

Aub. Such villany wou'd silence one with wonder,
Did not the joy that this discovery brings
Work stronger far, and raise me into transports.
Oh! hear itt freinds, receive the happy sound,
I am no Hypocrite, no secrett sinner;
Louder then victory, and swift as fame,
Proclaim itt to the world, I am not wicked.
And lett this lady, this fair injur'd lady   [*To* Mar.
Partake the joy and share the reparation.   80

Blan. Tis I my Lord, tis I must make her that,
[Kneels to her.
And beg all help, to win a pardon from her,
Oh! now we will not part, we will not part,
Shall we Marina, thou art silent still,
Oh! speak, for till that time, tho' twere for ever,
I wou'd n'er speak more—

Mar. My Lord, what I have done, enough has spoaken,
And told the World, my love outrun my prudence,
That paper speaks, and says I've given my hand
Already, giv'n itt, where my heart directed.   90
All I can do, is now but to restore itt,
[*Gives him her hand, he takes and kisses itt.*
And 'tis your fault, if e're again 'tis quitted.

Blan. I'll hold itt here for ever—

And tye my life, so fast to this soft charm,
That Death, and nothing else, shall e're dissolve itt.
  Aub. Seize on his Ship, tis forfeit by the Law,

                                    [*To an officer.*

For quitting of the port without a Passe.
A third of itt shall be thy share Capriccio,
But let it not be spent my freind in drink,
I'll ha' no more of that—   100
  Capr. Take itt again my Lord if drinks deny'd
I know no use, either of gold or silver.
Oh! world ungratefull world, to spurn att Blessings,
What mighty good, has not been done by drink,
What Plotts, have not been brought to light by drink,
The Goose, that sav'd the Capitol was drunk,
Or ne'r had gabbl'd loud enough to do itt.
Had I not now been drunk
I had not slept upon my charges bed,
And made you all as drunk, with love and joy,   110
And must I drink no more—
                      to death I'll pine,
And spend this money all in funeral wine,   [*They all laugh.*
  Aub. Before your death, release your prisoners Captain,
Your crimes wou'd reach imprisonment for ever,
But since against myself, they are comitted,
I'll pardon ye, but upon this condition,
That of your selves ye freely leave this isle,
The habitts, and the names of what ye were,
And least necessity still make ye wicked
I give ye back your wealth, his part excepted,   120

                                    [*Pointing to* Capr.

Away, and in three days, be seen no more.
  Riv. I ought to thank you, for this grace, but cannot,
I'm fal'n so much below my expectations,
That all your Jayles, can add no suff'rings to me,

I'll leave this place, for all I hate is here,
And all I lov'd, is now most hatefull to me.   [*Exit*.
   Vil. My Lord, this Devil has not damn'd us quite,
Your orders we'll obey, and blesse your mercy. [*Exit* Vil: Lin
   Aub. Now fair Marina, own me for your kinsman,
And all our errours, tow'rd your birth and sex   130
Forgive, and think we'll ever try to mend them.
   Queen. My lord. I beg to joyn in that request,
And thus embracing, court you for my freind   [*To her.*
   Mar. I fear I shall grow proud, with all these honours.
   Aub. I'll send to tell the Duke, your noble Father,
How you intend to blesse my Nephews Love,
He's not yett vow'd, nor shall be, but to you,
And to his own, my lands shall all be added,
To make him still become more worthy of you,

                   [Blan. *offers to speak.*

No thanks, dear Youth, I ever meant itt for you,   140
And cou'd not give itt, att a time more propper.
    To harmlesse revells, lett us now repair,
    Whilst mirth and musick, eccho throo' the air,
    And bear our tryumphs, to the blest above,
    That spring like theirs, from innocence, and Love.

THE END

ARISTOMENES: OR, THE ROYAL SHEPHERD
A TRAGEDY

PROLOGUE TO ARISTOMENES

To my Lord Winchilsea, *upon the first reading the Play to him, at* Eastwell *in* Kent

When first upon the Stage a Play appears,
'Tis not the multitude a poet fears,
Who from example, praise, or dam̄ by roate,
And give their censure, as some Members vote.
But, if in the expecting box, or pitt,
The wretch discerns one true, substantial witt,
Tow'rds him, his doubtful sight, he'll still direct,
Whose very looks can all his faults detect.
So, though no croud is gather'd here, today,
And you my Lord, alone, must Judge this Play,   10
Much more the ign'rant Author is concern'd,
Then if whole troops, of vulgar Critticks swarm'd;
Since Horace, by your mouth, must all condemn,
And 'tis her losse, that you're so great with him.
But, when good Plays scarse pleas'd our Charles's Court,
(So nice him self, and the refin'der sort)
A droll, wou'd att Newmarkett make them sport,
Where rusty copper, dect the strouling Vermin,
And flannel dash'd with Ink, make princely Ermin,
Then lett not this poor Poem, quite dispair,   20
The country asks but plain, and homely fare;
And if this please, by a good winter's fire
More then a visite from a neigh'bring squire,
Or tedious sheet, of doubtful news from Dyer,
The Writer's too well, paid for all her pain,
Who'll now begin, in King Cambyses' strain,
Heroicks, such as Falstaffe heretofore

Repeated, when a cusheon crown he wore;
Yet, those the Hostesse mov'd her eyes to wett,
These lines, she fears, no passions will begett,   30
But 'twill appear, in spite of all inditing,
A woman's way to charm is not by writing.

DRAMATIS PERSONÆ

MEN

Aristomenes, Prince of the *Messenians* and *Arcadians*.
Aristor, Son to *Aristomenes*.
Alcander, a Principal Officer under *Aristomenes*.

Demagetus,
Or the { Son to the Prince of *Rhodes*, under the Disguise
Royal Shepherd, } of a Shepherd call'd *Climander*.

Arcasius, An old Lord, under the Habit of a Shepherd, Councellor
to *Demagetus,*
Anaxander, one of the Kings of *Lacedemon* (for they had always
Two) and Leader of their Forces against *Aristomenes*.
Clariathus, Chief Councellor to *Anaxander*, a Lord of *Sparta*.
Clinias, A Shepherd keeping his Flock on the Plains of *Messenia*,
close to the Walls of *Phærea*, with other Shepherds.

WOMEN

Herminia, Daughter to *Aristomenes*.
Barina, Her Woman and Confident.
Amalintha, Daughter to *Anaxander*.
Phila, Her Woman and Confident.
Thæta.)
and } Shepherdesses on the Plains of *Messenia.*
Lamia,)
Soldiers. Officers. Guards. and Attendants. several Lords of the
Spartan Council.

The general SCENES are *Aristomenes*'s Camp near the Walls of
Phærea; sometimes the Town of *Phærea*, and sometimes the
Plains among the Shepherds.

ACT I SCENE I

A pleasant Plain by a Wood-side; beyond it are seen, on one side, some of the Shepherds Hamlets; on the other (at a distance) the Walls of Phæræa, *a Garrison of the* Lacedemonians.

Enter Climander *meeting* Arcasius; *both drest like Shepherds.*

Clim. Hast thou provided me a Horse and Arms,
A Sword, *Arcasius*, that when Time has freed me
From the Severe Injunctions of a Father,
May fill my Hand, instead of this vile Hook,
And fit it for the Work, a Prince is born to?

Arca. Unwillingly, I have obey'd your Orders;
But, 'till to-morrow's, and the next day's Sun
Shall light the angry, and contentious World,
Your Promise to your Father is in Force;
As well as the Assurance, which you gave,   10
That in my Custody these Arms shou'd rest,
Until that fatal Time demands their Use.

Clim. Call it not Fatal; Oh! that 'twere arriv'd!
That *Aristomenes*, the *Spartan* Terrour,
Were leading me, this moment, bravely on
Through Dangers, equal to the Cause he fights for,
Preserving these free Plains from foreign Bondage!
Though in the Strife this Body strew'd the Ground,
To Fame, and Publick Good an early Victim.

Arca. O wretched *Rhodes!* Thy Ruin is pronounc'd,   20
And thou beneath th' impending Plagues may'st perish;
Since He, whom Oracles appoint to Aid thee,
Thus wishes with his Own, to sell Thy Safety,
For the rash Praise of an intruding Warriour.

Clim. No more of Oracles!
Which oftner we fulfil by heedless Chance,
Than the vain Study to pursue their Meaning;

Which makes me banish, from my lab'ring Thoughts,
Those Mystick Words, which serve but to perplex them.
   Arc. From Mine they will not part, nor shou'd from
     Yours;   30
Which to prevent, ev'n now I will repeat them;

    The Isle of Rhodes *shall be of* Peace *bereft,*
    Unless it by the Heir thereof be left,
    And that He wed, ere he returns agen,
    The Beauteous Daughter of the Best of Men;
    Whose Father's presence there shall save the State,
    And smooth the threatning Brow of angryFate.

   Clim. But, Who this Man, or, Where his Daughter is,
Was left in Darkness, to employ our Search:
Yet, in Obedience, Hither did I come   40
To feed a Flock, and mix with simple Swains;
Because the Priests, who sway in Princes Courts,
Declar'd, that perfect Innocence, and Virtue
Was to be found but in their lowly Rank,
And There, the Best of Men was to be sought for.
   Arc. 'Tis True, they did; and therefore urg'd our Prince;
That slighting (in a Case of such Importance)
The Pride of Titles, and of equal Birth,
You might espouse One of these Rural Maids,
Whose Parents harmless Presence in our Land   50
Might bring the Blessings of the Gods upon us;
And, lest the Wars (which still infest these Countries)
Shou'd tempt you from from the Fates, and his Design,
How strictly did He Charge it on your Duty,
That, 'till the Time, which now, Two Days must end,
You shou'd not leave these Plains, to seek the Camp!
   Clim. Nor have I done it, as Thyself can witness;
But here have spent the long and lazy Hours,
Carelesly stretch'd beneath some *Sylvan* Shade,

And only sent my Wishes to their Tents: 60
But ere the Battle (which is soon intended)
Shall meet in glorious Tryal of their Right,
I will be there, and side with the *Messenians*.
   Arc. Oh! that you wou'd not!
That first your Native Country might be serv'd,
Think on her Danger, and your Sovereign's Will:
'Twas to the Reed, and not the wrangling Trumpet
He bid you listen, to secure his Peace;
Nor have you look'd with Love, as he requir'd,
On any Shepherdess, tho' ne'er so Fair, 70
Or born of Parents, harmless as their Flocks.
Low on my Knees, my Lord, let me prevail,   [*He Kneels.*
That, when the Time, decreed you, do's expire,
You will not prosecute this rash Design;
But go with me yet farther on these Plains,
And seek to please your Father, and the Gods,
In such safe, humble ways, as they direct us.
   Clim. Nay, prithee, do not kneel; it grates my Nature:
                                 [*Raises him.*
But trust me, when we have subdued these Countries
When *Lacedemon's* Kings shall sue for Peace, 80
And make great *Aristomenes* Returns
Agreeing to his Merits, and their Wrongs,
And I have gain'd such Honour as becomes me;
Whate'er thou dost request shall be observ'd:
And tho' my Soul finds such vast disproportion
Betwixt the Thoughts, with which she is inspir'd,
And those, that lodge in these poor Country Maids;
    Yet shall my Duty o'er my Temper rise,
    I'll trust (like Others) only to my Eyes,
    And think, that Women in Perfection are, 90
    Tho ne'er so Ignorant, if Young and Fair,

Arc. Ha!   [*A Noise is heard of distant Drums. Aside.*]
Sure I hear the distant Sound of Drums.
Heav'n grant what I've been told, and kept so secret,
Of a Design this Day to end the War,
Be not a Truth too tempting for my Reasons!

     Enter frighted, Thæta *and* Lamia, *Shepherdesses.*

  Thæ. Oh! may we here be safe, tell us *Climander?*
For all the Lawns, that lie beyond the Hill,
Where still our Flocks were us'd to feed in peace,
Are fill'd with War, and dark with flying Arrows :   100
The Sheep disperse, whilst none regard their Safety,
But call on *Pan,* to shield th' advent'rous Chief,
The noble *Aristomenes* from Danger.
  Clim. Hear me, *Arcasius,* hear and do not thwart me;

                            [*Aside to* Arc.

Not tye me to a few remaining Hours:
For, by the horrid Shield, that bears the *Gorgon,*
I Swear; if thou refuse to arm me now
With what I sent thee lately to provide,
These feet shall bear me sandal'd to the Battle,
This flow'ry Wreath shall mix with their stern Helmets, 110
And Death I'll take, if not impower'd to give it.
  Arc. Oh! do not ask my Aid; but in this Tryal,
Call all your fainting Virtue to assist
And help you keep your Promise to your Father.
  Clim. I did not promise him to be a Coward,
To let the Sound of War thus strike my Sense,
Yet keep my Heart in a cool, even Temper.
Hark! this way comes the Noise, and I will meet it.

    [*As he is going, a confus'd Noise and Cry is heard within.*

  Arc. They're Cries of Grief, and not the Shouts of Battle.
I hope All's past, lest He and *Rhodes* shou'd perish.   120

Enter meeting, Climander, Clinias, *and other Shepherds.*

1st Shep. Ruin'd, Undone!

Clin. Let every Shepherd weep!
Turn their sweet Harmony to Sighs and Groans!
To the fierce Wolves deliver up their Flocks,
And leave *Messenia* to the cruel Victor!

. *Clim.* The Victor, *Clinias!* is the Fight then over?

Clin. It is, and We again the Slaves of *Sparta.*

Clim. Then *Aristomenes* must sure be breathless,
And, if he's Dead, fall'n in his Countries Cause:
The Gods have giv'n Him Fame, whilst We are Wretched. 130

Clin. Oh! He's not Dead, but Living in their Power,
Which, 'tis believ'd, they'll use with utmost Rigour:
Pressing too far on the Auxiliary Troops,
The Foe surrounding bore him from his Horse,
Then with the Thongs of their curs'd *Cretan* Bows
Bound his strong Arms, and lead him off, in Triumph.

Clim. Convert, ye Powers, to Blood and Tears that
Triumph!
Rescue from their vile Hands the noble Prey,
And send him warmer Friends than *Demagetus*,   [*Aside.*
Who, knowing not his Person, lov'd his Valour!   140
O ill-tim'd Duty, how hast thou betray'd me!
Where is *Aristor?* Where's the brave *Alcander?* [*To them.*

Clim. The first may share in his great Father's Fate,
For ought, as yet, the Army can discover:
Alcander heads, but cannot lead them on,
And 'tis believ'd they quickly will forsake him;
Such cold Dismay and Terrour has possess'd 'em!
Yet ere we part, forever part from hence,
(If so the cruel Tyrant shou'd Decree)
Let us appoint one sad and solemn Meeting,   150
Where all the Ensigns of our former Mirth
May be defac'd and offer'd to His Praise.

That made our Nights secure, and bless'd our Days.
   1st Shep. So let it be!
                Again, one Ev'ning on these Plains we'll meet,
  2nd Shep. But never tread them more with chearful Feet.
                          [*Exeunt Shepherds and Shepherdesses.*

   Clim. Cruel *Arcasius*! How hast thou undone me,
Charming me, with thy Tears, to this soft Circle,
Whilst the bright Spirit, Honour is gone by,
And borne away on never-turning Pinions!   160
Why wou'd'st thou thus contrive against my Fame,
And rob my fiery Youth of this first War,
(For which it languish'd with a Lover's Fondness)
By saying still 'twou'd last, 'till Time had freed me?
But I will yet pursue it thro' Despair,
And share their Ruin, tho' deny'd their Glory.
                        [*As he's going* Arc. *kneels.*

   Arc. Yet, this last time, behold my bended Knees,
Which if you slight shall of the Gods implore
A hasty Death, to fall on old *Arcasius*:
Nor think, this Posture means to cross your way;   170
For, by those Powers I swear; if they will Fight
As much, we hear 'tis doubted by the Shepherds,
I will not sue, to keep you from the Army,
Or bring on me your future Life's Reproaches.
Let me obtain but This, for all my Service,
To be first sent to sound their Disposition,
Which I'll relate with Truth, and help your Purpose:
In this Attempt Two Hours will not be lost;
Oh! give so much, to save his Life, that loves you.
   Clim. Thou hast obtain'd it, by thy promised Aid,   180
And my long Knowledge of the Truth that guides thee.
About it then, whilst in that shady Grove,
I with impatience wait for thy Return.
   Arca. Which shall not be prolong'd my Lord, believe me.
                        [*Exeunt severally.*

Enter several Soldiers, running over the Stage, and throwing
away their Arms.

1st Sold. Away, away, haste to the Woods for Shelter.

2d Sold. Do they begin to sally from the Town?

3d Sold. I know not; look behind him, he that will.
Here lies my Way—   [*They run into the Wood.*

Enter more, doing as the former.

1st Sold. Farewell the Wars! Oh! never such a General!

2d Sold. Never such Sorrow! never such a General! 190

Enter more.

2d Sold. What, is the Army all dispers'd, and broken!
                                        [*To them.*

3d Sold. No, but the Wisest of them do as We do.
Away, away—

Enter Alcander *meeting them.*

Alcand. Why do ye fly my Friends, and cast these
    from ye?
For shame! like Men, that once have known their Use,
Take 'em again, and wait, or seek the Foe.

3d Sold. Seek 'em, for what?
We cannot find our General out amongst 'em:
'Tis thought they've made sure Work with him already;
And now you'd have us run upon their Swords.   200
We thank you, Captain.   Come away, away!
                            [*Exit follow'd by some others.*

Alc. Oh! yet my Fellow-Soldiers, stay and hear me;
Can ye so soon forget your Noble General,
Your *Aristomenes,* whose Courage fed ye,
And by whose Conduct, ye have slept securely
In reach of Foes, that trebled ye in Number!
Can ye forget the Care, that heal'd your Wounds;
The Tongue, that prais'd them; or those Liberal Hands,
That pour'd down Gold, faster than they your Blood!

1st Sold. No; were he but amongst us, we'd Dye with him.

2d Sold. We are no Cowards, Captain, nor Ungrateful. 211
But since they say, He's Dead, What can we do?

Alcand. Go back, and keep a little while together;
At least, 'till there are Tydings from the Town:
Then, if he lives, we may attempt his rescue;
Or, if he's Dead, in a most just despair
Burn their accurst *Phœrea* o'er their Heads,
And then disperse, when we're so far reveng'd.
Do this my Friends; Come, come, I know you will:
You lov'd the General—   220

1st Sold. Curs'd be He, that did not!

2d Sold. We will go back, but ne'er shall see him more.

3d Sold. Then we will Fight no more, that's sure enough.

4th Sold. Howe'er, let's follow the brave Captain here,
And stay, 'till we're inform'd as he advises.

Alcand. Come, I will march before you.
Take up your Arms and trust, my Friends, to me:
Your Lives shall not be set on idle Hazards;
Lose no more time, but let us join the Army.
                    [*They take up their Arms, and Exeunt.*

Enter Herminia *and* Barina, *Disguis'd like Shepherdesses.*

Herm. Alas! *Barina,* whither wilt thou lead me?   230

Bar. To Safety, Madam, poor and humble Safety,
Which in those Hamlets, now within our Sight,
The Shepherds find, with whom we may partake it.

Herm. Thus far indeed thou'st brought me on to seek it,
Urging the Danger of a Virgin's Honour,
When left defenceless to the Conqueror's Will:
But dost thou think, we may not through these Woods
Find out some gloomy Cave to Men unknown,
And there expiring, sleep secure for ever?

Bar. Why shou'd we Dye,   240
Since *Aristomenes* may yet be Living?

Herm. Oh! that thou hads't not named him!

[*She starts and weeps.*

'Till we were lodg'd, where Grief
Might have its Course; for now 'twill flow
And stop our farther Passage, barring the Sight
Which shou'd conduct our Steps.

Bar. It must not Madam, nor must you indulge it,
But put on chearful Looks to suit this Habit,
And make the World believe you what you seem.

Herm. I cannot do it.   250
In the midst of Sport
I should forget the gay, fantastick Scene,
And drop these Tears, when Smiles were most expected.

Bar. Then 'tis in vain farther to seek for Shelter:
Let us return and wait in your Pavilion,
'Till *Anaxander* shall command you thence
To serve the base Delight of some proud *Spartan.*

Herm. Oh! yet avert that Fate, ye angry Powers!
I yield, *Barina*; make me what thou wilt:
See, I no more am sad; look on this Brow;   260
Canst thou read there that I have lost a Father,
The best, the fondest, and the dearest Father?
Forgive the tender Thought, that breeds this Change;
I'll weep it off, and smile again to please thee.

Bar. No; I'll weep too, for his, that's past,
And your approaching Ruin.

Herm. Alas! I had forgot, but now am Calm:
What must I do? indeed I will observe thee.

Bar. Then not far hence, conceal'd within this Grove
Wait my Return, who must go find the Shepherds,   270
And frame some Story; that when you appear,
Thro' no Enquiries we become suspected:
And in my absence, be your Thoughts employ'd
To bend your Mind to what the Times require.

Herm. To Fate and thy Advice I will submit,
Suit to my alter'd State my low Desire;
My Fare be plain, and homely my Attire,
My Tresses with a simple Fillet bind,
Face the hot Sun, and wither in the Wind;
In my parch'd Hand a rural Crook be found,   280
The Trees my Curtains, and my Bed the Ground:
That Fortune (who at Greatness aims her Blow)
When thus disguis'd may not a Princess know.
                                        [*Exeunt.*

The SCENE *changes to a Street in the Town of* Phærea (*the*
Lacedemonian *Garrison*) *a Rabble and many common Soldiers
in the Street.*

1st Sold. All's done, all's done my Fellows.
We may now go home to our Wives and our Shops.

1st Rabble. Ay, that we may; we have caught him at last,
That has been our Back-friend so long,
As one may say—

2d Sold. Nay, I'll be sworn,
Thou ne'er look'd'st him in the Face:
But we shall have the tossing, and the tumbling of him
Assoon as ever the sowre-fac'd Senators
Have dismiss'd their Judgments upon him.

3d Rabble. Ay, I'll warrant ye, shall we;   10
Here, here he comes; bear back, bear back.

[Aristomenes *bound and guarded is conducted over the Stage, the
Rabble crouding and following him with confus'd Cries and
Shouts, Exeunt.*

The SCENE *changed, discovers a Council-Chamber in* Anaxander's *Palace:* Anaxander, Clarinthus, *and several Lords of*
Sparta.

Anax. Most happily, my Lords, we now are met,
To see those Hands in servile Fetters ty'd
Which broke the Bondage of the proud *Messenians,*

Whom *Sparta* long had held in hard Subjection.
Ere yet their Captive General do's appear,
Be it amongst your selves, My Lords, resolved
What Course will answer best our Ends upon them.
Speak you, *Clarinthus*, for'most of the Assembly;
And then, let ev'ry one add what he pleases.

   Clar. Short be my Speech, and plain, as is the way   10
Which must secure what *Lacedemon* toils for:
Let him resign that Country, kept by him
From the entire Subjection, to our Yoke;
Or let his speedy Death deliver to Us
What his too active Life has long kept back.

   Anax. What say the rest?

   All the Sen. All, all agree to this.

   Clar. No middle Course can be of use to *Sparta.*

   Anax. It is enough; Call for the Prisoner there.   19

   A Lord. Bring in the Pris'ner; 'tis the King's Command.

Aristomenes *is brought in by the Guard.*

Aristor *in a* Spartan *Dress presses in amongst the Croud, whilst*
Phila *appears at the Door.*

   Anax. At last, we see the Hero can be Conquer'd,
[*To* Clar.

   Clar. Not in his Looks; for they are haughty still,
And so his Mind will prove, if I mistake not.

   Anax. That you, our Pris'ner now, of late our Foe,
Have urg'd that Country, where you rule in Chief,
To break our Yoke, and make Incursions on us,
Since known to all, will justify our Sentence
Which is; That you shall meet the Death deserv'd,
Unless to keep our Quiet for the future,
You bring again *Messenia* to our Sway,   30
Paying such Tribute, as shall be impos'd
By Us, the Lords of that offensive State.

This is the Choice, we kindly set before you,
And wish, that you would take the safest Part,
  Aristom. Enslave my Country, to secure my Life!
That Pow'r forbid it, under whose Protection
I've often fought her Battles with Success,
And drove th' ill-grounded War home to your *Sparta!*
  Clar. He braves us in his Bonds: then you wou'd Dye.
  Aristom. I do not say I wou'd;   40
I am a Man, and Nature bars that saying:
Yet I dare Dye; no *Spartan* here, but knows it.
But since the Fates (whose Wills we best can read,
When thus unfolded in their dire Events)
Tell me by these vile Bonds I must submit;
Propose the gentlest Bargain you can make,
And if I find my Life bears equal Weight,
I am content to take it, else 'tis Yours.
  Anax. 'Tis not for Us to wave, or change our Terms,
Mistaken Man, who think not of our Power,   50
And that we may command what we propose:
Since the first Sally, now, must take Possession
Of what your frighted Rout will soon abandon.
  Aristom. My frighted Rout!
Ye basely wrong with foul reproachful Names
Those valiant Troops, which yet ye cannot·Conquer:
For know, thou proud insulting *Anaxander,*
There's at their head a resolute young Man,
That will not 'bate thee in his strict Account
One Sigh or Groan, thy Tortures or thy Dungeons   60
Shall wrest in Dying from his Father's Bosom.

Anaxander *and the Senate talk among themselves, whilst* Aristor
          comes forward upon the Stage.

But there he stands!   [*Aside seeing* Aristor.
Aristor thro' that *Spartan* Dress I view,
And ne'er till now, wish'd not to see my Son.

Protect him from their Knowledge, some kind Pow'r,
If Youth, or Virtue e'er engag'd your Pity!

Clar. Let it be so, and speedily perform'd,   [*Aloud.*
For He'll ne'er yield to what has been demanded.

Anax. You nam'd the Dungeon, with a Threaten too
Of swift Revenge, thinking to fright our Justice: 70
But we'll take care, first, to perform our Part,
Then, venture what your daring Son can offer.
The Dungeon is his Sentence, thither bear him.

Aristor. Not till this Hand has done a swifter Justice.
                    [*Draws and runs at* Anax.

Anax. Ha! what means this, my Guards!
                    [*He avoids the thrust:* Phila *runs in.*

Phila. Help, Soldiers, help; seize that distracted *Spartan.*
Who now has got a Sword; Disarm, and take him.
                    [*They disarm him.*

Aristor. 'Tis false; stand off, ye Slaves, and know I
am—

Phila. Oh! stop his Mouth; for if he raves, he Dyes.
                    [*They stop his Mouth with a Handkerchief.*

Aristom. As sure as now he Lives, had he spoke more [*Aside.*
Therefore be blest the Stratagem that stopt him!   81

Anax. What means this, *Phila;* speak, Who is this Madman?

Phila. One by a Friend entrusted to my Care,
Sent from the Country here to find a Cure;
But hearing, as the Croud pass'd by his Lodgings,
That *Aristomenes* wou'd soon be Sentenc'd,
He broke his Ward, and fancy'd He must save him.
I have pursu'd him, 'till I'm faint with Crying,
And am confounded at his frantick Passion.
Oh! Royal Sir, forgive it—   90

Anax. We do, and pity him: remove him hence,
Then, to thy Mistress, my dear Daughter, Go
And say we now again shall soon see *Sparta.*

Phila. I shall my Lord!
Now follow me, I'll lead ye to his Lodgings.   [*To the Guards*
                [*Exit* Phila *with the Guards bearing off* Aristor.
Aristom. Whoe'er she be,
May Heaven reward her, if she means his Safety.   [*Aside.*
Now I can meditate on my own Fortunes,
And slight the worst can reach me.
   Anax. He's deep in Thought which may produce a
     Change.   100
Again I'll try him—   [*To* Clar.
Now, *Aristomenes*, that this wild Chance
Has given you time to think upon our Sentence,
Have you enough considered of its Horror,
To bend your stubborn Will to our Demands?
   Aristom. Yes, *Anaxander*, I have weigh'd it well:
That active Faculty, which we call *Phancy*,
Soon as you spoke, dragg'd me thus bound by Slaves
Thro' the throng'd Streets, exciting several Passions;
The Barb'rous Croud shouted their clamorous Joy,   110
Because unpunish'd they might sport with Blood;
Old Men and Matrons, destin'd long for Death,
With envious Pleasure saw me forced before them
To tread that Path, in spight of vigorous Nature,
Whilst tender Virgins turned aside their Heads,
And dropt, in Silence, the soft Tears of Pity:
But, Oh! the Soldiers; from the Soldier's hands
Methoughts I saw their Swords neglected thrown,
When Fortune shew'd they cou'd not save the Bravest
(If once she frown'd) from such a Fate as mine.   120
   Clar. He'll move the Croud; urge him to speak directly.
   Anax. All this is from the purpose; plainly tell
Whether you'll meet our Mercy, or the Dungeon.
   Aristom. My Train of Thoughts to that dark Cave had
     led me;

I stood reclined upon the horrid Brim,
And gaz'd into it, 'till my baffl'd Sight
Piercing beyond the many jetting Rocks
That help to break by turns the falling Body,
Was lost in Shades, where it must rest for-ever:
And ready now to be pushed rudely off,   130
This was my last, and best Reflection on it,
That there dwelt Peace, which is not to be found
In his dark Bosom, that has sold his Country.

    Anax. Away with him to instant Tryal of it:
See this obey'd, and plunge him headlong down;
There, he'll have Time, if Life, for such fine Thoughts.
Away, and bring me word it is perform'd.

                              [Exeunt Anax. *and Lords.*

                    Aristomenes *born off.*

    Rabble and Sold. Away, away; the Dungeon, the Dun-
geon.
Peace and Prosperity to *Lacedemon!*   *[Exeunt.*

ACT II   SCENE I

A Room in the Palace. Aristor *alone.*

    Arist. I've torn with Cries the Roof of this vile Mansion.
And from that Window, barred too closely up
To give me leave to leap upon their Heads,
Have curs'd the Croud, and told 'em whose I am:
At which they laugh and cry, 'tis *Phila's* Madman.

                    [He attempts but cannot force the Door.
Confusion! that she dares confine me thus!
Whilst my free Thoughts, unfollow'd by my Hand,
Must see that cursed Deed, they can't prevent.
Oh! *Aristomenes,* my noble Father!
Hear me, ye Fates, and let me but Revenge him;   10
Give me Revenge; and now, methinks, I grasp it,

Broke thro' his Guards, I seize upon the Tyrant,
And stab him thus, and thus —   [*He acts all this.*
Then bear him to the Ground, thus falling on him,
And to his Heart thus tearing my wide way.
Oh! O', O', O',—   [*Throws himself upon the Ground.*

Enter Amalintha, *the Door by one without immediately lock'd
after her.*

  Amal. Where is this wretched Mourner?
Oh! let me find him, tho' to raise his Sorrows
With the sad Sound of my repeated Groans.
Ha! on the Ground! then be it too my Seat!   20
        [*Sits on the Ground by him.*

For I will share in this Excess of Grief,
As well as in the Days of milder Fortune,
I bore a part in Love, that knew no Measure.
O *Aristomenes!* oh! my *Aristor!*
        [*She puts her Handkerchief before her Eyes weeping.*

  Aristor. Whoe'er thou art, repeat again that Sound:
Such Groans shall hourly issue from his Dungeon,
And fright the bloody *Spartans* into Madness.
        [*He looks up.*

Ha! sure I shou'd know that Form, that Shape, those Limbs,
That lab'ring Bosom, and those Locks dishevel'd:
But take not from thy Face that friendly Cloud;   30
Do not expose it, lest thro' all its Charms
My deep Revenge find out whose Stamp it bears,
And urge me on to something Dark and Fatal.
  Amal. This from *Aristor!* this to *Amalintha!*
        [*She rises and shews her face.*

  Aristor. Why wou'd'st thou tempt me thus advent'rous
Maid,
And bring the Blood of *Anaxander* near me?
        [*Coming up fiercely to her.*

Canst thou too fondly think, that Love's soft Bands,
His gentle Cords of Hyacinths and Roses,
Wove in the dewy Spring, when Storms are silent,
Can tye these Hands, provok'd by horrid Murther!   40
Oh! do not trust it—
But fly this Ground, while I have Power to bid thee.
   Amal. Aristor, no; my Flight shall not preserve me:
The Life, I've kept but to indulge your Love,
Now to this loud, mistaken Rage I offer.
Take it, Oh! take it; Means cannot be wanting,
Altho' no Instrument of Death be near you:
This Hair, these flatter'd Locks, these once-lov'd Tresses
Round my sad Neck thus knit will soon perform it;
Or, on these trembling Lips your Hand but prest   50
Will send the rising Breath down to my Heart,
And break it, telling who deny'd it Passage.
   Aristor. Tryal beyond the Strength of Man and Lover!
   Amal. Or, if you wou'd be quicker in Dispatch,
Speak but a few such Words, as now you utter'd,
And my poor hov'ring Soul will fly before 'em.
Farewel *Aristor*, see! the Work is done:
I did but think I heard their killing Sound,
And the bare Fancy saves you farther Study.
                [*She faints, he catches her in his Arms.*
   Aristor. Oh! stop the glorious Fugitive a moment;   60
And I will whisper to it such Repentance,
Such Love, such Fondness, such unheard-of Passion,
As shall confine it to it's beauteous Mansion.
Thus let me hug, and press thee into Life,
And lend thee Motion from my beating Heart,
To set again the Springs of thine in working.
   Amal. I hear your Summons, and my Life returns:
But tell me, ere again so firm 'tis fixt
That it must cost an Agony like this,

To let it out to Liberty and Ease,   70
Will you not hate me for my Father's Guilt?
 Aristor. By the soft Fires of Love, that fill my Breast,
And dart through all the Horrors of my Soul,
Like Heaven's bright Flashes in a Night of Shadows,
I will not hate, or e'er reproach thee more:
Yet let me breathe so gently one Complaint,
So gently, that it may not break thy Peace,
Tho' it for ever has discarded mine,
And ask, why you thus cruelly wou'd use me,
Why, have me seiz'd, and bound with frantick Fetters, 80
Snatch'd from my Duty by a Woman's wile,
And here confin'd, whilst my great Father perish'd?
 Amal. 'Twas none of mine, by your dear self I swear;
It was the Fates design and *Phila's* action;
She saw you thus disguis'd amongst the Croud,
And, ere she would acquaint me with your Danger,
Follow'd to watch the means how to prevent it.
 Aristor. I will believe you to my Heart's relief,
Which must have broke, had your Consent been with her.
But, *Amalintha*, now my Rage is gone, 90
And Love thro' this mistake has forc'd his way,
It spreads before my Thoughts the gaudy Scene
Of those Delights, which have been once allow'd it;
Brings to my Phancy in their softest Dress
The gentle Hours, that told our private Meetings;
Shews me the Grove, where, by the Moon's pale Light
We've breath'd out tender Sighs, 'till coming Day
Has drawn them deeper, warning us to part,
Which ne'er we did, 'till some new Time was set
For the return of those transporting Pleasures. 100
 Amal. And so again, *Aristor*, we'll contrive,
And so again, we'll meet, and sigh, and love.
 Aristor. Oh! O', O',—*Amalintha!*

Amal. Oh! why that Groan, that deep, that deathlike
   Groan!

Aristor. When Soul and Body part, it can't be softer;
And I must leave thee, Soul to sad *Aristor,*
With all those Pleasures which I but repeated,
As Dying Friends will catch one last Embrace
Of what they know, they must forego forever.   109

   Amal. Indeed, you've call'd my wand'ring Fancy back
From those Delights, where 'twou'd have endless stray'd:
But, my *Aristor!* (for I'll call you mine,
Though all the Stars combine against my Title,
And bar fulfilling of the Vows they've witness'd)
Tell me, tho' we must ne'er in Nuptials join,
May we not meet, and at this distance sigh?
And when I've hoarded up a Stock of Tears,
Which in the *Spartan's* sight I dare not lavish,
Oh! tell me, if I may not seek you out,
And in large Showers thus pour them down before you? 120
                                            [*She weeps.*

   Aristor. Cease to oppress me more; thou weeping Beauty,
And think with what vast Storms my Soul is toss'd!
                              [*Comes up to hear earnestly.*
Think too, that but to gaze upon thee thus,
To stand in reach of thy Ambrosial Breath,
And hear thy Voice, sweet as the Ev'ning Notes,
When in still Shades the Shepherds sooth their Loves,
I wou'd not mind an Army in my way,
Or stop at raging Seas, or brazen Towers.
Yet, *Amalintha,* tho' I Dye to speak it,
Yet we must part, we must, my *Amalintha!*   130

   Amal. Never to meet agen? Tell me but that.

   Aristor. Alas! not I, the Fates can only tell it:
Let them make even one Account betwixt us,
And give this Hand the Liberty to seal it.

And we'll in spight of vengeful Thunder join,
If then, thy Heart be as resolv'd as mine.

   Amal. No: on those Terms you mean, we must not meet:
But since those Fates deny it to your Power,
The Will I to your mighty Wrongs forgive,
[From without the Door.

   Phila. Madam, you'll be surpriz'd; haste to return: 140
Your Father's now just going to your Lodgings.

   Aristor. All Plagues and Curses meet him!   [*Aside.*

   Amal. Oh! then I must be gone.
A little time will call the State to Council;
And when the Croud by that is thither drawn,
One I will send to wait on your Escape:
And if you tempt new Dangers, know *Aristor*
That *Amalintha* too will perish in them.

   Aristor. Fear not, my Love.

   Phila. Haste, Madam, haste, or we are all Undone.   150
[From without.

   Amal. So from his few short Moments calls away
A gasping Wretch, the cruel Bird of Prey;
Bids him make haste th' Eternal Shades to find,
And leave like me, all that is Dear behind.

   Aristor. Whilst, like the Friend that's sadly weeping by,
I see the much lov'd Spirit from me fly;
And with vain Cries pursue it to that Coast,
Where it must land, and my weak Hopes be lost.

   [*He leads her to the Door, and returns speaking as he's going
out at the Other.*
Now, let Revenge awhile sustain my Heart,   159
And Fate yet close my Life with some exalted part! [*Exit.*
The Stage darken'd represents the Inside of a Dungeon, Aristo-
   menes *lying down in it, and struggling as coming out of a
   Swoon.*

   Aristom. At last 'tis vanquish'd; and my soaring Spirits
Dispel the gloomy Vapours, that oppress'd them,

And cloath'd my Dreams with more than mortal Horrour.
So low in my deep Phancy was I plung'd,
That o'er my Head impetuous Rivers rush'd,
And Mountains grew betwixt our World and me:
Hungry and Cold, methought I wander'd on
Thro' fruitless Plains, that Food nor Comfort nourish'd,
'Till hideous Serpents twisted me about,
And drew me to their Den all foul and loathsome; 10
But I will quit the Bed, that breeds such Visions,
And summon all my Officers to Council;
For with to-morrow's Dawn we'll storm *Phærea.*

[He walks about feeling for the Door.

Ha! where's the Door, my Tent is sure transform'd,
And all I touch is Rock that streams with Dew.
Oh! that I'd slept, that I had slept for ever! *[He starts.*
Yes, *Anaxander,* yes! thou worst of Furies!
I know thy Dungeon now, and my dark Ruin:
Yet why, ye Fates, since fall'n below your Succour,
Wou'd ye thus cruelly restore my Senses, 20
To make me count my Woes by tedious Moments,
Dye o'er again, choak'd by unwholsome Damps,
Parch'd up with Thirst, or clung with pining Hunger,
Borne piecemeal to the Holes of lurking Adders,
Or mould'ring to this Earth, where thus I cast me?

[Throws himself on the Ground.

Musick is heard without the SCENE, *after it has play'd awhile
and ceases, He speaks.*

How, Harmony! nay then the Fiends deride me:
For who, but they, can strike Earth's sounding Entrails,
Or with low Winds thus fill her tuneful Pores?
Oh! that some Words of horrid Sense wou'd join it,
To tell me where I might conclude my Sorrows! 30

A Voice within Sings.

1st Voice. Fallen Wretch! make haste, and Dye!
        To that last Asylum fly,
        Where no anxious Drops of Care,
        Where no sighing Sorrows are,
        Friends or Fortune none deplore,
        None are Rich, and none are Poor,
        Nor can Fate oppress them more.
        To this last Asylum fly,
        Fallen Wretch! make haste and Dye!   39
                            [*The Voice ceases.*

Aristom. Thou counsell'st rightly; show me but the way,
And with the Speed thou urgest I'll obey thee.   [*He rises.*

The Voice Sings again.

1st Voice. A pointed Rock with little pains
        Will split the Circle of thy Brains.
        To thy Freedom I persuade thee,
        To a wat'ry Pit will lead thee,
        Which has no glorious Sun-beam seen,
        No Footstep known, or bord'ring Green,
        For thousand rolling Ages past.
        Fallen Wretch! to this make haste,
        To this last Asylum fly.   50
        Fallen Wretch! make haste and Dye!

Aristom. I come, thou kind Provoker of Despair,
Which still is nearest Cure, when at the Highest.
I come, I come—

*Going towards the Voice, another Sings at the other side, upon
which he stops and listens.*

2d Voice. Stay, oh! stay; 'tis all Delusion,
        And wou'd breed thee more Confusion.
        I, thy better Genius, move thee,
        I, that guard, and I, that love thee;

I, who in thy rocky way,
Cloth'd in Eagles Feathers lay,   60
And in safety brought thee down,
Where none living e'er was known.
Chearful Hope I bring thee now,
Chearful Hope the Gods allow,
Mortal, on their Pleasures wait,
Nor rush into the arms of Fate. [*The Voice ceases.*

Aristom. To hope, is still the Temper of the Brave:
And tho' a just Despair had dispossess'd it,
Yet, thus encourag'd, will I trust the Gods
With those few Moments, Nature has to spare me;   70
Nor follow thee, thou bad persuading Spirit.
Yet tell me, who thou art, and why thou tempt'st me?

1st Voice. I thy evil Genius am,
          To *Phœrea* with thee came;
          Hung o'er thee in the murd'ring Croud,
          And clapp'd my dusky Wings aloud;
          Now endeavour'd to deceive thee,
          And will never, never, leave thee.
2d Voice. I'll protect him from thy Pow'r.
1st Voice. I shall find a careless Hour.   80
2d Voice. Laurels He again shall wear,
          War and Honour's Trumpet hear.
1st Voice. For one fatal, famous Day,
          He his dearest Blood shall pay.
          Hear it ye repeating Stones,
          And confirm it by your Groans!
          [*A dismal Groan is heard round the Dungeon.*

Aristom. What all this Bellowing for a Conqueror's
     Death!
The Field of Honour is his Bed of Ease;
He toils for't all the Day of his hard Life,

And lays him there at Night, renown'd and happy: **90**
Therefore this Threat was vain malicious Fury.
1st Voice. Now away, away I fly;
>   For hated Good is rushing by.
>   *[Here the Voice ceases quite.*

*A Machine, like a Fox, runs about the Dungeon smelling, and
rushes against* Aristomenes, *who taking it for his evil Genius,
catches at it, and speaks.*

   Aristom. What! hast thou Substance too, and dar'st
      assault me!
Nay then, thou shalt not 'scape; I'll seize and grapple with
      thee,
And by my conqu'ring Arm o'ercome thy Influence.
Fool that I was! to think, it cou'd be vanquisht.
This is some rav'ning Beast; the Fur betrays it;
A *Fox*, I think, teach me to be as subtle,
Extremity, thou Mother of Invention!   *[He catches it.*   **100**
I have it now; and where it leads, will follow.
My better Genius do's this Hour preside:
Be strong that Influence, and thou my Guide.
>   *[Exit, led out by the* Fox

>   *The* SCENE *changes to the Plains by the Woodside.*
>   *Enter from the Wood* Herminia *alone and faint.*

   Herm. Here 'twas she left me; but so far I've stray'd,
Unheeding every thing, but my sad Thoughts,
That my faint Limbs no longer can support me.
Oh! let me rest; and if 'tis Death I feel,
A Guest more welcome none yet entertain'd.
>   *[She sits down, leaning against a Tree.*

Enter Climander *looking towards the Camp, as expecting the
returns of* Arcasius.

   Clim. He has exceeded much the time prefixt;
And yet, I wou'd not doubt him:
I've climb'd the Hill, better to view the Camp;

And all are fixt, and motionless as Death.
Therefore awhile I will command my Patience: 10
He cannot now be long—
> [*He turns and sees* Herm. *and gazes earnestly on her.*
—Ha! Who lies there?
A lovely Shepherdess; but faint she seems.
Say, beauteous Maid, if so much Strength is left,
How best a Stranger, may assist, or serve you!
> [*He kneels down by her.*
She do's not speak; but looks into my Heart,
And melts it to the softness of her Eyes.
Hard by, a Spring clear as the Tears she drops,
Runs bubbling under a delicious Shade:
Water, thence fetch'd in a Pomegranate's rind,
May call her fainting Spirits to their office.   20
> [*He goes out.*

  Herm. He's gone, but quickly will return again;
Yet he's so gentle sure I need not fear him:
Tho' at his first approach my Heart beat high,
'Till *Halcyon* sounds, and words of Pity calm'd it;
Nay, something courtly in them was imply'd:
And if the Swains are polish'd, all like him,
Their humble Sheds may scorn our ruder Greatness.

  Enter again Climander *with Water in a Pomgranate-Shell.*

  Clim. Pan! if thou e'er did'st hear a Shepherd's Prayer,
Endue this Water, sacred to thy Name,
With all the Vertues, needful to restore her.   30
> [*She drinks.*

  Herm. Your Pray'r is heard; kind Shepherd take my
    Thanks,
And He, whom you invok'd, reward you largely!
  Clim. Oh! You may far outdo all He can grant,
In but declaring where you feed your Flocks,
And to what Shade, when *Phœbus* hottest shines,

You lead those happy Sheep, to 'scape his Fury;
That I, exposing mine to the wide Plains,
May seek you out, and sigh till Night before you.

   Herm. Alas! I have no Flocks, or Skill to guide them;
No leafy Hamlet, strew'd with painted Flowers;   40
Or mossy Pillow, to repose my Head:
But wander from a distant, fatal Place,
Where I have lost my Parents, and my Succour,
And now, in such a Habit as becomes it,
Seek the low Plains, to learn the Art you practice.

   Clim. She may be Noble then; and for her Form,
'Tis sure the fairest that my Eyes e'er fix'd on.   [*Aside.*
Who were your Parents, gentle Maid, declare?

   Herm. They were not mean, and yet I must conceal them:
My Mother early Dy'd; but Fame has told me,   50
She'd all Perfections, which make others Proud,
Yet wore them, as she knew not they adorn'd her.
And be, in this, my Father's Praise exprest:
That by an Oracle He was confest
Of all the Grecian Race to be the Best.

   Clim. The Best of Men! and you the Fairest Woman!
And in a Moment I the greatest Lover!

   [*He speaks this transportedly and seizes her Hand, which he
kisses.*

Whilst to complete my Bliss, by Heav'ns decree
These Beauties all are mine, and thus I claim them.   59

   Herm. Protect me all ye Powers, that wait on Virtue,
From the dark Ends of such unruly Transports!

                 [*She takes her Hand away hastily and rises.*

Nor dare, presumptuous Swain, once to renew them,
Or tempt more Dangers than a Crook can answer!

   Clim. A Man there lives not, shou'd have urg'd that to
    me,
Built round with Steel, or plung'd all o'er in *Styx*.

Then, let your Beauty's Triumphs be complete,
Which, after such a Threat, can bend my Knee,
And make me sue for Pardon, as for Life.

Herm. I can forgive, whilst I forbid such Language;
Since She, who yields to have her Beauty worshipp'd,   70
Must pay too much to him, that brings the Incense.

Clim. To Me you cannot, 'tis a Debt to Fate.
Your Heart is mine; the amorous Stars ordain it,
Which smiling, hung o'er my auspicious Birth,
And not an angry Planet cross'd their Influence:
They bid me Love, aud the Harmonious God
When askt, what Path shou'd lead me on to Glory,
Sent forth a Sound, that charm'd the hoary Priest,
And said, a Passion, soft as that, must bless me.
Then, do not strive to disappoint their Purpose,   80
Or quench Celestial Flames with Scorn or Coldness.
Oh! that a Smile might tell me, that you wou'd not,
A gentle Word, a Look, a Sigh confirm it,
Or any sign, that bears the stamp of Love!
But 'tis in vain, and some more happy Youth
Has drawn my Lot, and mock'd foretelling *Phœbus.*

Herm. I must not leave you with a Thought that wrongs
   me:
For know, no Passion e'er possess'd this Breast,
Nor will the mighty Griefs, that now have seiz'd it,
E'er yield to give a softer Guest admittance.   90
But my Companion comes; Shepherd farewell!
When next we meet, if Heav'n that Moment sends,
For your Assistance lent, we may be Friends.

Clim. Heav'n can't be true, if it no more affords,
Nor Oracles explain themselves by Words.
Let talking Age the Joys of Friendship prove,
Beauty for Youth was made, and Youth alone for Love.

                                        [*Exeunt severally.*

ACT III   SCENE I

A Myrtle-Grove with a Fountain belonging to Anaxander's
Palace.
                Enter Amalintha *and* Phila.

Amal. Why had not I a barb'rous *Spartan* Soul,
Unapt for Love, and harsh, as our rude Customs!
Or why, ye cruel Fates, did you deny
My Birth to be among the neighb'ring Swains,
Where, on the flow'ry Banks of smooth *Panisus*
I might have sat, and heard the gentle Vows
Of some protesting Shepherd, uncontroul'd!
    Phila. 'Twas on those fatal Plains, I well remember,
That first your Eyes encounter'd with *Aristor's*.
    Amal. Yes, in a Chace we met, when Truce allow'd it, 10
Where the young Prince, whom I too much had mark'd
Thro' all the graceful Toils of that blest Day,
Redeem'd my Life, with Hazard of his own,
From the chas'd Boar, that now had almost seiz'd me.
    Phila. When I arriv'd the first of all your Train,
I heard you thank him for the gen'rous Rescue.
    Amal. I did; yes *Phila*, with my Heart I thank'd him,
And paid it down a Ransom for my Life:
Since when, how often in this Place we've met,
And with what Pleasure, thou alone can'st tell,   20
The only Friend, and witness of our Passion.
But, prithee go, and keep off all Intruders,   [*Exit* Phila.
Whilst with my Sorrows now I tread this Grove,
Which shou'd not thrive, when all our Hopes are blasted.
                          [*She walks into the Grove.*

From the other Door, the Fox *runs over the Stage, follow'd soon*
    after by Aristomenes, *his Hands foul with Earth.*
    Aristom. Farewell my wild Companion, and my Leader!
                          [*Pointing to the* Fox.
Henceforth thy figure, in my Ensigns borne,

Shall tell the World (if e'er I 'scape these Walls)
That 'twas thy Conduct drew me from my Bondage.
How fair this Grove appears to my loath'd Dungeon!
                              [He sees the Fountain.
Oh! welcome to my Sight, thou gentle Spring!   30
Ne'er did'st thou cool a Thirst, that rag'd like mine:
I bow my Knees upon thy mossy Brim,
              [He kneels and lays his Mouth to the Stream.
And, as they drank, ere Art had worsted Nature,
Draw thy refreshing Stream to my scorch'd Entrails.
                            [Drinks agen.
Again, O Nectar, most delicious!
This favour more, and then I quit thy Borders.
          [Washes the Earth off his Hands, and rises.

          Re-enter Amalintha

   Amal. Oh! 'tis all dismal, now that Love is absent,
Faded the Flow'rs, and with'ring ev'ry Branch:
Whilst thro' the Leaves the sad, and sighing Winds,
Methinks, all say, the Hours of Bliss are past;   40
And here, we ne'er shall meet each other more.
                      [Aristom. *comes towards her*
Ha! what Intruder do my Eyes behold?
A Stranger, and invade my private Walks,
The Doors too all secur'd! Tell how you came.
   Aristom. As comes the Mole, by painful working upwards,
Till the the sweet Air beat on my clammy Brows.
   Amal. There's something mystical in what you utter;
Which (tho' offended with your Presence here)
I wou'd be glad farther to have Unriddl'd.
                        [Draws her Dagger.
This be my Guard; and now you may proceed,   50
And, if you dare, discover who you are.
   Aristom. I'd not deny my Name, to 'scape that Dungeon,
                     [Pointing behind the Scenes.

From whence these Hands have dug my way to Light.
'Tis *Aristomenes* that stands before you.
  Amal. O blest and strange Surprise!   [*Aside·*
  Aristom. Now, if you have a Soul for noble Deeds,
As 'tis reported of you *Spartan* Ladies,
By my Escape your Fame shall rise so high,
That ne'er an ancient Heroes shall outsoar it:
If not, I know the Place from whence I came,   60
And 'twill be told with more uncommon Things,
Which shall make up the Story of my Fortunes,
That I alone liv'd to be there twice Bury'd. [*She looks about.*
Nay, look not round; for if you fear you wrong me,
I wou'd not injure you, to gain my Safety.
  Amal. Nor wou'd I fail to help you to secure it,
For all that *Lacedemon* holds most Precious.
I gaz'd about, lest any were in sight,
That might prevent my dear Design to save you.
Support me, as I walk, like one that serv'd me,   70
And when they have unlock'd that Postern-door,
I'll give you some Command before the Guard,
Which to perform they shall admit your Passage:
Or this must force it, if your evil Stars
                          [*Gives him her Dagger.*
Have plac'd such there, as know and wou'd detain you.
  Aristom. As long as Life, I'll proudly wear this Favour.
  Amal. Oh! haste, my Lord, lose not this precious moment.
  Aristom. No, stay; and ere I take one step tow'rds Free-
    dom,
Let me be told, to whose blest Aid I owe it;
And how I may discharge so vast a Debt: 80
Tho' I, and all that's dear to me shou'd perish,
I wou'd not stir, 'till satisfy'd in this.
  Amal. Know then, my Lord——
Tho' whilst I speak, I tremble for your Danger,

That to declare my Name, might work my Ruin:
But since such Gratitude crowns your great Virtues,
I have a Blessing to implore from you,
When the full Time shall ripen and reveal it;
Harder, I fear, to grant, and much more dear
Than what I now assist you to preserve.   90
   Aristom. By Liberty, which none like me can value,
By new-recovered Light, and what it shews me,
Your brighter Form, with yet a fairer Mind,
By all the ties of Honour, here I swear;
Be that untouch'd, and your Request is granted.
   Amal. Of you, my Lord, and of the list'ning Gods
I ask no more—but, that you haste to 'scape:
Without that Gate the open Champain lies.
May Fortune, which the hardest Part has done,
Crown her great Work, and lead you safely on!   100
                [*Exit* Aristom. *leading her.*
        Enter Phila *weeping.*
   Phila. What shall I say, or how reveal this to her?
Is't not enough, ye Gods, we bear our own,
That thus you suffer the vain trifler *Love*
To bring the Griefs of others too upon us!
        Amalintha *returns.*
   Amal. Oh! *Phila,* I such Tydings have to tell thee,
But thou hast chill'd them in a Moments space
With that cold dew that trickles from thine Eyes.
Is not *Aristor* safe?—
Thou say'st he is not, in that weeping silence:
But lives he yet? if this thou do'st not answer,   110
My Death shall free thee from all farther Questions.
   Phila. Yet he do's live:
But oh! that some free Tongue, that lov'd you less,
Cou'd tell how little time that Life must last
To you so precious, and I fear so fatal!

Amal. Go on; and if thou kill'st me with the Story,
Believe thou'st crown'd the Kindness of thy Life,
By giving endless Rest to her that wants it.
     Phila. I cannot speak——   [*Weeping.*
     Amal. Then one, that can, I instantly must seek for. 120
                                        [*Going out.*
     Phila. Publick Enquiry pulls his Ruin on her.
Stay, Madam, stay, and since it must be told,
Know that *Aristor*, soon as free to do it,
Again into your Father's presence rush'd,
And makes a new attempt upon his Person,
But miss'd his Blow, was seiz'd, and in Confinement
Now waits but the assembling of the Council,
Throughly to be examin'd, and discover'd.
     Amal. Darkness, and Night surround me.
With this Relief to my sad Bed I go,   130
                         [*Siezes* Phila's *Dagger.*
There wrapt in horrid Shades will lay me down,
And, when thou com'st charg'd with the heavy News,
Beware, no tedious Circumstance detain,
No fruitless Pray'r, or word of Comfort 'scape thee;
But with a Voice, such as the Dying use,
Bid me expire——
     ——Then to my Father go,
     And say, he kill'd his Daughter in his Foe;
     Who knowing, she his Temper cou'd not move,   140
     Th' excess of Hate paid with th' excess of Love.
                    [*Exit weeping and leaning on* Phila.

          The SCENE *changes to the Plains.*

               Enter Climander.

     Clim. All Patience this wou'd tire——
I will not wait the Trifler's slow return,
But go my self (tho' thus unarm'd) amongst them.
                    [*He is going and meets* Arcasius.

Art thou at length come back!
If 'twou'd not waste more time to blame thy stay,
Old loit'ring Man! I shou'd reprove thee for it.
   Arcas. 'Twas vain to move, 'till I had seen the utmost,
   Clim. The utmost! What was that, will they not Fight?
Not Dye for such a General!
   Arcas. My Lord, they will not—   10
Tho' brave *Alcander* tries to urge their Fury,
And wastes his own, to put new Life into them:
Sometimes he weeps, and throws his Helmet from him,
Kneels to his Troops, and wooes them to Compassion,
Which draws a gen'ral sympathizing Show'r,
And makes him think, he has obtain'd his Purpose:
Then on his fiery Steed in haste he leaps,
And cries, Come on; but not an Ensign waves,
Or any Motion seconds the Design.
The Meaner sort cry out aloud for Pay,   20
And mutiny to be discharg'd the Service.
   Clim. Base, mercenary Slaves! Yet these I'll use:
The Gold and Jewels which my Father gave,
Will fire their Souls, insensible of Duty;
And by it's aid, I'll gain what most I thirst for.
A king his Claim but to one Kingdom lays,
Wide as the Universe is boundless Praise.
This shining Mass shall buy a glorious Name,
They purchase all the World, who purchase Fame.
                                             [*He is going.*

   Arcas. Since you're determin'd to attempt these Dangers,
Let me declare the Time to be expir'd,   31
Which bound you in your Promise to your Father:
By Artifice I wrought you to believe
Those Days remain'd, which are indeed run out.
Your Soul may now be free, and Heaven protect you!
   Clim. For this discov'ry I'll return another

Worthy thy knowledge, when we meet again:
But now make haste, and from its deep concealment,
In the low Earth, fetch me the Wealth I mention'd.
About these Woods thy quick Return shall find me.   40
                                        [*Exeunt.*

Enter Herminia *and* Barina.

  Bar. See we are come to soon; I said 'twou'd prove so.
  Herm. It is no matter, long we shall not wait.

                          [Bar. *looks out for the Shepherds.*

I dare not tell her, that I like this Shepherd,
Nor yet indeed scarce own it to my self.
'Tis strange, my Mind shou'd sink thus with my Fortunes;
Yet he did talk above their humble strain,
And, as he knew that Nature had supply'd
What Fortune had deny'd him for Attraction,
Claim'd my weak Heart, and said he must possess it.
  Bar. Sure, they've put off this melancholy Meeting   50
Design'd in Honour of their lost Protector,
In which our share (tho' secret) must be greatest.
I see none move, nor hear their mournful Notes.
  Herm. Be not impatient: Where can we be better?
Have I not heard thee say sometimes, *Barina,*
That in a Dream, form'd by the Day's discourse
Of the sweet Life, that here they led in safety,
My Mother saw me wed one of these Swains,
And smil'd, tho' I had made a Choice below me?
  Bar. She did; and therefore never wou'd consent   60
That you, like others, shou'd behold their Revels:
Nor have I, since her Death left you my Charge,
Allow'd it, till worse Dangers forc'd us hither;
Tho' of myself, I ne'er observe such Trifles,
  Herm. D'ye call those nightly Visions then but Trifles?
  Bar. No doubt our Dreams are so; the work of Phancy,
Where things of Yesterday are odly piec'd

With what had pass'd some twenty Years before,
Knit in a weak and disproportion'd Chain,
Which cannot hold to lead us to the Future. 70
Whate'er I've said, I wish this had no meaning, [*Aside.*
And that some other Place cou'd give us shelter.
  Herm. We'll walk a while—
Great *Aristomenes*, now cou'd I meet thee!
But that's a Blessing which I must not know, [*Aside.*
'Till where thine is, my Spirit too shall go.
Oh! that my Grief wou'd force it to retire,
And Tears for him quench this new-kindl'd Fire!
                    [*They go off the Stage.*
        Enter at the other Door Climander.
  Clim. Either my Eyes, indulgent to my Love,
Deceive my Hopes; or now, within their reach 80
That unknown Beauty moves, which lately charm'd them.
'Tis she! and with the speed that suits my Passion,
I will o'ertake, and farther urge it to her. [*Exit.*
              Re-enter Herminia.
  Herm. She fears my Fate and fain wou'd have me go,
Before th' assembling Shepherds are arriv'd;
And having met one that can give her tydings,
Is busy to enquire about their coming.
Untimely Caution!—
              —'Tis too late to move,
When once o'ertaken by the wings of Love.
          Enter Climander *behind her.*
  Clim. From those fair Lips no sooner fell that word,
But all the neighb'ring Ecchoes caught the Sound, 91
And sent it doubl'd to *Climander's* Bosom:
The am'rous Streams have borne it down their Banks,
And the glad Plains breathe nothing, since, but Love.
Oh! speak it once again, and the fond Vine

Shall with a stricter grasp embrace the Elm,
Whilst joyful Birds shall hail it from the Branches.
   Herm. No; I have spoke too much—
Since on these Plains no syllable is secret.
Hereafter my close thoughts shall be confin'd,   100
And in this Breast lock'd up from all Men's Knowledge.
   Clim. Oh! not if Love be there; it cannot be:
Silence can ne'er last long, nor yet conceal it,
A thousand ways 'twill speak without a Voice,
And, whilst it struggles to obtain that Freedom,
Betraying Sighs will 'scape, and more declare it;
'Twill speak in list'ning to the Lover's Tale,
And say, 'tis Sympathy that makes it pleasant.
   Herm. He shakes my Soul, whilst thus he do's describe it:
For all he speaks I feel, and he must find.   [*Aside.* 110
Oh! yet, let me reflect upon my Birth,
And quit, in time, the Ground I can't maintain!
                                 [*She's going.*
   Clim. Nay, do not fly me, and I will be Speechless:
For if I speak, whilst on your Eyes I gaze,
It must be all of Love, and that offends you;
Yet since, perhaps, I ne'er may meet you more,
I wou'd have told the Story of my Heart,
And e'er it breaks, have mov'd you to Compassion.
   Herm. Meet him no more! then, what can Crowns afford
     me,
Amidst the noisie Pomp, that waits their Lustre?   120
Still shou'd I vainly listen for the Sound   [*Aside.*
Of such soft Words which charm my Sorrows from me.
Oh! that our Births were equal, as our Thoughts!
Yet I will pity him, and Fate be guilty.
                       [*She stops and turns towards him.*
   Clim. Blest be the Thought, that thus retards your steps,
And turns again those gentle Lights upon me!

If Pity 'twas; Oh! yet indulge that warmth,
And Love 'twill soon produce, to meet my Wishes.

[She looks kindly on him.

'Tis done, 'tis done! be witness ye still skies,
That all her Looks are calm, and smooth as yours,   130
And not one Frown forbids my forward Hopes:
Let this fair Hand be added to confirm them,
And ease the mighty longings of my Passion.

[Kneels and kisses her Hand.

Herm. Take, freely take this first and last of Favours.
Now, Shepherd rise, and hear what I've to say;
And if a Sigh mix with the fatal Sentence,
Believe, 'tis from the Grief, with which I give it.
You must not love me—   *[She sighs.*

Clim. I must not love you, tho' you Sigh to speak it!
Shou'd *Pan* pronounce it, in a Voice so loud   140
'Twou'd rive the knotty Oaks, that shade his Altars,
I wou'd to *Syrinxes* oppose your Beauties,
And ask the Gods, whose Loves had best Foundation?

Herm. Those Gods, who made our Births so disproportion'd,
Wou'd say, they ne'er design'd our Hands shou'd join.
But see! the Swains are gath'ring tow'rds this Place:
Yet, Shepherd, know, that if a Prince wou'd Love,
'Tis in your Form he must successful prove.

Enter Arcasius *with a Casket.*

Clim. Then in this happy Form, since you approve it,
Behold—   *[She interrupts him.* 150
Herm. No more! as you wou'd keep th' Esteem I've
shown you.   *[Exit.*
Clim. Another time must tell this Secret to her.
Th' Ambition of her Mind charms like her Person,   *[Aside.*
Nor can the Blood, that breeds such Thoughts be abject.

But welcome good *Arcasius* with that Bait,
Which shall be soon dispers'd among the Soldiers:
And if it win them to my great Design,
'Tis worth the Kingdoms which its Price might ransom.

           [Exeunt with the Casket follow'd by Arcasius.

         Enter Thæta *and* Lamia.

Lamia. The Dews are falling, and the Sun declin'd,
Whilst from this neighb'ring Grove are heard the Notes 160
Of that sweet Bird, that warbles to the Night,
Now telling us her Shadows are approaching:
And yet the tardy Shepherds are not come.

   Thæta. When all our Hours were gay, it was not thus:
But who can haste to break his chearful Pipe,
Tear the sweet Garland, made by her he sighs for,
And sing of Death, when Love is all his Passion?

   Lamia. Now thou dost talk of Love, yet ere we part,
Or fall into our melancholy Strains,
Lend to that Eccho, greedy of thy Voice,   170
Some moving Words, upon so soft a subject.

   Thæta. Rather that Song I'd chuse, which do's prefer
To all things else the Joys of these sweet Plains;
Since, now perhaps, we must too soon forsake them.

   Lamia. A better can't be chose; haste to perform it,
Lest the sad Ceremony break our purpose.

THE SONG.

(1.)

She Sings   A young Shepherd his Life,
           In soft Pleasure still leads,
        Tunes his Voice to his Reed,
           And makes Love in the Shades.   180
        To be Great, to be Wise,
           To be Rich, to be Proud,

To be loaded with Bus'ness
  Or lost in a Croud,
He ne'er seeks, or desires:
  Let but Silvia be won,
He is Great, he is Rich,
  And his Bus'ness is done.

(2.)

Whilst their Nymphs are as happy,
  As Happy as Fair;   190
For who has most Beauty,
  Has of Lovers most share.
Some will stay, some will fly,
  Some be false, some be true:
For the Lost we ne'er grieve,
  But still cherish the New.   [*Shouts.*
'Tis vain of their Frailties,
  Or Falshoods to mind 'em:
Mankind we must take,
  We must take, as we find 'em.   200

Thœta. What Shouts are these!   [*Shouts.*
Lamia. They're loud, and speak some Joy; and still
  repeated.
         Enter Herminia *and* Barina.
Lamia. Fair Stranger, know you whence these Shouts
  proceed?
Herm. I do not; but these coming, sure, can tell us.

Enter with great Signs of Joy Clinias *with other Shepherds and Shepherdesses, &c.*

Clim. Swell, swell, *Panisus*, o'er thy spacious Bounds,
Flow like our Joy, and chear the Meads about thee.
Pan, take in thankful Sacrifice; our Flocks,
And ev'ry rural Swain proclaim his Praises!
Lamia. Such Sounds, as these, meet with a gen'ral welcome:

But yet, the Cause we wish to hear explain'd. 210
Good *Clinias*, tell the Cause —
   Clin. He is return'd, and stands, like Fate, amongst 'em,
The Plain's Protector, and the Army's Genius,
The Virgin's Refuge, when the Town's in Flames,
And Shield to those whom Fortune makes his Vassals.
   Herm. 'Tis *Aristomenes* thou hast described:
No other e'er cou'd fill a Praise like this.
   Clin. 'Tis He indeed, next to the Gods, our Succour.
   Herm. Transporting News! how did the Army meet him?
   Clin. Just as a long stopt Current meets the Sea, 220
And rushes on, when once't has forced a Passage.
   2d Shep. Heav'n has their Plumes; for high as that they
     toss 'em:
And not a dusty Soldier in the Host,
That has not hugged him to his swarthy Bosom.
   Clin. No Voice is what it was an Hour ago;
And their hoarse Joy sounds like their distant Drums;
His Hands, as if the *Cretan* Thongs still held them,
Are useless made, and fetter'd now with Kisses;
Whilst neighing Steeds think that the War surrounds them,
And prance in Air light as their Master's Minds. 230
   2d Shep. How he escap'd, all ask in such Confusion,
That their loud Questions drive his Answers back,
And will not let them reach the nearest to him.
   Herm. It is enough, ye Powers that guard *Messenia!*
We now must change our Habits, and return. [*Aside to* Bar.
What did I say, return! O yes! I must,
And never hope to see *Climander* more: [*To herself.*
Yet will I give my Heart this last Relief
(Since Fate will have it bear th' unequal Passion)
To let him know my Love, and endless Flight, 240
And live on the dear Thought that he laments it.
                    [*Exit with* Bar.

Lam. Where is *Aristor?* Is he too return'd?
Clin. That question did the Gen'ral ask aloud;
And 'twas the only one that cou'd be heard:
But no reply was made; I think he is not.
Theata. Then we're but half restor'd—
For he so heavily will take that Loss,
Our Joys will not be long, nor he amongst us.
Lamia. Fear not the worst—
2d Shep. I met a rumour of a stranger Prince,   250
That with large Sums new fir'd the trembling Host,
And from the Camp had led on some Design
A Party, that for ·Wealth wou'd risque their Lives,
Tho' cold and dull to Thoughts of gen'rous Duty.
Clin. 'Tis true; of *Rhodes* they say,
And some I heard that call'd him *Demagetus.*
Thick flew his Gold, as swarms of Summer-Bees,
And 'twas to succor or revenge the Gen'ral.
He ask'd their Aid —
But whither he has led them, none can tell.   260
Ere *Aristomes* return'd, he went
And is not heard of since.
2d Shep. The Gen'ral's safe, and that 's enough for us:
Now therefore *Clinias*, you that guide our Sports,
Tell us what we're to do to shew our Joy.
Clin.   To Laugh, to Sing, to Dance, to Play,
          To rise with new appearing Day;
          And ere the Sun has kiss'd 'em dry,
          With various Rubans Nosegays tye.
          Deckt with Flow'rs and cloath'd in Green,   270
          Ev'ry Shepherdess be seen:
          Ev'ry Swain with Heart and Voice
          Meet him, meet him, and rejoice:
          With redoubl'd *Pæans* sing him,
          To the Plains, in Triumph bring him:

And let *Pan* and *Mars* agree,
That none's so kind and brave as He.   [*Exeunt.*

ACT IV   SCENE I

The General's Pavilion.

Enter Drest in the Habit of an Officer Demagetus *with* Arcasius.

Dema. Sh' has left the Plains, and is not to be found.
How cou'd'st thou bring this cruel Story to me,
Ere thou had'st search'd *Messenia*'s utmost Bound,
And travell'd o'er the spacious World of Shepherds?
She must be yet amongst their Shades conceal'd;
And thro' them will I pierce, like prying *Phœbus*,
To find my Love, or lose myself for ever.
    Arca. You will not hear (so much your Passion sways) ·
The Reasons, why I chose to see you first,
Ere I proceeded to pursue her Paths.   10
    Dema. There spoke the sixty Winters, that have froze
        thee,
And turn'd swift eager Love to Icy Reasons.
I must be Cold as thou art, if I hear thee,
Or lose one moment more in doating Questions. [*He's going.*
    Arca. Behold these Tokens, and let them retard you.
    Dema. Tokens of Love, sent to the fond *Climander.*
Oh! thou hast found a way indeed to stay me.
    Arca. Take that, to you directed;   [*A Letter.*
And 'twas my Hopes from thence of some discovery,
That kept me here 'till you had broke and read it.   20
    Dema. Then thou shalt hear it.   [*Reads the Direction.*
This to Climander *from the Nymph that leaves him
To everlasting Grief,* shou'd have been added,
For so 'twill prove, if no more Comfort's here. [*He reads it.*
        To love, yet from the Object fly,
        Harder is, than 'tis to Dye:

Yet, for ever I remove,
Yet, for ever will I love.
Shepherd, seek no more to find;
Fate, not I, has been Unkind. 30
We pluck on Fate. by striving to avoid it.
To shun the low Addresses of a Swain,
For ever has she left a Prince despairing.
Why didst thou not, as I at parting bid thee,
Find out, and let her know my fair Intentions,
And that my Birth was Noble as her Wishes?
   Arca. I was not negligent, nor wou'd be thought so:
But full of Transports when I heard your Story,
Thinking the Fates wou'd now fulfill their Promise
Thro' her the Daughter to the best of Men, 40
Fled to discover what you gave in Charge,
Travers'd the Plains in a long fruitless Search,
But cou'd not find that Beauty born to Bless us.
   Dema. I shew'd thee, as we pass'd, her new rais'd Hamlet.
   Arca. Thither at last I went, but Oh! too late:
For ere I reach'd it, the fair Guest was vanish'd;
Upon the Floor lay her neglected Hook,
And o'er the Door hung Boughs of fading Willow,
To shew, as Shepherds use, the Place forsaken.
That Paper there I found, and near it lay 50
This precious Gemm, that bears a well-cut Signet,
                       [Shews him a Ring.
By chance sure dropt, yet may assist your Purpose.
   Dema. Give me that Emblem of my fatal Passion:
For without End is that, as is this Circle.
Oh! that my way to Bliss shou'd seem so plain,
Yet in a moment thus be lost and wilder'd!
Now in the midst of Crouds and loud Applauses,
That greet me for restoring them *Aristor,*
Must wretched *Demagetus* sigh for Love,

And hang his drooping Head tho' wreathed with Laurels.

> [*A sound of Drums and Trumpets.*

But hark! the Gen'ral comes —
To him the Oracle I have reveal'd,
And all the Story of my rural Life.
I'll tell him too the Cause of my new Grief,
Which to relieve, I instantly must leave him.

A FLOURISH.

Enter Aristomenes, Aristor, Alcander, *and other Attendants.*

Aristom. Why, *Demagetus*, art thou from my Sight,
From these fond Arms, that ever thus would hold thee!

> [*Embracing him.*

Thou kind Restorer of my lov'd *Aristor.*
Come to the Camp, and hear them shout thy Name,
Whilst I declare thee equal in Command   70
With him, who owes his Life to thy young Valour.

Dema. Alas! my Lord —

Aristom. A Soldier sigh, when courting Fame attends him!
I know you Love, by your own kind Confession:
But that too must succeed, since now your Birth
Is known to answer all the great Desires,
Which, to my Wonder, did possess the Breast
Of that fair rural Maid, whose Beauty charm'd you.
We'll send, and with the Pomp that suits a Princess,
(Since such your gen'rous Passion means to make her)   80
Have her conducted to a rich Pavilion,
And join your Hands, as Heav'n has join'd your Hearts.
This, my *Aristor*, be your pleasing Task.

Enter an Attendant to Aristomenes.

Attend. The Princess is without, and waits your Pleasure.
Aristom. Conduct her in —
I sent for her, to see the generous Stranger.   [*To* Alcander.

Enter behind the Company Herminia *and* Barina.

Aristor. My Lord, what you command I take in charge.
[To Aristomenes.

Tell me, my best of Friends, the way to serve you.
[To Demagetus.

Dema. I know it not my self, and that's the Torture.
Hear me, my Lord, nor think my Sorrows light: 90
[To Aristomenes.

For Love, the only Comfort of fond Youth,
Is lost for ever to the poor *Climander*.

Herm. Climander —   [To Barina.

That Name and Voice bears down my fainting Spirits.
I shall be known, yet have not Strength to fly:
Where will this end, and where's *Herminia's* Honour.
[To herself.

Aristom. So sad a Pause still keeps us in Suspence:
Proceed, and if there's help on Earth, we'll find it.

Dema. At my return, made joyful by Success,
With hasty Steps, and in my Heart soft Wishes,   100
Love, and a thousand flatt'ring Expectations,
I fled the clam'rous Praise prepar'd to meet me,
And sought the Path that led to my Desires:
But ere I was advanc'd beyond the Camp,
The Voice of this Old Man
Cross'd my sad way, and cry'd, She's gone for ever.

Aristom. Perhaps 'tis some Mistake,
If other Proofs are wanting to confirm it.

Dema. Oh! far too many for *Climander's* Peace.
She own'd her Love, and with this Signet bound it,   110
And in the Folds of this dear Paper left
At once the tokens of my Joy and Ruin.
[Gives the Letter and Ring to Aristomenes.

Herm. The Character and Signet will betray me;
And now Necessity must make me Bold.   [*Aside.*

Oh! yet, ere you proceed to view that Paper,
[*She throws herself at* Aristomenes *Feet.*
(Wrapt in Confusion) hear your Daughter speak,
[*As he is opening the Letter.*
And pity in her Fate all Women's Frailty.

Aristom. Ha! Thou dost much surprize me; but go on,
And, 'till she has finish'd, let no Word be utter'd.

Dema. By all my fleeting Sorrows 'tis my Love: 120
Nor cou'd I, but to hear her speak, be Silent.   [*Aside.*

Aristom. Proceed, and 'bate those Tears, that stay thy
    Speech.

Herm. That I have stoop'd below the Blood you gave me,
And cast my doating Love upon that Shepherd,
(For such he is, altho' a Plume adorns him)
My wretched Hand, and now my Tongue confesses:
For by that Paper, indiscreetly penn'd,
The Secret wou'd be told, shou'd I conceal it.
But Oh! my Lord, since you can ne'er forgive me;
A sad Recluse for ever let me live,   130
Or Dye for Love, to do my Birth more Justice.

Aristom. Be comforted, and farther yet unfold
How first you came acquainted with this Shepherd.

Herm. To 'scape the Fury of prevailing Foes,
Disguised, I in your absence sought the Plains,
And in that Habit heard the pow'rful Sighs
Of one that knew not then his own Presumption.

Aristom. Were he a Prince, and still would urge his Suit
Wou'd'st thou receive 't, and bless the Pow'rs that sent him?

Herm. I shou'd not hide my Thoughts, or blush to own
    them.   140
Yes, I cou'd bless those Pow'rs which now undo me.
[Demagetus *comes forward.*

Demag. I cannot wait these Forms; Love plead my Pardon,

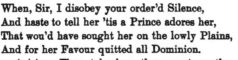

When, Sir, I disobey your order'd Silence,
And haste to tell her 'tis a Prince adores her,
That wou'd have sought her on the lowly Plains,
And for her Favour quitted all Dominion.

   Aristom. Then take her, thou most worthy Prince of
    Rhodes!   [*Giving her to him.*
And know, *Herminia*, to encrease thy Passion,
Thou hold'st that noble Hand, that sav'd thy Brother,
And gives thy Father in this new Alliance,
More Joy than when he first receiv'd and bless'd thee.   150

   Dema. Let all the Joys of Earth give place to mine,
Whilst in deep, silent Raptures I possess them:
                         [*Taking her from* Aristomenes.
For *Demagetus* is above Discourse,
And will not wrong his Love with faint Expressions.

   Herm. So let mine flow, and O *Barina*, see
I smiling give my Hand now to a Shepherd,
Yet fear not to offend my Mother's Ghost.

   Bar. No; that smiles too, and all that love and serve you.

   Arca. The Fate of *Rhodes* is clear and chearful now;
And old *Arcasius* has outliv'd his Cares.   160

   Aristor. Now as a Brother, take this new Embrace;
                         [*To* Demagetus.
Tho' all the Love, it shews, you had before.

   Aristom. Conduct her, *Demagetus*, to her Tent:
I'll soon be there, and see those Rites perform'd,
That shall confirm her Yours; be Kind and Happy.

    [*Exeunt* Herminia *and* Demagetus *leading her follow'd by*
    Arcasius, Barina *and others.* Aristor *is going too but is*
    call'd back by his Father.
Come back *Aristor*, and the rest withdraw:
For something I wou'd say to you in private.
                         [*The Attendants go off.*
Free from the Croud, and unobserv'd my Transports,

I wou'd embrace, and welcome thee to Life,
And with a loud repeated Blessing pay   170
The pious Care, that brought it to such Dangers.
Oh! that the Love of Women shou'd be thought
To pass the Fondness which a Father feels,
When thus he grasps a Son of thy Perfections,
                                    [*Embracing him.*
My Dear, my Lov'd *Aristor!*
    Aristor. My Prince, my Gen'ral, and the Best of Fathers!
    Aristom. Thy Heart speaks loud, and knocking at my
        Breast
Seems as 'twould close in conference with mine.
    Aristor. It would, my Lord, and strives to force its Passage.
            [Aristomenes *looses his Arms from embracing him.*
    Aristom. Oh, no my Son! for now I must be plain,   180
And tell thee, thou dost lock some Secret there
Which all my depth of Kindness ne'er could fathom:
I see it in the Cloud, that shades thy Brow.
And still thy pensive Eyes are downwards cast,
As thou wou'd'st seek the Grave, or something lower:
Long have I this observed —
And thought whole Nights away to find the Cause,
Which now, my Son, I urge thee to reveal:
And think that He who best can love thee asks it.
    Aristor. Oh! that you did not love, or would not ask it!
I cannot speak, for speaking must offend: 191
Yet shou'd my Silence grieve such mighty Goodness,
'Twou'd break that Heart, which thus you seek to succour.
Upon my Knees a strange Request I make,
            [*Offering to Kneel but his Father takes him up.*
That you would quite forget and think me Dead;
Which the approaching Battle shou'd confirm,
And leave you to possess your other Comforts.
    Aristom. My other Comforts! All are light to Thee:

And when I would have shar'd amongst my Race
Impartial Kindness, as their Birthrights claim'd,   200
Still to my Heart *Aristor* wou'd be nearest,
Still, with a Merit not to be withstood,
Wou'd press beyond my cool and equal Purpose,
And seize a double Portion of my Love:
And wilt thou lose it now, to keep thy Silence?
   Aristor. My Life I rather wou'd; but Oh! my Lord! [*Sighs.*
   Aristom. Another Sigh, another yet, my Son!
And then, let Words relieve this mighty Passion:
They will, they will; the Sweetness of thy Temper
Will melt before a just and warm Persuasion.   210
Now, let me know it —
   Aristor. Believe that if 'twere fit, it shou'd be told:
But Oh! my Lord, 'tis what you must not know.
   Aristom. Not I, *Aristor!* if thy Soul were bare
As is thy faded Cheek now to thy Father,
It were most fit—
Oh! think, my Son, who 'twas that made it Noble,
And train'd it in the Paths of Truth and Honour:
Else, what had hinder'd, but thou might'st have been
(In spite of all the Virtues with thee born,   220
For Education is the stronger Nature)
A bragging Coward, or a base Detractor,
A Slave to Wealth, or false to Faith or Friendship
Lull'd in the common Arms of some Seducer,
And lost to all the Joys of Virtuous Love.
   Aristor. Ha! Virtuous Love!
   Aristom. What, dost thou start? why, so I meant thou
    shou'dst.
When hastily I press'd that Word upon thee,
To catch that flushing Witness in thy Face,
Was all this Bait contriv'd; no more, my Son,   230
No more dissembling of a Truth so plain:

I see 'tis Love, the best of all our Passions.
And fram'd like Thee; sure none cou'd e'er Despair,
Nor can I fear thou'd'st make a vulgar Choice.

 Aristor. On *Ida*'s Top not *Paris* made a nobler,
When of three Goddesses he chose the Fairest.

 Aristom. Will she not hear thy Love?

 Aristor. Oh yes! with all the softness of her Sex,
And answers it with Vows, more strong than Ours.

 Aristom. If thus it be, what hast thou then to fear? 240

 Aristor. A Father's Wrath, more dreadful to *Aristor*
Than is the frown of *Jove*, that shakes the Poles,
And makes the Gods forget they are Immortal.

 Aristom. Thou wrong'st my Love in that mistaken Terror.
By all those Powers I swear, I will not cross thee;
Be she a *Spartan* Dame, 'bate me but One,
And tho' a Foe, I yield thou shou'd'st possess her.

 Aristor. I dare not ask; my trembling Love forbids it.
Who is that One, so fatally excepted?

 Aristom. Then, I'll by telling thee prevent that Trouble.
It is the Tyrant *Anaxander*'s Daughter,   251
Whom, tho' I ne'er beheld, I must abhor,
As borrowing her Blood from such a Fountain.

 Aristor. Take mine, my Lord, then to wash out that
  Stain   [*Offers his Breast.*
You'll think it has contracted by her Love:
For 'tis that Tyrant's Daughter I adore,
And ne'er, while Life is here, will change my Purpose.

 Aristom. Confusion seize those Words, and Her that caus'd
  'em!
Not Groans of Earthquakes, or the Burst of Thunder,
The Voice of Storms urging the dang'rous Billows, 260
E'er struck the Sense with sounds of so much Horror.
It must not, Oh! it must not, shall not be:
Sooner this Dagger, tho' my Soul lives in thee,
      [*Drawing* Amalintha's *Dagger.*

Shou'd let out thine with this prepost'rous Passion,
Than I wou'd yield, it e'er shou'd meet Success.

Aristor. Of all the Instruments by *Aulcan* form'd,
That Poinard best is fitted to my Heart,
Since Her's it was, whose Eyes have deeper pierc'd it:
Quickly, my Lord, let me receive it here,
And see me proud in Death to wear that Favour.   270

> [Aristomenes *amaz'd looks on the Dagger, and speaks to
> himself.*

Aristom This Dagger Her's, this *Anaxander's* Daughter's!
Fate then is practicing upon my Soul
What sudden Turns and Tryals Man can bear.

Aristor. Oh! do not pause—
Lest fainting with the Weight of what I feel,
I poorly fall, unlike your Son or Soldier.

Aristom. If this were Her's, Her's were the grateful Vows,
With which I rashly charg'd the Life she gave me.

> [*Still to himself.*

Aristor. Ha! not a Look, not one sad parting Word!
Then my own Hand thus sets me free for ever.   280

> [*Offers to Stab himself, but is stay'd by* Aristomenes.

Aristom. Hold! by Love and Duty yet a moment hold!

Aristor. My Life they've sway'd, and must command a
   Moment
But let it not exceed, lest both I cancel,
And only listen to my wild Despair.

Aristom. Shall I perform them? shall I hear her plead?
And to a Woman's Claim resign my Vengeance?
No; let my Ear still fly the fatal Suit,
And from her Tears be turn'd my harden'd Face.
What did I say! a hasty Blush has seized it,
For but imagining a Thing so vile.   290
Turn back my Face from Her that shunn'd not mine,
When it was Death to know, and to preserve me!

No; let the Fiends be obstinate in Ill,
Revenge be their's, while Godlike Man is grateful.

Enter an Attendant.

Attend. Pardon, my gracious Lord, this bold Intrusion.
Two Ladies veil'd, escaping from *Phœrea,*
Ask with such earnestness for Prince *Aristor,*
That, sure, their Bus'ness is of mighty Moment.
From one this Ring at her entreaty, Sir, I must deliver.
                    Gives it to Aristor *and Exit.*

Aristom. Retire, and if not call'd, return no more.   300
Aristor. 'Tis *Amalintha's* Ring, my *Amalintha's:*
She's come in time, to see me fall her Victim.
Aristom. No; to receive her from my Hand, my Son;
Since 'twas from her's, I took this healing Weapon,
That has cut off the Hate in which I held her.
'Twas she that met me rising from my Grave,
And fearless freed the Foe to her and *Sparta:*
Then in a grateful Promise was I bound
Not to deny whate'er she shou'd request;
And sure thy Love, before the Pomp of Crowns,   310
Is what a Maid must ask, that knows its Value.
Aristor. The Transports of my Soul be thus exprest;
Then let me Dye, for having griev'd such Goodness.
                    [*Embracing his Father's Knees.*

Aristom. No; rise my Son, go meet and chear thy Love,
And to this Tent conduct the Royal Maid,
Whilst in that inner Part I stand conceal'd,
And hear her tell why thus she comes to seek us:
Thence will I issue, as occasion calls,
And giving thee, give all I hold most precious.
            [*He goes into the inner Tent.* Aristor *goes out at the other
            Door and re-enters immediately leading* Amalintha *veil'd
            follow'd by* Phila.

Aristor. Dismiss that Cloud, and with it all your Fears,
Safe in this Camp, and in *Aristor's* Love,   321

Which ne'er was truly bless'd, 'till this glad Moment.
Now *Amalintha*, let my Joys o'erflow;
And ere I ask what brought thee to my sight,
Let it be filled with thy amazing Beauties,
And with this Hand my longing Lips be clos'd.

[Kisses her Hand.

   Amal. Thus, after each short absence, may we meet,
Thus pleas'd, thus wrapt in Love, thus dying fond.
But Oh *Aristor!* since I last beheld you,
So has this Life been threaten'd by the Fates,   330
That to your Arms 'tis forc'd for Peace and Safety.

   Aristor. Still may they prove a Haven for my Love,
Too strong for all the Shocks of rig'rous Fortune.
But what beneath thy Father's Roof cou'd fright thee?
Or what bold Danger break thro' his Protection?

   Amal. 'Twas from Himself, and all the Lords of *Sparta*.
When *Aristomenes* they found escap'd,
High was their Rage as Billows in a Tempest;
And all the Arts of State were put in use
To find who had assisted in his Flight: 340
But still in vain, 'till subtle, vile *Clarinthus—*

   Aristor. That Villain will be first in Blood and Mischief.
But cou'd he pry into thy generous Heart,
And find it there, that you had nobly done it?
And are not secret Thoughts secure against him?

   Amal. I did believe them so, 'till he disprov'd it:
For 'twas his Counsel, when all others fail'd,
To know by speaking Gods the deep Contrivance;
And from the Oracle, in some few Moments,
The full Discov'ry will have reach'd *Phœrea.*   350
Which ere it does, I was advis'd to leave,
By one that heard the horrid Voice accuse me,
And with a Speed unmark'd outflew the rest.

   Aristor. As swiftly may the bounteous Gods reward him.

Amal. This, my *Aristor*, brings me to your Tents,
But not to save my Life, or 'scape their Fury:
For shou'd your Heart, which boldly I will claim,
Be yet deny'd me by your injur'd Father,
Not all his Army shou'd retard my Steps
From leading to the Town, and certain Ruin;   360
For they have sworn it (with this Imprecation,
That 'till 'tis done, no Victory may bless them)
To sacrifice the Soul that sav'd the Gen'ral.

Enter Aristomenes *from the inward Tent.*

Aristom. That Army you have nam'd, shall first in Flames
Consume the utmost Town of *Lacedemon.*
Take your Security, and softest Wishes,
Your dear *Aristor* take, and if ought more
The fair Preserver of his Father claims,
Be it but nam'd, and at that instant granted.

Amal. Beyond *Aristor's* Heart there's no Request,   370
No longing Thought, no Hope for *Amalintha:*
For still his Love prescrib'd their tender Limits.

Aristor. Oh! let it not be thought irrev'rent Passion,
If in the awful Presence of a Father
I run upon my Joys, and grasp 'em thus.   [*Embraces her.*

Aristom. Thou well dost intimate I shou'd retire;
For Privacy is only fit for Lovers.

Aristor. Pardon my Transport, Sir, nor thus mistake it.

Aristom. No more, my Son! but when the Trumpet calls,
Which must be soon, remember thou'rt a Soldier,   380
And that the Battle, we shall lead to morrow,
Will ask our best of Care and Preparation.

Aristor. Never was I yet wanting to my Charge.
But give me leave here to attend that Summons.
                                    [*Exit* Aristomenes.
For Oh! my *Amalintha,* since thou'rt mine,
Since I can tell my Heart that darling Truth;

The Moments that must take me from thy sight,
Will pass for lost, and useless to *Aristor*.
And this War done, which we now soon shall finish
(For You not there, what God will fight for *Sparta?*)   390
I'll swear the Sun and radiant Light shall part,
Ere I will once be found from this lov'd Presence.

Amal. Confirm it, all ye soft and gentle Pow'rs!
And let the pattern of a Love so perfect
Reform Mankind, and bless believing Women.
But can I think it is *Aristor* speaks?
That I behold, and hear you safe from Danger,
Whom late I saw assaulted so with Death,
When from the Guard a Weapon you had snatched,
And but that brave Swords length cou'd keep him from you?
Hope and fond Expectation all had left me: 401
Arm'd with this Dagger full I stood in vain,
And from my Window watch'd the fatal Stroke,
Which soon was to be copy'd on my Heart;
Then, had I meant to own your noble Love,
And told mine Dying, whilst the Croud had trembl'd.

Aristor. I saw your dire Intent, and that preserv'd me:
For 'twas to stop your Arm, that mine perform'd
What else had been above the Force of Nature;
And when the Drums of *Demagetus* thunder'd,   410
As thro' the shiver'd Gates he rush'd to save me,
You may remember, that I wou'd not meet him,
Till I had told my Love what meant the Tumult,
Which since has given me Fears, cold as pale Death,
Lest some Observer might have charg'd it on you.

                                    [*Trumpets sound.*

Amal. No; for too much their own Concern engag'd them.
But Oh! already hark! the Trumpet calls,
And jealous Fame no longer lets me keep you.
Must you be gone, must you obey this Summons?

Aristor. Oh! yes, I must; it is the Voice of Honour. 420
Yet, do not weep—
Be this Embrace the Earnest of a Thousand.
Now let me lead you to *Herminia's* Tent·
Then think, I go more to secure your Charms,
And fight to rest with Peace in these fair Arms.

[*He leads her off.*

ACT V SCENE I

The SCENE is the Camp. A Noise of Drums and Trumpets.
Enter Aristomenes, Aristor, Demagetus, Alcander, several
Officers and Soldiers.

Enter an Officer from the other Door, and speaks to the General.

Officer. My Lord! I'm from *Alcander* bid to say,
The Battle he has marshall'd as you order'd;
And that your Presence now is only wanted.
    Aristom. Tell him we come; and let the Drums beat higher.
Now, my brave Followers, be your selves to Day,
And more I need not ask, that know your Valour;
Who've seen you at the backs of *Spartans* ride,
Till their long Flight, and not your Conquest, tir'd you.

[*The Soldiers shout.*

And Oh! my Sons, since they who bravely seek it,
May meet with Death, when all his Darts are flying,   10
Let me Embrace, and breathe my Blessings on ye.

[*Embraces* Demagetus.

Yet, *Demagetus*, if I 'scape him now,
And Victory attends my great Endeavour,
Thou shalt Triumphant lead me into *Rhodes*,
Where we'll obey the Gods, and save thy Country.
    Dem. Still you're the Best of Men, as they declared you.
    Aristom. Now let me fold thee thus, my Life's best Treasure!

[*He embraces* Aristor, *but seems disorder'd, and not to feel him in*
his Arms, which he often clasps about him.

Thou dost not fill my Arms, 'tis Air I grasp:
Nor do my Eyes behold thee—
Where is my Son, ha! where is my *Aristor?*   20
   Aristor. Here my dear Lord, here pressing to your Bosom.
[*His Voice seems to* Aristomenes (*still under his disorder*) *to be
   low and different to what it was usually.*
   Aristom. From what far distant Valley comes thy Voice?
It sounds so hollow, scarce my Ear receives it.
   Aristor. What means my noble Father!
   Aristom. Till now, my faithful Senses never fail'd me.
They talk of Omens, ha! I must not think on't;
Such chilling Damps would blast a Day of Battle: [*Aside.*
Yet let my evil Genius but be true,
And a fam'd End is all it can portend me.
   Aristor. You reason with your self, and turn from us. 30
May we not know what thus disturbs your Thoughts?
   Aristom. Nothing—a Vapour crossed me, but 'tis gone:
And now the Field, the dusty Field, my Sons,
Must be the Scene, where we shall nobly act
What our great Spirits, and our Country urges.
The Trumpet calls, with the impatient Drum;
And He that loves his Honour, let him come.
[*He draws his Sword and goes off followed by the rest with their
   Swords drawn, Drums and Shouts of Battle immediately suc-
   ceed.*

   *The Noise continues, the SCENE changes to a fine Tent.
   Enter* Amalintha *followed by* Phila.
   Amal. Not yet enough! when will this Discord end!
Is there no happy Land,
Where only Love, and its kind Laws prevail?
Where the false Trumpet flatters not to Death,
Nor the more noisy Drum outcries the Dying?
Oh! *Phila,* why shou'd Men with Hearts unmov'd
Seek the bold War, and leave ours trembling for them?

Now whilst I speak, a chilling Fear surrounds me;
And ev'ry Tread I hear, is hast'ning on,
Methinks, to tell me, all my Hopes are perish'd.   10
  Phila. Why shou'd you, Madam, who have pass'd already,
Unhurt by Fortune, thro' more threat'ning Dangers,
Now faint, when Reason bids you think the best?
The Sound goes from us, and the lucky War
(Since you've the Promise of your Father's Life)
Proceeds, as we cou'd wish, for the *Messenians.*
  Amal. So do's it seem; but yet my failing Spirits
Sink to my Heart, and bid it think of Ruin.
Last Night my Dreams shew'd me *Aristor* bleeding;
And o'er my Head a screaming Voice proclaim'd   20
That *Amalintha's* hasty Fate had kill'd him:
I clos'd my Eyes to catch another Vision,
That might interpret, or prevent the first;
But all in vain, no Help or Comfort found me,
And wrapt in Fears, I wak'd and still continue
For what's foretold so fatal to my Love.
  Phila. Your Fate work his? it rather will protect him.
But here come Tydings, and the Bearer smiles;
Good let them be, and these vain Fears will vanish.

Enter an Officer.

  Amal. From Prince *Aristor?* Do's he live, and send you?
  Officer. Madam he does—   31
And bids me say, what I my self can witness,
That *Lacedemon's* Battle breaks to pieces,
And soon will give him leave to find you here.
  Amal. Take this, and wear it, Soldier, for your News;
[*Gives him a Jewel.*
And may your Honours still outshine its Lustre.
Stay here, whilst I report this to *Herminia,*
If *Demagetus* too be yet in safety.

Officer. He is; and near *Aristor* did I leave him.

Amal. Come with me *Phila;* yet my Heart is heavy,   40
And wou'd be forcing Tears to my sad Eyes:
But I'll repel them with this welcome Message,
And put on all the smiles of Love to meet him.

       [*Exit with* Phila *into the Tent.*

Officer. The Centinels have all forsook the Tents,
In hopes to share the Plunder of the Foe,
Finding by their retiring we prevail:
But I'll report it loudly to the General.
Oh! here are some returning; are they *Messenians?*
They wear the Habit, yet no Face I know;
Their Haste and Looks do seem to point at Mischief: 50
I will conceal my self, and watch their Purpose.

       [*He conceals himself.*

Enter Clarinthus *with others disguis'd like* Messenian *Soldiers.*

 Clar. You heard the King, and the chief Lords of
   Sparta
Wish, that no Victory might bless our Arms,
Till we had sacrificed the Traytor's Life,
That freed this Lyon, which devours us all.

 Sold. We did, we did—

 Clar. You've also heard, 'twas *Amalintha's* Action.

 Sold. Yes, and the King then said, his Vow shou'd stand:
And she had Dy'd, I think, had she not fled for't.

 Clar. 'Tis true; therefore when I reflected on our Curse,
And saw that Conquest wou'd no more attend us   61
Till we perform'd what to the Gods we swore,
I mov'd the King—
To let me with your Aid attempt the Camp,
Which if I found unguarded,
I would to *Sparta* soon convey the Traytress,
Where she should meet the Rigour of the Law.

These are the Royal Tents, where she must be;
Therefore no more remains, but to secure her.
[They follow him into the inner Tent and the conceal'd Officer
comes out.

Officer. Curst Conspiration, not to be prevented   70
With but my single Arm against their Numbers!
But to the Battle, and *Aristor's* Ear I'll fly for Help;
That may o'ertake, and cross the bloody Purpose. *[Exit.*

The Women shriek in the inner Tent, and Re-enter Clarintha
&c. leading in Amalintha and Phila.

Amal. *Messenians* are ye, and yet treat me thus!
Restrain those Hands, that gave your Gen'ral to you.
Let me but hear you speak, and name the Cause;
Which, if a just one, I'll submit to Fortune.
    Clar. 'Tis but too just, and do's not ask explaining.
    Amal. Oh! now *Clarinthus* in your Voice I read
The cruel Sentence of an angry Father.   80
Turn not away that Face, but hear your Princess;
I can't resist, no Force, no Help is near me:
Therefore command, that but my Arms be freed,
And let me not be dragg'd, where I must follow.
    Clar. Will you, relying then on me for Safety,
Forbear to cry for Help, as we conduct you?
    Amal. By *Castor's* Soul I swear it.
    Clar. Then taking first her Dagger, free her Arms.
Give me your Hand, and now perform your Promise,
To follow where I'll lead you—   90
[Just as Clarinthus is offering to take her Hand, she snatches
Phila's Dagger, and then answers Clarinthus.

    Amal. No, stay *Clarinthus;* that I did not Promise.
My Voice, and not my Feet, my Word engag'd;
And whilst my Hand holds this, I will not follow.
    Clar. So swift and subtle? yet disarm and take her.

Amal. Hear me but speak, *Clarinthus:*
My Father's Life already I've secur'd;
And if you yet will quit this dang'rous Purpose,
Yours with Rewards, as great as your Desires,
Shall too be given you, and all Wrongs lie bury'd.

Clar. More than I love Rewards, I hate *Messenia;* 100
Therefore alive or dead will bear you from 'em.

[*He offers to sieze her, she keeping him off with her Dagger
    kneels.*

Amal. Oh! Pity yet my Youth, and wretched Fortunes:
A Princess at your Feet behold in Tears,
And Spare the Blood, the Royal Blood of *Sparta.*

Clar. Yes, and be lost our selves to save a Trayt'ress?
For, such you've been to that high Blood you've boasted.
I will not spare nor pity, but thus seize you.

[*He wrests the Dagger from her, she rises hastily and follow'd by
    Phila escapes into the Tent,* Clarinthus *pursues her, and
    immediately the Cries of Women are heard.*

Enter at the other Door Aristor *and Soldiers.*

Aristor. Oh! we are come in time. Detested Villains,
Your Deaths are all that you shall meet with here.

[*They fight.*

Re-enter Clarinthus.

Clar. The Victim's struck which could not be borne off.
Now my next Task 111
Must be to rescue those, who shar'd the Danger.

[*He runs at* Aristor, *who kills him, he speaks falling.*

Thou'st kill'd *Clarinthus;* And
The Fiends reward thee.

Aristor. Dye; and those Fiends thou call'st on meet thy
    Spirit.
I askt but that, to crown the War we've ended.

[*He and his Men fall on the rest, fighting off the Stage.*

Enter Amalintha *wounded and supported by* Phila.

Amal. Phila thy Hand; help me to reach that Couch,
The dying Bed of wretched *Amalintha!*
Nay do not weep, since 'tis the Fate's Decree,
Who let one luckless Moment interpose   120
Betwixt *Aristor's* coming, and my Ruin.
Here, set me down; and let this last Embrace   [*Sits down.*
Reward the Cares and Fears, my Life has cost thee.
Now leave me, *Phila,* to perform a Part
Which must not be prevented by thy Tears.
   Phila. Thus pale, thus faint, thus dying must I leave you!
   Amal. Yes; if thou wilt obey, thou must retire.
But be not far, and when thou seest me fall'n
Dead in *Aristor's* Arms, who'll soon return,
Come forth, and tell him 'twas my last Request   130
(By all our Love, by all our Sighs and Sorrows,
By our new Vows, and swiftly faded Joys)
That He wou'd yet survive his *Amalintha;*
Nor let my fatal Vision prove a Truth,
That 'twas my Fate, my hasty Fate that kill'd him.
   Phila. Let me but stay, at least 'till he's arriv'd.
   Amal. 'Twou'd cross my Purpose, hark! I hear him
     coming.
Quickly retire and let me hide this Stream,
Lest he shou'd swell it with a Flood of Tears,
And waste in Grief my small remaining Life,   140
Which I design to lavish out in Love.
   [Phila *goes off.* Amalintha *pulls her Garment over her Wound.*
About him let my dying Arms be thrown,
Whilst I deny my parting Life one Groan.
My failing Breath shall in soft Sighs expire,
And tender Words spend my last vital Fire;
That of my Death Men this Account may give,
She ceas'd to Love, as others cease to Live.

Enter Aristor *hastily, and sits down by her.*

Aristor. How fares my Love? sink not beneath your Fears,
When this most lucky Hand has made them groundless,
Securing to my Life its greatest Blessing,   150
Your matchless Love and all its dying Transports.

Amal. Its dying Transports, did you say *Aristor?*
I would be glad to know, that Death has Transports.
But are there none, none that do live and Love?
That early meet, and in the Spring of Youth,
Uncross'd, nor troubl'd in the soft Design,
Set sweetly out, and travel on to Age
In mutual Joys, that with themselves expire?

Aristor. Indeed, there are but few, that are thus Happy.
But since our Lot it is, t'encrease the number;   160
Let us not lose a Thought on other's Fortunes,
But keep them still employ'd upon our own;
For in no Hearts, sure, Love e'er wrought more Wonders.

Amal. Oh! no, to mine I gladly did admit it
Thro' the stern hazards of a Father's Wrath,
And all the Hate of *Sparta* and *Messenia.*
If e'er I wept, 'twas Love that forc'd the Dew,
And not my Country, or my colder Friendships;
And on my Face (when *Lacedemon* mourn'd)
Suspected Smiles were seen to mock her Losses;   170
Because that Love was on the adverse Party.
Thus fond, thus doating have I pass'd my Hours,
And with their dear remembrance will I close
My Life's last Scene, and grasp you thus in Dying.
                                        [*She embraces him.*

Aristor. Far be that Hour; but Oh! my *Amalintha,*
Proceed thus to describe thy tender Soul,
And charm me with thy mighty Sense of Passion;
For know, 'twas that which fix'd me ever thine,
When with a Pleasure, not to be express'd,

I found no Language of my Love escap'd thee,　　　180
Tho' wrapped in Myst'ry to delude the Croud;
When ev'ry longing Look cou'd raise a Blush,
And every Sigh I breath'd heave this lov'd Bosom,
Which held such soft Intelligence with mine,
And now o'erflows with a like Tide of Pleasure.
　　Amal. Oh! yes, it do's; it meets the vast Delight,
And takes the Thought ev'n of *Elysium* from me.
Nor will I, as some peevish Beauty might,
Take light offence, that mine you did not mention;
Since 'tis my equalling *Aristor's* Love　　　190
Is all the Charm, I wou'd be proud to boast of.
　　Aristor. Believe not, that I slighted such Perfections.
I saw you Fair, beyond the Fame of *Helen;*
But Beauty's vain, and fond of new Applause,
Leaving the last Adorer in Despair
At his approach, who can but praise it better:
Whilst Love, *Narcissus*-like, courts his Reflection,
And seeks itself, gazing on other's Eyes.
When this I found in yours, it bred that Passion,
Which Time, nor Age, nor Death, shall e'er diminish.　200
　　Amal. For Time, or Age, I think not of their Power.
But, after Death, *Aristor,* cou'd you love me,
Still call to me your Thoughts, when so far absent,
And mourn me sleeping in that Rival's Arms?
　　Aristor. Yes; if I cou'd outlive my *Amalintha,*
Still shou'd I turn my Eyes to that cold Grave,
Still love thee there, and wish to lie as low.
But why do's ev'ry Period of thy Speech
Thus sadly close with that too mournful Subject?
Why, now I press this Question, dost thou weep,　　210
Yet in my Bosom strive to hide thy Tears?
Paleness is on thy Cheek, and thy damp Brow
Strikes to my Heart such sympathizing Cold,

As quenches all its Fire, but that of Love.
Oh! speak my Life, my Soul, my *Amalintha;*
Speak, and prevent the boding Fears that tell me
Eternal Separation is at hand,
And after this, I ne'er shall clasp thee more.

                  [Embraces her, and she starts and groans.

  Amal. Oh! O', O', O'.

  Aristor. Nay, if the gentle foldings of my Love,   220
The tender circling of these Arms can wound,
'Tis sure some inward Anguish do's oppress thee,
Which too unkindly thou wilt still keep secret.

  Amal. Secret it shou'd have been, 'till Death had seal'd it;
Had not that Groan, and my weak Tears betray'd me:

                       [Speaks faintly.

For Death, which from *Clarinthus* I receiv'd.
Is come to snatch my Soul from these Embraces.

  Aristor. Oh fatal sound! but let me not suppose it,
Till Art is weary'd for thy Preservation.
Haste to procure it *Phila:* all that hear me   230
Fly to her Aid; or you more speedy Gods
The Cure be yours, and Hecatombs attend you.
But none approach; then let me haste to bring it,
Tho' thus to leave her is an equal Danger.

                    [Endeavours to go.

  Amal. Aristor stay; nor let my closing Eyes
One Moment lose the Sight that ever charm'd them.
No Art can bring relief; and melting Life
But lingers till my Soul receives th' Impression
Of that lov'd Form, which ever shall be lasting,
Tho' in new Worlds, new Objects wou'd efface it.   240

  Aristor. No, *Amalintha;* if it must be so,
Together we'll expire, and trace those Worlds,
As fond, and as united as before:
For know, my Love the Sword of War has reach'd me;

And none wou'd I permit to bind the Wound,
Till to thy gentle Hand I cou'd reveal it.
The Blood uncheck'd shall now profusely flow,
And Art be scorn'd, that cou'd but half restore me.
   Amal. Oh! let me plead in Death against that Purpose,
Employ my Hand, yet warm, to close the Wound,   250
And with my suppling Tears disperse the Anguish.
Your Country asks your stay, and more your Father:
This Blood is his, ally'd to all his Virtues,
By him more priz'd, than what supports his Frame,
Nor shou'd be lavish'd thus without his Licence.
Oh! *Aristomenes* haste to preserve it,
Since Life from me departs, and Love is useless
Aristor—   *[She Dies.*
   Aristor. Her fleeting Breath has borne far hence my
       Name:
But soon my following Spirit shall o'ertake her.   260
My Godlike Father gave her to my Arms,
And then resign'd to her more powerful Claim
This purple Stream, which wafts me to possess her.
May every Power, that shields paternal Goodness,
Enfold his Person, and support his Sway:
His dear remembrance take these parting drops,   *[He weeps.*
And then be free, my Soul, for ties more lasting,
Eternal Love, the faithful Lovers due,
In those blest Fields, which stand display'd before me.
My *Amalintha*—   *[He takes her in his Arms and dies.* 270

Enter Phila.

   Phila. I shou'd have come, and urg'd his Preservation,
If when I saw her fall my Strength had served me:
But all my Cares departed with her Life,
And mine I hope is now for ever going.
                [She falls in a swoon at Amalintha's *feet.*

Shouts of Victory. Enter Demagetus, Arcasius, Alcander, *and several officers, their Swords drawn as coming from Battle.*

Demag. A glorious Day, and warmly was it fought:
Nor ever did a Victory more complete
Stoop to the General's Valour—
Some Troops are order'd to secure *Phærea;*
And with to-morrow's Sun he enters there
To take the Homage of the conquer'd *Spartans.* 280
    Alcand. They say, that *Anaxander* he has freed
As generously, as he'd ne'er known the Dungeon.
    Demag. He did, at Prince *Aristor's* kind Request;
And now, with the high Marks of Conquest crown'd
Is coming to declare to *Amalintha*
That all her Wishes, and her Fears are ended.
            [Turning to go into the Tent, he sees the Bodies.
They are, indeed; for ever, ever ended.
Oh! turn and see where that pale Beauty lies,
And faithful, dead *Aristor,* bleeding by her!
    Alcand. O sudden Horror! where's our Conquest now,
Our lofty Boasts, and brave expected Triumphs? 291
Lie there, my Sword, beneath my Leader's Feet;
            [Lays his Sword at Aristor's *Feet.*
For under him I fought, and now weep for him.
    Dema. We'll all join to encrease the mournful Shower.
A Soldier for a Soldier's Fall may weep,
And shed these Drops without unmanly Weakness.
            [A Sound of Trumpets.
But hark! the Gen'ral, how shall we receive him?
Awhile we'll with our Bodies shade this Prospect,
And tell him by our Looks, some Grief attends him;
Lest all his Fortitude shou'd not support 300
A Change so sudden in his wretched Fortune.
Nor can we learn from whence this Loss proceeds.

Phila. Yes, that you may from me: Life yet remains,
And will admit of the too dire Relation.

    Demag. Then gently bear her hence, and hear it from her;
                             [They lead off Phila.
That when the Sorrow, which at first must bar
All cold Enquiries, shall awhile be past,
The Gen'ral may be told to what he owes it.
But see! he enters; be we Sad and Silent:
For Oh! too soon this fading Joy must vanish.   310
            [They stand all together before the Bodies.

  A FLOURISH *of Drums and Trumpets, with Shouts of Joy.*

Enter several Officers and Soldiers, the Shepherds and Shepherd-
    esses strewing flowers, followed by Aristomenes *his Sword*
    drawn in his Hand, and a Wreath of Victory on his Head.

    Aristom. Enough my Friends! enough my Fellow-Soldiers!
And you kind Shepherds, and your gentle Nymphs,
Receive my Thanks for the Perfumes you scatter,
Which yet shall flourish under our Protection.

    Shepherds, &c. Great *Aristomenes!* Live long and happy!

    Others. Live long and happy, Father of *Messenia!*

    Aristom. Now to fair *Amalintha* wou'd I speak
The joyful Tydings of this Day's Atchievements:
Therefore let her be told, we wish her Presence.
                            [Seeing none move.
Ha! what none stir! perhaps *Aristor's* with her: 320
Why let him tell it; from a Lover's mouth,
'Twill bear a Sound more welcome and harmonious.
And sure in Love and Battle none exceeds him,
The last you all can witness; you saw him Fight,
Saw the young Warrior with his Beaver up
Dart like the Bolt of *Jove* amongst their Ranks,
And scatter 'em like an Oak's far-shooting Splinters.
Will none confirm it? this is envious Silence.
                            [Walks up and down.

Thou *Demagetus*, ha! thou'rt all in Tears,
And so are these that make a Wall about thee: 330
The Cause deliver, Oh! declare it quickly.
   Demag. Enquire it not, my Lord; too soon 'twill find you.
   Aristom. I must prevent it by my hasty Search.
Reveal it you, or you, since all partake it:
                                 [*To* Alcander, &c.
What silent still!—
If yet ye do not speak, ye do not love me;
I find you do not, since ye all are Speechless.
Aristor would have spoke, had he been here.
   Demag. *Aristor's* here, but Oh! he cannot speak.
You have it now, my Lord, and must weep with us.   340
   Aristom. Thy Tongue has warn'd my Eyes to seek the
      Centre: [*Looks down.*
For round this Place I dare not let them stray,
Lest they explain too soon, thy fatal meaning.
Oh! *Anaxander*, had such Trembling seiz'd me,
When at the Army's Head I met thy Fury;
The poorest of thy Troops had cry'd me Coward.
Why so we're all, there's not a Man that is not;
We all dread something, and can shrink with Terror:
Yet he that comes a Conqu'ror from the Field,
Shall find a vain Applause to crown his Valour,   350
Tho' fainting thus, and sweating cold with Fear.
                    [*Pauses and leans on an Officer.*
But didst thou say, *Aristor* cou'd not speak?
Oh! that I live to ask it! not answer to his Father!
   Demag. Oh! never more!
   Aristom. The Sun will keep his Pace, and Time revolve,
Rough Winters pass, and Springs come smiling on;
But Thou dost talk of Never, *Demagetus:*
Yet ere Despair prevails, retract that Word
Whose cloudy distance bars the reach of Thought,

Nor let one Ray of Hope e'er dawn beyond it.   360
Never, Oh never!
  Demag. This Passion must rise higher, ere it falls.
Divide and let him know the worst.   [*To the Officers.*
  Aristom. Where is my Son? my Grief has pass'd all
      Bounds,
All dallying Circumstance, and vain Delusion,
And will be told directly where to find him.
  Demag. Oh! then behold him there!
  [*They divide. He seeing the Bodies stands awhile amaz'd and
      speechless, drops his Sword, then speaks.*
Aristom. So look'd the World to *Pyrrha*, and her Mate;
So gloomy, waste, so destitute of Comfort,
When all Mankind besides lay drown'd in Ruin.   370
Oh! thou wert well inform'd, my evil Genius;
And the complaining Rocks mourn'd not in vain:
For here my Blood, my dearest Blood I pay
For this poor Wreath, and Fame that withers like it;
          [*Tears the Wreath, and throws himself upon his Son.*
The Ground, that bore it, take the slighted Toy,
Whilst thus I throw me on his breathless Body,
And groan away my Life on these pale Lips.
Oh! O', O', O',—
Thus did I clasp him, ere the Battle join'd,
When Fate, which then had Doom'd him, mock'd my Arms,
Nor in their folds wou'd let me feel my Son.   381
Oh! that his Voice (tho' low as then it seem'd)
Cou'd reach me now!—But the fond Wish is vain,
And all but this too weak to ease my Pain.
  [*He takes the Sword that lay at* Aristor's *Feet, and goes to
          fall upon it,* Demagetus *takes hold of it.*
  Demag. Oh! hold, my Lord; nor stab at once your
      Army.
          [*All the Officers and Soldiers kneel,* Alcander *speaks.*

Alcand. We're all your Sons; and if you strike, my Lord,
The *Spartans* may come back, and take our Bodies;
For when yours goes, our Spirits shall attend it.

[They all prepare to fall on their Swords.

Aristom. Wou'd you then have me live, when thus unbow-
  ell'd,
Without the Charms of my *Aristor's* presence,   890
Without his Arm to second me in Fight,
And in still Peace his Voice to make it perfect?

[He rises in a Passion and comes forward on the Stage.

Yes I will live, ye Sov'reign Pow'rs, I will:
You've put my Virtue to its utmost Proof;
Yet thus chastis'd, I own superior Natures,
And all your fixt Decrees this Sword shall further,
'Till *Rhodes* is rescu'd, and my Task completed.
Who knows, but that the Way to your *Elysium*
Is Fortitude in Ills, and brave Submission;
Since Heroes whom your Oracles distinguish,   400
Are often here amidst their Greatness wretched?
But yet my Heart! my lov'd, my lost *Aristor!*

Demag. Let me succeed him in his active Duty,
And join with all the Earth to bring you Comfort.

Aristom. Comfort on Earth! Oh! 'tis not to be found.
My *Demagetus*, thou hast far to travel;
The Bloom of Youth sits graceful on thy Brow,
And bids thee look for Days of mighty Pleasures,
For prosp'rous Wars, and the soft Smiles of Beauty,
For generous Sons, that may reflect thy Form,   410
And give thee Hopes, as I had, of their succour.

Demag. With these indeed my Thoughts have still been
  flatter'd.

Aristom. Then let me draw this flatt'ring Veil aside,
And bid thee here, here in this Face behold,
How biting Cares have done the work of Age,

And in my best of Strength mark'd me a Dotard.
Defeated Armies, slaughter'd Friends are here;
Disgraceful Bonds, and Cities laid in Ashes:
And if thou find'st, that Life will yet endure it,
Since what I here have lost—   420
So bow'd, so waining shalt thou see this Carcass,
That scarce thou wilt recall what once it was.
Then be instructed Thou, and All that hear me,
Not to expect the compass of soft Wishes,
Or constant Joys, which fly the fond Possessor.
Since Man, *by swift returns of Good and Ill,*
In all the Course of Life's uncertain still;
By Fortune favoured now, and now opprest,
And not, 'till Death, secure of Fame, or Rest.

A SONG

Designed to have been brought into the part between Climander
and Herminia.

> Wretched Amintor with a flame
>   Too strong to be subdu'd
> A nymph above his Rank and Name
>   Still eagerly pursu'd.

2

> To gain her ev'ry art he try'd,
>   But no return procur'd,
> Mistook her prudence for her pride,
>   Nor guest what she endur'd.

3

> Till prostrate at her feet one day
>   Urging in deep dispair,
> Thus softly was she heard to say,
>   Or sight itt to the air.

4

Witnesse ye secret cares I prove,
Which is the greater tryal,
To sue for unrewarded love,
Or dye by self denyal.

EPILOGUE TO ARISTOMENES

An Epilogue, after a tedious Play,
Is like the last long mile in dusty way,
That trys your patience, and that wearies more,
Then all the irksome road you passt before.
Or like the Stirrup cup, a Bumkin forces,
When men already scarce can sitt their horses.
Yett for one here, good arguments prevail;
And since the Play so many ways does fail,
For her own sake, the Author thought itt fitt
To lett the Audience know when this was writt,
'Twas not for praise, or with pretense to witt:
But lonely Godmersham th' attempt excuses,
Not sure to be endur'd, without the Muses;
Then if what was compos'd within that shade,
(And has no farther from itts limmitts strayde
Then Eastern Beautys, which are only shown
To the dear spouse, and family alone)
Can gain your Pardon — cancell but the past,
And of this kind, this fault shall be the last.

NOTES

[Notes by Lady Winchilsea are inclosed in brackets]

P. xviii: "*Sketch of Lady Winchilsea's Life.*"— The chief authorities quoted in this sketch are *Genealogist*, New Series, ed. Keith Murray, Vol. XII, "The Royal Descent of Kingsmill;" *Genealogist*, ed. Marshall, Vol. I; Burke, *Landed Gentry; Harl. Soc. Pub.*, Vols. XXIV, XXVI; Doyle, *Official Baronage;* Collins, *Peerage*.

P. xxii, l. 28: ". . . . *the list of ladies.*"—This list is quoted in Miss Strickland's *Lives of the Queens of England* from the original document. The maids of honor were Frances Walsingham, Catharine Fraser, Anne Killigrew, Anne Kingsmill, Catharine Walters, and Catharine Sedley. In other references to Anne Kingsmill Miss Strickland makes curious blunders. On p. 283 of the *Life of Mary of Modena* Anne is spoken of as the wife of the Heneage Finch who stopped the flight of James II. at Faversham, but that Heneage Finch was Anne's father-in-law. On p. 476, under the date of 1712, Miss Strickland calls Anne Finch "Queen Anne's learned lady of the Bed-chamber," and says : " Her Jacobite influence with Queen Anne is never calculated in general history, but those versed in the signs of the times know that it was considerable. The dislike that her royal mistress had to the war is alluded to in some lines playfully addressed to her by Pope. . . . . Lady Winchilsea, recently left a widow with a small provision, was a devoted partisan of the house of Stewart: she was always near the royal person. This lady was a pleasant rhymstress, and possessed of some personal influence, but was without territorial power." In *Notes and Queries* (Eighth Series), Vol. V, p. 5, is a note on Lady Winchilsea, evidently based on Miss Strickland, for it repeats all her errors. In point of fact, the Lady Winchilsea "lately left a widow" in 1712 was Sarah, the wife of Charles, the third Earl of Winchilsea, and the nephew of Anne's husband.

P. xxv, l. 11: "*Heneage Finch . . . . aged ab. 27 years.*"— In Doyle's *Official Baronage* the date of Lord Winchilsea's birth is given as 1654, which would make him thirty at the time of his marriage; but his *Journal* has the entry, "Jan. 8, 165$, I was born, 11th I was christened." Add. MSS. 5507, Brit. Mus., also gives 1656 as the date of his birth.

P. xxvii, l. 27: ". . . . *the following statement.*"—Quoted in Nichols, *Literary Anecdotes of the Eighteenth Century*, Vol. I, p. 529.

P. xxix, l. 18: "*Heneage Finch . . . . as a non-juror.*"—"Heneage [fourth Earl of Winchilsea] a man of great worth and honor; he was a Non juror. His lady was Maid of Honour to King James 2nd Queen. She was a poetess; publisht a book of poems." *Mem. on the Peerage*, by Edward Harley, Earl of Oxford. See *Notes and Queries*, Second Series, No. 17, p. 325.

P. xliv, l. 8: "*Lady Marrow to her Daughter Lady Kay.*" Letter quoted in MSS. of Earl of Dartmouth, 3:147, Brit. Mus.

P. xlvi, l. 5: "*The Parallel.*"—The full title is: The Parallel; or, A Collection of Extraordinary Cases Relating to Concealed Births, and Disputed Successions. Containing, I. The History of Richard Plantagenet, Son to Richard III. II. An Account of Mrs. M. Cognot, etc., *London*, 1744.

P. xlvii, l. 4: "*Lord Winchilsea's antiquarian zeal.*"— In Nichols, *Illustrations of Literary History of 18th Cent.*, a note, Vol. II, p. 770, says that "Daniel, the fifth Earl of Winchilsea" was the author of the antiquarian letters: but the letters date October 20, 1722—October 18, 1725; and Heneage Finch, the fourth earl, did not die till 1726. This error is corrected by Nichols, Vol. IV, p. 496. But in *Gent. Mag.*, August and October, 1802, certain inquiries about a Commonplace Book "kept by Lord Winchilsea in 1721" are answered in a note attributing the book to the Lord Winchilsea who died January 1, 1730. But this again was Daniel Finch, who held the earldom 1726–30. The book was by Heneage Finch, the fourth earl.

P. xlvii, l. 6: "*Mr. Creyk.*"—See *Archæologia*, Vol. I, p. xxxvii, for note on "Mr. Creyke." Also Clarke, *Life of James II.*, Vol. II, Appendix, for signed statement by "J. Creyk" January 10, 172$, concerning the disposition made by him of important historical documents formerly in the possession of the late earl of Winchilsea. Also letters in which the earl of Winchilsea refers to Mr. Creyk, in Nichols, *Illustrations of the Literary Hist. of 18th Cent.*, Vol. II, p. 769 ff. The letter by Mr. Creyk on Lord Winchilsea's death (quoted p. lxxxvi) is in Vol. II, p. 788.

P. xlviii, l. 4: "*Lord Winchilsea was elected President of the Society of Antiquaries.*"—See Granger, *Biog. Dict.* 4 vols. Continuation by Noble, 3 vols. 1806. In "A Catalogue of Engraved British Heads" is the statement: "On the revival of the Society of Antiquaries in 1717, the Earl [of Winchilsea] was chosen president, when he procured the excellent artist, Vertue, the office of engraver to that respectable body. His lordship was well acquainted with his skill, which he had eminently shown in engraving his lordship's portrait, before mentioned.

P. xlix, l. 11: "*Books which I have subscribed for.*"

(*a*) "*Carm. Quad.*" This is doubtless the *Carmina Quadragesimalia* referred to by Coleridge in a note on his poem *Kisses.* A copy in the Bristol Library is catalogued as in "2 vols. *Oxon.* 1723-48, 4to."

(*b*) "*Recuille des Piers,*" etc., is probably the book by Stosch, entitled, *Pierres antiques gravées . . . . Dessinées et gravées . . . . par B. Picart, Tireés des principaux cabinets de l'Europe,* 1724.

(*c*)"*Monfaucons Supplim.*"—Bernard de Monfaucon published *L'Antiquité expliquée et representée en figures* in 1719. A *Suppliment au livre de l'Antiquité,* etc., appeared in Paris, 1725, 5 vols.

(*d*) "*Cardinal Wolsey's Life.*"—Doubtless the *Life* by Fiddes, published by subscription in 1724.

(*e*) "*Querels Testament.*" — Probably Quesnel's *Réflexions morales sur le Nouveau Testament,*" published 1694; condemned by Pope Clement XI., 1713.

(*f*) "*Sr. Ra. Winnwood's Letters.*"—In 1725 Edmund Sawyer published in London (3 vols.) *Memorials of Affairs of State . . . . collected chiefly from the original papers of the Hon. Sir Ralph Winnwood,* etc.

(*g*) "*Rev. Lewis' Isle of Thanet.*"—One of Lewis's topographical works, published 1723.

(*h*) *Mr. Breval's Book.*"—John Durant Breval wrote *The Confederates,* and so would doubtless be well known to Lord and Lady Winchilsea. The book mentioned here is probably Breval's *Remarks on Several Parts of Europe,* 1723, 4 vols.

(*i*) "*Dr. Barwick's Life.*"—Probably the *Vita J. Barwick* written by Peter Barwick in Latin, and published 1721 ; or perhaps the translation by Hilkiah Bedford, published 1724.

P. lii, l. 1: "*An Ode on Love.*"—In *Report of Hist. MSS. Com-*

mission, Vol. VIII, is a notice of this ode. It is in a package containing many papers relating to Steele and Addison, among them one hundred letters to the authors of the *Tatler* and the *Spectator*.

P. lvi, l. 3: ". . . . *her Spleen had attained the dignity of a second edition*."—See *The Spleen: A Pindarique Ode, By a Lady. Together with a Prospect of Death: A Pindarique Essay*, 1709. The *Prospect of Death* was by John Pomfret who had died in 1702.

P. lvi, l. 31: "*Courthope conjectures*," etc.—See Pope, *Works* (Elwin and Courthope), Vol. I, p. 20, note; Vol. VI, p. 198, note.

P. lxxvii, l. 16: "*The note runs thus*."—Throughout these letters by Wordsworth the page references were to the edition of 1713. They have been changed here to correspond with the pages of this edition.

P. lxxxix, l. 3: "*Versification*."—for the following references to Swift, Pope, and Dryden see Pope, *Works* (Elwin and Courthope), Vol. I, p. 338. In *Essays of John Dryden* (ed. W. P. Ker, Oxford, 1900) see "Dedication" to *Aeneis*, Vol. II, pp. 215–30 (*passim*) and "Dedication" of *Examen Poeticum*, Vol. II, pp. 10–11.

THE PREFACE

P. 8, l. 24: "*From their new Worlds, I know not where*."—[Cowley.] The lines occur in Cowley's *Complaint*.

P. 9, l. 31:   ". . . . *correct Essay Which so repairs our old Horatian way*."

[L⁴ Roscommon on L⁴ Mulgrave's Essay on poetry.] The quotation is from Roscommon's *Essay on Translated Verse* (1684). Mulgrave's *Essay on Poetry* appeared in 1682.

P. 10, l. 26: " . . . . *the two short pieces of that Pastoral*."—[A scene or two more have been translated from the Italian and since added, at the end of the first part of the Book.] The two short pieces from the *Aminta* are *Though we of small proportion see* and *Then by some Fountain's flow'ry side*. They number 5 and 6 in the folio MS. The other three pieces from the *Aminta* number 60, 61, 62, in the MS., and just precede the religious poems.

P. 10, l. 27: " . . . . *the Songs and other few lighter things*."—In the MS. "*Fables*" is inserted in pencil after "Songs," the list of "lighter things" having apparently been made before the writing of the Fables.

P. 11, l. 6: "*My Lord Roscommon under the name of Piso*."

"A noble Piso does instruct us here," is a line in Waller's *Upon the Earl of Roscommon's Translation of Horace* (1680).

P 11, l. 18: ". . . . *the Triumphs of Love and Innocence.*" — [Which title I have since given to that play called by me at first the "Queen of Cyprus; or love above ambition."] This note is one of many slight indications that the folio MS. was revised by Lady Winchilsea herself.

FRAGMENT

L. 17: After l. 17 in the MS. the following lines have been crossed out:

> Nor feeds a hope that boasts but mortal birth,
> Or springs from man though fram'd of Royal earth.

L. 23: *Abandoned pleasures in Monastick Walls.*"—[Wye College in Kent, formerly a Priory.] The parish-church of Wye was, in 1447, endowed by Archbishop Kempe and converted into a college for the education of the youth of that district. At the close of the sixteenth century the site and buildings of the college were willed to the master of the grammar school and the master and mistress of Lady Joanna Thornhill's charity school. The manor of the vicarage of Wye had long been in the possession of the Finches of Eastwell. It is the children of the Free School of Wye whom Lady Winchilsea celebrates in *Fanscomb Barn*. See W. H. Ireland, *History of the County of Kent* (London, 1829), Vol. II, p. 413.

A LETTER TO DAFNIS

The title in the octavo MS. is, *A Letter to Dapnnis from Westminster, Ap: the 2d, 1685.* The "Daphnis" is a substitution for "Mr. Finch," partially erased.

TO MR. F., NOW EARL OF W.

L. 41: "*In Haste th' affrighted Sisters fled.*"—[The Muses— Erato, Melpomene, Thalia, Urania.]

L. 73: "URANIA *only lik'd the choice.*"—[Urania is the Heavenly Muse, and suppos'd to inspire thoughts of Virtue.]

UPON ARDELIA'S RETURN HOME -

L. 8: "*Have threaten'd Hanging, Horn, or Drowning.*"— "To put to the horn" is to proclaim one an outlaw. "Makbeth . . . syne confiscat Makduff's guddis, and put him to the horn"

(Jamieson's *Etymol. Dict. of Scot. Language*). The phrase origi-
nated from the manner in which a person was proclaimed an outlaw. The King's Messenger, after the formalities, must give three
blasts on a horn, in announcement of the decree of outlawry.

L. 48: "*But he reply'd she'd break the Glasses.*"—"Glass
coaches," as coaches with glass in the doors and in the front of the
coach were called, were still comparatively rare in the early eighteenth century. Advertisements speak of coaches as having full
sets of glasses, or having the glasses entire. In Mrs. Centlivre's
The Basset Table, Act. III, scene 1, a despairing lover throws
himself so violently into his coach as to "break all the glasses."

AN INVITATION TO DAFNIS

L. 25: "*Come and let Sanson's World no more engage.*"—
An edition of the *Description de tout l'Univers*, etc., by Nicholas
and Guillaume Sanson, appeared in 1700. That this is the volume
to which Lady Winchilsea refers is indicated by l. 27. This reference helps to date the poem and so the MS. in which it occurs.

UPON THE DEATH OF WILLIAM LORD MAIDSTONE

William, Lord Maidstone, the oldest son of Heneage, the
second Earl of Winchilsea, was killed in the twenty-first year of his
age. In Add. MSS. 30,999, Brit. Mus., is a curious memorial to him.
Its heavy black borders and sketch of a tomb are crudely done by
hand. The proposed epitaph begins,

> Here William Lord of Maidstone lies, whose end
> The greatest Navies of the World did tend
> With eight hours Prologue to his Tragedy.

The closing lines are,

> Youth = Beauty = Honour = Courage = Wit = Good Nature
>   All ly enclos'd together
>   In his Tombe
> Who for his King and Country suffer'd Martyrdome.

The English Iliads, a poetical tract of 361 pages, printed in 1674,
also commemorates the death of Lord Maidstone. (*Kentish Garland*, chap. cxx.)

FROM THE MUSES AT PARNASSUS

The Lord Winchilsea of this poem is Charles, the posthumous
son of William, Lord Maidstone. He came into the title on the
death of his grandfather in September, 1689, when but seventeen

years of age. This poem was probably in honor of his eighteenth birthday.

L. 16: "*And trace his blood, until itt mix with Kings.*"— [A Daughter of Henry the Sevenths, when Queen Dowager of France, married to the Earl of Suffolk, by whom she had a Daughter that married to the Earl of Hartford, Great-grand-Father to the late restor'd Duke of Somersett, from a Daughter of whom my L⁴ Winchilsea is descended.]

UPON MY LORD WINCHILSEA'S CONVERTING THE MOUNT, ETC.

The Lord Winchilsea here eulogized is the Charles of the preceding poem. The improvements made by him at Eastwell may be approximately dated by the following letter from Edward Southwell, who wrote from Eastwell, July 22, 1702, "My Lord Winchilsea has been making very fine gardens which added to the beauty of the Park makes it a very fine seat."

L. 25: "*Where late it stood the Glory of the Seat.*"— In Murray's *Handbook for Kent and Sussex*, 1868, under "Eastwell" there is a parenthetical reference to "an edifying story of the misfortunes which resulted from the felling of a most curious grove of oaks here by one of the Earls of Winchilsea." The authority for Murray's "edifying story" is probably the following passage in John Aubrey's *The Natural History and Antiquities of the County of Surrey* (London, 1718), Vol. II, p. 37:

I cannot omit here taking notice of the great Misfortunes in the Family of the Earl of Winchelsea, who at Eastwell in Kent, felled down a most curious grove of Oaks, near his noble seat, and gave the first blow with his own hands. Shortly after, the Countess died in her Bed suddenly, and his eldest son, the Lord Maidstone, was killed at sea by a cannon-bullet.

The destruction of the oak-grove took place, then, about 1669 or 1670. The earl referred to would be Heneage Finch, the second Earl of Winchilsea. In the MS. after l. 77 the following lines have been crossed out:

> When by a Consort's too prevailing Art,
> The Park was rifl'd of so fair a part,
> Which now restor'd like itt's new Master's Mind
> Is with the whole, but in just bounds confin'd.

The "consort" here referred to would be the second of the Earl's four wives, Mary Seymour, daughter of William, Duke of Somerset.

A SONG UPON A PUNCH BOWL

Leslie, or Lashley, Finch was born in 1669, the year of his father's and mother's return from Turkey. At thirty he married Barbara Scroop. He died without issue at Longleat. This poem was first published in Mr. Gosse's *Gossip in a Library*.

THE BARGAIN

On the margin of the manuscript is written in pencil, "Made at my request by Ardelia." The handwriting is the same as that of many of the corrections in the text.

TO MY SISTER OGLE

"From Kyrby, Dec. 31, 88" is added in the earlier MS. There is also a note in pencil: "Also found on p. 5 of folio MS.," showing that the two manuscripts have been at some time in the same hands. Christopher Hatton, the owner of Kirby Hall, had, in 1685, married as his third wife Elizabeth Haselwood, Anne's cousin.

ARDELIA'S ANSWER TO EPHELIA

L. 75: "*And some few Authors old and dull to me.*"—The following lines were added here in the margin of the MS.:

> Ev'n Wicherly admires whose biting pen
> Reveals our Frailty to insulting men,
> And speaks of Otaway with such delight
> As if no other pen could move or write.

L. 78: "*Ere twelve was struck she calls me from my bed.*"—The hours observed by a fashionable lady are somewhat variously indicated in the satire and the comedy of this period. Lodowick in *Sir Patient Fancy* (Mrs. Behn, 1678) in describing how a married woman of quality ought to live, says: "From eight till twelve you ought to employ in dressing, till two at dinner, till five in visits, till seven at the play, till nine in the Park, at ten at supper with your lover." In *The English Lady's Catechism* (1703) the lady says: "I lie in Bed till Noon, dress all the Afternoon, dine in the Evening, and play at cards till Midnight" (quoted by Ashton: *Reign of Queen Anne*). In *The Basset Table* (Mrs. Centlivre, 1705) Lady Reveller says: "Why does anybody dine before Four o'Clock in *London*? For my Part, I think it an ill-bred Custom to make my Appetite Pendulum to the Twelfth Hour;" and her Maid adds, "Besides 'tis out of fashion to dine by Daylight." In *The Rape of the Lock* (ed. of 1712) Belinda wakes "when striking watches the tenth hour resound," but in the edition of 1714 she wakes "just at twelve." Prior's *Hans Carvel* (published 1709, but written probably several years earlier) says of the fashionable lady,

> She without fail was wak'd at Ten,
> Drank Chocolate, then slept again.
> At Twelve she rose, with much ado
> Her cloaths were huddled on by Two.

Then she dines, makes a tour of interesting places in the city, and closes the day by a turn in Hyde Park much after the fashion of Almeria in the poem of Lady Winchilsea.

L. 85: "*Of the best China Equipage, be lost.*"—Concerning the rage for china and the custom of boarding the India ships before the cargo was unloaded so as to have the first chance to pick up novelties, see Sydney: *Social Life in England, 1660–1669*, p. 270. *Cf.* description of Leonora's library (*Spectator*, April 12, 1711) and Gay's *Fan* (1714).

L. 133: "*But Noble Piso passes.*"—[Ld Roscommon.]

L. 161: "*Whilst all he sung was present to our eyes.*"—[In my Ld Roscommon's Sylenus.]

L. 208: "*Which through all ranks, down to the Carman, goes.*"—Carmen have traditional notoriety for singing and whistling. For an assemblage of literary references similar to this one by Lady Winchilsea, see Chappell: *Popular Music of the Olden Time*, Vol. I, p. 138.

TO THE HONORABLE THE LADY WORSLEY

The Utresia of this poem is Frances Thynne, only daughter of Viscount Thynne of Longleat and Frances, his wife, the daughter of Heneage Finch, second Earl of Winchilsea. Frances Thynne married Sir Robert Worsley in 1690. This poem was evidently written very soon after her marriage. The tone of ll. 1–16 would seem to date the poem before the final settlement at Eastwell.

L. 72: "*His genius who th' original improv'd.*"—Baron Thynne of Warminster, made Viscount Weymouth in 1682. He came into possession of Longleat in 1682 on the murder of his cousin Thomas Thynne. Viscount Weymouth lived much at Longleat, where he laid out gardens in the Dutch style. The new English larch, introduced into England in 1705, was named after him the Weymouth pine. He was noted as a peer who maintained "the splendour and hospitality of the ancient peerage of England."

THE MARRIAGE OF EDWARD AND ELIZABETH HERBERT

Elizabeth Herbert, great-great-granddaughter of the fourth Earl of Pembroke, married Edward Herbert of Swansea, county Glamorgan. The "Worsley" of the poem is the Frances Worsley who became Lady Cartaret in 1710. Hence the marriage of Edward and Elizabeth Herbert must have occurred before that date, or when Edward was nineteeen and Elizabeth sixteen.

ON THE DEATH OF THE HONOURABLE MR. JAMES THYNNE

L. 28: "*And his renowned Ancestors repose.*"

(a) "*Coventry.*"—[Lord Keeper Coventry.] Lord Keeper Coventry's second wife had four daughters, one of whom, Mary, married Sir Henry Frederick Thynne, the grandfather of the young James Thynne of the poem.

(b) ". . . . *his Paternal Predecessor.*"— Sir John Thynne, who bought Longleat in 1541, and was occupied in the years 1567–79 in building the mansion, said to have been the first well-built house in the kingdom. The whole of the outside and the interior from the hall to the chapel court were completed by him.

(c) "*Essex.*"— Robert Devereux, second Earl of Essex, had a daughter Frances, who was married (April, 1618) to Sir William Seymour, afterward Marquis of Hertford and Duke of Somerset. Their daughter, Mary Seymour, the second wife of Heneage Finch, the second Earl of Winchilsea, was the mother of Frances Finch, who married Viscount Thynne.

(d) "*Somerset.*"—The Sir William Seymour of the preceding note. He was one of the three lords who prayed the court to lay upon them, as the advisers of Charles I., the entire responsibility for his acts. Upon his execution they gained permission to bury his body at Windsor. At the Restoration the dukedom of Somerset and the barony of Seymour (declared forfeit in 1552) were revived and conferred upon Sir William Seymour by act of Parliament September 13, 1660. He died October 24 of the same year.

(e) ". . . . *that matchless Female.*"—[The Lady Packington supposed by many to be the author of *The Whole Duty of Man.*] Dorothy Coventry, daughter of Lord Keeper Coventry and wife of Sir John Packington, a lady of great learning and piety. The tradition connecting her name with *The Whole Duty of Man* was persistent. Her grandson caused to be engraved on her monument, "justly reputed the author of *The Whole Duty of Man,*" but the

proof seems strong that the book was really written by Richard
Allestree. See *Journal of Sacred Literature*, July, 1864.

CLEONE ILL-PAINTED

The "Theanor" of this poem, Henry Thynne (*cf. A Description of one of the Pieces of Tapestry at Longleate*), son of Viscount
Weymouth, died, *vita patris*, 1708. "Cleone" is his wife Grace,
the daughter of Sir George Stroud. This poem was apparently
written not long after the marriage of Henry Thynne and Grace
Stroud, which took place in 1695.

TO THE RIGHT HONORABLE THE COUNTESS OF HERTFORD

Frances, the daughter of Henry Thynne, married Algernon
Seymour, Earl of Hertford, in "about 1713," according to Doyle's
Official Baronage, but "in 1715," according to the note in Lord
Winchilsea's private journal. Lady Hertford was the correspondent
of Henrietta Louisa Fermor, countess of Pomfret, and of Mrs.
Elizabeth Rowe. Dr. Watts published four of her pieces under the
pen-name "Eusebia" in his *Miscellanies*. Thomson dedicated his
Spring to her in 1727. In 1728 she befriended Savage. It is
implied in the poem that the volume sent to Lady Hertford was
largely made up of poems that had been seen by her father Henry
Thynne; hence it would seem to be the volume of 1713. But manuscript poems were also sent to Lady Hertford.

UPON THE DEATH OR SIR WILLIAM TWISDEN

Sir William Twisden (or Twysden), the third baronet of Roydon
Hall, East Peckham, Kent, died November 27, 1697, and the poem
was probably written soon after. Sir William's grandfather had
married Anne Finch, the daughter of Sir Moyle Finch and Elizabeth Heneage. The qualities attributed to Sir William Twysden
by Lady Winchilsea are the qualities for which his father, Sir
Roger Twysden, was especially noted. During the years 1650–60
Sir Roger was living quietly on his estate and occupying himself
chiefly with historical and antiquarian researches. During these
years his son William was from fifteen to twenty-five years of age,
and was closely associated with his father's interests. In 1672 the
baronetcy devolved upon Sir William, and he evidently kept up the
family traditions in the way of learning.

L. 70: "*A heavyer Immage of our Country drew.*"—[A person

y^t has been chosen Kt. of the Shire to the exclusion of Sir Wm Twisden.]

L. 178: "*Beneath the covert of a moving wood.*"—[This is a poetical allusion to the common Proverb that Kent was never conquer'd.] According to a historic legend, the Kentish men assembled with boughs in their hands (*circa* 1067) and demanded of William the Conqueror a recognition of their rights, when that monarch was on his way from London to take possession of Canterbury and Dover Castle. In 1795 was circulated a Kentish halfpenny bearing on its obverse the mounted figure of the Conqueror confronted by three men holding boughs. The legend on the coin was "Kentish Liberty preserved by Virtue and Courage." *Invicta* is the motto of Kent. Drayton, in his *Polyolbion* (song xviii, l. 737), says of Kent: "Of all the *English* shires be thou surnamed the Free." See Lambarde's *Perambulation of Kent* (1576); *The Kentish Garland*, Hertford (1881).

L. 191: "*As much the Poet's Friend, as much the World's Delight.*"—[This line is an immitation of Spenser's thought of St. Phil: Sid[n]ey whom he calls "Astrophel" in his poem.] The line referred to is probably "Sidney is dead, dead is my friend, dead is the world's delight," in the poem (ascribed by Lamb to Lord Brooke) entitled *Another of the Same* in the *Astrophel* volume of 1595.

AN ENQUIRY AFTER PEACE

The title in the MS. is: *Verses incerted in a Letter to my Lady Thanet; being an enquiry after Peace; and shewing that what the World generally persues, is contrary to it.*

THE PETITION FOR AN ABSOLUTE RETREAT

L. 59: "*The Luxurious Monarch wore.*"—[Josephus says that every *Monday Solomon* went to the House of *Lebanon* in an open *Chariot*, cloath'd in a Robe most dazling White, which makes that allusion not improper, and may give us Grounds to believe that the *Lilly* mention'd by our Saviour (compar'd to *Solomon* in his Glory) might really be the common white *Lilly*, altho' the Commentators seem in doubt what Flowers are truly meant by the Lillies, as thinking the plain *Lilly* not gay enough for the Comparison; whereas this Garment is noted by *Josephus* to be wonderfully Beautiful tho' only White; nor can any Flower, I believe, have a greater Lustre than the common White Lilly.]

L. 89: "*As gather'd from Fidentia's vales.*"—[These circum-stances are related by *Plutarch* in the Life of Sylla.]

L. 206: "*Thus had Crassus been content.*"—[The Description of this Cave is exactly taken from Plutarch in the Life of Crassus.]

L. 238: "*Nor had he who Crouds could blind.*"—[Sertorius.]

L. 255: "*Truly Fortunate, and Blest.*"—[The *Canary* Islands, called by the Ancients the *Fortunate* Islands, and taken by some of the Poets for *Elysium.*]

TO THE R^T HON^{BLE} THE LADY O. TUFTON

In this and the next poem "Serena" is Catharine Tufton, (born April 24, 1692, daughter of "Arminda," the Countess of Thanet).

A POEM FOR THE BIRTHDAY OF THE LADY CATHERINE TUFTON

L. 19: "*How Great that more distinguish'd Peer.*"—The sixth Earl of Thanet, known as "the good Lord Thomas." "He is a good country gentleman, a great assertor of the prerogatives of the monarchy and the church; a thin, tall, black, red-faced man, turned of 60 years old.— *Of great piety and charity.*" Macky, *Characters in the Court of Queen Anne* (Swift's additional comment in italics).

L. 33: "*Of Her, whose Fav'rite she appears.*"—[The Lady Coventry.] Margaret Tufton, sister of the second Earl of Thanet, married to Lord Coventry in 1653.

L. 63: "*When Hothfeild shall (as heretofore).*"—Hothfield, the family seat of the Tuftons in Kent. The five daughters of Thomas, the sixth Earl of Thanet, married early and into noble families, thus maintaining the reputation of the family for "illustrious Hymens."

UPON THE DEATH OF KING JAMES THE SECOND

L. 37: "*Earlier than Cæsar far.*"—[The king was born in the year 1633, and in 1642 He was in the Battel atEdge-hill.]

L. 41: "*Which Cæsar never prov'd nor his tenth Legion knew.*"—[The Tenth was the most vaillant and favour'd of Julius Cæsar's Legions.]

L. 45: "*Whil'st the best General which the World cou'd boast.*"—[The King when very yong was in the French service and Lieutenant General under Mareschall Turenne against the Spaniards where he behaved himself with that Valour and Conduct that in a sicknesse of Turenne's when 'twas thought he could not live, the King of France sending for his advice who should command his Army, if he shou'd not recover, He answer'd the King. that if he wou'd have his affaires prosper, he shou'd make choice of a noble, valourous and fortunate General and cou'd chuse no fitter Person than the thrice Heroick Duke of York. In that famous Action when Turenne forc'd the Spanish Trenches (altho defended by the Prince of Condé) and reliev'd Arras, the D. of York behaved himself with remarkable bravery and was wounded, as may be seen in the French translation of Card. Mazerin's Life, written in Italian by Count Gualdo.]

L. 53: "*Which to the skies was borne in Opdam's fiery blaze.*"— [In our first Dutch war after the Restoration the D. of York commanded our Fleet, beat the Dutch, and blew up Opdam their Admiral, for which service the Parliament with great applause of his Vallour and Conduct made him a magnificent Present as apears upon their Journals.]

L. 102: In stanza 6, before l. 102, three lines have been crossed out, and the sense of those that follow consequently left imperfect. These lines seem to read:

> Weep then ye Realms who once his sway confeast,
> Who had he been of your Belief possest
> Amongst your Kings that have laid down.

L. 104: "*Then Alfred's Piety had form'd his Praise.*"— [Alfred was one of our Saxon Kings famous for his Piety and application day and night to the publick affaires.]

L. 108: "*Unto our frugal Henry's been preferr'd.*"—[Hen. the Seventh.]

L. 111: "*What even Eliza's dayes brought in.*"—[Cambden sais that the custom of excessive drinking was brought amongst us out of Holland by those Troops which Queen Elizabeth lent the States.]

L. 112: "*The wasting foul Excesse Miscall'd Good-natured Sin.*"—[Drinking.] After l. 112, twelve lines are crossed out so effectually that it is impossible to restore them. Decipherable words and phrases indicate that these lines have to do with the private life of James II. Lines 9–11 seem to read:

> In his own Breast a rebell world to find
> Where such embattled troops of vices grew
> As the Souldier did at length subdue.

But in what connection they were used is not apparent.

L. 139: After l. 139 are these two lines which have been crossed out:

> Least Ruin'd by their complicated charms
> Mankind had laid on Fate their unprevented Harms.

THE CIRCUIT OF APPOLLO

L. 11: "*He lamented for Behn o're that place of her birth.*"—[M⁏ Behn was Daughter to a Barber who liv'd formerly in Wye, a a little market Town (now much decay'd) in Kent: though the account of her life before her Works pretends otherwise; some persons now alive Do testify upon their knowledge that to be her Original.] See Mr. Gosse on this point in the *Athenæum*, September 6, 1884. He finds the statement verified by the records of the parish of Wye.

A POEM OCCASIONED BY THE SIGHT OF THE 4ᵀᴴ EPISTLE OF HORACE

The Mr. Richard Thornhill here referred to is the one who afterwards killed Sir Cholmley Deering, his intimate friend, in a duel, May 9, 1711, and was himself, in consequence, assassinated August, 1711. See Swift's *Journal to Stella* under these dates. This famous duel is fully described by Ashton, *Reign of Queen Anne*, pp. 392–4. Mr. Thornhill's remorse is described under the character of "Spinamont," *Spectator*, 84, June 6, 1711. See also Wotton, *English Baronetage*, 2 : 21. The "Orania" of the poem is Frances Coell, daughter of Thomas Coell, Esq.

Ll. 58–62: "The Vine" was a tavern in Long-Acre. The two men supposed to meet Mr. Thornhill there were probably Nicholas Rowe and Charles, Earl of Winchilsea.

TO A FELLOW SCRIBBLER

L. 10: "*The night-shade with a dismal flow'r.*"—This is probably the *Solanum Dulcamara*, the woody night-shade, "a climbing plant found in moist hedges and thickets with purple flowers in drooping clusters." See Catlow, *Field Botany*, London, 1848.

L. 12: "*Or honesty with feather'd down.*"—A local name for wild clematis, the full name being "Maiden's Honesty." "About Michalmass all the hedges about Thickwood (in the parish Colerne) [Wilts] are as it were hung with *maydens honesty*, which looks very fine." Aubrey's *Wilts*, Royal Soc. MS., p. 120. Quoted in *English Plant Names*, English Dialect Society.

L. 19: "*With beauteous Eglantine imbrac'd.*"—"Eglantine" and "honey-suckle" (l. 21) seem to be used as synonymous. The plant probably referred to is woodbine. Prior in *Popular Names of British Plants* (1879) says that honey-suckle in "poetry and popular usage" is *Lonicera periclymenum*, but that the name "honey-suckle" seems to have been given to the woodbine "because of the honey-dew so plentifully deposited on its leaves." "Eglantine" is a name much discussed and not certain of application. Its usual signification at the present day is the sweet-briar. But Prior says that the "twisted eglantine" of Milton's *L'Allegro* was probably the woodbine. And the *English Plant Names* (Eng. Dialect Soc.) says that woodbine is still called eglantine in N. E. Yorkshire. *Cf.* Ellacombe, *Plant-Lore and Garden-Craft of Shakespeare*, 1884, pp. 83, 125.

TO DR. WALDRON

In the *Oxford and Cambridge Miscellany Poems* (Bernard Lintot, 1709), p. 112, is *An Essay on Death* by Dr. W—— of All Souls.

TO MR. JERVAS

Charles Jervas, a popular portrait painter, was on intimate terms with Pope, Swift, Arbuthnot, Addison. He painted several portraits of Pope. After the return of Jervas from Italy in 1709 his house in Cleveland Court was a meeting-place for his literary friends. Lady Winchilsea's town-house was close by in Cleveland Row. Of Mrs. Chetwynd Swift, in a letter dated London, March 22, 1708–9, and addressed to "A Monsieur Monsieur Hunter," says: "The beauties you left are all gone off this frost, and we have got a new set for spring, of which Mrs. Chetwynd and Mrs. Worsley are the principal."

A SONG OF THE CANIBALS, OUT OF MOUNTAIN'S ESSAYS

This love song of the cannibal chieftain is in *Les Essais de Montaigne*, Paris, 1886, Vol. II, chap. 31, p. 145.

AN EPISTLE FROM A GENTLEMAN TO MADAME DESHOULIERS

Madame Deshoulières (Antoinette de Ligier de la Garde) was one of the chief female poets of France. Her works were published in 1687–88, and again in 1695, the year after her death, by her daughter. The letter here translated is included in her works and is there entitled *Lettre de M. de Senecé, premier valet-de-chambre de la Reine, à Mme Des Houlieres, en lui envoyant de l'argent qu'elle lui avoit prête à la Bassette.*

RALPH'S REFLECTIONS

L. 19: "*But throw our stockins at our heads.*"—For the customs and superstitions connected with "flinging the stocking" and drinking the "sack-posset" see W. C. Hazlitt, *Popular Antiquities of Great Britain* (1870), Vol. II, pp. 112, 114.

THE OWL DESCRIBING HER YOUNG ONES

L. 50: "*At length he cry'd with Vultur's Becks.*"—In Tusser, *Husbandry* (1573) "bex" is the plural form, as in the lines, (chap. 34, st. 11):

> So doing, more tender and greater they wex
> If peacock and turkey leave jobbing their bex.

Murray (*Dict.*) gives "beck" as still in use in the eighteenth century.

Ll. 52–4: "Palatines" were fur tippets. *Cent. Dict.* quotes from *Ladies Dictionary*, 1694: "*Palatine*, that which used to be called a sable tippet, but that name is changed." *Doily* was a woolen stuff introduced for summer wear in the latter part of the seventeenth century. Dryden speaks of "Doily petticoats" (*Limberham*, Act IV, Sc. 1, 1678). *Spectator*, 283, speaks of doily as a stuff at once genteel and cheap. Arbuthnot (*John Bull*, I, vi) says: "His Children were reduced from rich silks to Doily stuffs," and Congreve speaks of "a fool and a doily stuff" (*The Way of the World*, Act III, Sc. 3), but Gay makes doily synonymous with silken drugget (*Trivia*, 1:43), and Lady Winchilsea classes her "Doily stuffs" with silks as opposed to calicoes. Dr. Johnson (*Dict.*) defines "calico" as "an Indian stuff made of cotton; sometimes stained with gay and beautiful colors." Murray (*Dict.*) quotes from J. Roberts, *Spinster*, 347 (1719): "A tawdry, pie-spotted, flabby, ragged, low-priced thing, called Callicoe, made by a parcel of Heathens and Pagans that Worship the Devil, and work for half a penny a day."

THE EAGLE, THE SOW, AND THE CAT

Ll. 27–9: "*Lest Pettitoes should make,*" etc.—William King in *Art of Cookery*, chap. 9, in his pretended excerpts from a great work by Cælius Apicius, puts emphasis on the sumptuous dishes prepared by the ancients from "hog-meat" in various forms.

Apicius is represented as lauding the "liver, lights, brains and pettitoes" of a black China pig, and as speaking of a dish much in favor with certain Roman emperors, one of the elements of this dish being "a wild sow's hock and udder."

L. 46: "*A Pestilential Sow, a meazled Pork.*"—"Measles" was a name for several diseases of swine or sheep. Butler (*Hudibras*, Part I, Canto II, l. 688) has: "As e'er in measled pork was hatched." Tusser (*Good Husbandry*, chap. 17) has:

> Hog measeled kill
> For Fleming who will,

With evident derogatory estimate of the discrimination of the "Flemings."

FANSCOMB BARN

L. 7: "*Through Ages pass'd consigned for Harbour meet.*"— [Fanscomb-Barn, near Wye in Kent, is a privileg'd Retreat for Beggars.]

L. 97: "*Where the White Sparrow never soiled her Plumes.*"— [Fanscomb-Barn is famous for breeding white mice and white sparrows.]

L. 100: "*That flows near Pickersdane renowned Stream.*"— [Pickersdane, is a point of Wye-Downs, where there is an excellent spring, much frequented by the scholars of the Free-School at Wye; who meet there to drink the water with sugar; which has been an ancient custom and a great diversion to them.]

L. 111. "*Nor shou'd, quoth he, that Well o'er-hung with shade.*" —[A very deep well, within a little wood near Fanscomb Barn.]

JEALOUSIE IS THE RAGE OF A MAN

L. 14: "*Smooth, ev'ry clinging plume with anger lies.*"—[A dove when angry or going to fight lays her feathers close.]

THE SPLEEN

L. 41: "*We faint beneath the Aromatick Pain.*"—Mr. Saintsbury (*Short History of Eng. Lit.*, p. 563) suggests that Lady Winchilsea borrowed her phrase "aromatic pain" from Dryden. The reference is probably to Dryden, *Annus Mirabilis*, st. 29, reads:

> Amidst whole heaps of spices lights a ball,
> And now their odours armed against them fly;
> Some preciously by shattered porcelain fall
> And some by *aromatic splinters die.*

Mr. Gosse, in Ward's *English Poets*, called attention to the fact that Pope borrowed from Lady Winchilsea his phrase "aromatic pain." The line in Pope is (*Essay on Man*, 1:200):

> Die of a rose in aromatic pain.

Mr. Gosse now further calls my attention to the following lines in Shelley's *Epipsychidion*:

> And from the mass violets and jonquils peep,
> And dart their arrowy odour through the brain,
> Till you might faint with that delicious pain.

This is almost certainly a conscious recollection of Ardelia's lines.

A PINDARICK POEM UPON THE HURRICANE

L. 96: "*O Wells! Thy Bishop's Mansion We lament.*"—[The Bishop's Palace at Wells was blown down, and kill'd Bishop Kidder with his lady.]

L. 233: "*Ye Clouds! that pity'd our Distress.*"—[We had a great shower of rain in the midd'st of the storm.]

L. 247: "*Which to foreshew the still portentous Sun.*"—[The ancients look'd upon the Sun (or Phœbus) as prophetick.]

L. 248: "*Beamless and pale of late his Race begun.*"—[One day of the summer before the storm we had an unusual appearance of the sun (which was observ'd by many people in several parts of Kent). It was of a pale dead colour, without any beams or brightness for some hours in the morning, altho' obstructed by no clouds; for the sky was clear.]

PROLOGUE TO ARISTOMENES

This *Prologue* was not published with the play in 1713. The Lord Winchilsea to whom it was addressed was doubtless Charles, the third Earl of Winchilsea.

L. 17: "*A droll wou'd at Newmarket make them sport.*"—Cartwright's ed. of Sir John Reresby's *Diary*, March 22, 1684, describes the diversions of King Charles at Newmarket as a progress 'from the cock-pit to the horse-race, back to the cock-pit, and then to the play, though the commedians were very indifferent." Shadwell's "Prig" in *The True Widow* enumerates among the delights at Newmarket the "play in a barn" (Sidney, *England, 1660–1669*). Ashton (*Social Life in Reign of Queen Anne*, ch. 20)

describes the shows at the various fairs. Among them was what Ward called "a dwarf *Comedy*, Sir-named a *Droll*."

L. 24: "*Or tedious sheet, of doubtful news from Dyer.*"—In the MS. this line is written over the earlier form, "*fulsom lyes from Dyer.*" Dyer's *News-Letter* was discontinued September, 1718.. For references to this *News-Letter* see *Tatler* (18), where Dyer's skill in manufacturing exciting news is commented on; *Spectator*, Nos. 48 and 127; and Ashton. *Reign of Queen Anne*, p. 300.

INDEX

9 781377 754970